GOVERNOR

JOHN WENTWORTH

& THE AMERICAN

REVOLUTION

GOVERNOR JOHN WENTWORTH & THE AMERICAN REVOLUTION

The English Connection

BY

PAUL W. WILDERSON

UNIVERSITY PRESS OF

NEW ENGLAND:

HANOVER &

LONDON

University Press of New England, Hanover, NH 03755

© 1994 by University Press of New England

Printed in the United States of America

1 2 3 4 5   5 4 3 2 1

Set by Tseng in Matthew Carter's
Galliard & Mantinia types

CIP data appear at the
end of the book

This publication has been funded, in part,
by the New Hampshire Historical Society
with contributions from Stanley A. Hamel,
the Lord Henniker, Mr. and Mrs. Edward
Tuck, and in memory of Lucy Putnam Bell.

FOR MARILYN

In the Course of the long American Business from the Year 1765 to 1782 I had occasion to observe the Conduct of all the Governours, and without meaning to disparage any I must say that not one of them has done his Duty in a more clear and manly a Style [than John Wentworth]: That he shew'd a mark'd Zeal for the Crown at the same time that he made not one Enemy to the Interests of Great Britain by any thing intemperate in that Zeal; that he lost a Noble Situation a large fortune and the hopes of an indefinite encrease to it, and that I have reason to be convinced that if he had join'd in the Revolt, he would have been in one of the most commanding and most distinguish'd Situations in the United States.

EDMUND BURKE, 1792

CONTENTS

ILLUSTRATIONS

ACKNOWLEDGMENTS

Many people and institutions provided invaluable assistance in the completion of this book. Three in particular deserve more thanks than I can offer. Frank C. Mevers, the state archivist of New Hampshire and a historian of New Hampshire's Revolutionary period, read and commented on the original manuscript and over many years continued to offer unrelenting aid in identifying and supplying important source materials. James L. Garvin, architectural historian for the state of New Hampshire, steered me to numerous additional sources through the years, unceasingly offered his encouragement and enthusiasm, and consistently provided in his own work an example of diligent and exemplary scholarship. Stephen L. Cox, former editor of publications at the New Hampshire Historical Society and now senior historian at Connor Prairie, unfailingly responded to repeated requests for information in the society's collections and helped me keep it all in perspective through his welcome sense of humor.

I would like to thank Jere R. Daniell of Dartmouth College, who at the beginning of the project loaned me his personal collection of microfilms and photocopies of documents in Britain relating to New Hampshire. His assistance was a great help in research and writing at home and allowed me to make the best use of my research time in England. He read an early draft of the manuscript and provided many valuable suggestions for improving it. A late version of this work has also benefited from his comments.

I am grateful to Diane R. Tebbetts of the University of New Hampshire library, whose persistent effort helped me obtain a microfilm copy of the John Wentworth Letter Book Transcripts at the New Hampshire State Archives. That source proved indispensable to both the research and writing stages of my

xiv

project. Colonel Henry B. Margeson of Portsmouth, New Hampshire, generously donated his time to provide access to the collections of the Portsmouth Athenaeum and copies of key documents. Peter Drummey, librarian of the Massachusetts Historical Society, promptly and graciously responded to my request for photocopied material. Robert Calhoon of the University of North Carolina at Greensboro suggested additional sources on loyalists; Brian Cuthbertson, public records archivist of the Public Archives of Nova Scotia, kindly answered questions about material in his book on John Wentworth's life in Nova Scotia.

Archives personnel at the New Hampshire Historical Society, the Baker Library of Dartmouth College, and the New York Public Library were efficient and helpful. The same holds true for the Sheffield Central Library, the Sheepscar Library in Leeds, the Public Record Office, the House of Lords Record Office, and the British Library, assuring that my research time in England was well spent. I am particularly indebted to the Director of Libraries and Information Services of Sheffield and to Olive, Countess Fitzwilliam's Wentworth Settlement Trustees, for access to the all-important Wentworth-Woodhouse Muniments. I am also grateful to the manuscript librarians of the University of Bristol library, the University of Nottingham library, and the Lambeth Palace Library for providing information and photocopies of documents by mail.

I owe much to Charles E. Clark, professor of history at the University of New Hampshire, who encouraged me to undertake this project. His knowledge of early America and especially northern New England was always a valuable resource.

Without the help of John Frisbee and the New Hampshire Historical Society this book might not have been published. I am deeply grateful for that support.

Finally and most importantly I want to thank Marilyn, who over the years has selflessly devoted a great deal of her own time and effort to this book. From her own work she has brought consistently helpful advice and an understanding and sympathy for the many difficulties and discouragements involved in such a project.

GOVERNOR
JOHN WENTWORTH
& THE AMERICAN
REVOLUTION

INTRODUCTION

The royal governor in eighteenth-century America was by the nature of his office an isolated individual. The sovereignty of the English crown was vested in him alone. In most matters his decisions were final and irrevocable. In fact, his legal power in relationship to the legislature was greater than that of the king of England to Parliament. Many royal governors commanded respect. Some were able to generate good will and a few even affection among the people. But after 1763, the increasingly restrictive and threatening colonial policies of the British government magnified fear of the governors' absolute powers and guaranteed rising antagonism between each executive and the inhabitants of his province.[1] By 1774 that submerged hostility had in several cases erupted into open warfare, and over the following two years every royal governor lost all effective power.

One of the first to leave the colonies was Thomas Hutchinson of Massachusetts. Although the people of Boston were too much upset with the closing of their port on 1 June 1774 to express any feelings of joy at their governor's departure for England that day, no royal governor in America had aroused more negative sentiment than Thomas Hutchinson. Hutchinson's biographer Bernard Bailyn describes his subject as "one of the most hated men on earth—more hated than Lord North, more hated than George III, . . . and more feared than the sinister Earl of Bute."[2] Although not all of the royal governors provoked as much hostility as Thomas Hutchinson, it is difficult to identify one for whom any good feeling could be found in America after 1776.[3] There was, however, one clear exception—a colonial governor at the outbreak of the American Revolution who, though only sixty miles from Boston, stood at the opposite end of the scale from Thomas Hutchinson in the amount of ill will he engendered. That governor was John Wentworth of New Hampshire.

Mercy Otis Warren, a patriot and a historian of the Revolution, described Thomas Hutchinson as a "dark, intriguing, insinuating, haughty and ambitious" man, one who "diligently studied the intricacies of Machiavelian policy."[4] The Reverend Jeremy Belknap, a Congregational minister in Dover, New Hampshire, also a historian of repute who ardently supported the American cause in the years preceding the Revolution, later discussed the last royal governor of his own province in very different terms. Belknap found it "easy to conclude" that John Wentworth's

> intentions were pacific; and whilst the temper of the times allowed him to act agreeable to his own principles, his government was acceptable and beneficial; but when matters had come to the worst, his faults were as few, and his conduct as temperate, as could be expected from a servant of the crown. If a comparison be drawn, between him and most of the other governors on this continent, at the beginning of the revolution he must appear to advantage. Instead of widening the breach, he endeavored to close it; and when his efforts failed, he retired from a situation, where he could no longer exercise the office of a governor.[5]

In the early nineteenth century, the Reverend Timothy Dwight, passing through New Hampshire on one of his many travels in New England, reflected favorably on John Wentworth. According to Dwight, Governor Wentworth "retired from the chair with an unimpeachable character, and with higher reputation than any other man who at that time held the same office in this country."[6] In the 1860s, Lorenzo Sabine, the chronicler of the loyalists of the American Revolution, wrote that John Wentworth had always maintained "the respect of his political opponents," that "not one of the public men of the time who clung to the Royal cause will go down to posterity with a more enviable fame. Had Bernard, Hutchinson, Tryon, Franklin, Dunmore, Martin, and the other Loyalist Governors been like him, the Revolution might have been delayed."[7] More than a century later, Robert Calhoon, a prominent historian of the loyalists, could still write: "John Wentworth brought unusual insight and ability and a cool head to the difficult task of royal governor."[8]

Was John Wentworth significantly different from other governors of the time? Not all of the colonial governors were royal governors: several were elected, others, proprietary. Of the royal, or crown-appointed, governors, some were English—professional placemen with no special ties to the American colonies. Their primary allegiance was to their own advancement within the British government. But a few Revolutionary period governors were colonial-born, appointed royal officials like Wentworth.

James Wright of Georgia was an intelligent, sensible, and moderate man. He was also determined to uphold what he saw as an immutable constitutional principle of the absolute supremacy of British law and authority throughout the empire. Wright was the only governor to actually enforce the Stamp Act, and though radical activity was never very pronounced in Georgia, he became increasingly hostile in his response to any anti-British sentiment.[9]

3

William Franklin of New Jersey was the one governor who probably came closest to John Wentworth in his beliefs and his desire to find some kind of rational accommodation between the extreme positions taken by radical colonists on the one hand and a stubborn and insensitive British administration on the other. Franklin was not motivated by an arbitrary view of the English constitution. His ability to see both sides of difficult issues led him to emphasize practical, workable solutions that he hoped would reduce the chance of conflict in the future. As a native colonist, Franklin, like Wentworth, had a good understanding of colonial views and an appreciation of the role and rights of colonial assemblies. And, also like Wentworth, before taking the governorship Franklin had spent considerable time in England, where he became acutely aware of the ignorance of British officials about the American colonies.

Nonetheless, William Franklin was not as successful as John Wentworth in maintaining the favor of his fellow colonists. Franklin has been described as "vain, ambitious and authoritarian."[10] Wentworth was young and he was vain, but he did not have the ambitions of William Franklin, and he was not authoritarian. Franklin was solidly middle class, but as royal governor he had access to the elite society of New Jersey into which he dearly desired acceptance. John Wentworth represented the establishment in his colony; William Franklin longed to be acknowledged by the establishment in his. As the illegitimate son of a prominent, self-made man, Franklin craved identity, which he found as a royal governor. Yet his background left him thin skinned, with little tolerance for criticism during a period of rising animosity toward royal officeholders. He lacked the equanimity possessed by John Wentworth, a trait of great value during the difficult years of the 1760s and 1770s.

William Franklin had little base of support in New Jersey. Unlike John Wentworth, he had no established family or mercantile roots in the province. In fact, when he came to New Jersey, he was faced by a party that already opposed him. The East Jersey proprietors were in close league with the proprietary party of Pennsylvania, which viewed the Franklin family as deadly enemies. Benjamin Franklin, William's father, was in the forefront of a growing movement to replace proprietary authority in Pennsylvania with royal government. As the son of Benjamin Franklin and a royal governor himself, William Franklin could count on the enmity of a large number of influential people in New Jersey.

4   Though James Wright and William Franklin were both born in America, neither was governor of the colony that had been his birthplace and home. Other than John Wentworth, the single Revolutionary period royal governor who had the kind of physical and emotional ties to his province that could develop only over generations was Thomas Hutchinson. Hutchinson's situation was like Wentworth's in many ways. His forebears migrated to New England in the 1630s, the same time as Wentworth's, and in fact it is likely their ancestors knew each other. Thomas Hutchinson descended from a line of successful merchants in Massachusetts, just as John Wentworth did in New Hampshire. Other aspects of the two men's backgrounds are remarkably similar. Hutchinson's family before him was actively involved in provincial politics, and they sent young Thomas to Harvard College. It was about that time that Hutchinson made some trading investments of his own, which multiplied significantly and became the basis of his personal fortune. While still in his twenties, Hutchinson, again like Wentworth, began a political career that lasted until he left the province. Both men were intelligent and industrious.

Beyond those general similarities, however, the two royal governors had little in common. Hutchinson was a generation older than Wentworth and vastly different in personality. Though Thomas Hutchinson was first a merchant and then long active in the everyday give-and-take of colonial politics, he had a strong intellectual bent. He was a collector and compiler of information and an indefatigable writer. His output of letters and other manuscripts was prodigious. He kept notebooks and diaries, and he wrote political treatises, legal opinions, and an exceptional history of the Massachusetts Bay colony. Hutchinson was not an innovative thinker, but few were better at analyzing the fine points of a legal tract or following the lines of logic in a political argument. He had the bookishness of a scholar and the personality to go with it.[11]

No one would ever have characterized Thomas Hutchinson as garrulous. Descriptions of him most often include adjectives like cold, aloof, humorless, reserved. Hutchinson was uncomfortable with those outside his immediate circle of family and friends, and he had little admiration for people in general. It is not surprising that his political views were hierarchical, that he placed great importance on the locus of authority and obedience to it. Hutchinson was conservative, he was cautious, and he readily accepted the received political wisdom of his age.

Hutchinson had served in the Massachusetts assembly for many years, and he did not quarrel with the idea of colonial rights within the British system. He believed, nevertheless, that because of their great distance from the seat of empire, the American colonists simply could not enjoy all of the rights of English people at home. Moreover, whatever rights the colonists did have could never take precedence over the policy of the British government. Hutchinson felt strongly that the location of ultimate authority must be clearly established and that such authority could lie only with the king in Parliament. British policy might not be beneficial at the local level, it might override what colonists traditionally considered to be their rights, but it was to be obeyed as the supreme law. The alternative, Hutchinson believed, was anarchy, the breakdown of all government and authority. If government policy brought hardships for colonists, they could seek redress through established political channels. But those channels were not effective in the 1760s and 1770s, and events led relentlessly toward revolution as Thomas Hutchinson's unyielding dedication to an arbitrary principle backed him ever more tightly into an inescapable corner.

John Wentworth was no more of an original political thinker than was Thomas Hutchinson, but his reaction to the political crisis enveloping British America was far different from that of his neighboring governor. Wentworth was not given to thinking in abstract terms such as principles, rights, or even authority. Although he appreciated books and relished the discovery of new information, he was not studious. He was a man of action for whom physical activity was an integral and important part of life. No better example can be found than his exertions to help his good friend Jeremy Belknap write a history of the province of New Hampshire. Not interested in writing himself but devoted to the project, Wentworth, on horseback and on foot, painstakingly collected facts about fauna, flora, geology, weather, and other physical features of the colony that found their way into the natural history portion of Belknap's work. Dedicated to education in his province, Wentworth regularly rode over the mountains to visit and inspect Dartmouth College, an institution he felt particularly responsible for. He was personally involved in all stages of the creation of his sumptuous estate in Wolfeboro. As surveyor general of the woods, Wentworth made many long and arduous forays into the interior to inspect timber and enforce the mast laws.

John Wentworth was a hands-on leader. He did not seek answers in abstract political ideas but looked for practical solutions to problems as they arose. His response to a challenge commonly involved taking some kind of personal action. As a result, he often dealt directly with people himself, something that was not difficult for Wentworth. Unlike Thomas Hutchinson, John Wentworth liked people, and evidence indicates that they responded positively to him. John

Wentworth seemed to have the common touch, something that could not be said of James Wright or William Franklin, and certainly not of Thomas Hutchinson. The inhabitants of New Hampshire found it hard to dislike their governor, even through difficult times.

It is not surprising that John Wentworth saw the answers to political problems in terms of people. For Wentworth it was beside the point to split constitutional hairs. The main requirement for a smoothly functioning and profitable empire, in his view, was to have practical people on both sides of the Atlantic—wise and thoughtful ministers in England and intelligent, sensitive royal officeholders in the colonies—who were dedicated to finding workable solutions. Wentworth believed it was important to have officials in government with the right attitude and the right approach, that is, men who could see beyond their own special interests and focus on what was best for all parts of the empire. Royal officials should demonstrate common sense, good will, and a willingness to accommodate differing views to reach a common goal. John Wentworth knew the importance of responsive, concerned governors in the colonies. He took his own responsibility to make the system work very seriously. The role of the ministers in London was even more important, and Wentworth continued to hope that they would take the right path or be replaced by men with a larger vision. People made things work. Only people could solve problems. John Wentworth did not relate to abstractions, but he understood people very well.

Wentworth made mistakes and he created enemies, but those eventualities were certain for all royal governors. He also retained the good will of his province more successfully than did any other royal governor during the Revolutionary period. While Hutchinson stood rigidly behind his idea of the English constitution until he was almost totally ineffectual and reviled by most of the people in his province, Wentworth looked for accommodation by focusing on people and achievable goals. In that sense, John Wentworth was a true politician. It has been suggested by modern political scholars that "the form or style of political ideology—favoring force or persuasion, compromise or arbitrary dictation, being tolerant or narrowly prejudiced, flexible or highly dogmatic in policy—is determined largely by personality considerations."[12] Though conditions for royal officials were unquestionably more favorable in New Hampshire than in Massachusetts (and other colonies as well), the New Hampshire governor's personality must be recognized as a factor in the persistence of positive feelings for him in his colony.

Like the other royal governors, however, John Wentworth could not escape the course of history. Appointed in 1766, he assumed the governor's responsibilities in New Hampshire the following year and vigorously and conscientiously carried them out until late summer 1775. At that time, no longer able to forestall in his small northern colony the crescendo of the revolutionary events that were engulfing British America, fearing for his family's safety and his own, Wentworth fled New Hampshire, fully expecting to return. He had no idea that he would never see his native province again.

* * *

This book emerged from a desire to understand why John Wentworth consistently appeared in a light different from that of other royal governors of the Revolutionary period. Why did both contemporary and later observers, on both sides of the Revolution, perceive him as an able, honest, forthright individual who happened to be caught in the wrong place at the wrong time? Why were opponents willing to praise him? Was Wentworth, in fact, as universally popular as those accounts seemed to indicate? If so, what were the sources of his popularity? I have indicated that personality must be considered a contributing factor. Political, economic, and other conditions also figured significantly in determining the tenor of John Wentworth's term as governor, and they have been closely examined.

Wentworth's early life has been explored. Into what sort of milieu was he born? What influence did his parents, other family members, and his friends have on him? How did his schooling affect his life? How were travel, romance, and other experiences significant in his development? All of these considerations help in understanding how Wentworth dealt with people and situations at the time of the Revolution.

Most of the answers to these questions unfolded logically in the course of research. One central question, however, was more difficult to resolve: Why did John Wentworth choose the side that he did? Why, when the American Revolution came, did he break with his family, his friends, and his native land? Why did he become a loyalist?

At first glance the answer appeared obvious. Wentworth possessed every attribute of a typical loyalist. He was a Crown officer, the highest in his province. His family had been closely connected with royal authority since early in the eighteenth century. Benning Wentworth, John's uncle, was governor of New Hampshire for a quarter of a century, longer than any other governor in the history of Britain's American colonies. The Wentworths made their home in Portsmouth, the only seaport in New Hampshire. They had accumulated great wealth through mercantile trade, mainly in timber, and had long been at the center of the elite in the province. John Wentworth was an adherent of the Anglican faith, which looked to London for authority and support and which was still regarded with suspicion in New England. Since birth, John Wentworth's fortunes had been closely tied to the mother country. The Wentworths' social and economic position at the top of New Hampshire society was dependent on political influence in England and on trade within the British Empire.

It seemed that there was really no choice for John Wentworth as the colonies proceeded ever faster down the road to revolution. Yet other factors made his loyalism less than a foregone conclusion. For one thing, Wentworth was a native of the colonies. Not only was he born in New Hampshire, but by his birth in 1737, the Wentworth family had already been in the province for a century. John Wentworth's long lineage in New Hampshire created ties with the colony that could not easily be severed. The same could also be said of Thomas Hutchinson in Massachusetts.

But it was Wentworth's own interests and inclinations that provided an even stronger bond with New Hampshire. The best example is the country estate he began building shortly after becoming governor. The mansion itself, when completed, was among the largest and most elaborate dwellings in New England. More remarkable, though, was its location in Wolfeboro, an unsettled town fifty miles northwest of Portsmouth, deep in the New Hampshire woods. During the warmer seasons, Wentworth spent as much time as possible at Wolfeboro, supervising the construction of his house, clearing land, planting crops, raising animals, observing and capturing native American wildlife, and in general enjoying nature.

John Wentworth's love of the outdoors gave him a special affection for New Hampshire. He took pride in the extraordinary natural attributes of his province—the forests, lakes, mountains, and seashore. He went out of his way to collect geographical and topographical information for Jeremy Belknap's history of New Hampshire. Instead of assigning his duties as surveyor general of the woods to a subordinate, Wentworth performed them himself, riding horseback hundreds of miles at a time through the forest with as much intention of greeting new settlers in his province as of apprehending violators of the mast laws.

During his years as governor, Wentworth made great efforts to develop the interior of New Hampshire. He promoted the building of roads and the division of the province into counties, both with an eye toward luring farmers to the virgin lands of the west and north. He encouraged the production of raw agricultural materials that New Hampshire could profitably trade to become a stronger, more self-sufficient member of the British Empire. The establishment of Dartmouth College within New Hampshire's borders owed much to Wentworth's efforts, an accomplishment he took great pride in. One of the roads he commissioned connected Wolfeboro, the site of his country home, with Hanover on the

Connecticut River, where the college was situated. Each spring he and a group of friends rode their horses over the mountains to attend commencement at the college and inspect the improvements made during the preceding year.

In North America, there was probably no governor who took a more genu- ine interest or greater pride in his colony than John Wentworth. His roots were five generations deep in New Hampshire soil, and he had developed a strong affection for the province on his own terms. That affinity made the growing rift between the colonies and Great Britain after he became governor in 1767 an especially wrenching experience for him. Moreover, at no time during the period up to 1775, when he left New Hampshire, was Wentworth in ready agreement with the colonial policies handed down from Whitehall. As an active merchant from a leading mercantile family, John Wentworth could see as well as anyone the great discouragements to trade caused by the recent regulations. Why, then, did he abandon New Hampshire in support of British authority and imperial policies about which he had strong negative feelings?

To fully understand John Wentworth as he left New Hampshire in 1775, one additional, deciding factor must be taken into account. Wentworth had developed a special connection with England as well. That link had not only influenced much of his personal life and his activities as governor but had also colored his view of the relationship between Great Britain and the American colonies during the critical period leading up to the American Revolution. Specifically, the connection was his close bond with Charles Watson-Wentworth, the marquis of Rockingham.

John Wentworth became acquainted with Rockingham in England during the mid-1760s. When the two men discovered they had many interests in common and were also distantly related, their friendship grew rapidly. In 1765, when George III placed Rockingham at the head of the government, thereby saddling him with the responsibility for resolving the Stamp Act crisis in America, Wentworth was one of the first people Rockingham turned to for information and advice about the colonies.

As first minister and leader of the whig faction, Rockingham deliberated carefully over proper policy for America. When finally formulated, that policy was both moderate and practical. Strangling economic restrictions on the colonies were to be lifted in the interest of welding the British Empire into a single prospering unit. What was good for trade in the colonies would also benefit Britain. Early in 1766, the Rockingham administration pressed for and gained the repeal of the Stamp Act.

John Wentworth could not have been happier. He himself had decried British barriers to colonial economic development, and months earlier he had been among the first to recommend repeal of the Stamp Act to Rockingham. Rockingham's assiduous study of the situation, the meetings he held, the political dinners he attended, his eventual commitment to repeal, and the support he mustered to achieve it, all served as proof to John Wentworth that here was a British official with a broad vision. Rockingham was committed to a strong empire, one to which the American colonies would make a major contribution. Restrictive trade and tax policies would only hinder the development of the struggling provinces and diminish their ability to support a thriving British system. Wentworth's later efforts as governor to develop agriculture and transportation within New Hampshire reflected his commitment to Rockingham's vision of a profitable, healthy empire in which the colonies played a vital role.

With the repeal of the Stamp Act, John Wentworth had seen firsthand the significance of an enlightened administration at Whitehall. A short time after the repeal of the Stamp Act, however, the Rockingham ministry was turned out for political reasons, unfortunately for New Hampshire and the colonies from Wentworth's point of view. The succeeding government, under the influence of Charles Townshend, the chancellor of the Exchequer, proceeded by adopting new revenue measures that brought immediate negative repercussions in America and caused John Wentworth some of his earliest difficulties as governor of New Hampshire. As relations between Britain and her colonies deteriorated in the ensuing years, Wentworth consistently marveled at what he considered the unwise policies emanating from the home government and the injudicious enforcement of those policies by Crown officers in America. At the same time, the conduct of the Rockingham government during the Stamp Act trouble served as an enduring example to Wentworth of the way in which sound formulation and administration of colonial policy could redound to the benefit and happiness of everyone.

The solution that Wentworth envisioned to the growing problems in the colonies during the early 1770s was the return to sober, rational government in Britain. He had himself observed that kind of government at work and was convinced that such a change in administration could again restore amity between the mother country and her North American provinces.

This is not the story of a loyalist. That portion of John Wentworth's life came later. This book describes how an American colonist who was also a high royal official dealt with the difficult and traumatic situation created by revolutionary events in the 1760s and 1770s. When John Wentworth left New Hampshire in the midst of crisis in 1775, he was not choosing one side over another. There was no idea in his mind of a permanent break between the colonies and England. He had no perception of himself as a loyalist, for it was only a matter of time until sound government and reasonable policies would be restored at White-hall. Then the problems in America could be rationally resolved. He had been present during an earlier period of such resolution with Rockingham and the Stamp Act. The gravity of events in 1775 now demanded a similar course. What other choice could there be? Perhaps Rockingham himself would be called back to head a conciliatory government.

John Wentworth's English connection, his experience in England in the 1760s and his subsequent attachment to the marquis of Rockingham, blinded him to the stark reality of what had happened to the British-colonial relationship since the time of the Stamp Act. It was this English connection that led him to leave New Hampshire in full expectation of an eventual peaceful settlement and his return to the province. In 1775, John Wentworth did not realize that the remainder of his life would be spent in permanent exile from his native land.

»I«
SERVANTS OF THE KING

The Wentworths in England and America

John Adams had gone to the theater that evening to see a performance of Voltaire's *Brutus*. "As I was coming out of the Box," he later remembered, "a Gentleman seized me by the hand. I looked at him.—Governor Wentworth, Sir, said the Gentleman.—At first I was somewhat embarrassed and knew not how to behave towards him. As my Classmate and Friend at Colledge and ever since, I could have pressed him to my Bosom, with the most cordial Affection. But we now belonged to two different Nations at War with each other and consequently We were enemies." [1]

The date was the second of May 1778. The place, Paris. Adams was at the theater trying to improve his rudimentary French. As a minister of the infant United States government seeking badly needed French aid in the struggle to throw off British rule, Adams needed all the subtleties of language he could muster. The man who greeted him was John Wentworth, the last royal governor of New Hampshire. Adams and Wentworth had first met at Harvard College, where they graduated together in the class of 1755. After college the two maintained their friendship, despite disturbing changes that drew them down rapidly diverging political paths.

Beginning as a small town lawyer, Adams became an outspoken and influential leader of the mounting colonial resistance to British rule through the 1760s and 1770s. As a member of the Continental Congress, he played a vital role in declaring America independent from Great Britain in 1776. Wentworth, on the other hand, followed in his family's footsteps and became a royal officeholder. As the king's governor of New Hampshire from 1767 to 1775, he tried desperately to reconcile the British and colonial points of view. In the summer of 1775,

Wentworth paid for his continued allegiance to the Crown when a growing distaste for English domination erupted into mob violence, driving him from his own province. Since then he had worked actively in both America and Europe for the restoration of British authority in the colonies. By 1778 he was living in London and now was in Paris with Paul Wentworth, his distant kinsman and close friend—and premier British spy.

As Adams fumbled for words at this awkward meeting, he realized that spies of the French police were watching. He was relieved when his old friend took the initiative and made small talk, inquiring after his father, Mark Hunking Wentworth, and friends whom he had left behind in America nearly three years earlier. The governor then asked Adams about the health of Dr. Franklin and promised he would come out to Passy and pay his respects to the gentleman. Wentworth had known Franklin since 1765–1766 when they had both worked against the Stamp Act in London.

After Wentworth's visit to the Paris suburb several days later, Adams seemed quite pleased to report of his old friend, "Not an indelicate expression to Us or our country or our ally escaped him. His whole behaviour was that of an accomplished Gentleman."[2] It is hard to imagine John Adams, a man of volatile passions, without a strong prejudice against any British supporter, particularly at this critical time with the fighting still going on and the result still very much in doubt. Yet it is clear that Adams held no ill-will toward John Wentworth.

Unlikely friends in 1778, John Adams and John Wentworth were improbable friends from the beginning. Adams was descended from a long line of Puritan farmers. Although his mother was a Boylston and his father a prominent citizen and deacon of the Braintree church, the Adams family was little known beyond the confines of the community.

Wentworth, by contrast, was the scion of the most powerful mercantile and political family in New Hampshire. His grandfather, for whom John was named, had been lieutenant governor of the province. His uncle, Benning Wentworth, had been governor of New Hampshire for ten years by the time John rode off to Harvard in 1751. Benning Wentworth would continue in office another fifteen years, making his term longer than that of any other governor in the history of Britain's American colonies. John's father, Mark Hunking Wentworth, through political influence and lucrative mast contracts with the Royal Navy, was the richest man in New Hampshire.

In addition, the Wentworths were Anglican, a religious affiliation politically correct for a family dependent on royal patronage but anathema to most New Englanders, including the Adamses, who held to the faith of their Puritan forebears. The broad social gap between the two young men was apparent in their college standing. In the mid-eighteenth century, Harvard did not rank students according to their scholastic achievements but by the economic and social status of their families. In the class of 1755, Wentworth was number five; Adams, fourteen.[3]

John Adams and John Wentworth are clear examples of the stratified society that had evolved in colonial America since the first settlements over a century earlier. In that distant past, however, their roots were remarkably similar. In the late 1630s, the great-great-grandfathers of both men, Henry Adams and William Wentworth, unknown to each other, had migrated from England to Massachusetts to pursue common Puritan beliefs. In 1640 Adams was farming his own land in Braintree. Wentworth, by that time, had already headed north to New Hampshire.

* * *

On 15 March 1616, William Wentworth of Rigsby and his wife, Susannah, took their baby, William, to be baptized in the market town of Alford in eastern Lincolnshire, a low-lying part of England characterized by fens and canals and often likened to Holland just across the North Sea. Young William was destined to be the first Wentworth to go to America. He was distantly related to the Wentworths of Wentworth-Woodhouse in Yorkshire's West Riding. From that branch of the family came many of the great English Wentworths, including Sir Thomas Wentworth, earl of Strafford, beheaded in 1641 in the cause of King Charles I, and Charles Watson-Wentworth, second marquis of Rockingham, head of the British ministry in 1765 at the time of the Stamp Act furor in America.[4]

The first evidence of William Wentworth in America is his signature, among a number of others—headed by that of the Reverend John Wheelwright—on a mutual compact of government at Exeter, New Hampshire, dated July 1639. Wentworth probably was among a group of Wheelwright's relatives and friends who disembarked at Boston in July 1637.

In 1632 John Wheelwright, a Puritan minister, lost his benefice at Bilsby near Alford because of alleged unorthodox opinions emanating from his pulpit. Four years later he left for New England, where others with similar spiritual views had already gone, most importantly his wife's brothers, William and Edward Hutchinson, and their families. Wheelwright did not know that he had left a religious and political controversy in England only to step into another in Massachusetts.

Within months he found himself, along with his sister-in-law Anne Hutchinson and a group of followers, accused of spreading heretical religious ideas that were considered a threat to the Puritan oligarchy of Massachusetts Bay. As a result, in late 1637 the Antinomians, as they were derisively labeled by their accusers, were banished from the colony. Mrs. Hutchinson and her family followed the example of Roger Williams and moved to Rhode Island. Choosing a different course, John Wheelwright gathered some twenty of his adherents and their families together, apparently including young William Wentworth, and in the chill of late November 1637 set out north to found the community of Exeter in the wilds of New Hampshire.[5]

By 1650 William Wentworth had married and made a permanent home in Dover, New Hampshire, then under the jurisdiction of Massachusetts. He acquired a generous quantity of land through grants and gained mill rights on a nearby stream. He soon became involved in the developing lumber trade, a business that would play a key role in the future of New Hampshire as well as in the rise to prominence of the Wentworth family in the province.[6]

Of the eleven known children of William Wentworth, Samuel, born in Exeter in 1641, was the oldest and the progenitor of the later governors of New Hampshire. Samuel Wentworth moved to Portsmouth in 1678 and, five years later, purchased the large and unusually fine home of Lieutenant Governor Cranfield. Built in 1671, the house had served previously as a tavern, and Wentworth now returned it to that purpose. Samuel presided over his public house for seven years, but in March 1691 he succumbed to one of the deadly killers of the colonial period, smallpox. The responsibilities of both family and business were left to his wife, Mary Benning Wentworth, and his nineteen-year-old son, John.[7]

More than seventy-five years later, in 1767, when Samuel's great-grandson John Wentworth came to the governor's chair, he assumed the leadership not only of New Hampshire but of the Wentworth family, whose wealth, position, and political power had dominated the province for five decades. That legacy had its real beginnings with Samuel Wentworth's son, John. In 1693 in his father's spacious tavern, John Wentworth married Sarah, daughter of a prominent Portsmouth sea captain, Mark Hunking. Their sixteen children were born in this same building, among them a future governor of New Hampshire, Benning, and the father of yet another governor, Mark Hunking.[8]

John Wentworth, like many others in the seafaring community of Portsmouth, started his career as a ship's captain, moving with advancing age to the more sedentary role of merchant. In 1712 he was appointed to fill a vacancy in the New Hampshire council and, a short time later, was chosen as a judge of the court of common pleas. Although New Hampshire had been dislodged from the jurisdiction of Massachusetts in 1679 and made a separate royal province, from the early eighteenth century it had shared a governor with its larger neighbor to the south. Because the governor of Massachusetts and New Hampshire rarely ventured above the Merrimack River, executive responsibilities in the northern province were largely in the hands of the lieutenant governor. In 1717, when Lieutenant Governor George Vaughan was removed after antagonizing both Governor Samuel Shute and the New Hampshire council and assembly, John Wentworth was chosen for the post.[9]

Wentworth served as lieutenant governor of New Hampshire from 1717 until his death in 1730. He made particularly good use of the period between 1722 and 1728, when there was no governor in Massachusetts, to consolidate his power and advance his family's position in the province. When Wentworth granted new townships, his close associates and members of his family, as well as every member of the assembly, became landowners. During his tenure, according to one historian, "the Wentworths and their associated clans," who composed "the ruling clique of Portsmouth merchants," developed "a tightly woven coterie of wealth and political power."[10]

Wentworth was the leader of the New Hampshire faction pushing for complete separation from the province to the south. That desire was tied directly to the fact that the Massachusetts governor had made grants of land in territory claimed by New Hampshire, land that otherwise could be granted by Lieutenant Governor Wentworth to his relations and members of the legislature. Governor Shute, however, had covered himself in New Hampshire by distributing land and political appointments to certain influential families, primarily to the Waldrons and Sherburnes, thus setting the stage for future strife in New Hampshire between the Massachusetts party and those agitating for a total break with the Bay Colony. When Lieutenant Governor Wentworth died in 1730, leadership of the Portsmouth group dedicated to the independence of New Hampshire fell to his oldest son, Benning, soon to be a member of the assembly and later advanced to the council. It is not surprising that Governor Belcher of Massachusetts found Benning Wentworth a "rascal" and a "contemptible simpleton."[11]

Born in 1696 and a graduate of Harvard College, Benning Wentworth was a merchant, first in Boston and later in his native Portsmouth, who dealt largely in the New Hampshire timber trade with Spain. In 1732 Wentworth was elected to the House of Representatives, where he and Theodore Atkinson, who had married Benning's sister Hannah the same year, created as much trouble as possible for Governor Belcher. Lieutenant Governor Dunbar, though not a native of New Hampshire, was equally opposed to Belcher and had recommended Wentworth and Atkinson for places on the council. Belcher managed to block those appointments for two years, but in 1734 he was forced to accept the inevitable.

Wentworth, however, soon became more concerned with his own business affairs. In 1733, as a result of the deteriorating relations between Spain and England, the Spanish reneged on a huge payment due Benning Wentworth for a valuable shipment of New England oak delivered to Cadiz. To satisfy his Boston creditors, Wentworth borrowed money in London and then badgered the English government to press the Spanish for payment, but to no avail. Benning Wentworth was bankrupt in 1738 when New Hampshire's English agent, John Thomlinson, came to his rescue. Thomlinson had convinced Wentworth's creditors that their best chance of being repaid lay in backing him as the independent governor of New Hampshire. Jonathan Belcher had other enemies besides the Wentworth faction, and in 1741, when William Shirley replaced Belcher as governor of Massachusetts, New Hampshire also received a new governor—this time one of its own—Benning Wentworth.[12]

More than anyone else, Benning Wentworth was responsible for making the name Wentworth nearly legendary in New Hampshire. He literally ruled the province for twenty-five years, the longest reign of any governor in the history of England's American colonies. But Wentworth did not go unchallenged throughout this period. A remnant of Belcher's party remained in New Hampshire, led by Richard Waldron and determined to undermine the new governor's authority at any cost. When Waldron contrived a plan to have the governor replaced and filed a complaint against him in England, Wentworth effectively countered the charge.

More serious was the threat mounted by Waldron and his cohorts in the assembly elected in 1748. Earlier that year, the governor had issued precepts to a number of new towns to return representatives to the House, which they did. The Waldron faction, charging that this was a violation of the House's own prerogative, organized a majority of old members to vote against seating the new representatives. Wentworth, in response, disallowed the House's choice of speaker, Waldron himself, and would not recognize the House as a legally constituted body. With the battle lines drawn, the House took up the offensive; the representatives petitioned the Crown and wrote to their agent, Thomlinson, leveling serious charges against the governor and asking for his removal. What they did not know was that Thomlinson, a mast contractor for the Royal Navy, had a close working relationship with Benning Wentworth, who, besides being governor of the province that shipped out most of America's white pine masts, had in 1743 also received the commission of Surveyor General of His Majesty's Woods in North America. In addition, Wentworth, expecting just such a challenge to his authority, had requested and received additional instructions specifically granting him the power to issue election precepts to new communities.

The opposition's efforts in England failed, but they continued to hold out hope in America. Wentworth kept the assembly in session, but because of its "notorious and unjustifiable . . . Act of disobedience," he refused to grant it legal recognition. As a result, public affairs in New Hampshire, including the collection of taxes, payment of militia, occupation of new lands—even the payment of the governor, which by this time Wentworth felt he could weather—came to a virtual halt for three years. Under the province's triennial act, Governor Wentworth finally called for new elections, and when the new assembly met early in 1752, the sentiment for conciliation was obvious. The new members were seated, and Wentworth had won a victory for the royal prerogative unparalleled in American colonial history.[13]

Wentworth's triumph ended the only serious threat to his consolidation of power in New Hampshire, and under his leadership and patronage an elite group of Portsmouth merchants, primarily close family members and friends, came to dominate the highest political offices and most lucrative economic opportunities in the province.[14] The council and judicial offices were controlled by his relatives, who also were made proprietors in nearly all of the numerous townships granted by the governor. Mark Hunking Wentworth, as the brother of the surveyor general of the woods, monopolized the New Hampshire mast trade as agent for the Royal Navy's contractor, Thomlinson, and as a result became the wealthiest man in the colony.

Yet Benning Wentworth was too clever a politician to ignore areas where criticism might emerge. After the Waldron faction had dissipated its strength in the three-year controversy, the governor saw to it that land, lesser offices, military commissions, and supply contracts were distributed liberally among House members. To further placate the assembly when the occasion demanded, Wentworth ignored his instructions and let bills that he knew would be disapproved by the home government pass into law without the precautionary suspending clause. There were few representatives, most themselves men of property, who did not benefit from Wentworth's rule in New Hampshire.

The people in general too were satisfied. Land was always in demand, and Benning Wentworth, buoyed by the belief that New Hampshire's jurisdiction extended almost as far west as the Hudson River, viewed the supply as nearly endless. As a result, he placed the terms of acquisition and occupation—small fees or sometimes no fee at all and a quit rent of one ear of Indian corn for the first ten years—within nearly everyone's grasp.[15] Wentworth, governor of a colony that depended for its prosperity on the timber trade more than on any other industry, in his other role of surveyor general might have alienated large numbers of people by a strict enforcement of British mast laws that restricted the cutting of New Hampshire's valuable white pine. Yet, as long as the

Wentworth interests received their masts and maintained their profits, he conveniently overlooked legal irregularities that constantly occurred in New Hampshire's forests. Thus Wentworth maintained the loyalty of his constituents, both large and small.

One of the delicate tasks of every royal governor was the need to satisfy both the people of his province and the government in England. For most of his twenty-five years as governor, Benning Wentworth was able to do that. He convinced London that there was no illegal trade in or out of the Piscataqua and that no one was more diligent than he in enforcing the mast laws. He was active in prosecuting the war against the French and Indians, and his support of Anglicanism, including the practice of setting aside one lot in every new town for the Society for the Propagation of the Gospel, further endeared him to those in power in England.

Finally, but not least important, was the influence wielded by the agent John Thomlinson at court. Thomlinson, who was close to the duke of Newcastle and had contacts in most government agencies, including the Board of Trade, performed invaluable services for Benning Wentworth. When needed, he obtained additional instructions or permission to disregard instructions for Wentworth; he was able to prevent disputes involving Wentworth from reaching the Privy Council, and he kept the governor apprised of any adverse gossip circulating in England that might be detrimental to his position.

From Whitehall to the White Mountains, Benning Wentworth controlled his own political destiny. Through a monopoly of New Hampshire's prime resources, land and timber, he was able not only to enrich his relations but to accumulate a personal fortune large enough to offset any worry about the assembly's willingness to grant him a proper salary each year. He lived in a large, rambling house of fifty-two rooms two miles south of Portsmouth, hard by the water at Little Harbor.[16] One of those rooms, high ceilinged with an elaborately carved mantel, served as a council chamber, especially during the latter part of his administration when he was afflicted with severe attacks of gout. Occasionally he even invited the members of the assembly out for refreshments, no doubt including a toast to the king, the ostensible source of all their good fortune.

Benning Wentworth had created a highly effective political machine, notable for its stability and the general harmony it produced. A noted historian has termed New Hampshire "the exception that helps explain the rule" of American colonies torn by factionalism and political strife during this period, important elements in the "latently revolutionary" character of eighteenth-century America.[17] But Wentworth could not go on indefinitely, and in the 1760s new

Benning Wentworth, by Joseph Blackburn
(New Hampshire Historical Society)

circumstances, some beyond his control, began to produce small fissures in his well-organized system.

John Thomlinson's health declined and, with it, his influence and effectiveness on Wentworth's behalf in British government circles. Exacerbating that situation, Newcastle and his supporters fell from power in 1761 when young George III brought in his favorite, Lord Bute. Governor Wentworth not only lost his leverage in England but also had to contend with the efforts of an avowed enemy, John Huske, whose father Wentworth had forced to resign from the chief justiceship of New Hampshire in 1754. Huske, who had influence among the new elements in English government, was elected to Parliament in 1764. Adding to those problems were hearings opened by the Board of Trade in 1763, at the request of New York, into the legitimacy of New Hampshire jurisdiction and land grants west of the Connecticut River. As a result of the inquiries, those lands were forfeited to New York, and further investigations into Governor Wentworth's activities persuaded British officials by 1765 that Wentworth's abuse of power required his removal.

As the governor became aware of the gravity of his situation, he sought help in salvaging at least his dignity if not his position. He was fortunate that his vigorous, intelligent nephew, Mark Hunking Wentworth's son John, was at that time in England. John Wentworth had become an intimate of the marquis of Rockingham, who in 1765 rose to the head of the British ministry, and he was willing to intercede with the government on behalf of his uncle. In 1767, amidst an unsettling background of increasing hostility between the colonies and Great Britain, when old, gouty Benning Wentworth finally relinquished his responsibilities as governor of New Hampshire after twenty-five long and eventful years, young John Wentworth was there to take his place.[18]

A VARIED EDUCATION

Portsmouth,
Cambridge, and Boston,
1737–1755

The birth of a son, John, in Portsmouth, New Hampshire, on the ninth of August 1737 must have been especially pleasing to Mark Hunking Wentworth and Elizabeth Rindge Wentworth, since two earlier children had died. Hoping to change what was seemingly a bad omen in naming the first two sons Mark after their father, the parents named this child for his grandfather, John Wentworth, the lieutenant governor of New Hampshire from 1717 until his death in 1730. Five days later the boy was baptized in Queen's Chapel by the Reverend Arthur Brown, a missionary for the Society for the Propagation of the Gospel who within the previous year had been appointed rector of New Hampshire's only Anglican congregation.[1]

On the paternal side, John Wentworth was born into one of the province's most politically important families. His mother's lineage was notable as well. Elizabeth Wentworth was the daughter of John Rindge, a prominent Portsmouth merchant. As province agent in Britain in the early 1730s, Rindge had initiated proceedings that eventually led to the settlement of the long-standing New Hampshire–Massachusetts boundary dispute. Rindge also was responsible for hiring the influential London merchant John Thomlinson as New Hampshire's permanent agent in England.[2] Thus, through both parents John Wentworth inherited a highly respected place in the mercantile aristocracy that governed Portsmouth and New Hampshire.

Little is known of Mark Hunking Wentworth beyond the fact that he was a merchant and shipowner who eventually acquired great wealth. When his son was born in 1737, the Wentworths' circumstances were not what they had been nor what they would become in the future. Mark Hunking's father, the lieutenant governor, had died seven years earlier. His brother Benning, thirteen years his senior, had been a member of the assembly and the council but was now struggling under the burden of a great debt verging on bankruptcy as a result of his losses in the Spanish timber trade. Although Mark was involved in trading ventures with Benning, his brother-in-law Theodore Atkinson, his father-in-law John Rindge, and others, at the age of twenty-eight he probably was still considered a junior partner. Even so, by 1737 he had done well.[3] Moreover, his fortunes were about to take a turn for the better.

In the late 1730s, fortuitous circumstances combined to improve the position of all the Wentworths, including Mark Hunking. During the thirties, he and Theodore Atkinson had been trading with the English merchant and New Hampshire agent John Thomlinson. Toward the end of the decade, Thomlinson, through his influence at court and connections in New Hampshire, was able to get a contract from the navy board to supply the Royal Navy with New Hampshire pine masts. To help him fulfill his obligations to the navy, Thomlinson turned to Mark Hunking Wentworth, whom he made his chief subcontractor, or agent, in New Hampshire, the man responsible for supplying him with sturdy white pine logs suitable for naval use.[4] It was also in the late thirties that a dispute with Spain, the War of Jenkin's Ear, followed by the broader conflict with France known in America as King George's War created what one authority has called "a demand of unprecedented proportions" by the British navy for New England's white pines.[5]

Added to those events, in 1741 Benning Wentworth, through the good offices of Thomlinson, was handed the governorship of New Hampshire. Even more important for the fortunes of Mark Hunking Wentworth was the purchase by Benning, just two years later, of the office of Surveyor General of His Majesty's Woods in North America. The surveyor general's job was to protect potential mast trees for the British government, and only he could grant the license needed to cut those masts. Thus by 1743 Mark Hunking Wentworth had a virtual monopoly over the mast trade, a lucrative business even in slow times but especially so during periods of war. By 1763, when the Peace of Paris finally brought an end to the British-French struggle in North America, Mark Wentworth was the richest man in Portsmouth.[6]

Born into a family of position and wealth, John Wentworth enjoyed close bonds with his parents. Many years later, long after he was forced from New Hampshire and upon hearing that he had virtually been left out of his mother's will, he wrote to his cousin John Peirce in Portsmouth: The news "can never for a moment extort an unfilial tho't from my heart, which is dutifully & kindly attached to the memory of a venerable parent, whose parental care & attention to my earliest childhood & youngest days implanted in my mind sentiments of reverance."[7] Beyond his immediate family, John formed close relationships among the many uncles, aunts, and cousins who made up the intricate network of Wentworth relations in the small society of Portsmouth. Some of those ties, such as that with the Peirces, lasted a lifetime, even though Wentworth no longer lived in New Hampshire and by law could never return. John Peirce was the son of Daniel Peirce, whose wife, Ann Rindge, was a sister of John Wentworth's mother.[8] Wentworth's mother's brother, Daniel Rindge, a respected merchant and only five years his senior, was also one of John's confidants. From England in 1765 he wrote to Rindge for advice and emphasized their "friendship which has been my peculiar happiness to have enjoyed from my earliest youth."[9] John Wentworth's youth, spent amidst prosperity and familial warmth, was by all appearances happy. That assumption is reinforced by many later descriptions of him as a gracious and even-tempered adult.

In April 1740 another son, Thomas, was born to Mark and Elizabeth Wentworth. At about that time, with their growing family in mind, the Wentworths moved to a large house at the corner of Daniel and Chapel streets in Portsmouth.[10] The two-story house, built some years earlier by Captain Thomas Daniel, for whom the street was named, had a gambrel roof, "massive chimneys," and a wine cellar large enough to hold a year's supply of the best Portuguese port and madeira. Shortly before it was demolished in the midnineteenth century, an observer called it "a mansion of the highest class." From its description, it sounds remarkably similar to a house built directly across the street in 1716 by the Scottish-born merchant and iron manufacturer, Archibald Macphaedris. Constructed of brick and still standing, the Macphaedris house is one of the most elegant examples of early Georgian architecture in New England, and it seems probable that Captain Daniel kept his eye cast in that direction as he built his own home.[11] Giant elms in front of the Wentworths' new residence shaded passersby on the busy thoroughfare between the wharves on the river and Market Square at the center of town. Living just halfway along that short route, young John Wentworth, with little brother Thomas tagging along, must have often headed for the docks to catch a glimpse of sail downriver on an inbound schooner or to hear sailors boasting of their exploits in Tobago or Cadiz as they lowered down a butt of wine or heaved on a quintal of cod.

Outbound vessels, as they slipped away from the Piscataqua wharves and threaded their way down the deep, narrow tidal channel among numerous islands, through the pool, past Newcastle at the mouth of the harbor, and into the open sea, most often carried products from New Hampshire's forests destined for the West Indies. Other items too were shipped out, such as beef, fish, rum, and horses, but the indispensable export was timber. It went as staves and hoops for barrels; as building materials such as planks, joists, clapboards, and shingles; or sometimes as a completely finished large chest of drawers or a delicate comb-back Windsor chair crafted by one of Portsmouth's fine cabinetmakers. New Hampshire's products were exchanged at Barbados, Antigua, Jamaica, and other ports of call in the Caribbean for sugar and molasses, which might be brought directly back to Portsmouth to be made into rum. More often, however, the West Indian produce was either transported to the southern and middle colonies and traded for foodstuffs and naval stores or carried to England to be sold along with the Piscataqua-built ship to pay earlier debts incurred there with merchants for British manufactured goods.[12]

There were, of course, variations and permutations of that trade. Occasionally ships headed directly for England loaded with enumerated materials, such as mast timber, and returned with sundry items for the shelves of local shopkeepers—Irish linen and German serge, bone lace, buttons, pins, ribbons, tea, coffee, nails, powder and shot, Staffordshire or porcelain dishes, East Indian spices. They also brought ship fittings—canvas, cordage, iron ware—to complete vessels built from New Hampshire timber.[13] At other times, Piscataqua captains, such as those in the employ of Benning Wentworth, might steer for the Wine Islands, Portugal, or Spain with fish or lumber to trade for casks of madeira, sherry, and port destined for the tables of Portsmouth merchants. Some ships were sent north to Newfoundland to take on fish for the Caribbean or Iberian trade; in addition, there was an active commercial intercourse with the colonies to the south. Still, the mainstay of the Portsmouth trade was lumber to the West Indies, which allowed New Hampshire to import the food it needed to supplement its own supply and to procure the manufactured niceties and necessities that it could not produce for itself.

The lure of the sea and images of faraway places were not the only sources of excitement for a boy growing up in Portsmouth, New Hampshire, in the 1740s. The fierce struggle between England and its bitter rival France for control of the North American continent was too close to home for the residents of New Hampshire to ignore. From Quebec and the St. Lawrence in the northeast, through the Great Lakes and down the Mississippi to New Orleans in the southwest, the French had virtually cordoned off the English seaboard colonies and were gradually edging eastward. Alliances with the many tribes of Indians in that vast hinterland were fostered by French fur traders and Jesuit missionaries, and it was only a matter of time until the conflict, which had stirred sporadically in the late seventeenth and early eighteenth centuries, would break out again. The War of the Austrian Succession in Europe gave the French an excuse,

26

and in 1744 they attacked Nova Scotia, taken from them by the English in the Treaty of Utrecht of 1713, thus beginning in America what was known as King George's War.

New Hampshire was in a vulnerable position. Its sparse population was con-   27
centrated near the seacoast. The frontier was no farther than twenty miles from Portsmouth, the capital and commercial center of the province. Sitting at the top of the tier of English colonies, closest to Canada, it was obviously open to attack from the French and their Indian allies. There was good reason, then, for John Wentworth's uncle, Benning, as governor of New Hampshire, to back a plan conceived by Governor William Shirley of Massachusetts. Shirley hoped to raise a large force among the New England colonies and any others that could be induced to contribute men and money for the purpose of capturing the formidable French fortress of Louisbourg. From its strategic location on Cape Breton Island, Louisbourg commanded the Gulf of St. Lawrence and protected Canada. Massachusetts voted fifty thousand pounds and raised 3,250 men for the expedition. Tiny New Hampshire could hardly match that, but Governor Wentworth did manage to wheedle thirteen thousand pounds out of the assembly and to raise 500 men and an armed sloop to carry them. In keeping with the purely colonial nature of the operation, William Pepperrell, a merchant from Kittery, Maine, just across the river from Portsmouth, commanded the entire force of more than 4,000 men.[14]

The Louisbourg expedition of 1745 marked the greatest achievement in intercolonial cooperation before the American Revolution, and American colonists, especially New Englanders, had cause to be proud of their effort. The New England forces, including New Hampshire's troops, arrived at Louisbourg at the end of April and laid siege to the French bastion. On 17 June, the French commander, Duchambon, ill supplied and with a mutinous garrison on his hands, surrendered to the motley New England militia of carpenters, farmers, and fishermen. When word of the stunning victory traveled back down the coast—to Falmouth, Portsmouth, Boston—there was great rejoicing. A day of thanksgiving was declared in Massachusetts, Thomas Prince in Boston prayed that this would be "the *dawning Earnest* of our DIVINE REDEEMER'S carrying on his Triumphs thro' the *Northern Regions*," and while still at Louisbourg, William Pepperrell was made a baronet by George II, only the second American colonist to receive that honor. As historian Jeremy Belknap claimed some years later, the conquest "filled America with joy, and Europe with astonishment."[15]

The French were not the only menace feared in Portsmouth. Even though the seacoast area of New Hampshire had been settled as early as 1623, conflicts with Indians continued in the province more than a hundred years later.

In 1744, Samuel Lane, only five miles from Portsmouth, jotted in his journal: "Many people Driven out of the Woods by Indians and people kept Garrison at Newmarket; Alarms Made often. Where I live, we heard Alarms often, & Horns Sounded on the other Side the River, and People much Distress'd by Indians." The following year, Louisbourg was taken, and the war on the frontier correspondingly heated up. Beginning in July, several incidents occurred near isolated settlements in western New Hampshire. At Great Meadow (later Westmoreland) on the Connecticut River, William Phips, attacked while weeding corn, shot one Indian and wounded another with his hoe before three of their comrades killed him.[16]

Such hostilities were commonplace. People huddled in garrison houses, afraid to work their fields, while Indians slaughtered their livestock. By 1746 the terror had moved eastward from the Connecticut to the Merrimack, and in June Indians struck within twenty miles of Portsmouth at Rochester. Again, men working in a field were surprised, and four were killed, including one John Wentworth, a distant cousin of young John in Portsmouth.[17] With the very real threat of invasion by a foreign power and with kinsmen being tomahawked only a few miles away, a boy growing up in eighteenth-century New Hampshire did not have to rely entirely on his imagination for drama in daily life. Maturity developed rapidly on the colonial frontier.

But a young man could not spend all his time dreaming of places with romantic names or even considering the stark realities of a frontier that seemed almost too close. Most of his youth would be devoted to the abstractions demanded by schooling, especially if his family's means and position dictated that he go to college, as John Wentworth was expected to do. We do not know where or from whom John received his early education, but a hint lies in a later statement when, as governor, he was praised as one whose "birth and education have been in the province."[18] His parents were in a position to provide him with private tutors, but it is just as plausible that he attended the small school only a block and a half south of his home, particularly since Portsmouth as early as 1701 required a schoolmaster who could teach children not only the basic reading, writing, and arithmetic but also "the tonges and other learning as may fit them for the colledg."[19]

Before beginning his college preparatory classes, John Wentworth spent his first several years learning to read, perform basic arithmetic, and form his letters carefully. He must have taken the penmanship lessons to heart for his writing as an adult is large and easy to read, a characteristic not always common in the eighteenth century. Once the fundamentals were mastered, classical studies made up a major part of the preparation for college and usually took about seven years.

College rules still required that applicants for admission be able to "read, construe and parse Tully, Virgil, or Such like common Classical Latin Authors, . . .
to write true Latin in Prose, and . . . verse, . . . and to read, construe and parse
ordinary Greek."[20]

Prospective freshmen at Harvard College were examined by the president
and tutors shortly before commencement, which traditionally was held on a
Wednesday in July. By 1751, before he was fourteen, John Wentworth and his
schoolmaster decided that he had progressed far enough in his studies to present
himself for admittance. The exams that year were scheduled for Friday and Saturday, the fifth and sixth of July. Wentworth left no account of his journey south
to Cambridge, but we can gain some insight into the experience of a young
man facing that crucial test from the remembrance of his future classmate, John
Adams, who rode north from Braintree the same July. With his instructor ill
and unable to go with him as planned, Adams was mortified at the thought of
"introducing myself to such great Men as the President and fellows of a Colledge" and almost turned back.[21]

During the examination, Joseph Mayhew, tutor for the incoming freshman
class, handed Adams a passage in English to be translated into Latin. Adams
glanced at it and immediately saw some unfamiliar words. In that brief agoniz-
ing moment, he saw his future slip away and his father's hopes for him dashed.
But then Mayhew, motioning Adams to follow, stepped into his study, pointed
out paper and pen, a grammar book, and most importantly a dictionary, and
told the young man he could have as much time as he needed. With great relief, Adams hurriedly set about his task.[22] Whether John Wentworth was better
prepared than his future friend from Braintree no one can know. He did take
the same exam, and he obviously performed adequately, for he was admitted to
Harvard in the fall of 1751.

Cambridge, on the Charles River west of Boston, was little more than a vil-
lage of about fifteen hundred people and a few taverns and churches. As the seat
of the oldest college in America, however, and until the second quarter of the
eighteenth century one of only three colleges throughout all the colonies, the
importance of the town in the eyes of the colonists, especially New Englanders, was disproportionate to its size. The governor of Massachusetts, his staff,
and important members of the legislature not only visited annually but took
a strong interest in the welfare and development of the college. Deliberately
modeled after the University at Cambridge in England, Harvard had attracted
the most distinguished sons of New England for well over a century. Founded
in the Puritan age of the seventeenth century, Harvard's original purpose had
been to provide an educated clergy. But in the more secular eighteenth cen-

tury, although the ministry was still the career choice of many students, college education was seen more and more as preparation for the professions of law and medicine or as an essential ingredient in the background of an increasingly wealthy New England mercantile class.[23]

30

In the early autumn of 1751, John Wentworth, like all college freshmen beginning the break from home and immediate family, was assigned a room and a roommate. In his first year he lived with an upperclassman, Thomas Malbone, a senior from Newport, Rhode Island, described as "an ardent lover of literature and the arts, learned, wise, and pious above his years." Another senior who befriended Wentworth in his first year at college was Ammi Ruhamah Cutter of North Yarmouth, Maine. As was common practice, John probably attached himself to Cutter for protection from the unreasonable demands predictably made on freshmen by the sophomores and juniors. Cutter was apparently so favorably impressed by Wentworth and some other students he knew from Portsmouth that, when he graduated at the end of the year, he moved there to learn and practice medicine. He remained in Portsmouth, and the friendship between the two young men flourished.[24]

Malbone and Wentworth roomed together in number twenty-four Massachusetts Hall, a four-story structure completed in 1720. Massachusetts was one of only four buildings that composed the campact Harvard campus. Directly across the yard to the north stood the center of most activities at the college, old Harvard Hall, built in 1677 of brick and destroyed by fire in 1764. Subject matter and modes of teaching at Harvard in midcentury were undergoing gradual change in an effort to keep abreast of enlightenment thought, but the general curriculum was not greatly different from that of the seventeenth century. Still of first importance were the classical languages, Latin and Greek, both grammar and literature. The emphasis was on Greek, although much of the classroom recitation was conducted in Latin and a thorough knowledge of the latter language was assumed. Right methods of thinking were developed through the study of logic, metaphysics, and ethics. Rounding out the core curriculum were natural philosophy (science that could range from physics and chemistry to geometry, meteorology, and biology), mathematics (usually geometry), and astronomy. In addition, some study of divinity was required of all students.[25]

Each of Harvard's four tutors was assigned to an incoming class to instruct its members in the whole range of subjects for the entire four years. The tutor in charge of John Wentworth's class in 1751 was Joseph Mayhew. Mayhew had graduated from Harvard in 1730 and had been a tutor since 1739. He suffered the indignities that all tutors came to expect, including "Heinous Insults" and threats of physical violence by drunken students. His brandy and beer were stolen, rocks were thrown through his window, and logs were rolled down the stairs next to his study. There is no reason, though, to question his ability as a scholar and a teacher. One of his contemporaries praised him as "a man of superior abilities and learning." The class of John Wentworth and John Adams was to be Mayhew's last, for he resigned in 1755 shortly after commencement.[26]

Not all instruction was carried on by the tutors. The more subtle and complicated points of theology were explicated by the Hollis Professor of Divinity, Edward Wigglesworth, whose deafness, "small still voice," and slight lisp may have prevented him from acquiring a permanent pastorate. In college teaching, however, he probably found a vocation even more suitable to his temperament and considerable talent. He possessed the qualities of all great teachers, depth and breadth of knowledge, "clearness and strength of argument," and a lack of dogmatism that allowed him to present conflicting views to stimulate the minds of his students. Wigglesworth was an intellectual gadfly whose cool, satirical lectures taught students to think before they believed.[27]

John Winthrop, Hollis Professor of Mathematics and Natural Philosophy, also greatly influenced students' minds by infusing them with the orderliness and rationalism demanded by the rapidly expanding scientific thought of the eighteenth century.[28] Known among the learned scientific circles and societies of Europe, Winthrop was the single scientist in the colonies who could be considered on a level with Benjamin Franklin. He was a religious man, but he could not brook the simple-minded ascription of any remotely complicated occurrence of nature to providential causes. When New England was rocked by an earthquake in 1755, Winthrop tried to raise his listeners above superstition and religiously inspired ignorance by explaining earth tremors as natural events that were at least partly beneficial and not "scourges in the hand of the Almighty" inflicted on a people for spiritual backsliding or any other reason. Winthrop demanded much of himself and of his students but, according to one student, "had the happy talent of communicating his ideas in the easiest and most elegant manner, and making the most difficult matters plain." He was Harvard's single claim to fame during that period, and it was a privilege for colonial students such as John Wentworth, isolated from the leading thinkers of Europe, to be exposed to such a penetrating, analytical mind.[29]

Presiding over the professors, tutors, and students in the middle of the eighteenth century was Edward Holyoke, president of Harvard. At 235 pounds, Holyoke was called by Ezra Stiles a man of "commanding presence"; the students referred to him as "Guts." Learned and worldly but not a great scholar, his administration has been described as one of "aggressive liberalism." The terms "agressive" and "liberal" must be understood within the context of the eighteenth century, but there is a sense that the college in that period, though still definitely denominational, was characterized by a nonsectarian openness. That orientation was important for students of other faiths such as John Wentworth, who had been brought up an Anglican, and contributed to a general sense of intellectual freedom that encouraged students to find their own truth in the world, whether in God or politics. Thus, Harvard could produce in the class of 1755 (a class with the reputation as the most able since 1721) a man identified with the republican spirit of the future, John Adams, and another who through the difficult times ahead would adhere above all else to traditional order and authority, John Wentworth.[30]

One of the most common offenses for which students were punished was tardiness to chapel or to lectures, or absence from school altogether, often as a result of failure to return after a vacation. Each student, if he lived within ten miles of Cambridge, could go home four days each month. John Wentworth did not qualify for monthly trips home, but he could take advantage of the provision allowing those outside the ten-mile radius to take a twenty-one-day leave twice a year to visit home. In the spring of his junior year, though, Wentworth did not bother to sign out when he left school. On 30 March 1754, the president and trustees fined him "for going out of Town without Leav" and for an unauthorized absence of twelve days. He probably did not register his departure because he was not going home; it is unlikely that a young man of his means was much concerned with the relatively paltry penalty of eighteen shillings nine pence. Spring fever may have sent Wentworth (and probably friends—his roommate William Warner, a senior from Portsmouth, was fined at the same time for absence) off on an adventure to explore previously unseen sights. It is possible he visited his friend John Temple to mingle with some of Boston's socially prominent people at Temple's five-hundred-acre estate, Ten Hills Farm, in Charlestown. More likely, though, he went to the home of his uncle, Samuel Wentworth, a successful merchant in Boston. John seems to have been a frequent visitor there while an undergraduate at Harvard.[31]

When John Adams later reflected on his college days and attempted to recall "several others, for whom I had a strong affection," Wentworth was the first name that came to his mind. When he listed "some better Schollars than myself," however, John Wentworth's name was not mentioned. It is difficult to know what kind of student Wentworth was at Harvard. He was certainly intelligent enough to have done well in his studies. Later in life, when he was in a position of responsibility and power, he went out of his way many times to promote education, especially higher education. He always maintained a strong curiosity, at times bordering on boyish enthusiasm, about the outdoors and natural occurrences, from seemingly exotic animals to unusual geological formations. It seems logical that his interest was developed, or at least heightened, by the lectures and experiments of Professor Winthrop. Wentworth was an avid supporter of the project of his friend the Reverend Jeremy Belknap to write a history of New Hampshire and was assiduous in collecting information, both natural and historical, for the minister. As a boy, John had been exposed to books in his father's home and as a college student had a library of his own, although he did not take it with him to Cambridge. In 1755, after following up a request by his uncle Daniel Rindge to price certain books in a Boston book store, he wrote to Rindge, "I have most of them of my own at Portsmouth the use of which you may freely have, and as long as you please, in the Preceptor you'll find Fordyce's Mor[al] Philos[ophy] abridg'd. If you have a Mind to use any of my Books; my uncle Wm. has the care of them and will lend them to you."[32]

Opposing these indications that Wentworth, like his friend Adams, might have welcomed the opportunity provided by Harvard to expand and develop his intellectual awareness through serious study is his own interpretation of college life during his junior year. Writing to his good friend Ammi Ruhamah Cutter, by then a physician in Portsmouth, John lamented that "the observation you make of the great Variety of pleasing scenes we pass thro' is unjust, as it is now entirely chang'd from what it then was when your presence bless'd us." He went on to complain that "the College now is filled up (allmost) of Boys from 11 to 14 Years old and they seem to be quite void of the Spirit & life which is a general concomitant of Youth, so you may Judge what kind of life I now live, who was won't to live in the gayest and most Jovial manner, when I was first admitted one of this Society which I then thought was a Compound of Mirth and Gaiety as it is now of Gravity." Unfortunately, in Wentworth's eyes, serious scholarly discussions centering especially on religious dogma had become the rule "instead of the sprightly turns of Wit & Gay repartees which the former Companys used to have, which makes me cry out . . . Oh Alma Mater, how hast thou degenerated from thy Pristine Glory!" It may have been just a youthful pose or his Anglican background or both that led Wentworth to make such statements and, later in the year, to invite Cutter to commencement "to celebrate my entrance upon the last year of my Pilgrimage among the Heathen." Whatever the cause, there is no reason to believe that John Wentworth was unhappy during his days at Harvard; one historian's interpretation of his complaints as "arrogance which was entirely foreign to his nature" seems plausible.[33]

In 1754 John Wentworth, probably with more enthusiasm than he would admit, returned to Cambridge for his final college year. As a senior at Harvard, Wentworth had reason to be concerned with military and political develop-

33

ments, for by that time it was apparent that a war was coming between Britain and France that would determine domination of North America. Indians, egged on by the French, were again conducting bloody raids on New Hampshire's frontier. Also, Wentworth's roommate that year was Theodore Atkinson, Jr., a cousin from Portsmouth and the son of one of New Hampshire's delegates to the congress called in Albany in the summer of 1754 for the purpose of cementing an alliance between the English colonies and the powerful Iroquois tribes of the Six Nations.[34]

From Boston during his winter vacation in January 1755, Wentworth wrote to Daniel Rindge in Portsmouth: "We have a Rumor of War here, & Men raising; but no one knows why as the Council & Representatives, have been sworn to secrecy." The Massachusetts legislature had probably received word of the two British regiments under the command of General Edward Braddock that had embarked for America to remove the French forcibly from the Ohio country. That was not, however, a particularly well-kept secret. France was well aware of England's intent and was raising a much larger force of its own. Wentworth reported that some of the local politicians were convinced there would be a war in the spring because "two Armies of Different Nations, and Interest, cannot live together without coming to Action." He was confident that if there were any news he would hear it "at my Uncles" in Boston.[35]

Two months later when he wrote again to Daniel Rindge from Cambridge, he had still heard nothing. Men were enlisting, there was a great deal of "noise," but who could tell if anything would come of it? Wentworth was fairly certain conflict would break out, but he had his own theory about the tactics of the French. He told Rindge they might try to "evade" war "by Laying Bullets of Gold to the hands of those that shou'd annoy them with Bullets of Iron & Lead, Which yellow Balls properly applied have hitherto been found to be very usefull in turning the just resentment of their Neighbors. . . . Historians relate that Philip of Macedon, said when he was beseiging a City, that he was never afraid of being disappointed of taking it, provided he cou'd but introduce into it a Mule laden with Gold, (so great is the power of that Metal!) It seems from the Conduct of the French that they have adopted The Maxim of that Prince, tho' not his Bravery." Wentworth hoped the French would not have the same success they had had in the past with the "dispersion of their Coins." The French did wish to avoid war as long as possible, but it is not clear who John Wentworth thought they might be attempting to buy off.[36]

In January Wentworth told Daniel Rindge that in spite of ill health he had gone to Boston, "as I want to be at Schools, where I never can have another

Opp[ortuni]ty of going." We don't know for sure what those schools were. But many young men, especially those of John Wentworth's social position, felt it necessary as budding gentlemen of an aristocratic society to acquire certain refinements and skills that were not included in a Harvard education. In Boston, as in the other major colonial cities in eighteenth-century North America, a substantial number of private instructors taught a variety of subjects from art and music to dancing and fencing. It is reasonable that Wentworth was preparing himself for his return, in the near future, as a full-fledged member of an elite society in the small but relatively cosmopolitan seaport of Portsmouth. He had maintained his Anglican affinity throughout his four years in the Calvinist community of Cambridge, apparent from his reference in the spring of 1755 to the "Heathenish and Popish Fast day" slated to be observed by his "Presbyterian Brethren in N. Hampshire." He hoped they would be reminded of the scripture passage, " 'Many are the Afflictions of the righteous.' "[37]

John Wentworth and his fellow seniors ended their classroom recitations in March but were required to remain on campus until their final exams were completed in June. Those were followed by valedictories, accompanied in the time-honored manner of graduating seniors by entertainment, reveling, "drunkedness and confusion." Harvard commencement, which in 1755 fell on 16 July, was more than just a day for graduates and their parents. It was a festive occasion that came closer to being a regional celebration than any other holiday in New England. For several days before the ceremonies, the roads were dusty and the ferries packed with people pouring into Cambridge. Taverns and boarding houses overflowed. When commencement for a time was changed to Friday, the clergy as well as the public demanded that it be returned to Wednesday to ensure participants time to get home and sober up for Sunday services.[38]

Maintaining his indifferent demeanor, John Wentworth was noticeably unimpressed by this annual academic ritual. On writing to Daniel Rindge in June to invite him to commencement, he declared, "I shall promise myself the Pleasure of your Company to see me perform a number of ridiculous Ceremonys, which Custom has render'd necessary if we intend to keep on good Terms with the World, & you know that is very necessary." In fact, most of the seniors had more weighty matters on their minds than the activities of graduation day. Once the commencement dinner in Harvard Hall was over and final farewells had been said to close friends of the last four years, the new graduate had to have a good idea of where he was going and what his life's work would be. When John Adams, the son of a farmer, began his education at Harvard, he planned to follow his father's wishes and become a minister. In the intervening period, his developing talents indicated to him that he would be better fitted for the legal profession, but by commencement he was still undecided between law, medicine, or the clergy.[39]

36   Adams's friend John Wentworth did not share his problems or concerns. Wentworth's family had not had to save and sacrifice to send him to college. He had not gone to Harvard to prepare for a profession that would lift him above his father's station in life. His father was a successful and wealthy merchant, and there was no reason why John should not follow in his footsteps. A college education was more or less expected of a young man destined to be an active member of Portsmouth's small, largely mercantile upper class. And one did not have to be a lawyer to take an active part in public affairs and politics. In fact, the greater share of that responsibility was expected of and borne by men in commerce and trade. John's uncle, Governor Benning Wentworth, had been a merchant, even a bankrupt one, before coming to office. John Wentworth thus had few worries as he bid his friends in Cambridge goodbye and readied his horse to carry him back to Portsmouth and an adult role in the society of a thriving colonial seaport.

»3«
THE MAKING
OF A GENTLEMAN
MERCHANT

Portsmouth,
1755–1763

John Wentworth, eighteen years old and about to embark on a career, had as good a college education as a young man could acquire without leaving the English colonies. Now it was time for more practical learning. Wentworth had inherited a place in the small Portsmouth aristocracy, but as in most colonial cities, that was not an idle class. It was built on hard work, shrewd commercial sense, participation in political affairs, and knowing the right people. John Wentworth thus entered his father's business with much to learn about bills of lading, shipping manifests, and the best prospects for the highest percentage of profits; about how to make up a cargo, buy into a ship, and choose a captain; most importantly, about who to trade with and who not to. It also took capital to become a trader in one's own right, and that was something that Wentworth, even though his father possessed great wealth, would have to work hard to accumulate. The sums required for a trading investment were substantial. Although Wentworth had saved six hundred pounds by late 1757, he would need another year, as he told Daniel Rindge, "before I can reach to the moderate height of 1/20 of a lumber laden Ship; & perhaps then not be able." So he lived at home and worked for his father, learning the business and building up a reserve of cash to make trading investments of his own.[1]

During the years immediately following his graduation from college, Wentworth kept up a regular correspondence with classmate John Adams. Adams was serving an apprenticeship of his own in Worcester, Massachusetts, in the law office of James Putnam, while continuing to support himself by teaching school. Adams valued Wentworth's friendship highly and welcomed his stimulating missives from New Hampshire. He replied to his friend, "dear Jack," in

1758: "I should have forgotten that I had a mind and that there is a Temple of Knowledge, if your letters and the letters of Some other Friends, did not recall them sometimes to my memory." Adams also enjoyed his friend's compliments, although he told Wentworth, "When I first read your Letter I resolved very nearly to drop the correspondence." He went on to explain, "my Vanity could not bear to be feasted with such a variety of the greatest delicacies, by a Friend whom poverty disables me to entertain with any better fare, than lean beef and Small Beer.—On a second Reflection, however, I found my naughty appetite so keen for your Dainties, that Vanity and Envy must go a foot." Later in the year, Adams implored Wentworth to continue his letters, "which always raise a full Gale of Love, sometimes almost a Tempest of Emulation and some times a Breeze of Envy." Nevertheless, as happens so often with college acquaintances, time, distance, and more pressing obligations took their toll. The friendship remained, but the correspondence began to wane.[2]

In July 1758, John Wentworth had an opportunity to see Adams and most of his other classmates again as they returned to Cambridge to take their Master of Arts degrees. That commencement also marked the graduation of Wentworth's brother, Thomas, who as class orator delivered the valedictory of the class of 1758. The M.A. at Harvard was generally considered a formality that followed "in course" three years after graduation. About the only students who remained in residence during that period were those studying for the ministry. For others the degree was supposedly related to the profession or career they had been pursuing and may or may not have involved any study. To actually receive the degree, however, the candidate had to be present on commencement day and be prepared to argue, in either the affirmative or the negative, a "Quaestione," which was printed with others on a "Quaestio Sheet" for the afternoon ceremonies. John Adams, as we might expect from his growing interest in law, government, and politics, took the affirmative of the question "Is Civil Government absolutely necessary for Men?" Here also was the first indication of John Wentworth's concern with public affairs and political theory. For his M.A. he argued against the idea that the status of the citizen and the authority of the state were completely dependent on the whims of the rulers. Not a radical position in the mideighteenth century, its deference toward the rule of law had a decidely whiggish tone.[3]

Now with two college degrees, Wentworth, at twenty-one the heir apparent to New Hampshire's greatest mercantile and political fortune, moved to acquire one of the requisites of all established gentlemen. Although he felt he did not have enough capital to buy into a trading venture on his own, he could, merely by knowing the right people, become a landowner. Virgin land was a plentiful commodity in New Hampshire in the 1750s when the frontier still began not many miles from the seacoast. In 1749 John's uncle, Governor Benning Wentworth, had begun making grants almost as far west as the Hudson River. But John Wentworth did not have to go that far afield for his land; he knew a source   39 even closer than his uncle. In 1622 Captain John Mason had received a patent from the Plymouth Company in England for a tract of land, extending from the sea sixty miles into the interior, that would eventually make up a substantial part of New Hampshire. When Mason died in 1635, his title fell into dispute, and over the course of the next century the family lost control of the land. In the 1730s, however, a descendant, John Tufton Mason, revived the Mason claim. John Thomlinson, New Hampshire's agent in London, seeing the advantages for the province, convinced Mason to sell his claim to New Hampshire for one thousand pounds as soon as complete separation from Massachusetts was assured.

In 1741 Benning Wentworth was appointed the separate governor of New Hampshire, but the legislature was not apprized of the agreement until three years later, and then it was slow to act. Despite continued urgings by the governor and council for ratification, the assembly procrastinated. Mason threatened to sell the title to others if the legislators were not interested. In July 1746 the legislature finally voted to buy Mason's claim with the stipulation that the assembly would have granting power over the lands involved. That incurred a dispute with the governor and council, who claimed that, under the commissions and instructions from the Crown, only they had lawful power to dispose of lands. It made little difference, though, for on the day following the assembly's vote, Mason sold his claim to twelve private persons for five hundred pounds more than the legislature was going to pay him.

The purchasers, known as the Masonian proprietors, were among the most powerful and wealthy men in the province and included John Wentworth's father, Mark Hunking Wentworth. They now controlled a vast portion of land, roughly half the area of what would eventually fall within the borders of New Hampshire. The boundaries of their land corresponded closely to those of the original grant to Captain Mason, which "gave him the lands contained within a line following up the Merrimack, and then westward to a point sixty miles from the sea," connected by what "was always generally understood to be a curved line everywhere distant sixty miles from the sea."[4]

The fact that the twelve Masonian proprietors had stolen from under the nose of the legislature all New Hampshire land not previously granted within sixty miles of Portsmouth angered more than a few people. The governor himself was so incensed that in 1751, when four vacancies opened up on the council, he sent a list of persons to London that he did not want appointed to the positions. Among the names was that of his own brother, Mark Hunking Went-worth, who did not gain a councillor's seat for eight more years. But the new owners argued that the assembly had had its chance, and to show that they had the interest of the people in mind, they relinquished claim to lands already occupied within the tract. At least the issue had been settled, and the transaction was soon accepted if not applauded by most people. The proprietors shortly began attempts to settle their lands, and within the next forty years they established thirty-seven new towns.[5]

At one of the regular meetings of the Masonian proprietors, on 5 October 1759, at James Stoodly's tavern in Portsmouth, discussion centered around a recent application by "sundry young Gentlemen" of the seaport for a grant of land. Dr. Ammi Ruhamah Cutter, John Wentworth's friend from Harvard, and David Sewall, a member of Wentworth's college class, along with Henry Apthorp and William Treadwell, hoped to become proprietors of a new town in New Hampshire. Their bid was successful. They received a six-square-mile tract of land at the southeast corner of Lake Winnipesaukee, some forty-five miles northwest of the capital.

The Masonian proprietors applied their usual terms to the grant. They charged no fee and demanded no quit rent but stipulated that a portion of each new town, in this case one quarter, be reserved for themselves. That was how they expected to obtain a return on their investment; as each town gained settlers and prospered, their own land would correspondingly increase in value. The land was exempt from taxation until actually improved. Within the proprietors' own section, one lot was reserved for the first minister, one for other ministers, and one for a school. The grantees were expected to have ten families settled in their part of the town within three years after the end of the current war. Although by the end of 1759 it looked as if the French would be soundly beaten, no one expected yeomen to test the New Hampshire frontier until a peace had actually been signed. Within eight years, there were to be forty families on the land, a church, and passable roads. Unless good cause could be shown why those conditions had not been met, title would revert to the original proprietors, who would then be free to regrant the land.

Three weeks after receiving the grant, Cutter, Sewall, Apthorp, and Tread-well admitted twenty associates to their proprietorship, among them John Went-worth and his brother, Thomas, now also back in Portsmouth after graduating from Harvard. On 14 November, the twenty-four fledgling proprietors met at John Stavers's inn and voted to name their town Wolfeboro, after the British hero, General Wolfe, who had died in the decisive victory at Quebec earlier that year. John Wentworth, with no sacrifice in his slowly accruing personal fortune, was now a landowner, a role that carried not only a certain amount of prestige but also the very real possibility of future profits.[6]

One of the excuses accepted from either proprietors or settlers for not meeting the requirements of their grants within the specified time was interference by Indians, which had become commonplace on the frontier of New Hampshire since the opening of hostilities between the French and British in 1755. Just one week before Wentworth's graduation from Harvard, his speculation that war was near was borne out when General Braddock with his British troops and American volunteers marched into an ambush by French and Indians near Fort Duquesne on the Monongahela River. The ensuing Battle of the Wilderness, in which Braddock lost his life and Colonel George Washington led the retreat, marked the overt beginning of the last struggle between two empires for the North American continent. 41

In that same year, an expedition, including two New Hampshire regiments, sent against the French fortress at Crown Point merely provoked the Indians in Canada to resume hostile incursions on the New Hampshire frontier. Property was destroyed, people murdered, and prisoners carried off as settlers found themselves in a state of siege. In 1756 another regiment was raised in New Hampshire, and its commander, Colonel Nathaniel Meserve, was placed in charge of Fort Edward on the Hudson just below Lake George. Wentworth's friend Dr. Cutter served with the regiment at Fort Edward, and when Lord Loudon, impressed with the special capabilities of the New Hampshire soldiers, formed them into bodies of rangers to reconnoiter the enemy in the woods, gather intelligence, and perform special missions, Cutter was appointed surgeon of the group placed under the command of Major Robert Rogers.[7]

John Wentworth would have been well supplied with the latest military intelligence during Cutter's occasional visits to Portsmouth. Unfortunately the news was not very good. Fort Oswego was lost to the French in August 1756, and a year later Montcalm captured Fort William Henry. Adding to the increasing consternation of the English colonists was the fact that Montcalm had been unable to restrain his Indian allies from savagely attacking the unarmed soldiers to whom he had granted safe passage to Fort Edward. New Hampshire lost eighty men out of its regiment of two hundred in that bloody debacle. Dr. Cutter was fortunate not to have been among them. He had sailed to Canada, where in September a British attempt to take Louisbourg was foiled by the French navy and a hurricane that scattered the English fleet. Another force, including Cutter and more than a hundred carpenters from New Hampshire under the command of Nathaniel Meserve, was dispatched to Louisbourg the following spring. That time the enemy was smallpox. Many died, including Meserve and his son. Cutter contracted the disease while treating others and nearly fell victim to it himself. John Adams wrote to Wentworth in April 1758 that his thoughts were on the war. The future for English fortunes in North America seemed extremely bleak.[8]

42   But changes were in the wind. The indomitable William Pitt had taken command in England and was devoting all his energy to a strategy designed to defeat the French. In July, in spite of the smallpox, the British forces under Generals Amherst and Wolfe recaptured Louisbourg. A month later, Fort Frontenac fell, and the French were finally driven from Fort Duquesne. In 1759 there was a growing sense of relief and optimism in Portsmouth as reports of Amherst's succeeding victories—Niagara, Crown Point, Ticonderoga—reached the seaport. When news arrived in October of the fall of the French capital of Quebec the town broke out in a general celebration marked by the firing of cannon, fireworks, a bonfire, and a parade.[9] The English victory, which marked virtually the end of French influence and Indian depradations on New Hampshire's borders, was especially pleasing to Dr. Cutter and others who had served faithfully in the war. It was also good news to settlers, who could now head west and north to make a new start on virgin land of their own, and to men like John Wentworth who held western lands and had a strong interest in developing them.

The war had been on everyone's mind, but it had not impeded development in Portsmouth in the years following John Wentworth's return from college in 1755.[10] The prosperity of the mercantile class was displayed in the construction of increasingly elegant Georgian homes. The town built several new public buildings, including an almshouse and a badly needed jail. The provincial legislature had never had a place of its own to meet. The assembly usually gathered in one of several public houses, and the council, after 1750, conducted its business in a specially furnished chamber at Governor Benning Wentworth's mansion at Little Harbor. Finally convinced that any provincial capital worth its salt should have a dignified home for the government, the House of Representatives in 1757 voted to build a state house. The result was a frame structure eighty-four by thirty feet and two stories tall, the upper floor divided into three chambers to house the assembly, the council, and the courts.

Although to inhabitants of Boston, Philadelphia, and New York, Portsmouth must have seemed perilously close to the barbarous frontier of the north and east, the New Hampshire capital had begun to enjoy some semblance of a cultural and intellectual awakening. From what we know of John Wentworth, his father, Mark Hunking, and his friend Dr. Cutter, many of the Portsmouth gentry probably had libraries of their own. Nevertheless, in 1750, apparently inspired by Benjamin Franklin's Philadelphia Library Company and a similar venture in Newport, thirty-four citizens subscribed 936 pounds for the formation of a "Library Society." They considered it a necessity, "As the Advancement of Learning and the Increase of all useful Knowledge is of great Importance both to the Civil and Religious Welfare of a People and as all Gentlemen who have any Taste for polite Literature or desire to have any Aquaintance with the vari- 43 ous Affairs of Mankind, . . . cannot but look upon it to be a great Privilege to have always a good Collection of Books at hand." Despite the subscribers' eclectic goals, literature and books dealing with the "affairs of Mankind" remained strictly secondary to theological, especially Anglican, treatises.

Most important for the growing sense of cosmopolitan awareness in Portsmouth during the period was the establishment in 1756 of a printing press, a newspaper, and a book shop by Daniel Fowle, a native of Boston. The *New Hampshire Gazette*, first printed in October, was the small province's first newspaper and probably did more than any other one thing to break down the narrow insularity of this budding but still isolated society on the edge of the wilderness. The sense of communication provided by a newspaper should not be underestimated. It not only was the vehicle for the diffusion of news, ideas, and culture but gave New Hampshire residents a sense of belonging to a larger community, especially in relation to the other American colonies, but also to England and Europe. That connection was particularly important, as an anonymous contributor emphasized in one of the first issues of the *Gazette*, in a region characterized by a "Prevalance of Ignorance" and "People that have no Acquaintance with any thing beyond the narrow Limits of the Family or Parish where they were born."

In addition to printing his newspaper once a week and publishing numerous pamphlets and books, Fowle broadened the reading taste of the public by offering for sale works by Bunyan, Locke, Addison, Shakespeare, and many classical authors, along with books on such diverse subjects as medicine, shipbuilding, architecture, and navigation. Another sign of Portsmouth's growing importance and interest in the outside world came in 1761 when John Stavers began running a weekly stage to Boston, the first operated north of that city. Passengers could board the coach at Stavers's Earl of Halifax Inn early Tuesday morning, conduct their business in Boston, and be back in Portsmouth in time for dinner Friday night.

Another kind of stage was involved the following year when a group of Portsmouth citizens petitioned the governor to allow the establishment of a playhouse that had been proposed by some actors from New York and Newport. John Wentworth was one of the signers, along with a number of other young men including his brother, Thomas; his cousin and friend Theodore Atkinson, Jr.; and John Fisher, who married John's younger sister, Anne. They argued that the dramatists would "act no obscene or immoral plays, but such as tend to the improvement of the mind and informing the judgment in things proper to be known." But Portsmouth, although it was showing signs of increasing sophistication, was not ready for a theater. A counter petition expressed the fear that "sundry entertainments of the stage . . . would be of very pernicious consequences, to the morals of the young people, (even if there should be no immoral exhibitions) by dissipating their minds, and giving them an idle turn of attachment to pleasure and amusement." [11]

Indicating a definite generation gap, Mark Hunking Wentworth was among a number of the town's most established citizens who signed another protest against such a useless frivolity as a playhouse. Instead of emphasizing the moral threat of the theater, they turned to more immediately practical considerations. A severe drought in 1761 had resulted in a serious shortage of food during the following year. Samuel Lane of Stratham called it the "Most Remarkable" year he could remember; the only thing that saved many people from starvation were the shiploads of grain brought in from other colonies. During those difficult times, opponents of the playhouse felt that people encountered enough trouble just paying their taxes and buying food without being tempted to squander what little they had on worthless amusements. Accordingly, the House of Representatives voted to request the governor "to discountenance and deny" any proposals for a theater. John Wentworth and the other young people of Portsmouth would have to seek their entertainment elsewhere. [12]

Wentworth's membership in St. John's Masonic Lodge consumed some of his spare time. Meeting regularly at Stavers's inn, the lodge provided a good chance for young merchants to fraternize socially with some of the older, more established businessmen of Portsmouth. Any interruption of the weekly ritual was not welcomed but was borne with patience when the circumstances were unavoidable. In December 1757, Wentworth wrote to Daniel Rindge: "Mrs. Stavers lies dead in the house of John her Husband, who, by her being there is impeded from vending his Punch, he therefore determined to put her under ground this afternoon or tomorrow, . . . & then I suppose we may again assume our lodge, that, Since last Wednesday, has been cover'd with the Show of Sorrow." [13]

John Wentworth had now reached an age and a position in the community that dictated marriage and a family as his next logical step. In November 1761 his younger brother, Thomas, who had taken his M.A. at Harvard the previous summer and returned also to work in his father's business, married Anne Tasker, the daughter of a judge in Marblehead. For her son and daughter-in-law and their prospective family, Wentworth's mother generously had a magnificent

Georgian home built directly on the Portsmouth waterfront. Every attention was paid to detail, from the large quoins at the corners and dentil molding under the roof, to the finely carved scroll pediment over the door and the unusual carved block front meant to simulate stone. Even more elaborate was the interior, which took fourteen months to complete. The house, termed one of the finest examples of Georgian frame architecture in America, was a fitting symbol of the Wentworths' wealth and indicative of the grandeur they strove for in the essentially simple trading community of Portsmouth.[14]

John Wentworth undoubtedly would have been provided with an equally fine dwelling had he chosen to marry at that time, but he did not. It is difficult to judge the validity of a report that a romance was budding between John and his cousin Frances Wentworth, daughter of his uncle Samuel in Boston, but in May 1762 she married their mutual cousin, Theodore Atkinson, Jr., before she was seventeen years old. John had no doubt become acquainted with her when she was a child during the frequent visits he made to his uncle's house while a student at Harvard. If there was in fact any early affection between the two, he may have thought her too young to marry in 1762, or more likely, at the age of twenty-four he valued his independence too highly to be tied down with family responsibilities.[15]

Wentworth remained occupied by his business activities and the increasing demands made on him as one of the Wolfeboro proprietors. By 1762 a peace was assured, and the frontiers were again habitable. At a meeting of the proprietors at Stavers's inn in April, Wentworth, Paul March, and Ammi R. Cutter were made a committee to get the development of Wolfeboro under way. They were directed to settle five families in the town by offering a total of up to a thousand acres of land. Nevertheless, by 1764 not one family had yet moved to Wolfeboro.[16] But by that time more pressing concerns had drawn John Wentworth's attention and were requiring his presence outside the province.

In November 1761, Captain Samuel Willis of Connecticut rode into Portsmouth to see Benning Wentworth. Willis, an emissary for Jared Ingersoll, brought a mast contract from the navy board, procured by Ingersoll during his recent mission to London as Connecticut's agent. Willis also carried a request for Wentworth, as surveyor general of the king's woods, to have appropriate trees marked for felling, in particular along the upper valley of the Connecticut River from about Deerfield in Massachusetts northward through that unsettled region claimed by New Hampshire on both sides of the river. The seriousness of this challenge to his control and his family's dominance of the lucrative New England mast trade was not lost on Governor Wentworth. All licenses for cutting masts had to come from the surveyor general, and since Mark Hunking

Wentworth had been the primary mast agent in New England, masting had become pretty much a Wentworth affair. By the early 1760s, the forests along the Piscataqua and near the New Hampshire and southern Maine coasts were beginning to recede under the persistent swing of the woodsman's ax. That left the best mast trees further east in Maine and, of special interest to the Wentworths because New Hampshire claimed the territory, to the west along the Connecticut River, a region said to contain some of the finest virgin white pine timber in North America. The presumptuous Jared Ingersoll and his loggers now proposed to invade that Wentworth preserve.

Ingersoll's objective was to wrest the mast business from the control of the Wentworths and to provide Connecticut with an exportable staple commodity that would serve to keep badly needed specie in the colony. To do so, he would divert the flow of mast pines from Portsmouth by cutting them on the Connecticut River and floating them downstream to be shipped out of the Connecticut port of New London. An important part of his scheme was the establishment of a separate vice-admiralty court for Connecticut, which currently was under the jurisdiction of a court in New York that also covered New York and New Jersey. All assaults against the king's reserved timber were prosecuted in the vice-admiralty courts. An exclusive Connecticut court, or a deputy judgeship for Ingersoll for Connecticut, would discourage the ever-occurring illicit cutting of royal timber, protect the contractor's masting agents from the hostility of settlers who considered the trees their own, and most important serve as a foil against the tremendous influence of the Wentworths, which was sure to be leveled against them.

Since Ingersoll possessed an official mast contract from the navy, Benning Wentworth had no choice but to grant him the license needed to cut trees. But now aware of the danger, the Wentworths were not about to let this threat to their dominance of New England's forests go unchallenged. Early in 1763, Ingersoll's agents, who were in the process of collecting the logs for shipment, were harassed by a Colonel Symes, who said he was a deputy of the surveyor general but later admitted that Mark Hunking Wentworth had sent him. Symes proceeded to measure the smaller sticks, leading the agents to fear that the Wentworths were going to inform the navy board not only that Ingersoll's masts were inferior and not up to contract size but that many small trees had been illegally cut. In July Governor Wentworth complained to Governor Thomas Fitch of Connecticut about the tremendous waste of timber by people who were transporting it to Connecticut and demanded from Fitch protection for his deputies as they proceeded against the offenders. On 18 October, Wentworth sent a recommendation to the Board of Trade for a single vice-admiralty judge with jurisdiction over the forests in all the colonies. A friendly superior judge would nullify for the Wentworths any threat posed by a separate Connecticut court under the influence of Ingersoll.[17]

In addition to those measures, the Wentworths thought it prudent, in light of the ailing condition of their faithful agent John Thomlinson, to have an effective representative in London to protect their interests and advance their cause at all the proper agencies. It would have to be someone fully knowledgeable about the family business and the current situation, someone who would be completely dependable. Because that representative would need to meet persons of influence in government circles, he must appear competent but not overbearing. Above all, in an age so dependent on appearances, he should leave a positive impression of the Wentworths with whomever he spoke. Since a close member of the family would be best, the only logical choice was twenty-six-year-old John Wentworth. Besides having the best possible American education and experience in the small social world of Portsmouth, he had worked in his father's business for the past eight years and knew exactly what family interests must be guarded. So in the autumn of 1763, Wentworth prepared to take his first trip abroad.

The threat to the Wentworth mast trade, however, was not the only family crisis that demanded John Wentworth's presence in England. By 1763 there were indications that Benning Wentworth, who had already served longer than any other English governor in America, might not hold his office much longer. He was getting old, and recurrent sieges of gout kept him immobilized for months at a time in his home at Little Harbor. The fact that his major source of influence with the home government, agent John Thomlinson, was also "Broken Down & Past his Labour" and forced to stay away from London much of the time did not help his political fortunes. In 1761 a friend in London wrote to the province secretary, Theodore Atkinson, that upon seeing an address from the New Hampshire Assembly, Lord Bute, the confidant of the new king, had asked "if their was Noe Govr in the Province." Atkinson, who had been trying to have his office transferred to his son, Theodore, Jr., was enough worried about Governor Wentworth's future in 1762 to urge Thomlinson to push the affair through as speedily as possible before it could be blocked by a new governor.[18]

Benning Wentworth's old enemy from New Hampshire, John Huske, now residing in England, gained a powerful ally in 1763 when his political patron Charles Townshend was placed at the head of the Board of Trade. Even more significant that year was the move by the Board of Trade, after persistent urgings by successive governors of New York, to open hearings into the dispute between New York and New Hampshire over the land west of the Connecticut River that would later become Vermont. Since 1749, Benning Wentworth,

Theodore Atkinson, by Joseph Blackburn
(Worcester Art Museum, Worcester,
Massachusetts)

under the bold assumption that New Hampshire's jurisdiction carried to within twenty miles of the Hudson River, had been making grants in the region and had accumulated thousands of acres there himself. To make matters worse, since Governor Wentworth had taken his young housekeeper for his wife in 1760, nasty rumors had circulated in London that he "had Maried a Dirty Slute of a Maid." [19] Thus by 1763 there was valid cause for concern among the Wentworths, not only for their mast business but, more importantly, for the political hegemony they had maintained in New Hampshire since Benning Wentworth became governor in 1741. It was doubly important that they have a reliable representative in England during this crucial period.

Yet those very pressing, practical considerations may not entirely account for John Wentworth's departure for England. Although the difficulties in family affairs provided Wentworth with a compelling reason to make the trip abroad, it seems safe to assume that he eagerly volunteered for the assignment. Just as the grand tour of the Continent added the finishing touches to the education of young English gentlemen, a trip to England did much the same for young men of standing in the colonies. This requirement was particularly evident in the South, where planters fashioned a self-image based on the English squirearchy, but such attitudes toward travel were also prevalent among the wealthier classes in other regions. John Wentworth had all the advantages of his position: two degrees from Harvard plus an honorary M.A. from the College of New Jersey (Princeton) awarded in 1763, private instruction in certain amenities considered too frivolous to be taught at Harvard but deemed necessary by persons with the rank of the Wentworths, and an exposure to as much social life as the mercantile elite of Portsmouth could muster. He lacked only a sojourn within English aristocratic society to become a complete, well-rounded cosmopolitan gentleman. [20]

Late in October 1763, the elder Theodore Atkinson sat down to pen a note to John Thomlinson and Barlow Trecothick concerning his account with their mercantile establishment in London. "My kinsman John Wentworth," he wrote, "by whom you will receive this is taking a Trip to England. I know I need not recommend him to your House. Youl finde him deserving every Favour granted." [21] Supplied with all the necessary letters of introduction, Wentworth a short time later departed from Portsmouth on what would be a momentous adventure.

»4«
SIGHTS, SOUNDS, AND A FORTUNATE ACQUAINTANCE

England, 1763–1765

A transatlantic voyage was a serious undertaking during the colonial period. Given the rigors and hazards involved, it is remarkable how many and how often Americans made the trip "home" to England. Reports of the crossing were enough to deter some completely; fear of the sea led Benjamin Franklin's wife to adamantly refuse his entreaties to accompany him to London. In 1766 William Samuel Johnson of Connecticut wrote back from London that the sight of the British capital was not worth the shipboard experience required to attain it.

Conditions and the time required for passage had not changed appreciably since the early seventeenth century, when Englishmen first began to venture across the ocean in any number. Accommodations below deck were often extremely primitive, and even if the passenger purchased a separate cabin, as no doubt John Wentworth did, it would be cramped and he would still be subject to the many dangers of the voyage. Food often turned rotten and wormy, and water would go bad before land was sighted. Sanitation was a constant problem, and illness, ranging from seasickness to dysentery and smallpox, was common. If fevers and agues did not overtake the traveler, heavy seas, slack winds, pirates, or warships of enemy nations might. Very occasionally the trip could be made in three weeks, but at least one voyage took twenty-four weeks, during which most of the passengers died. Four weeks was considered fast; the average crossing took somewhere between one and two months.[1]

Embarking on the turbulent North Atlantic in the winter took special courage, but that did not stop John Wentworth, who took advantage of a departing mast ship. Running regularly, the "masters" normally carried passengers and mail between the colonies and England. Wentworth's destination was London, but the disembarkation point for mast ships was Portsmouth, on the south coast, where the timbers were unloaded at the great English naval shipyard. From there it was an easy coach ride to London.

On his arrival in the metropolis in December 1763, Wentworth's first order of business was to seek out the firm of Thomlinson and Trecothick and to present his papers.[2] John Thomlinson, the senior partner and New Hampshire agent, had been ill for several years and thus spent little time in the city, so the chances are not great that Wentworth found him in. Thomlinson's son, John, who had been appointed joint agent with his father in February, was also in poor health. Wentworth, however, carried a letter of introduction from his uncle Theodore Atkinson to Barlow Trecothick, Thomlinson's energetic and influential business partner. Atkinson solicited the London merchant's hospitality and "Canded Advice" for his young nephew.[3]

Wentworth's first need was for suitable lodgings. Once that chore was taken care of, his next immediate requirement—to satisfy the inevitable curiosity of a visitor from the colonies on his first trip to London—was a tour of the great city. John Wentworth doubtless considered himself cosmopolitan and urbane by colonial standards. Nevertheless, having spent most of his short life in a town of fewer than forty-five hundred persons on the edge of the North American forest, he must have been astounded by the sights and sounds of London. Little more than a year earlier, the young Scotsman James Boswell had exclaimed on his second trip to the city: "The noise, the crowd, the glare of ships and signs agreeably confused me. I was rather more wildly struck than when I first came to London."[4]

Even visitors from other European capitals were impressed by the constant traffic and throngs of people that filled the streets. One observer at midcentury reported, "Most of the streets in Paris are as little frequented on week days as those of London on Sundays."[5] More shocking to first time visitors, especially those from the relatively homogeneous society of colonial America, were the great contrasts in London, from the wealth and fashion of the City and St. James's to the squalid filth found all too frequently on narrow side streets and lanes and around the edge of the town, especially to the east in the area of the docks.

One of the first stops for any American visitor in London was the appropriate coffeehouse. Familiar faces and names from the colonies were sure to be found there. Merchants patronized the coffeehouses in the City near the Royal Exchange, where familiar colonial names were found: the Pennsylvania, the Virginia, the Carolina, and the New England Coffee House in Threadneedle

Street. Coffeehouses played a major role in the dissemination of information in eighteenth-century London. Because reading the newspaper was deemed an absolute necessity by both Englishmen and visitors from the colonies, most coffeehouses had ten or twelve copies of the same paper. Business was conducted there, and appointments arranged. At most of the colonial houses, the arrivals and departures of ships were reported, along with information about what American was now in London. Anyone who frequented a particular coffeehouse could use it as a mailing address. John Wentworth directed his correspondents in New Hampshire to address his mail to the New England Coffee House. The coffeehouse was especially useful to young men like Wentworth who were new to London. It provided a place to meet people with experience and influence, men who knew their way about town and politics and who could help make the important contacts necessary for business success. Wentworth had good reason to spend time at the New England Coffee House during his first weeks in London.[6]

From Threadneedle Street, it was a short walk to the Thames, which with its voluminous traffic was one of the major sights of London. From time to time the sails were thick on the Piscataqua, but it was nothing compared to this. The area below London Bridge, where the docks of the East and West India merchants and other major commercial houses lay, was once described as harboring "such a prodigious forest of masts, for miles together, that you would think all the ships of the universe were here assembled." Above the bridge, "the whole surface of the Thames" was covered with barges and other smaller boats. Here was entertainment to delight the eye for hours.[7]

Wentworth could not linger too long, however, for London boasted too many other sights. Foremost among those for travelers from America were the city's architectural wonders. Nowhere in the colonies could one see buildings to compare with St. Paul's Cathedral, Westminster Abbey, or the ancient Tower of London with its dark historical associations. A visit to the Houses of Parliament was a requisite for any visitor, particularly for those interested in politics and government. John Wentworth did not know that before long he would have compelling reasons to spend more time there.

Another major attraction for visitors to London was the large number of fine shops with their alluring windows. By general consensus, they were far superior to anything in Europe, even in Paris. One traveler insisted, "The magnificence of the shops is the most striking thing in London." Behind the large glass display windows lay the latest fashions in English manufactured goods: elegant clothing, rich leather articles, fine ceramic ware for the gentleman's table. John Wentworth had instructions from a number of his friends, as did most colonists who journeyed to England, to do some shopping for them. Theodore Atkinson informed his London merchant friends, Trecothick and Thomlinson, that he "desired Mr. John Wentworth to purchas Some particular things for me & to apply to you for reimbursement." Shortly after arriving in London, Wentworth sent a bill to his uncle Daniel Peirce for a number of items, including silk, brocade, a suit, and a saddle.[8]

During his stay in the city, John Wentworth never lived far from one of its best known parks, St. James's. By late 1765 he was residing on Charles Street directly at St. James's Square. What astounded most visitors was the heterogeneous collection of people found in the park. The mall in St. James's Park has been referred to as "pre-eminently the 'public walk' of the century—both of 'the World' in the limited sense of 'the Great' and . . . of the people who went to stare as well as to amuse themselves in ways not always decorous." Within minutes a stroller might be hounded by the open solicitations of both beggars and prostitutes and treated to a view of the king and queen riding by in their carriage.[9]

In 1762 James Boswell recorded frequent trysts with women of the park, even though he claimed he "had a low opinion of this gross practice and resolved to do it no more." St. James's was also the scene of brutal floggings of soldiers found guilty of various crimes and misdemeanors. Thus the park was a microcosm of what has been called the "curious mixture of fashion, squalor, and the macabre" that characterized London in the eighteenth century.[10]

More purely for entertainment were a variety of pleasure gardens located around the city, Vauxhall and Ranelagh primary among them, and the theater. If one could put up with the unruly mob clamoring to get in and the often rude behavior of the audience during a performance, drama could be an enlightening and exhilarating experience. In spite of those drawbacks and the small number of theaters, stage plays were one of the chief entertainments in London. Wentworth, with some of his friends, had tried to start a theater in Portsmouth and would not have missed a chance to see the century's greatest actor, David Garrick, perform a Shakespearian tragedy or one of Goldsmith's new comedies at Drury Lane.[11] For a young man from a small and thinly populated colony in North America, the opportunities for diversion in London were endless. John Wentworth, however, had business to attend to and the rest of Britain to see.

The most pressing concern for the Wentworths in early 1764 was the immediate danger posed by Jared Ingersoll to their control of the mast trade. John Wentworth made clear to the Thomlinsons and to Trecothick the seriousness with which Benning and Mark Hunking Wentworth took that threat. They in turn applied pressure where they thought it might do the most good and in the process gave John Wentworth a useful introduction to practical English politics.

One of the first people who had to be made aware of the situation was John Henniker, a member of Parliament and one of the navy's major mast contractors through whom the Wentworths had worked. Most suppliers of naval timber went through contractors such as Henniker. Occasionally, however, single shiploads of masts were purchased directly by the navy board. Such seems to have been the case with Ingersoll. His contract was for one load of masts on a trial basis; if the navy liked what he delivered, there might be orders for more. He had at least one supporter on the board, for in August 1763 the comptroller expressed "great hopes" that through Ingersoll "the Government will, not only in what He has contracted for but in the future, be furnished with Masts on better terms than heretofore." Henniker would not worry about one load of masts bypassing him, but if his main suppliers in America believed their monopoly threatened by Ingersoll, his own position might be in jeopardy. Thus, in April 1764, not long after John Wentworth arrived in England, a friend of Ingersoll's wrote to him from London that he had "the greatest reason to believe that Mr. Hennika and others in Contact with Mr. Wentworth are Determined to break all your measures and frustrate your designs." [12]

The Wentworths in America were active as well. In that same month, one of Benning's deputies signed a deposition in the New York vice-admiralty court charging that Ingersoll's loggers, in the process of collecting the eighty sticks called for in his contract, had felled twice that number of trees "to the great waste of the King's woods." The deposition went on to declare Ingersoll "an Improper person to set as the Judge of the Vice Admiralty Court in the Colony of Connecticut concerning or relating to any pine Logs or Masts that may be seized or Libelled." With John Wentworth organizing the opposition in England and Benning Wentworth applying relentless pressure in America, Jared Ingersoll's plans to make Connecticut the principal mast exporting colony in America slowly dissolved. Although Ingersoll had received his contract in early 1761, by the beginning of 1764 no mast ship had yet been sent to pick up the load. In February he wrote to the navy to express his concern. By summer, there still was no sign of a ship. It finally arrived in the fall, and the masts were loaded by the end of October. They did not reach England until almost 1765. [13]

The delay of the ship can be attributed to pressure put on the navy board by the Wentworth interests in England, urged on by Benning Wentworth's energetic nephew John. It was also in 1764 that, as the Wentworths wished, a single vice-admiralty court with final authority for all America was established at Halifax. Ultimate testimony to the Wentworths' success in consolidating control over their mast interest lay in the fact that, following his arrival in England, Jared Ingersoll, rather than pursue the matter, concerned himself with other issues. [14]

It is difficult to know exactly what role John Wentworth played in defeating Ingersoll's masting plans, but with both of the Thomlinsons ill and others like the contractor Henniker unaware of the gravity of the situation, his presence was crucial in keeping the issue before the right parties and in seeing that they persisted until victory was won.

Another reason for his success may lie in what seems to have been a chance but fortuitous event, one that affected Wentworth's stay in England and also went far toward determining his entire future. That event was a meeting between Wentworth and the marquis of Rockingham at the racetrack, probably Newmarket. Rockingham, whose full name was Charles Watson-Wentworth, reportedly was intrigued by this young man who was placing large bets. Following an inquiry, Rockingham and Wentworth struck up an acquaintance.[15] They soon found that their love of horses was not the only thing they had in common. The discovery of their mutual name led to the realization that they were related. In order to establish more exactly what that relationship was, Wentworth sent a letter to his uncle Daniel Peirce asking him to trace the Wentworth lineage in America. In July 1764, John again wrote to Peirce, this time to thank him for "Your kind endeavors to ascertain my Pedigree," even though those efforts had not been successful. The first encounter between Wentworth and Rockingham thus probably took place sometime between the end of March, which marked the opening of the season at Newmarket, and early summer 1764.[16] The two never seem to have discovered exactly how they were related, but it mattered little.[17] Rockingham found Wentworth engaging, invited him to his home, and they soon became close friends.

Charles Watson-Wentworth, second marquis of Rockingham, was the leading landed nobleman in Yorkshire, making him, according to a biographer, "one of the pillars of the ruling system of politics in the kingdom." Rockingham was a relatively young man, only thirty-four at the time he met John Wentworth, which undoubtedly played a part in their friendship. His country home, Wentworth-Woodhouse, set in the lush rolling landscape of Yorkshire's West Riding, was one of the great houses of eighteenth-century England. Consciously copied after the purest example of classical architecture yet built in Britain, Wanstead House in Essex, Wentworth-Woodhouse was clearly derivative in design. What it lacked in originality, however, it made up for in sheer size. Extended to the extraordinary length of more than six hundred feet, Wentworth-Woodhouse was nearly the largest house in the realm. It was indeed what one architectural historian has called a "collossal mansion." In the 1760s it was considered "one of the finest places in the kingdom," and even today, especially to the visitor from America, the sight of this palatial Georgian structure amidst the tranquil

Wentworth-Woodhouse, Yorkshire, England
(Photograph by Paul Wilderson)

Yorkshire countryside is awe inspiring. Rockingham's new friend from New Hampshire must have been deeply impressed when he first viewed Wentworth-Woodhouse.[18]

58   It is not surprising that the two men met at the racetrack, for horses were one of Rockingham's abiding interests. He bred them on his estate, and he was one of the early members of the exclusive Jockey Club at Newmarket. In fact, his schedule was apparently determined as much by the races there as by the meetings of Parliament at Westminster. But horses were not the only attraction for Rockingham at home. He was by nature a local person, one who preferred the secure familiarity of his estate and county to the demands of eighteenth-century politics in the kingdom's center, London. He was devoted to agrarian improvement, not only on his own lands but in the surrounding country. The marquis felt that agriculture in the West Riding was inefficient and wasteful, and he was determined to see it improved by setting a good example himself. He experimented with new methods of cultivation and conservation, tried various crops, used different tools, and manufactured needed items such as bricks and tiles. One observer commented that he had never seen "the advantages of a great fortune applied so nobly to the improvement of a country."[19] Rockingham loved the country and would like to have stayed there, but he was not allowed to indulge his desires. Instead, the sense of public duty incumbent in his station drew him into the mainstream of English politics.

As the leading lord of the important county of Yorkshire, with the influence that position implied, Rockingham wielded considerable power in the political system of Great Britain. That fact, coupled with the favor he had won at court by his firm but diplomatic handling of antimilitia riots in Yorkshire in the late 1750s, made him a man eagerly sought after by that consummate politician and manipulator of Parliament, the duke of Newcastle. In the early sixties, Rockingham had obtained the office of lord of the Bedchamber, while Newcastle presided as first lord of the Treasury. In 1762 Newcastle found himself at odds with the other ministers' opinions on the financing of Britain's continental alliances and, considering himself indispensable to the ministry's control of Parliament, resigned from government as Pitt had done the year before. George III's new ministers, Bute and Grenville, were now determined to push through their peace terms with France and to force the agreement of the friends of Newcastle who still remained in office. When the duke of Devonshire declined to join and was unceremoniously removed from office, Newcastle asked his remaining followers to resign. He soon found, however, that the devotion of many of them to their own positions far outweighed any personal loyalty to himself. The marquis of Rockingham, however, indicating his attachment to Newcastle, promptly resigned his post.

When Parliament overwhelmingly approved the ministry's peace proposals, Newcastle quickly realized he was not indispensable to the government and that his only political option was to go into opposition. Old and tired, the duke of Newcastle was not sure he was up to the challenge. Some of his young whig friends encouraged him, however, and by 1764 that group had considerably augmented its numbers and was holding regular "opposition dinners" at Wildman's Tavern in Albemarle Street.

The marquis of Rockingham, who had lost his position as lord lieutenant of Yorkshire as a result of his adherence to Newcastle's position on the peace with France, was a key member of that circle of close political friends. In fact, he soon emerged as the recognized leader and spokesman of the group. That position was not achieved because he was an especially talented individual. He was not the politician Newcastle was, nor could he aspire to be a public figure of Pitt's caliber or even to compete with some of the lesser lights then performing on the political stage. Rockingham was one of the great aristocrats of the realm with vast estates, a moderate man of conviction who considered himself in the mainstream of English whig tradition. As such, he could command a large following, and he had a special ability in reconciling disparate individuals and groups and inspiring their loyalty. He was thus a natural focus of attention for whigs who found themselves at odds with the ministry of George III, a government that to many seemed increasingly like the old toryism revived. In an age of factional politics, Rockingham maintained a surprisingly constant hold on those whigs, so much so that some historians have viewed the group as the original forerunner of the English political party. Whatever they were, the Rockingham Whigs were a political force to be dealt with.[20]

John Wentworth must have stopped, at least for a moment, to consider his recent stroke of good fortune. He, an unknown young man from a small American colony, had been befriended by one of the great landed nobles of England and, further, one of political consequence. In addition, the tie was all but guaranteed when it turned out that the two men were related. Had he been merely daydreaming Wentworth could not have conjured up such a favorable circumstance for his visit to Britain. The relationship was bound to have a profound effect on a man in his twenties, still impressionable and from a colonial family identified with leadership and British authority, who was still seeking his own fortune. In immediately practical terms, it meant access at the highest level to English politics and politicians and, most significantly, to ones of a certain hue. But for now, Wentworth still had concerns of business and travel to occupy him.

In July 1764, he was back in Portsmouth on the south coast where he could look after the Wentworth mast interests. In a letter sent via his brother-in-law, John Fisher, who was departing for America, he told his uncle Daniel Peirce that any political news he had would be reported by Fisher and "Mr. Livius— a good Young Man and well accomplished." Apparently, Wentworth was favorably impressed by Peter Livius, who was on his way to make his home in New Hampshire. He would later view Livius in quite a different light. He also sent a note of introduction for a Mr. Watts and his wife, who were sailing for New Hampshire with the intent of settling near Portsmouth as farmers. Showing a continued interest in his home, husbandry, and people in general, Wentworth asked that no "Civilitys" be spared the couple on their arrival.[21]

By the middle of August, John Wentworth was far to the north on the high bluffs of Scarborough, overlooking the North Sea. Known as "a watering place of some repute," Scarborough was a common stop for visitors from the colonies. Wentworth was extremely busy, but he managed to find time to jot a note to Daniel Peirce. In response to a previous query from Peirce, he expressed regret that the New Hampshire Council was full and that the next two vacancies had already been claimed. He promised, however, that if any more positions opened up before he left England, he would do everything possible to obtain one for his uncle, and, he continued, "[I] think it will be in my Power."[22] Wentworth was beginning to feel that he wielded some influence in places of importance.

That confidence may have prompted him to go on and complain to his uncle about the inadequacy of New Hampshire's representation in England. By his reasoning, it was only because of carelessness and inattention that Peirce's name, though placed in nomination for a councillor's post, had not been presented to the Board of Trade. Further, he was worried that this neglect might place "our property . . . in a precarious Situation." There is reason to believe Wentworth was referring specifically to the claims of the Masonian proprietors, of whom Peirce was one, and of those who held land from them such as himself. To remedy what he obviously considered the weak agency of the Thomlinsons, Wentworth thought it "highly necessary we have an addition of Integrity and Knowledge" in England.[23] He did not say it, but by that time he was thinking of himself for the job.

In January 1765, Wentworth set out to see the "Kingdom of Ireland." He visited Dublin and Cork, made the acquaintance of another Wentworth kinsman who lived near Carlow, and sought mercantile contacts that might be valuable for his father's trade.[24] By early March, however, he was back in London, settled in New Bond Street with more weighty concerns on his mind. On 20 July 1764, by order of the king in council, the disputed New Hampshire–New York boundary had been fixed at the Connecticut River.[25] This meant that all of the land west of the river that Benning Wentworth had assumed was his to grant was now forfeited to the province of New York. Worse, though not totally unexpected, the inquiry into the governor's land granting policies had led to the disclosure of numerous abuses of the royal prerogative in New Hampshire.

A report of the Board of Trade to the Privy Council clearly indicated that Benning Wentworth was in trouble. He had gone ahead with his grants west of the Connecticut River after being expressly ordered to desist until a determination on the boundary had been made. When the same proprietors turned up again and again in different grants and it was brought to light that the governor himself held title to five hundred acres in every new township, the Board of Trade had no choice but to conclude that Benning Wentworth's land granting policies were governed by a "view more to private Interest than public advantage." As such, they were deemed "totally inconsistent" with his official instructions. He was also found negligent in allowing laws to pass without the required suspending clause and in not forwarding those laws promptly to Whitehall for approval. As a result, a number of what the board considered "absurd, incongruous and unjust" laws had been in effect in New Hampshire for as long as five years without the knowledge of the home government.[26]

It was also believed that Wentworth had been neglecting his duties as surveyor general of the woods, allowing the king's best mast timber to be illegally cut and wasted. Adding to the general displeasure of the board with the governor was their belief that he had a personal interest, as opposed to the interest of the Crown, in the "waste and unimproved lands within the Limits of Mason's Grant," a subject that had been under consideration by the British government since 1753.[27] What had seemed probable in New Hampshire on John Wentworth's departure in 1763 was, from his vantage point in England, becoming a certainty by early 1765: the evidence was overwhelming that Benning Wentworth would be replaced.

John Wentworth knew there was no way to save his uncle. The governor was old, his transgressions too flagrant. Wentworth might, however, be able to salvage the aged gentleman's honor and that of the Wentworth family. Years later he recalled that when he learned of Benning Wentworth's imminent removal, he quickly composed a defense that he hoped would not only "blunt the edge of Misfortune" but gain the governor enough time to resign gracefully.[28]

In spite of its rhetoric, the case that John Wentworth drew up for his highly placed friend, the marquis of Rockingham, was not a strong one. He argued that Benning Wentworth's gout (which was indeed real) had prevented him from corresponding with the home government and transmitting the laws passed by the provincial legislature. Strangely, the affliction had "not the least impeded" his other duties as governor. As for the absence of the suspending clause, it had not seemed necessary in acts that involved two private parties who were in agreement. Wentworth did not try to explain why his uncle had continued to grant lands long after being ordered to stop. At the same time, he "failed to find the impropriety" of the governor's reservation of five hundred acres for himself in each of the grants he made. After all, Wentworth argued, a governor was under the same obligation as any other proprietor to satisfy the requirements of his grant. As long as those conditions were met, what did it matter who had title to the land? Wentworth ascribed the recurrence of other names in many of the grants to the large families of the proprietors. When a man's many children, and possibly servants, were ready to leave home, they would thus have a plot of land of their own. Furthermore, the governor could not possibly have received large fees for his land grants because of the "general Poverty" of the inhabitants of the province.

John Wentworth denied that the obviously vague wording in the town charters concerning the reservation of the king's timber was an encouragement to indiscriminate and illegal destruction of valuable mast pine. On the contrary, the laws were being enforced, and to prove that Benning Wentworth was doing his job as surveyor general, his nephew referred critics to notices in New England newspapers of timber seized and prosecutions made in the admiralty courts. Then Wentworth answered one more accusation that he said he had been "this very day surprised with"—that Governor Wentworth had made government in New Hampshire "a Family Affair." He categorically denied the charge of nepotism and family favoritism and substantiated his argument by claiming that he himself had been denied the grant of a township by his uncle "for no other Reason than my Connections with him."

Probably because he realized the case he had made was weak, Wentworth padded it with reminders of Benning Wentworth's unrelenting services during the war and, perhaps as an excuse for many of the charges he knew to be true, a claim that his uncle's meager salary had caused him to labor in office for many years "almost at his own expense." Whatever the effect of John Wentworth's efforts, he had done his duty for Benning Wentworth and the family, and now the affair was out of his hands.

On 8 April, Wentworth wrote to Daniel Peirce that he had nominated him for the first vacancy on the council. One name was ahead of Peirce's on the list, but Wentworth was going to change that the following day when he met with the president of the Board of Trade, Lord Hillsborough, who, he claimed, "is much my friend and has these appointments."[29] With that behind him, Wentworth considered his duties completed, and he was determined to be back in New Hampshire by summer. First, though, he wanted to see Europe.

From the company he kept in England, John Wentworth doubtless heard first-hand reports of the many attractions of the Continent. Descriptions of ancient architectural wonders, fabulous art, exotic food, and fine wine were bound to arouse wanderlust in a young man from America. When he departed England in the spring of 1765, Wentworth planned to travel across Europe to Italy, then back to New England. He even scheduled a five-hundred-mile diversion to Prussia to call on a cousin of Daniel Peirce in Berlin. He wrote home that he hoped to arrive back in New Hampshire "with a few little conveniences, and a vast amount of itinerary . . . amusement, for my friends assembled at the Office, over . . . a due proportion of cool Punch." Wentworth's itinerary was cut short, however, when news reached him in Brabant that cancelled his well-laid plans and sent him hurrying back to London.[30]

63

George III had reached the end of his patience with the Grenville ministry and had tried to forge a new one joining Pitt with the friends of Newcastle. When Pitt declined, the king had no choice but to place the government in the hands of the Rockingham Whigs. In July the marquis of Rockingham was appointed first lord of the Treasury; he was now the king's first minister and head of the administration. Wentworth reported that this news of "a general change of Men and measures, made it necessary to return directly to London, having some interests of my Friends, Which were likely to be affected by so universal a commotion."[31] Friends aside, Wentworth's own interests were at stake. With his patron now in the government's most powerful position, he would have as good a chance as anyone of replacing his uncle as governor of New Hampshire.

By August, John Wentworth was back in London, writing to his relatives in Portsmouth about the new situation. The change in government had brought the earl of Dartmouth to the Board of Trade in place of Lord Hillsborough. Because it was Hillsborough who had promised the first vacancy on the New Hampshire Council to Daniel Peirce, Wentworth would now have to renew the application. He was able to reassure Peirce, though, that there would be no problem. Dartmouth, a devotee of Newcastle and a member of the Rockingham group, had promised him any favor he desired from the Board of Trade. There was something more serious, however, that Wentworth wanted to discuss with his uncle: the reaction in America to the Stamp Act.

Since its passage in Parliament in March, the Stamp Act had produced a ground swell of opposition in the colonies. By the end of July, soon after taking office, the Rockingham administration was made aware of inflammatory resolves adopted by the Virginia House of Burgesses claiming that the people of that colony had been unconstitutionally deprived of their "ancient" right of self-taxation. Moreover, by late August, Massachusetts had called for a convention of delegates from all the colonies to meet in New York in October for the purpose of drawing up a petition to the Crown for relief from the measure. On 27 August, Wentworth wrote home, "I suppose N[ew] E[ngland] is deeply immersed in political discussion of Colony rights, and the principles of taxation upon the Stamp Act," and he wondered, "Where shall we poor N[ew] Hampshire men get the money to pay It?" He noted that he had talked with a "certain great man" who had concluded that the tax could not really harm the colonies. Wentworth had rejoined that it would not only hurt the colonies but England as well. He warned that if the act was enforced, British merchants should hope to be reimbursed by Parliament "as it wou'd be much more necessary than for their relief in time of War." The Stamp Act, according to Wentworth, would only exacerbate the perennial shortage of currency in the colonies, and the stamp commissioners should be prepared to accept "Boards, plank and joist, indian Corn and spanish potatoes" in payment. He then facetiously asked the English gentleman for his help in obtaining an appointment as "exporter general" of all those commodities. The Englishman apparently did not find the remark amusing and changed the topic of discussion.[32]

In all seriousness, Wentworth told Daniel Peirce, "The Prudence of our Province, in avoiding any warm resolves, and of the people not expressing an indecent resentment in their publication is very much commended, and may be of good Consequence to us."[33] Significantly, this opposition to British policies detrimental to the colonies, combined with a firm belief that the colonists should make no strong stand or statement against those policies, was a position that John Wentworth would hold consistently in the years to come.

»5«
A MODEL FOR THE
FUTURE

Rockingham and the Repeal
of the Stamp Act,
1765–1766

John Wentworth was concerned about the reaction to the Stamp Act in the colonies, and so was the marquis of Rockingham. Almost immediately on his accession to the head of the ministry, Rockingham was confronted with ominous portents of widespread resistance to British policy in America. He had had no previous reason to give much thought to American affairs, and his first question was logically: Is there any reasonable basis for this reaction against the Stamp Act? To answer that, he would need to know all he could about the colonies. Rockingham, of course, had immediate access to the Board of Trade and all other government agencies and officials who were involved with colonial matters. But what he needed was not an official report. It was possible, after all, that the current troubles stemmed from inadequate advice provided to the ministers who originally sponsored the Stamp Act. What Rockingham needed was a firsthand account of the colonies from an American point of view. It was natural, then, that he turned for this information to his close friend John Wentworth.

On 1 September 1765, Wentworth, in accordance with Rockingham's "commands," sat down in his London residence in New Bond Street to pen a lengthy description of the North American colonies along with his opinion on the recent trade and revenue acts.[1] The dominant theme in his letter repeated what he had written to Daniel Peirce only a few days earlier: that the greatest value of the colonies lay in their trade, and anything that interfered with that trade, including taxes and debilitating restrictions, was harmful both to the colonies and to the mother country. Stating this mercantile premise boldly at the beginning, Wentworth hoped his description would prove "that greater benefit would accrue to this country [England], from their trade, than can be expected from their present ability considerably to increase or rather create a revenue."

Plunging ahead, he worked systematically from north to south, beginning with Canada and Nova Scotia and finishing in the West Indies, with even some reference to nearly uninhabited East and West Florida. Although he devoted by far the largest portion of his account to New England, Wentworth showed a remarkable knowledge of conditions in all the colonies. Pennsylvania he described as the "most flourishing" of the provinces, Virginia the most "populous and opulent." Because of its relatively primitive state, Georgia's trade was negligible. New York, on the other hand, had great potential as an exporter of iron. Wentworth showed an awareness of the main exports and imports and the pattern and balance of trade in each colony. He was mistaken on a few counts, such as describing Virginia as "the only colony not indebted to Gr[eat] Britain," but his information overall was surprisingly correct. He even accurately estimated the colonial population at "about two millions of subjects."

Understandably, Wentworth showed the most interest in the New England provinces. He justified his bias on the grounds that "they are so great a division of the American dominions both in trade and number of inhabitants, and as the late regulations will more particularly affect them, than the other colonies." It was in relation to this region, in fact, that he went into the most detail concerning problems in the colonies and the probable effect of the recent British measures. New England's major exports went to the West Indian islands, some to be traded for goods brought back to the mainland. The majority, however, were exchanged for items loaded on board and carried to England. There, both ship and cargo were sold to pay for British manufactures. That trade produced little cash, and for the previous ten years, according to Wentworth, New England had continued at a "considerable loss." Compounding the problem was the fact that the New England colonies could not raise enough grain to feed themselves and were forced to import it, thereby draining off valuable currency already in short supply.

Recent restrictions on the trade of surplus goods to the foreign West Indies had also hampered New England's commerce and cut even more deeply into the merchants' ability to purchase manufactured items in England. And while he was on the subject of burdensome and unproductive restrictions on trade, Wentworth brought up an older regulation that required all commerce from the European continent to the colonies to flow through Great Britain. Every year New Englanders carried a quantity of codfish to Portugal, Spain, and Italy in return for salt, wine, oil, and fruit. The requirement of entering those products in England, paying a duty, and then reexporting them for home was unreasonable and, Wentworth claimed, "attended with insupportable expense." It certainly was not an encouragement to the trade of the empire and had resulted only in widespread smuggling.

John Wentworth recognized that the greatest problem in New England, and in almost all of the other colonies, was a shortage of circulating currency. It was also clear to him that the imposition of a direct tax such as that called for by the stamp tax and the three-pence molasses duty of 1764, if rigorously enforced, would "consume every shilling of specie in New England within two years, and will be as affectually draining them as if it was annihilated." The results would be catastrophic. With all their money gone, colonists would no longer be extended credit in the mother country. They would thus be forced to develop their own manufacturing and would not be able to produce goods for much less than twice the cost of buying them in Britain. This added hardship, according to Wentworth, would halt the growth and settlement of the colonies, allowing fertile land to "lay waste and useless" that might otherwise "support vast numbers of laborious people, and extend the commercial interest of England beyond their most sanguine expectations." The merchants and manufacturers of England would certainly feel the dire effects of the loss of so valuable a market. As proof of the value of the colonies to the British mercantile system, Wentworth suggested a comparison of "the present state of Gr[eat] Britain to her state one century back, at which time her colonies began to be useful."

Wentworth argued that without "some indulgence to their trade and an exemption from taxation, . . . [the colonies] will be depressed beyond recovery." Specifically, he proposed that the duty on foreign molasses be lowered from three pence to one. That would end smuggling, provide additional specie for the colonies with which to purchase British manufactures, and raise a real revenue that would not be eaten up by the cost of enforcement. Further, he suggested that wine, fruit, and oil from Iberia and Italy be allowed directly into the colonies under a "moderate duty." That would stop the "running" of those commodities and would also raise a revenue. Finally, and most important, John Wentworth told the marquis of Rockingham that the Stamp Act should be repealed. The great debt that the colonies were struggling under, increased by the current trade restrictions, made the attempt to collect a revenue by a direct tax a highly imprudent policy.

Wentworth's suggestions were not separately conceived; they were part of his integrated theory of the British Empire. He believed that his argument proved that the colonies' "advantage to Gr[eat] Britain must arise from their trade." As long as that trade suffered under such burdens, Britain could not expect to reap the full benefits of her colonial system. If, on the other hand, the hindrances were removed, trade would increase, prosperity return, and possibly "in a few years a more direct assistance [might be] obtained" from the colonies. Summarizing his position for Rockingham, Wentworth predicted that if the government in England would "rescue" the colonies "from the late imposed tax, and preserve them from new ones: also permit an indulgence of every trade which cannot prejudice Gr[eat] Britain, and some necessary assistance to that which tends directly to her advantage, the colonies will then flourish, their demand for British manufactures would increase and be paid for: dependence and fidelity will then be their indispensible interest."

John Wentworth's letter of 1 September 1765 is significant because, as well as can be ascertained, it was the first time anyone had suggested repeal of the Stamp Act to Rockingham since he had taken office. The actual decision of the administration for repeal was not made until well after the beginning of 1766, but it seems that the first minister was committed to the idea long before that. It is quite possible that John Wentworth's reasoned and well-balanced account of the difficult circumstances of the American colonies turned Rockingham's thoughts to the idea of repealing the Stamp Act, and that subsequent events only strengthened his inclination toward that solution.[2]

John Wentworth's suggestion of repeal was especially remarkable for its early date. It was known at the time that there were objections in America to the Stamp Act. It was not then known, however, that there had already been riots and destructive violence in the colonies and that the months ahead would bring widespread resistance and, eventually, blatant defiance of the law. Moreover, the results of the Stamp Act Congress, which called for repeal, did not reach England until late in the year. Those developments thus could not have influenced Wentworth. Rather, his assessment of the measures that needed to be taken was based on a thorough knowledge of economic conditions in the colonies and the trade disadvantages they labored under. As might be expected from a member of a prominent American merchant family, Wentworth was knowledgeable about Britain's system of empire and based his argument against further taxation entirely on sound mercantile principles. Unlike the earlier Virginia resolves and the later Stamp Act Congress petition, he made no mention of rights under the English constitution.

Although his letter was concerned with the future welfare of the colonies, it seems also to have carried suggestions portentous for Wentworth himself. The changes that he recommended in the trade and revenue regulations would start the colonial system back toward a harmonious and profitable operation. But that was not enough for Wentworth. He went on to argue that one of the guarantees of a smoothly running empire lay in a judicious choice of governors for the colonies. A good governor would maintain order and stability, foster economic growth that would complement rather than compete with the mother country, promote settlement and prosperity, and develop a sound defensive force that would not require British aid but could be called on to aid the British if needed. Wentworth told Rockingham, "It would be almost endless to enumerate the variety of essential service that a disinterested, diligent and faithful Governor can and ought to effect." Determining the best policies to follow was not nearly so difficult as finding the "integrity and resolution to carry them into execution."[3]

Wentworth presumably felt that he had those qualities essential to a colonial governor and was counting on Rockingham to recognize it. In fact, since at least midsummer he had been actively seeking his uncle's job. George Meserve, the new distributor of stamps in New Hampshire, who set sail for home no later than the middle of July, discussed the possibility with Wentworth before he left England. Writing from Portsmouth after his arrival in September, Meserve referred to Wentworth's "resolution" to become governor, and, on having broached the subject in the province, he had found the "People in General" in favor of the idea.[4]

But Meserve had more urgent news for Wentworth. Before he had even set foot on shore he was rudely awakened to sentiments running high against the Stamp Act in America. On 9 September, before his ship could dock in Boston, an officer and marines clamored on board to keep an angry mob from sinking the vessel, which they believed carried forty-five tons of stamp paper. Further, the harbor pilot carried a special note for Meserve from some "Principal Gentlemen" in Portsmouth, warning him that feeling was just as strong in New Hampshire as it was in Boston and that it would not be safe to return until he had renounced his position as stamp distributor. He was forced to write a letter to that effect before he was allowed off the ship, but he was still burned in effigy in Portsmouth. When he finally arrived there on 18 September, the local Sons of Liberty extracted a public resignation from him on the Parade in front of the state house. Nor was that to be the end of Meserve's troubles. He later reported that at the end of October a mob of some six hundred men bullied him into another oath of assurance that he would not execute his office, and the following January he was again threatened.[5]

It was not a motley rabble that confronted George Meserve. He found among his tormentors "the principal Inhabitants of the Town and the Representatives of the County." The local Sons of Liberty did in fact include some of the most important merchants in Portsmouth. The Speaker of the House, John Sherburne, and his two sons-in-law, Woodbury and John Langdon; Samuel Cutts; and even John Wentworth's two uncles, Daniel Peirce and Daniel Rindge, were all active against the Stamp Act. Meserve told Secretary of State Henry Conway that the oath he was forced to take in October was "administered by Daniel Warner Esq. one of his Majestys Council, Chief Justice of the Inferior Court and Lieut. Col. of the Town Militia," and went on to complain that this intimidation was countenanced by such significant people as Theodore Atkinson and Jonathan Warner.[6]

Just as John Wentworth had explained to the marquis of Rockingham, times were hard in the colonies, and the stamp tax only made them worse. The difficulties fell on the large merchants as readily as the small. Even Meserve described the condition of trade as "terrible"; cash was in short supply, and the molasses duty was working a very real hardship. In a statement puzzling from a man ready to enforce the Stamp Act, Meserve exclaimed to John Wentworth that "if something is not done for us on the other side [of] the water I don't know how these Colonies are to subsist." Benning Wentworth was well aware of the nearly universal opposition to the Stamp Act and, as he had done with so many inconvenient government directives before, chose to ignore it. He refused to accept Meserve's commission and later excused his action by claiming that he had never received official notification that the Stamp Act was law.[7]

The New Hampshire Assembly declined to send representatives to the Stamp Act Congress in New York in October, possibly because of ill feelings with that province over the recent boundary dispute. Nevertheless, on 22 November the assembly voted approval of the resolutions and the petition for repeal adopted by the congress. Further, those papers were to be signed and forwarded to two new special province agents chosen specifically to present the documents at the proper agencies and to use "their utmost Endeavors" to see that the Stamp Act was repealed. The two special agents were Barlow Trecothick and John Wentworth.[8]

Wentworth did not yet know of the appointment or of the petitions being forwarded to him when he wrote to Daniel Rindge late in November. He was now living in Westminster on Charles Street at the corner of St. James's Square. With an eye on the growing political agitation in England over America's response to the Stamp Act and his own designs for the future, Wentworth wanted to be as close to Whitehall and the houses of Parliament as possible. He was frankly alarmed at the "melancholy" state of things. The lion's share of the blame for the Stamp Act, which he found "totally obnoxious," he placed on the Grenville administration, which had "utterly misapprehended" colonial trade. But Wentworth did not believe the wretched legislation was entirely the fault of the ministers. Nearly as guilty were the colonists themselves, in particular those self-serving men who came to England for brief stays seeking positions or favors, who enjoyed "being noted by the Great Men," and who were willing to say anything to promote their own advancement. Wentworth felt that these men had only a superficial knowledge of America based on their own small vantage point and accomplished nothing but the spread of ignorance. The only way to really know all the colonies and the complexities of their commercial relationships within the empire was, Wentworth asserted, through "study, experience, and assiduous well directed inquiry."[9]

He did not know what action the English government would take, but he assured Rindge that the administration was sympathetic to the colonies. The problem lay with the opposition, many of whom had originally voted for the stamp bill and who, he had discovered, were still "very warm against us." Enforcement of the act was being championed merely because the colonists had resisted it with threats and violence. For many in England, the principle of parliamentary sovereignty was at stake. But Wentworth, too, felt that he could stand behind the constitution when attempting to "combat" the hundreds of such arguments he encountered daily. The fact was that the colonies were not represented in the body that was taxing them. Wentworth did not fail to point out to his English opponents that the citizens of London who were represented, who had their interests doubly protected by their immediate proximity to Parliament and who could claim "evry advantage to obtain redress," often broke out into riotous open opposition to Parliament's policies. In many such debates, he claimed, he did not shy away from holding forth the "inalienable right" of the colonies.[10]

When arguing the matter himself in Britain, John Wentworth was willing openly to defend the colonies in terms of basic rights and constitutional principles. He did not, however, think the colonists should do the same. At that time, in late autumn 1765, there seemed to be a wait-and-see attitude in England; what would the Americans do next? Word was expected from the Stamp Act Congress at any time, and Wentworth believed, though mistakenly, that the ministry's policy would be largely determined by the action taken in New York. Thus he expressed great concern over the imminent message from America. He earnestly hoped, he wrote to his uncle, that "it may be firm, decent, loyal and expressive, if possible evading all matter of right, a point too critically dangerous to discuss."[11]

Wentworth felt free to use the argument of right himself, but why did he deny that privilege to his fellow colonists? In England he saw firsthand the immediate negative feelings aroused by that line of colonial justification. Wentworth may have believed that he could handle the subtle distinctions demanded by the argument in face-to-face confrontations. Familiarity with British emotional reaction to colonial objections, however, may have told him that a flat statement of constitutional rights would, indeed, be "critically dangerous." Instead, he was convinced that the safest, most judicious, and most productive course of action for Americans was to stress, as he had done in his letter to Rockingham, "the inability of America" to pay the tax. That would, according to Wentworth, "put it in the power of our friends to labor for us, without the insidious objections of the opposition to the repeal of this odious Act."[12] He did not know when he wrote those lines that only a week earlier the representatives in his own province, in hopes of repeal, had signed a strong statement of colonial rights under the English constitution and chosen him as their agent to present it in England.

In his November letter, Wentworth also mentioned, for the first time in his correspondence home, the possibility of his appointment as governor of New Hampshire. He cautioned that the rumor was "premature" and that "indeed there has been no vacancy or expected removal from Jamaica to N.H. . . . for the last eight months, but has been given to me in public report, and many of them been the subject of News paper declamation." Nevertheless, he told Daniel Rindge, "it is more than probable I shall have N.H." If he did return as governor, he promised that he would be his own man, under no obligation to any person, party, or interest. Obviously sensitive to Benning Wentworth's recent troubles, John also felt obliged to renounce all possible influence by members of his own family. His only aim would be to advance the welfare of New Hampshire, something he would be in a particularly good position to do through his connection with the marquis of Rockingham. He was confident that the relationship would serve to procure "some special advantages" for the province. With the current dispute in mind, he assured his uncle that, if he was expected to carry out measures that ran contrary to the "real rights and truest interests" of the people of New Hampshire, he would refuse to serve. He would rather, he claimed, "retire to Wolfeborough and procure a scanty subsistence from hardest labour than either undertake so ungenerous an employ or not oppose any one that did." He was sure, though, that the present administration would make no such demands on any governor.[13]

The question by this time, in both England and America, was what would the government do in regard to the Stamp Act? As resistance in the colonies broadened and turned increasingly hostile, it became obvious that some kind of action would be necessary. The experience of George Meserve was not isolated. Even before Meserve's arrival in America, Boston had set the tone for demonstrating displeasure with the act and all officers who might attempt to enforce it. A mob hung stamp distributor Peter Oliver in effigy, then descended on his house and ransacked it after breaking down the doors and smashing the windows. Oliver resigned his commission. Several weeks later, another mob attacked Lieutenant Governor Thomas Hutchinson's stately Georgian mansion with even more gusto, believing (wrongly) that Hutchinson was a secret supporter of the Stamp Act. This lawless desecration of property was shocking even to many opponents of the British measure. Nevertheless, the violence spread. With few exceptions, similar hangings, riots, and forced resignations occurred throughout the colonies.[14] By 1 November, when the Stamp Act was to go into effect, the colonies had all declared their opposition to it, and there was no one left in America willing to carry the law out.

There seemed to be three choices before the Rockingham ministry: enforcement of the Stamp Act, which probably could not be done without the use of arms; modification of the act in hopes of making it more palatable to the colonies; or outright repeal.[15] John Wentworth was close enough to Rockingham to know that the first alternative was never seriously considered. By November, Wentworth could report that Rockingham "would give his Interest to repeal 100 stamp Acts, before he would run the Risque of such Confusions, as would be caused by Enforcing it."[16] Still, Rockingham realized that to make any kind of conciliatory policy possible he would need a strong and convincing argument. His caution is understandable given John Wentworth's comments about those who were "very warm against us." Not only was there a strong opposition in Parliament to a policy of relief, especially repeal, but Rockingham could expect a fierce battle from some of his own ministers, in particular the earl of Northington, Charles Yorke, and Charles Townshend.

By late November, in preparation for the reconvening of Parliament the following month, Rockingham had begun to formulate a strategy. Significantly, his plan emphasized what John Wentworth had recommended to him early in September. He hoped to keep the Stamp Act in the background "till Good Principles are laid down for Easing and Assisting N[orth] America and being well informed of the high Importance of the Commerce to N[orth] A[merica] respectively to the Mother Country."[17] The necessity for relieving America from the burden of the stamp tax might thus be made apparent.

Rockingham knew he would need pressing evidence to support his argument, and, with the aid of John Wentworth's co-agent, Barlow Trecothick, he was working to obtain it. Trecothick had an interest in America that went back to his early years. Born in England in 1720, he had emigrated to Boston with his family at the age of seven. An apprenticeship carried him into the world of commerce, and he eventually became associated with the mercantile firm of Charles Apthorp, a wealthy Boston merchant. As Apthorp's commercial representative, Trecothick traveled to the West Indies and to England. In London he worked with Apthorp's trading partner, John Thomlinson. By 1755 he had decided to stay in his native land in partnership with Thomlinson, who was also agent for New Hampshire and a close associate of the Wentworths, whom Trecothick had come to know in the colonies. In the 1760s, with both of the Thomlinsons ill, Barlow Trecothick became the most important member of the firm and by 1765 was considered one of London's leading merchants.[18]

Trecothick had been a vocal mercantile spokesman against passage of the Stamp Act in the first place, and in early November, when American resistance to it had become obvious, he wrote a letter to the marquis of Rockingham. He warned that if the Americans carried out their refusal to comply with the act, as almost surely they would, it would mean a halt to all trade that depended on stamped paper. That event would kill the demand for British exports, hurt merchants and manufacturers, and throw people out of work, leaving them hungry—all disastrous consequences for the nation. Rockingham's reply was to invite Trecothick to a private dinner party, one of his favorite means of collecting information and making decisions during this difficult period. From that point on, Rockingham and Trecothick worked together closely.

On 4 December, a committee of London merchants trading with North America was formed under the leadership of Barlow Trecothick to work for the repeal of the Stamp Act. On the sixth, the committee agreed on a circular to be sent "to the outports and to the manufacturing Towns." It outlined the crucial interests of the kingdom that were at stake and appealed for aid in the form of pressure on Parliament. This letter, the combined work of Rockingham and Trecothick, emphasized points that John Wentworth had been making since he first wrote to Rockingham about the Stamp Act in September. There was no mention of constitutional issues, and all arguments were based on the hardships caused in England by the restrictions placed on the colonies. The appeal was sent to thirty cities and towns and resulted in some twenty-five petitions to Parliament for relief. The importance of the circular can best be seen in the words of Rockingham's secretary, Edmund Burke, who called it "the principal Instrument in the happy repeal of the Stamp Act."[19]

English merchants and manufacturers did indeed have reason to be concerned with the colonial situation. Since 1764 there had been a recession in North American trade. It was well known that the colonists considered the stamp tax an added hardship and were deeply opposed to it. Warnings had emanated from some of the wealthiest and most highly regarded American merchants that the act might put a complete stop to trade and that the bills owed in England could well go unpaid. Thus the Stamp Act, though not a trade law, seemed to be very much involved in the present economic downturn, and the English mercantile community began to identify repeal with a return of prosperity. They had even more reason to desire the end of the Stamp Act when, shortly, word arrived that the colonists were taking actions to boycott British goods.[20]

Parliament met briefly before Christmas but postponed consideration of the
American question until after the first of the year. Avoiding consultation with his full official cabinet, Rockingham continued to hold his private dinners, seeking practical information and advice that might lead to a workable policy. One point by now was clear. If relief was to be gained for the colonies, an attempt would have to be made to placate a Parliament and public incensed at the violence and blatant disregard for British authority in America. During the week after Christmas, this portion of administration policy was decided. A declaration of absolute sovereignty of Parliament over the colonies would be proposed. Exactly what form of relief would be offered along with this pronouncement was still undetermined.

When Parliament reconvened on 14 January 1766, John Wentworth sat in the House of Commons as a spectator from one o'clock until ten in the evening. The American question was the main topic of discussion, and the session was dominated by a spirited and highly important debate between William Pitt and George Grenville. Pitt had not spoken in the Commons for over a year, and although his opposition to the Stamp Act was well known, no one was sure what form his argument would take. As England's most influential and charismatic political figure, his words were awaited with great interest, not least by Rockingham and his ministers, who, during the recess, had tried to get the great man to join the administration but had been rebuffed. Pitt, who Wentworth noted "spoke clearly and nervously," began by upholding the authority of Britain over the colonies "in every circumstance of government and legislation whatsoever." He went on, however, to point out one exception; he did not include taxation as part of the governing and legislative power. Taxes, he claimed, were "a voluntary gift and grant of the Commons alone." The Stamp Act, according to Pitt, "was founded on an erroneous principle" and should be repealed.[21]

Swayed by both the thrust of Pitt's argument and his persuasive oratorical powers, Wentworth was moved to report that the Great Commoner "never was half so great before. No Subject—scarce any Monarch even had such Homage paid him. The whole House of Commons *hung* upon him. He was happiest who made him the greatest Compliments. Great Ministers implor'd (openly) the Honor to serve under him, and inferior Luminarys wish'd only to shine, by reflection from this Sun." In contrast, Wentworth noted, George Grenville "made a weak, desultory defence, of weak and ruinous measures, but was little attended to."[22]

So impressed was Wentworth that he characterized Pitt's argument as exhibiting "the most profound and yet shining knowledge of the British Constitution."[23] Despite appearances, many members of Parliament did not agree. Even the administration did not concede that Parliament had no right to tax the colonies, but Rockingham had been hoping for a chance to propose the repeal of the Stamp Act. With Pitt's resounding rhetoric now leading the way, that course was finally resolved upon by the ministry at two of Rockingham's unofficial meetings on 19 and 21 January. By that time, the petitions solicited by Barlow Trecothick and the merchants committee began to arrive at the House of Commons asking for relief from the economic distress that seemed to be caused by the recent acts of Parliament aimed at the colonies. Large ports and manufacturing cities—London, Bristol, Liverpool, Leeds, Manchester, Birmingham, Glasgow—were represented as well as smaller towns—Leicester, Bradford, Wolverhampton, Stourbridge, Taunton, Witney, Dudley, Chippenham, and others. The petition from the Stamp Act Congress was presented to the Commons on the twenty-seventh. After a long discussion and many objections, including one that it "Strongly pointed at Independency upon [from] the Mother Country," the decision was made to ignore it.[24] For purposes of confidentiality, on 28 January the House of Commons resolved itself into a committee of the whole and called for the consideration of all information relevant to America. That material was to include official government papers, petitions from the various cities of Great Britain, and testimony from persons with specific knowledge of the colonies, especially the colonial agents.

London seethed with political controversy as the month of February was consumed by exhausting debates in Parliament over the repeal of the Stamp Act. Although Wentworth had not yet gained a political office, he claimed to have plans to sail home in the middle of the month. He now canceled those plans. An intimate of the Rockingham Whigs and deeply concerned about the outcome for his own province, Wentworth deemed his presence at Westminster a necessity. His attendance became even more necessary when news of his appointment as special agent for New Hampshire, along with Barlow Trecothick, arrived in England along with the province petitions for the repeal of the Stamp Act.

On 3 February, the House of Commons ordered some thirty persons to attend the following day to testify concerning the Stamp Act. John Wentworth was among those on the list, as were Barlow Trecothick and Benjamin Franklin.[25] It was also on the third that Secretary of State Conway proposed the ministry's first resolution, the one decided on in December stating that all laws passed by Parliament were binding on the colonies "in all Cases whatsoever." When the vote was taken at nearly three o'clock on the morning of the fourth, scarcely a voice was raised against it. On 11 and 13 February, when the petition of the London merchants was considered, Trecothick and Franklin were the administration's star witnesses, each taking the stand for four hours on those dates respectively. The evidence they presented delineating the severe straits of the mercantile community in England and America was well designed by Rockingham as the basis of a proposed repeal of the Stamp Act.[26]

Wentworth was not called on for evidence. He of course did not have the reputation of Dr. Franklin, nor, as he later lamented, did he represent an influential province. Neither was his friendship with Rockingham likely to carry much weight with those in opposition to the ministry's policies. Nevertheless, that did not diminish his interest in the proceedings, and he was diligent in his attendance in the Commons, sitting for sessions that sometimes lasted thirteen hours and often continued well past midnight. After a few hours sleep, he probably headed for the New England Coffee House for breakfast, his mail, and a discussion of the previous day's events with "a Club of Gentlemen" that included John Huske, formerly of New Hampshire, now a member of Parliament and an advocate of repeal. By 15 February Wentworth was able to sit down with pen and paper to congratulate Daniel Peirce on that "happy prospect." The resolution for repeal had not even been introduced yet, but Wentworth was confident that the whole process would be completed shortly, within a month at the latest. The testimonies of Franklin and Trecothick had no doubt impressed many in Parliament, but Wentworth thought the crucial evidence was in the petitions from the trading and manufacturing towns of England and Scotland. It seemed to him that "repeal appears to be more necessary for this Country than America. Such vast numbers of manufacturers being turn'd out of Employ unless it is done, who if they should not starve, from more idleness wou'd raise a dangerous Fever in the State, but will soon be press'd into tumult by Hunger and want."[27]

Unfortunately, Wentworth had to report that George Grenville was fighting "with the most malignant obstinacy" to prevent the extinction of the act that he had sponsored and worked so hard to bring into existence. Grenville seemed to be trying to stall, hoping that new evidence of "disorderly outrages" would arrive from America to inflame Parliament against the colonies again. It was not that there was such a great devotion to, as Wentworth termed it, this "abominable and justly odious Taxation"; rather, as he had explained before, enforcement was seen by many Englishmen "as the point on which the Honor of Parliament and Sovreignty of Gr[eat] Br[itain] materially rest." Wentworth said that he could not disagree with this idea more. One thing he did know, however, was that the "excesses" in the colonies had been detrimental to the cause of repeal, and he could not help regretting them. He heaped high praise on Rockingham and his ministers, who out of office were "Virtuous, independent and patriots," and now that they were in, remained "assiduous, uninfluenc'd and uncorrupt." From the beginning, Wentworth claimed, Rockingham had seen the inequity of the Stamp Act and been determined to redress it. He assured Peirce that news of the disorders in America had not changed the goal of the administration. Wentworth personally found the actions "reprehensible," especially because they provided ammunition for the Grenville faction's barrage against the ministry. It is not surprising that he attempted to keep word of George Meserve's ordeal in New Hampshire as quiet as possible. Rockingham did not need any more bad news to interfere with his Parliamentary offensive. Barring such further obstacles, Wentworth was confident that he would soon be able to report the complete success of the administration's efforts.[28]

But word of the probable repeal of the Stamp Act was not Wentworth's only news for home. He told Peirce that the governorship of New Hampshire was now his, if and when he wanted it. In fact, he had had the appointment delayed in hopes that Benning Wentworth would realize the futility of his situation and gracefully step aside, as much for his own honor as anything. Showing signs of impatience with his uncle, John went on to exclaim that Benning's resignation "is doubtful and immaterial to me." He had done his best for the old gentleman, and if the governor continued to be recalcitrant, he would just have to bear the consequences. But Wentworth had another reason for desiring a delay. He would not put himself in a position that required an oath to enforce the Stamp Act. He would never support the act, and if it was not repealed, he would refuse the governor's post. As he told Peirce, "If this commission shou'd be so circumstanc'd as to make my Duty to it incompatible with my Duty to the Province, believe me Sir, my Hands and Heart shall never be burthen'd with it." By this time, however, that possibility seemed remote. For the good of New Hampshire, Wentworth felt he should accept the position because, if he did not, it would probably go to a certain Scotsman with no particular interest in the province or its people. He did not identify this competitor for the governorship.[29]

Wentworth was still concerned about another position that he felt should be filled by a person with a genuine interest in New Hampshire—that of agent at Whitehall. The situation had not improved since his last report. The Thomlinsons simply were no longer up to the task, and, as a result, province interests were appallingly neglected. Referring to the Board of Trade's boundary decision in 1764, Wentworth lamented that New Hampshire "is near a fourth part of it given to N[ew] York, because No one said a Word to the Contrary." He also feared that New Hampshire's share of the reimbursement granted by Parliament to the colonies for their effort in the recent war had been lost. Seven thousand pounds gone because application for it was not made in time! Wentworth planned a trip to the Treasury to try to rescue the claim.[30]

The job of colonial agent was not easy. It took energy, devotion, and persistence. Wentworth had experience at Whitehall and spoke with authority when he said, "A man must have patience and resolution to resist the endless delays of Office, neither ought evasions or even Refusal to discourage him." The Thomlinsons wanted energy because of their poor health. Perhaps more crucial was their lack of interest, a fact traceable, Wentworth believed, to the trifling salary paid them by New Hampshire. He warned, "Unless our Province will appoint an Agent, and give him a handsome Salary, of at least Eight or nine hundred per annum Sterling or a thousand, whereby he may be independent of People here and have it his Duty to exert his utmost attention in your Service, your affairs will forever be neglected." A thousand pounds was a far cry from fifty, the sum allotted to the position by the legislature. Wentworth realized that it might "sound great to give an agent L1000 Sterling per annum," but he believed the province "wou'd very soon find that such a Salary wou'd be the best Expence they ever paid."[31]

Wentworth, in fact, had a specific person in mind for the job—himself—despite the fact that he was already guaranteed the governorship. Wentworth's willingness to remain as agent for two or three more years, or however long the province might desire, shows that he was thoroughly enjoying his stay in Great Britain. It is not difficult to understand why, for he moved in some of the highest political and social circles in England, an opportunity not afforded many colonials who set out for the mother country, especially young men from small provinces. His advantageous circumstance was, in fact, one of the reasons he thought New Hampshire should want him there. As he expressed it, "My Connections here have happily fallen with the first people in the Kingdom, whose particular respect enables me to do more than most Men, in any affair of public concern." Perhaps thoughts of the relatively primitive conditions of life in the small seaport of Portsmouth also raised twinges of doubt about returning so soon, even as governor. But he told Daniel Peirce he would do whatever was in the best interest of New Hampshire.[32]

Wentworth was also able to give Peirce the good news of the latter's acceptance for a seat on the provincial council, along with another of Wentworth's uncles, Daniel Rindge, and, somewhat surprisingly, an old enemy of the Wentworth family, Henry Sherburne. Less cheerful was his report on the "precarious state" of the Masonian proprietorship. The case, brought to the Board of Trade by persons interested in reverting of the private title to the Crown, had lain dormant for sixteen years. Now, however, it was in danger of being revived because of the focus on America brought by the Stamp Act. Through a friend at the board, probably Lord Dartmouth, Wentworth had been allowed to take the original papers home for study, and though he found the charges against the proprietors "far from satisfactory," he warned Peirce that they might "suffice to overturn your title unless refuted." If the proceedings were rekindled, Wentworth would do all in his power to squelch them, and, with the aid of Dartmouth, he was reasonably sure of success. In the meantime, however, Wentworth recommended that word of this not go beyond the proprietors, "lest an Idea of uncertainty shou'd depreciate the value of those Estates, and the People in general be apprehensive of the security of their settlements."[33]

On 21 February 1766, Secretary Conway introduced a resolution in the Commons to repeal the Stamp Act. In so doing, he stressed the importance of British-American trade and said that any revenue gained from the tax did not justify forsaking "the trade of this country and the liberty of America in the pursuit of it."[34] When a vote was finally taken at two A.M. on the twenty-second, the resolution was approved 276 to 168. Between 24 and 28 February, the Declaratory and Repeal Bills were read several times and finally committed. On 1 March, Wentworth wrote to Daniel Peirce that a "Bill pass'd a third reading in the Commons to repeal the Stamp Act in America, and I have scarce a doubt but will pass the Lords next week. Permit me to congratulate you upon this happy Event, obtain'd for us by the ablest and most patriotic Administration these Kingdoms have been bless'd with for many Centuries."[35]

With the king's signature on 18 March, the repeal of the Stamp Act became official. The great goal had finally been accomplished, and John Wentworth was justifiably ecstatic. He undoubtedly enjoyed himself at a great ball, "among the most brilliant ever seen in the City," that was given in honor of the event. Barlow Trecothick presided, and large numbers of the nobility were in attendance. All thanks, Wentworth told Daniel Peirce, belonged to Rockingham and his associates, who had persevered so long against such difficult odds to provide relief for the colonies. He suggested that New Hampshire adopt a resolution of gratitude to be sent to the marquis, "whose Labor and assiduity" had been "incredible." "Without him," he wrote to Peirce, "you may rely on it—we shou'd not have been releiv'd." Wentworth's greatest apprehension was that colonists would take this opportunity to gloat over their victory with unseemly celebrations. He knew this had been one of the principal fears of those who had opposed repeal, and if their predictions proved true Rockingham would be greatly embarrassed. Wentworth had given his word, he told Peirce, that the people of New Hampshire would indulge in no such demonstrations, and he asked his uncle's help in fostering an attitude of "prudent" thankfulness among the citizens of the province.[36]

A statement by Wentworth on this matter gives us a sharper insight into his perception of the relationship of the colonies to England within the British Empire. He hoped "we may continue obedient and affectionate Colonies," that the conduct of the citizens of New Hampshire would be "temperate and dutiful, and that they will rejoice to receive this relief from the parental care and justice of the mother country." For John Wentworth, England was the benevolent "parent," the colonies, "dutiful" children. In sharp contrast to one of the most widely disseminated ideas of the eighteenth century, that a parent's ultimate duty was to prepare a child for adulthood and independence, Wentworth foresaw no need for a change in this unequal relationship.[37] The "mother," from her superior wisdom and strength, dispensed justice and, when necessary, "relief." The obedient children received it thankfully and with humility. It was thus difficult for Wentworth to talk about "rights," even though he had been tempted to use that defense when arguing with obstreperous and overbearing Englishmen who showed no sympathy for the colonies whatsoever. In Wentworth's mind, children did not have rights, only duties.

But the parent, too, had responsibilities—the primary of which was to provide for the maximum welfare of the entire family. A judicious, informed government policy would result in mutual benefit for both England and America. According to Wentworth, that aim had been Rockingham's objective from the time he entered office, and now his goal had been achieved. The Rockingham administration, in Wentworth's eyes, served as proof that when the empire functioned as it should, there was no need to discuss matters of right. He seemed to agree heartily with Pitt's position that Parliament possessed all authority over the colonies except that of direct taxation. He apparently considered the Declaratory Act superfluous. Wisely, he never mentioned it in his correspondence with New Hampshire.

John Wentworth could not have been more pleased with the prospects before him in the spring of 1766. He would have the governorship or the agency of New Hampshire and, in either position, could count on direct access to the first ministers of the realm. Further, because this administration was the wisest and most prudent that could possibly sit at Whitehall, he saw nothing in the future of the American colonies but harmony and prosperity. But though he had an inside view of British government, Wentworth was still a novice in British politics. He could not realize, in the midst of the successful campaign in March, that Rockingham's position was weak. This ministry had not been the king's first choice but was forced on him for lack of alternatives. Although Wentworth would have disagreed, it was generally felt that the marquis of Rockingham's leadership abilities were, at best, mediocre. There had been divisions in the cabinet from the beginning. From the right, Lord Chancellor Northington had opposed Rockingham's conciliatory American policy during the Stamp Act controversy. On the left, the young duke of Grafton had taken the office of secretary of state for the North only with the idea that Pitt would soon be brought in as leader. When that failed to materialize, Grafton was clearly dissatisfied.

In April, Grafton resigned. Secretary of State Conway was leaning in a similar direction. The king and a growing number of politicians in the House of Commons saw the administration breaking apart and were concerned with the rapid turnover of ministries and what was beginning to seem a chronic unstable condition of government. George III knew that strong leadership was necessary, and Pitt, because he was independent of party connections, was his only alternative. Early in July, using Northington's resignation as a pretext, the king sent for Pitt, who had earlier expressed his willingness to form a new ministry, on his own terms of course. On 9 July, Rockingham and his ministers were informed by the king that their administration would continue only until Pitt could prepare to take over.[38]

The news was probably more of a blow to Wentworth than to Rockingham, who must have expected it. Wentworth now had some decisions to make. With his patron out of power, he would no longer be able to count on obtaining any office he desired, whenever he wanted it. He had expected Daniel Peirce to suggest his availability as sole agent for New Hampshire to the provincial assembly. It was their choice, however, and as yet he had received no word on the matter. He must also have reconsidered the attractiveness of that office and of staying in England without his close friend at the head of the government. His most obvious and logical step, the one he had leaned toward in the first place, was to take the governorship while he was still sure he could have it.[39] Nearly a year and a half had passed since Wentworth had written to Rockingham on behalf of his uncle, and he was still waiting for the governor's resignation. It appears that the decision was now made for Benning Wentworth. On 22 July, one day before Rockingham received official word that his government was at an end, the duke of Richmond notified the Board of Trade that a commission and instructions were to be prepared, "The King having been pleased to appoint John Wentworth Esq. to be Captain General and Governor in Chief of New Hampshire."[40]

Given the abuses practiced by Benning Wentworth, the reluctance of British officials to confer both the governorship and the surveyorship of the woods on the same man, especially another Wentworth, is understandable. More than a year earlier, Thomas Whately at the Treasury had suggested the second post for Robert Temple, the brother of John Temple, John Wentworth's old friend from Charlestown, Massachusetts, who had held the lieutenant governorship of New Hampshire as a sinecure since 1761. Robert was in England at the time. Whately reported that "it is probable Governor Wentworth may be removed from that office, and it is certain the Governor and the Surveyor of the Woods will never again be the same person."[41] Whately's prediction was not only premature, it was wrong. Before Rockingham turned over the reins of government to William Pitt, he saw to it that John Wentworth was made both governor of New Hampshire and Surveyor General of His Majesty's Woods in North America.

John Wentworth's commission, which was essentially the same as his predecessor's, was sent up for the king's signature on 29 July. His instructions would take longer to prepare, however, because they had to be altered to take into account the changes in colonial policy since 1741 when Benning Wentworth began his long tenure as governor of New Hampshire.[42] The appointment was safe now, though, and there was no reason for Wentworth to hurry home. With politics out of the way, he could take this time to enjoy the more relaxed aspects of English life, do some traveling, and reflect on the prospect of returning to the far different world of New Hampshire.

Once the great political question of America had died down, Wentworth moved from Westminster to Soho near Golden Square. Soho had not yet gained its bohemian notoriety of more recent times, but it was in the process of becoming London's artists' colony and was not far from Great Queenstreet, where Wentworth went to have his portrait painted by an artist named Wilson. In all likelihood, this painter was Benjamin Wilson, one of England's journeyman artists, who is known to have painted portraits in London between 1750 and 1770. Posing with his hand around a scroll representing his new commission, the words "New Hampshire" clearly visible, Wentworth intended the portrait as a gift for Rockingham. He did not have time to see it finished, though, and he later had to write to England to ask if it was a "likeness."[43]

By early August, Wentworth was on his way to spend time in Yorkshire before departing for New Hampshire in September. On the twelfth he received a doctor of common law degree from Oxford University, a highly prized honor even if it was primarily the result of his friendship with the marquis of Rockingham and his recent appointment as governor of one of England's colonies.[44] Then on to York. By late August, Wentworth had taken up residence at Bretton Hall near Wakefield, the home of another distant relative, Sir Thomas Wentworth, high sheriff of Yorkshire. He was pleased to hear from Daniel Peirce that New Hampshire had chosen him permanent agent, with Barlow Trecothick, but of course now he would not be able to accept the position. He did, though, recommend that Trecothick be retained. He thought the London merchant the "properest and most capable Man" for the job and would urge him to accept it.[45]

Wentworth had been gratified at New Hampshire's restraint in celebrating

83

John Wentworth, 1766, probably by Benjamin Wilson
(Courtesy The Lady Juliet de Chair. Photograph
by Desmond Moore)

the repeal of the Stamp Act, and he was glad to learn that the legislature had voted to send addresses of thanks to the king and Parliament. He was miffed, though, at the assembly's failure to send a similar note of gratitude to Rocking- ham, who he still strongly insisted was the primary benefactor in the good fortune of the colonies. A polite thank you was the least they could have done, he wrote to Peirce, although he had also hoped for a vote commissioning a statue or a full-length portrait of the former first lord of the Treasury. The fact that Rockingham was no longer in office was no excuse either, because future ministers would look to see if the Americans had appreciated what had been done for them. Of more personal matters, Wentworth could now tell Peirce that the Masonian question was looking better and that he hoped to have the proprietors' claim "upon a good footing" before he left England. He would board a ship soon, for he planned to be in New Hampshire by November.[46]

But as had happened so many times before during his years in England, Wentworth's planned departure for home was delayed. It is difficult to know exactly what kept him, although a reluctance to leave behind the close friends and the familiarity with English society and culture that he had cultivated is certainly understandable. Part of the reason, though, may lie in the aid he needed to provide for his sixteen-year-old cousin, Samuel Wentworth, son of his uncle Samuel of Boston. Young Samuel had been studying in England when news arrived in October of his father's death. The Reverend Henry Caner, rector of King's Chapel in Boston, wrote to John Wentworth asking for help so that the boy might continue his studies and not have to return home because of lack of funds. Caner was especially hopeful that Wentworth's influence might gain Samuel a fellowship at Oxford, where he was planning to enroll in the fall. Wentworth was happy to do what he could, and his connections did mean something. Following Samuel's matriculation in early November, Caner wrote to Wentworth that he was "well satisfy'd in the measures you [have] taken for his introduction to the university, and indeed greatly obliged to you for opening to him a prospect, perhaps beyond what my small interest might have accomplish'd."[47]

December found Wentworth still in England. He was now at Bath, convenient to Bristol where passage could be taken for the colonies. On the eleventh, he met with another American, Nathaniel Whitaker, who represented Eleazar Wheelock's Indian charity school at Lebanon, Connecticut. Whitaker, with Sampson Occom, had left for England late the previous year to raise money for the school. Wentworth had first learned of this fund-raising campaign when his father, Mark Hunking Wentworth, wrote to introduce Wheelock's emissaries and to request any aid his son could provide them on their mission. In July, Wentworth had discussed the matter with Occom, one of Wheelock's star Indian pupils, now a minister traveling throughout Britain delivering learned sermons designed to impress the worth of the project on doubting Englishmen. Because the school's present buildings were inadequate and the province of Connecticut had been completely overtaken by white civilization, Wheelock sought money for a future move to a more appropriate location nearer prospective Indian students. Also under consideration was the addition to the school of a college so that Wheelock might complete the education of his pupils and prepare Christian missionaries, both red and white, for work among the natives.

86

In July, Wentworth's greatest concern was his own future. Now, however, with his own course determined, and ready to return to America, he was able to give Wheelock's plan more thought. He summoned Nathanial Whitaker to Bath and, joining a list of prominent subscribers headed by Lord Dartmouth, made a pledge of twenty-one pounds to the school. He also offered to make a public statement in behalf of the project, which he did in Bristol on 16 December. Most important, he expressed his desire to see the school located in New Hampshire, and as governor he promised Whitaker the grant of a township if Wheelock should decide to move to his province.[48] The possibility that a college might be added to the school made the scheme especially advantageous for a frontier province like New Hampshire. Although Wentworth had been indifferent as an undergraduate, his attitude toward education now showed signs of the mature, urbane, well-traveled man who for several years had moved within the highest political and social circles of the British Empire.

When Wentworth did finally board ship in mid-January 1767, he was a considerably different person from the young, inexperienced colonial who had left home three years earlier. Not a small part of the transformation was traceable to his chance meeting and subsequent friendship with one of England's great lords, the marquis of Rockingham. Wentworth had gained polish, prestige, and important political offices, but those visible attributes were not the only results of the close relationship. During that time, Rockingham had risen to the pinnacle of English government and politics, and Wentworth held him in high esteem, one is tempted to say, as a younger brother might view an older one. Certainly Rockingham provided a personal and political model worthy of emulation. It seems reasonable, then, that in addition to the specific favors he bestowed on his friend from America, Rockingham also imparted certain English political principles and provided an example of a particular standard of conduct for persons holding high government office.

Rockingham and his political associates were adamant upholders of the old whig view. Once the insurgents, but now long established and increasingly reactionary, the whigs believed, above all, in the supremacy of Parliament.[49] Because they could conceive of no exception to this principle in any part of the British Empire, the whigs could not accept the American argument that Parliament had no right to tax the colonies directly. That belief also was why the Rockingham Whigs, though sympathetic to the colonial situation, could sponsor the Declaratory Act, which proclaimed parliamentary sovereignty over the colonies "in all cases whatsoever."

John Wentworth's ideas were largely in harmony with that position. He certainly believed in upholding parliamentary authority, and he had warned his friends in New Hampshire not to petition against the Stamp Act on the basis of right. Yet there are indications, at least in respect to the colonies, that Wentworth could not follow the whig view to its furthest extension. He himself had not shied completely away from arguing colonists' rights when discussing the Stamp Act in England. He also claimed close accord with the position of William Pitt, who unlike the Rockingham Whigs was not afraid to resort to Lockean principles of government. When Pitt spoke in the Commons declaring Parliament's total legislative sovereignty over the colonies but denying it the constitutional right to lay internal taxes on a people not represented in that body, Wentworth agreed with both parts of the assertion, for he stated that Pitt had "happily struck out the true distinction on what the Question rested." Wentworth believed, with Pitt, that direct taxation was at least one area in which Parliament did not have full authority over America. And in spite of his aversion to the colonial demonstrations against the Stamp Act, Wentworth was willing to concede that "the colonists refus'd submission to arbitrary impositions from noble principles of native unalienable Liberty which held property sacred."[50] So although he was in general agreement with the old whig principle of the supremacy of Parliament, he could not carry it to the ultimate claim of the Declaratory Act. His constitutional view was thus somewhat at odds with that of Rockingham and his whig followers, but that disagreement was not a significant factor in their relationship since neither Wentworth nor Rockingham were much concerned with constitutional arguments. Much more important than specific political beliefs in his influence on Wentworth was Rockingham's personal approach to politics and government.

Historians generally agree that the marquis of Rockingham lacked the requisite political skills and driving ambition to be a great leader. He was preeminently a private man who found himself in the government's highest position due to the strong sense of public duty that was an integral part of his role as one of England's leading landlords. His political rise was also attributable to the fact that he was the only one of Newcastle's close supporters who himself generated allegiance and was able to hold that group together. Rockingham had a reputation for fairness, honesty, and openhanded dealing. He did not have the will to bully or threaten political opponents, and he believed government functioned best under the direction of leaders tied together by respect and mutual confidence. That trust could best be engendered, he felt, by ending old vendettas and minimizing factional differences. He was thus willing to bring the great Pitt into office as well as supporters of Grenville, Bute, and Bedford. Upon becoming Rockingham's private secretary in 1765, Edmund Burke characterized his new employer as "a man of honour and integrity." The marquis had, a biographer has noted, a predilection for "the straight fair courses."[51]

At the local level, in his own county, Rockingham was known as a public-spirited man, interested in progress and improvement and the general welfare of the citizenry. He was a practical man who took a broad view and pursued aims that promised to prove profitable in the future. That was the outlook he brought to the administration of the country and empire. Rockingham was concerned with Britain's security vis-à-vis her continental and colonial rivals. He realized that the country's strength lay in the smooth functioning of its imperial system, a condition not fostered by the discord between England and her North American colonies over the Stamp Act. He also recognized that the colonial problem was not unrelated to difficulties at home. From his Yorkshire days, Rockingham had a strong interest in mercantile and manufacturing affairs, an important factor in his close contact with the merchants during the Stamp Act crisis.[52] He was well aware of the potential trouble in an economic downturn that left thousands of hungry laborers out of work. The key to avoiding these foreign and domestic dangers, in the eyes of Rockingham, was a harmonious empire ensured by well-reasoned policies characterized by moderation and an eye to the good of the entire system. He might believe in the absolute sovereignty of Parliament over the colonies, but he would go to almost any length to avoid a confrontation over the issue.

Rockingham's perception of the role and problems of Britain's empire reinforced and confirmed John Wentworth's own ideas. Again and again Wentworth applauded the first minister's painstaking efforts to find an answer to the colonial problem. Most praiseworthy in his eyes was Rockingham's far-sighted determination to arrive at a solution that would benefit both England and the colonies. Wentworth strongly believed that the decision for relief derived from "motives of Equity and Policy" and was based on "a knowledge of our real abilities and Inclinations." Any new regulations, he asserted, were designed "for the reciprocal welfare and connection of the Whole." Under Rockingham's close scrutiny, according to Wentworth, "the mutual interest of both Countries was

Charles Watson Wentworth,
Second Marquis of Rockingham,
by Sir Joshua Reynolds.
(National Portrait Gallery,
London)

diligently and impartially investigated, and the gross absurdity of separating it appear'd plainer than every other thing."[53]

Wentworth obviously agreed with Rockingham's emphasis on the need for mutual consideration and compatibility within the empire. Yet the two men's ideas on the subject did not flow in one direction only—that is, from Rockingham to Wentworth. In his description of America written for Rockingham in early September 1765, Wentworth had stressed that the welfare of Britain and the empire could not be separated from that of the colonies. John Wentworth may have been the first to firmly plant that idea in Rockingham's mind, certainly in such cogent and convincing terms and from the firsthand knowledge of a colonist's experience. Because of that input, and because he also seems to have been the first to recommend repeal to Rockingham, a case can be made that John Wentworth was one of the most, if not the most, important colonists involved in the repeal of the Stamp Act, Benjamin Franklin included. He was more than willing, however, to give all credit to Rockingham, who from an informed viewpoint had determined on a wise policy and, with ceaseless effort, skillfully guided it to fruition. Wentworth believed that this accomplishment, in sharp contrast to the efforts of the previous ministry, exemplified the way the government of the empire should be conducted.

But an enlightened, concerned administration in England was not the entire answer to a harmonious and profitable empire. One of the keys to the success of the colonies and thus of the empire, Wentworth had earlier told his patron, was the appointment of "disinterested, diligent and faithful" governors.[54] Now, at the age of twenty-nine, he was a governor and would have his chance to help make the system work. How would he conduct himself in that office? Evidence indicates that the marquis of Rockingham's philosophy of effective leadership had made a profound impression on him. The general terms Wentworth used to describe his intended behavior were strikingly similar to those both he and others employed when referring to Rockingham. Wentworth asserted that he would "endeavor with assiduous application to discover with honest disinterested zeal to pursue and with prudent firmness to maintain the general prosperity of the Province." The means to "conciliate the respect and affection of the People," he had determined, was through "a conduct plain, open and sincere, free from all cunning and intrigue, form'd upon Principles of integrity and pursued with prudent firmness."[55]

Consciously or not, John Wentworth seems to have found in the marquis of Rockingham a desirable model for the conduct of high public office. If not only the government in England but also those of the colonies were led by executives as "honest," "prudent," "assiduous," and "disinterested" as Rockingham, able to maintain "integrity" and "firmness," the British Empire would achieve every desired end of "power and wealth," to the benefit of all within it.[56] That happy eventuality would, from Wentworth's point of view, preclude any further debates over constitutional rights, an issue he believed strictly secondary to the proper operation of the empire. Thus, the volatile question of limits on parliamentary sovereignty in the colonies was not one he felt the need to submit to deep personal introspection or to refine definitively in his own mind. It would never come up if moderate, well-reasoned policies, such as those of the marquis of Rockingham, prevailed on both sides of the Atlantic. In January 1767, as his ship set sail for America, Wentworth was ready to do his part, and although his patron and friend was now out of office, he must have hoped that the new administration would have the foresight to follow Rockingham's example and do theirs as well.

»6«
MAKING THE THEORY WORK

New Hampshire and the British Empire, 1767–1770

John Wentworth again crossed the Atlantic at the worst possible time of the year. His duties as surveyor general of the woods dictated South Carolina as his destination instead of New England, but even the more southerly route did not ease the rigors of the winter voyage. Originally scheduled to stop at Lisbon, the ship was prevented from making port by "violent winds" and driven on to Tenerife in the Canaries, where it took on fresh water and food. The vessel proved unwieldy with its heavy cargo of passengers and animals, including both servants and horses Wentworth had brought from Yorkshire, some from Wentworth-Woodhouse as gifts from the marquis of Rockingham. Strong westerly winds combined to produce an excruciatingly slow and hazardous voyage. Fortunately, one of Wentworth's London friends had fortified him with a supply of wine, which he found a great relief for "the fatigue of Bad weather and other maratime distress." On 22 March 1767, sixty days out of the Canary Islands, Wentworth's ship landed at Charleston. It is not surprising that this "very Long and distressing Passage," as he described it, made "four Days rest at Charleston absolutely necessary." [1]

On his fifth day in South Carolina, when he could walk without feeling as though he were still on the deck of a rolling ship, Wentworth headed for the interior to begin his tasks as surveyor general of the woods in North America. The proper execution of this duty had been his purpose in not sailing directly for home. Traveling northward from Charleston would give him the opportunity to inspect the timber in the other colonies and register his commission as surveyor general with the other provincial governors. New Hampshire and northern New England were the source of the great white pine for main masts, but the all-important naval stores—tar, pitch, turpentine—were products of southern forests. On his tour, Wentworth also found that the yellow pine provided straight, strong logs for smaller masts, yards, spars, and bowsprits, and he reported favorably on the "Strength and Durability" of the live oak, a wood important for shipbuilding.[2] Unlike Benning Wentworth, his nephew took this job seriously and was intent on justifying the trust in and responsibility placed on him.

Carrying letters of introduction collected in England, Wentworth set out for New Hampshire. In North Carolina he made the acquaintance of Governor William Tryon and, while there, decided to ship two of his English mares home by water. That was a mistake, he later discovered, for although he paid seven guineas for the passage, one of the horses starved to death on the way to New England. In Virginia, Wentworth was extended the hospitality of one of the South's oldest and most prestigious landed families. The Byrds of Westover had come to epitomize the aristocratic southern planter class that was familiar to inhabitants of all the colonies. Pious New Englanders tended to consider the way of life of Virginia gentlemen such as the Byrds frivolous and morally objectionable, but after moving among England's elite for several years, John Wentworth had a less provincial view. Besides, he enjoyed cards and thoroughbred horses as much as his host did, William Byrd III. Westover, fronting on the broad James River, though not Wentworth-Woodhouse, was a perfect example of Georgian symmetry and certainly one of the finest buildings in the American colonies. Westover would not have been out of place anywhere in England, and Wentworth felt very much at home there.

Assuming his horses would fare better by water than by land, Wentworth left three more English mares with Byrd to be shipped home with the first vessel out. Before he left Virginia, he bought four additional horses from Colonel Peter Randolph, surveyor general of the customs for the southern district, with whom he stayed at Chatsworth, Randolph's estate up the James in Henrico County. Horses and servants in tow, Wentworth moved on through the tidewater of the Chesapeake to Annapolis, the capital of Maryland. Unfortunately, he arrived while the government was in session and, as he later exclaimed, found Annapolis "the only Town I had or have seen on this Continent where neither Money or Interest or Intreaty cou'd procure the least Accomodation for my Family or so much as a Single bed for myself." Governor Horatio Sharpe came to his rescue, however, and opened up his house to his fellow colonial governor.[3]

By the end of May, Wentworth was in Philadelphia, then on to Burlington in New Jersey where he stayed a night and spent a day fishing at Trenton Falls with Governor William Franklin. In New York City he enjoyed a rest at the home of William Bayard in Greenwich, overlooking the Hudson River from

94

lower Manhattan Island. Wentworth spent this welcome respite from the weariness of travel wandering in Mrs. Bayard's garden, turning music for Bayard's daughter as she sang and accompanied herself on the harpsicord, and just musing on the "pleasant views over to Hoebuck." Not eager to return to the dusty road, Wentworth boarded a ship in New York and enjoyed a leisurely three-day passage to Boston. There he planned to call on Joseph Harrison, whom he had last seen in England. Harrison, like Wentworth, had been one of the colonists whom Rockingham had turned to for advice during the furor over the Stamp Act. Serving as Rockingham's secretary for a period, he had lived at Wentworth-Woodhouse and become a close friend of Wentworth's. For his trouble he had received the post of collector of customs at Boston, where he had returned before Wentworth's appointment. Now Wentworth was looking forward to seeing Harrison again, but when he arrived at his home he discovered that his friend had been ill and had taken a trip out of town for his health.[4]

John Wentworth had sent a note to Benning Wentworth from New York to let him know that he was on his way. From Boston he wrote another, giving his expected time of arrival in just a few days. He would thus not catch the province unaware, allowing officials time to prepare a proper welcome for their new governor. Wentworth must have felt a mixture of excitement and curiosity as he and his entourage rode north from Boston toward New Hampshire on Saturday morning, the thirteenth of June 1767. He had left as a young merchant. He was returning, still young—not yet thirty—but as governor of the province. Would he recognize his many friends and relations? Would they know him—had his appearance changed much during his absence of more than three years? Would people treat him differently now that he was governor? He was anxious to see New Hampshire and Portsmouth—to see if they were as he remembered.

He knew he was getting closer as the Massachusetts hardwoods gradually gave way to the tall straight pines of the north. When he reached the New Hampshire line about noon, he was greeted by a troop of guards and another of horse, some members of the council, undoubtedly including Daniel Peirce, and a committee chosen by the assembly. They escorted him the rest of the way to Portsmouth, where he passed through throngs of people eager to catch a glimpse of their new governor. Upon reaching the state house, he was saluted by the First Regiment of Militia. Governor Wentworth produced his commission, which was read to the people by the high sheriff, and then went inside to the council chamber, where he and the members of the council took their oaths of office. Finally, he read a standard proclamation ordering all officers to carry on in their positions of government until notified further.[5]

With the formalities over, it was time to celebrate. Reports from the cannon

95

View of Portsmouth Harbor, sketched in the 1770s,
from *The Atlantic Neptune*. (New Hampshire
Historical Society)

at Fort William and Mary could be heard downriver, along with "three vollies of small arms . . . fired by the militia and three huzzas given by the multitude." An "elegant entertainment" had been planned for the occasion, and Wentworth, the council, and the chief magistrates, one hundred in all, dined together on turkey, duck, and beef washed down with generous amounts of punch, beer, and Benning Wentworth's best madeira. Of course, everyone was anxious to meet the new governor, and John Wentworth received an endless procession of well wishers. After his rough two-month voyage followed by nearly three more months on the road and through the forests from South Carolina, Wentworth would have appreciated some rest and solitude more than anything else. "I wish to God," he exclaimed, "that I was escap'd from all this Dust, Parade, shew and Ceremony." Nevertheless, the day was a success. As reported by one newspaper: "Such ardency and emulation prevailed among all ranks on this occasion, as gave the most promising hopes, that his Excellency's government would be crowned with the most cordial affections of the people, whose happiness and his own were now so intimately blended." The only negative note among the celebrations was the absence of Benning Wentworth. But that was not surprising, for it was common knowledge that his resignation had been forced. Apparently no one missed him, and he undoubtedly was thankful that he could claim his gout as an excuse for remaining at Little Harbor.[6]

In keeping with the nature of inaugural ceremonies, the euphoric hopes and expectations marking Governor John Wentworth's first day in New Hampshire dictated an eventual letdown. Even so, the passage of time did surprisingly little to diminish the respect and admiration of the people for their new governor. Some months later a prominent citizen of Portsmouth declared, "May we not expect Happiness under the administration of a Governour of an Ingenious, amiable, generous, Hospitable Disposition: The People in general are pursuaded they may."[7] This comment was characteristic of those made about John Wentworth. In fact, his personality played a large part in his popularity, which in turn was a major factor in his success as governor during difficult times. John Wentworth was warm, gregarious, and personable. Those qualities, combined with his generally open and forthright manner, were instrumental in keeping people loyal to provincial government throughout nearly his entire term as governor, a period marked by rising colonial suspicion of royal authority. Those most likely to oppose him—members of the assembly, merchants, others with influence—found they had little reason to fear or mistrust Wentworth. Though he was bound to enforce the law, there was little incentive to attack a fellow member of the mercantile class who understood their frustrations and who made no secret of his displeasure with British colonial policy and customs enforcement.

John Wentworth did not command respect, as some men do, by his physical size. From the few references to his stature that remain, we have to conclude that he was short, probably somewhat stout. The adjective most commonly used next to his name in this regard was "little." At the same time, he was a handsome man, and perhaps that partly explains why, unlike some other figures in history, his short stature has not been associated with any strong undesirable trait of personality or character. In fact, references to his size made directly to his face seem not to have bothered him. On one occasion, during one of his frequent expeditions into the interior, his host in a frontier cabin observed unabashedly that the governor seemed to be "getting leetler and leetler." Unoffended, Wentworth just grinned.[8]

Another story is told of a stranger to Portsmouth who, having heard about John Wentworth, was poking around in the vicinity of his house. Peering into the stables, he found a fellow taking care of the horses and, after expressing his interest in the governor, felt compelled to repeat what people commonly said about John Wentworth where he came from. "They say Johnny is short and thick," the stranger declared, and "that he is fond of his wine, but on the whole a pretty clever sort of a fellow—how I should like to see him." The man tending the horses said he thought that could be arranged and, after escorting the visitor into the house and showing him several of the richly decorated rooms, held out his hand and introduced himself as the governor. Only John Wentworth's affability kept the man from being completely embarrassed.[9]

These incidents in themselves are unimportant. As reflections of the character and demeanor of John Wentworth, however, they take on significance. The picture that emerges is one of a man of unusual equanimity, a well-balanced individual, self-confident with no need to retreat behind a facade of contrived hauteur that, given his station and office, no one would have faulted him for. Unaffected, he could mingle comfortably with shopkeepers, farmers, or woodsmen without making them ill at ease. This attribute was a far cry from the aloofness of his predecessor, Benning Wentworth, and from the expected behavior of royal governors in general. At the same time, as might be expected from his experience in England, Wentworth was equally at home in the most sophisticated society. Neither was he out of place in learned circles. He was intelligent, with an inquiring mind and broad interests, as was indicated in his treatise on the colonies drawn up for Rockingham at the time of the Stamp Act controversy. Jeremy Belknap, the first and still one of the best historians of New Hampshire and a contemporary of Wentworth's, owed much to the governor not only for political material but also for valuable information about the natural condition of the province: its flora, fauna, geography, and topography. As one admirer noted, John Wentworth "united the erudition of the scholar and the polite accomplishments of the gentleman."[10]

The fact that John Wentworth was comfortable at all levels of society does not mean that he was a democrat, interested in social change ahead of his time. By colonial standards he was an aristocrat. He accepted his position and fostered no leveling ideas. He was not an ideological person; he had no desire to change the status quo. In many ways Wentworth was a typical eighteenth-century politician—interested in using his office for personal gain. He had expensive tastes, and he seemed never to have enough money. He borrowed freely, particularly from close family and friends, and he saw to it, albeit less obtrusively than his uncle, that he did not leave himself out of the land granting process, which he controlled.

Nevertheless, self-gain was not the driving force behind John Wentworth's administration that it seemed to have been for Benning Wentworth. Though nephew and uncle, they each came to the governorship from different backgrounds. Benning Wentworth was one of twelve children. Although his father was a successful sea captain and merchant, there was no "Wentworth dynasty" in New Hampshire when Benning was born. Benning had to make his own way in the world, to scratch and struggle for wealth and position in society. His father later became lieutenant governor of the province, but by the time Benning himself became governor, his father had been dead for eleven years and Benning was bankrupt. When he took office he was indeed a man on the make. The result was the longest term as governor in the history of England's American colonies and the creation of a family hegemony over politics and wealth that was unrivaled in any other colony.

John Wentworth inherited that situation when Rockingham secured him the governorship in 1766. The oldest of only three children, John Wentworth's earliest remembrances were of an elite society created by his uncle's political power. His father, Mark Hunking Wentworth, was the richest man in New Hampshire because of lucrative mast contracts obtained through Benning's office. As John Wentworth grew up, he knew only warmth, security, and the best that colonial society could offer. When he took office at the age of twenty-nine, he was not hungry, and he was not ruthless. His goal was not to build a family empire but to protect the one already in place. Although he was interested in gain for himself, he had family wealth to fall back on, which he took advantage of throughout his term of office.[11] This secure background and sense of plenty allowed Wentworth to be more open and far-reaching in his outlook than Benning, less suspicious of potential competitors, and less concerned with stockpiling wealth for himself. It allowed him to develop an honest concern for his province and for persons beyond his own immediate milieu.

Wentworth's relative youth no doubt also contributed to his personal flexibility, and his age gave him the vigor to do things older men might not. The sight of the young governor galloping through the woods on his horse on his way to inspect a stand of virgin pine, stopping to chat amiably or inquire as to how the crops were coming along, undoubtedly endeared him to the people of the province.

But family position, youth, and vitality only partially explain his popularity; the focus needs to be on the overall character of the man. John Wentworth was one of those few individuals who can be completely natural regardless of the situation. He put up no barriers, he had nothing to hide. He listened as well as talked, and people sensed that his interest in them was genuine. He was open and honest, and it is not difficult to see why he inspired trust and affection. It is not surprising that John Wentworth and the marquis of Rockingham got along so well, because they appear to have been similar in nature. It is difficult to say exactly how much influence Rockingham had over his young friend, but it is certain that what Wentworth observed in England reinforced his own beliefs and behavior. In fact, a piece of advice that he gave to a cousin while still in the mother country might easily be seen as a motto that Wentworth held up for himself to live and govern by. In 1766 he recommended to Hugh Hall Wentworth that in his dealings he make "the plainest appearance and the most open declaration, as it will operate more in your behalf." [12] John Wentworth for the most part followed his own advice. By doing so he laid a solid foundation of respect and trust that served him in good stead through the inevitable periods of friction and the difficult times that lay ahead.

Yet those times, from 1767 to 1775, were too hazardous to allow any representative of royal authority in America to go unscathed. The one inescapable fact that affected to one degree or another nearly every aspect of John Wentworth's administration as governor was the continuing trouble between Britain and America. Although Wentworth instinctively operated in an open and forthright manner, the increasing disharmony between the colonies and England led him at times to act otherwise in the realm of government. Any person occupying an executive position of government with its inherent broad authority cannot realistically expect to avoid making enemies. Those that harbor such hopes are often forced into subterfuge and duplicity, eventually leading to their downfall. John Wentworth was not afraid of making enemies if the cause was just. He did, however, desperately want to reverse the direction of the slowly widening chasm between America and Great Britain. He had great love and respect both for his native New Hampshire and for the mother country, and to maintain harmony between the two, the object uppermost in his mind, he felt justified when necessary in resorting to secret political manipulations. Unfortunately, those few uncharacteristic actions, when discovered, served only to widen the breach further. John Wentworth was a man caught in the middle, trying to please and reconcile both sides. In this he was as successful as any governor on the continent, but he could not know that in the long run the situation was irreconcilable.

One of Wentworth's first concerns upon assuming the governorship was his place of residence. Because New Hampshire had been without its own governor before 1741, the province was under no obligation to provide a dwelling for an executive. When the governors came up from Boston, they normally rented rooms in a large brick mansion owned by the Packer family at the corner of Pleasant and Court streets.[13] Benning Wentworth had spent most of his time at his own rambling mansion at Little Harbor, so provincial taxpayers had again been relieved of the obligation of paying for a house for the governor. Now, however, there was a new governor, one who did not own a home. Rather than buying or building a house, the legislature chose the less expensive expedient of renting one, especially since the governor's father, Mark Hunking Wentworth, offered one of his properties at the highly reasonable rate of sixty-seven pounds a year. Several years later, the next owner complained that this amount was less than half the lawful interest on the money invested in the house.[14]

The house was a large frame structure built only a few years earlier. Two-and-a-half stories with a hip roof, dormer windows, and some classical detailing, it was typical of homes owned by prosperous merchants in New England's seacoast towns. From its location on a rise on Pleasant Street, about two-thirds of the way from the center of Portsmouth toward South Bridge, Wentworth enjoyed the view "over the town and down the river to the boundless Atlantic Ocean." Behind the house, a large garden with walks and ornamental shrubs sloped away more than four hundred feet to South Pond. Wentworth liked to stroll there in the mornings, enjoying the rural setting of fields and the sun sparkling on the small saltwater inlet. Along one side of the garden stood the coach house and the stables where Wentworth kept his horses, one of his great passions.[15]

In keeping with what he thought proper for a provincial governor, Wentworth was intent on making the interior of the house as fine as possible. He ordered furniture and personally selected the wallpaper. Window drapes he obtained from London, as well as paintings for his walls. The desired elegance was completed with six hundred feet of oak boards for wainscoting, nearly enough

The Governor John Wentworth House, Portsmouth
(Photograph by Douglas Armsden)

for every room in the house. The larder was stocked with Yorkshire hams, and the cellar, with Portuguese wine. Wentworth had his English servants to tend the house, cook, and take care of the stables. The final touch was added by two black slaves, Romulus and Remus, who played the French horn.[16]

Wentworth was clearly trying to mimic as best he could the splendor he had become accustomed to in England, and he was not afraid to admit it. He told his friend Joseph Harrison of his attempt to create a "Lilliputian" Wentworth-Woodhouse in Portsmouth. But in spite of his efforts—and he certainly was more than adequately prepared for any entertaining that might be required of a royal governor in New Hampshire—he was never satisfied with his residence. After Wentworth-Woodhouse, and even Westover, the house may have seemed small, and admittedly it was not as fine as his own brother's house a few blocks away on the waterfront or as large as the mansion built recently by Samuel Moffatt, a local merchant. Nevertheless, it hardly deserved to be called a "little Cabbin" or a "small hut," as Wentworth referred to it on one occasion. Three years after he moved in, Wentworth asked the assembly to consider "some means to Render this or some other house more convenient and Equal for my residence." Although a committee was appointed to look into building or buying another house for the governor, nothing ever came of it, and three years later Wentworth was still urging the legislature to provide "a Province House in which the Governor can reside with comfort to himself and respect to the Government."[17] On this point, Wentworth was destined to be disappointed for the duration of his term.

Another, and potentially more serious, point of friction between the governor and the legislature, one that was also never resolved according to John Wentworth's wishes, was the question of his salary. When he met with his first assembly on 2 July 1767, following his instructions he made a request for "an adequate, honorable, and permanent salary." Two days later, the House voted three hundred pounds for the cost of Wentworth's trip from England, but obviously realizing that the important matter of the salary would not be settled quickly, the members postponed debate on it until after the adjournment demanded by the agricultural season. When they reconvened again in late August, there obviously was little sentiment for granting the governor a permanent salary. No matter how well liked a governor was in America, provincial assemblies were extremely jealous of the one power—if only implicit—that they held over their executive: the annual grant of the governor's salary. New Hampshire was no exception. The House voted Wentworth seven hundred pounds for one year.[18]

One of the reasons given for not making the grant permanent was the expectation that Britain might institute a policy of paying royal governors out of the American customs revenue. The preamble to the recently passed Townshend revenue acts stated, as a sort of veiled threat, that this plan would be followed "in such Provinces where it shall be found necessary." Unlike wealthier, more populated colonies such as neighboring Massachusetts, New Hampshire saw this possibility as more of a blessing than a threat. What power the annual salary grant held over the governor they would happily give up for a reduction in taxes. As Wentworth well knew, his was a poor province. The salary of seven hundred pounds was among the lowest in all the American colonies, and although he considered it neither adequate nor honorable, he could hardly have been surprised. Had it been permanent, he would have been satisfied, but despite objections by himself and the council, nothing changed. The House was divided on the question, but Speaker Peter Gilman finally turned the vote against a permanent salary. The governor did not forget this. Although he and Gilman ostensibly were friends and he later nominated the speaker for a council seat, Wentworth disclosed to a confidant in England that he had offered the post because Gilman had been "troublesome" in the assembly. Among Wentworth relatives and friends on the council, he would have little opportunity to cause trouble.[19]

The following year John Wentworth was again voted seven hundred pounds for one year only, the reason still given as the expectation that payment might be made out of customs revenue. Although Whitehall had long been used to this situation in the American colonies, Wentworth felt compelled to apologize for this breach of his official instructions in a lengthy report to Secretary of State Shelburne. He explained that, because of rising opposition in America to the Townshend duties, he did not think this a good time to press the assembly on the issue of a permanent salary. He did find it somewhat ironic, though, that the assembly used as its reason those same Townshend revenue acts.[20]

As it became apparent in succeeding years that New Hampshire's legislators had no intention of granting him a permanent salary, Wentworth, as much as they, began to hope that the home government would indeed see its way to paying him out of the customs revenue. In 1770 he expressed this wish to the earl of Hillsborough, then colonial secretary, and added, "I am the more encourag'd in my hopes of a royal Independent establishment, as I have heard the same is amply granted for New York and Massachusetts bay," and especially as New Hampshire had "steadily adhered to the most perfect good Conduct, and testified their respect to the Laws of Gr[eat] Britain, when all the others were thrown into confusion and combinations against the commerce of the Mother Country." Lord Dunmore and Thomas Hutchinson, the governors of New York and Massachusetts, had been granted salaries from England, but precisely because there was trouble in their provinces. The cruel irony, which John Wentworth did not realize, was that as long as New Hampshire remained peaceful and obedient, he stood no chance of receiving an independent salary.[21]

In addition to his salary, Wentworth received four hundred pounds annually as surveyor general of the woods and approximately one hundred pounds from fees that were normal perquisites of a royal governor. This came to a total of 1,200 pounds. In spite of the fact that he told an English friend that an annual salary of 1,200 pounds in America made anyone "equal to a noble Man in Europe," he still complained to the assembly that his salary "hath not any one year come near to my support" and had forced him to "Retire to my own Estate in the Country." It is difficult to understand how building a lavish home in the interior, fifty miles from Portsmouth, helped Wentworth live on a more reasonable budget, but in any case he would have found it difficult to stay within his means. Wentworth had returned from England with expensive tastes; the horses, servants, and furnishings of his Portsmouth home were well known. It also took money to maintain the image of the dashing young governor, a role enjoyed and fostered by Wentworth, who was not yet thirty when he took office. Shortly after his arrival in New Hampshire, he ordered from Thomas Smith in Philadelphia a "Sulky one horse Chair for one person only on Steel Springs, with Wheels at least four Inches lower than our good friend Mr. Foxcrofts, to be painted the lightest Straw Color and gilt Mouldings with my Crest and Cypher . . . in a plain Oval without the least Ornament and rather in a small Compass, . . . the Carriage to be plain and neat." A local minister observed that the governor "lives in high style" and went on to lament that "too many endeavor to imitate his mode of living, whose circumstances would forbid it." [22]

John Wentworth's own circumstances could not support him in the manner to which he was accustomed, but that was not what bothered him most about the salary. He could always find other means for augmenting his income. The size of the salary was secondary to his belief that dependence on the legislature for a yearly grant of money undermined the authority and subverted the power of a royal governor. Little more than a year after he took up the burdens of office, he commented, "It is rather to be wonder'd that there are not more Riots, when we consider the natural Imbecility of Colony Government, where every civil Officer from the Governor to the Constable are dependant on the people for annual support." He went on to complain that it "destroys that respect and Confidence necessary to subordination." [23] This situation never changed. During the years before the outbreak of war in America, conditions in New Hampshire, at least in comparison to many of the other colonies, seemed too peaceful to the home government to justify an independent salary for the governor. To John Wentworth, however, the question of his salary remained a small but ever present element of discord underlying the generally harmonious relations between royal government and the people of his province.

The optimism prevalent in New Hampshire in the summer of 1767 made the salary dispute seem insignificant. Wentworth returned as something of a hero since it was well known that he had been close to the administration that repealed the Stamp Act. The same month that he arrived in the province, the succeeding administration at Whitehall passed another revenue act that would be of significant consequence to America. But that legislation was unknown at the time, and feelings of good will and hope for the future were at their peak, both for the governor and the people of New Hampshire. Wentworth had great faith in the cooperation of the assembly and the people and wrote to Stephen Apthorp in England, "I am extremely happy in the Universal Esteem of all this Province who emulate each other in obliging me and endeavoring to make my Administration honorable easy and as profitable as they Can."[24] This positive feeling was a good sign. Faith between his colony and Great Britain did not seem to have been shaken too badly by the Stamp Act episode. Now that he was in control himself, he could set about cementing that close relationship by making New Hampshire an exemplary part of the British Empire, as he had told Rockingham it should work, and by promoting the best possible relations between his province and England. Wentworth hoped that measures taken in England would match his own for foresight and prudence and that the theory of a smoothly functioning, profitable, and harmonious empire would in fact become a reality.

Wentworth was fortunate. His plan for New Hampshire coincided with and was greatly aided by a process already occurring naturally. With the end of the French and Indian War and the British acquisition of Canada in the early 1760s, colonists no longer had reason to fear attack on their northern frontier. That fact was especially significant for a previously vulnerable province like New Hampshire. It meant that thousands of acres of virtually virgin land were now open for settlement and cultivation. Migration into the western and northern wilderness areas of the province began even before the Treaty of Paris was signed, and between 1761 and 1775 New Hampshire grew faster than any of the other twelve mainland colonies to the south. When John Wentworth returned in 1767 the process was well under way, but during his governorship it became even more pronounced. From 1767 to 1773, population increased from fifty-two thousand to seventy-two thousand, and by 1774 the governor estimated it at over eighty thousand inhabitants. Most of the increase took place in the west and the north. Between 1767 and 1773, many of the towns in the older, southeastern part of the province grew little, and some, such as Portsmouth and Durham, actually lost population. In contrast, newer settlements such as those near the Connecticut River—Charlestown, Keene, Winchester, Cornish—saw substantial growth. Orford to the north saw its census more than triple during those six years.[25] Although the Wentworths had always been identified with Portsmouth and the seacoast, this strong demographic trend fit perfectly with John Wentworth's plans to make New Hampshire a vital part of Britain's system of empire.

The key to those plans was agriculture. Wentworth believed that New Hampshire had a great but as yet untapped potential for agricultural production. If this resource was encouraged and developed, it would play a large role both in bringing prosperity to his province and in making it a valuable part of the British trade system. As he viewed it in 1768, New Hampshire was all too dependent on its lumber exports. Those items were carried to the West Indies for rum, which was brought back and consumed, the inhabitants of New Hampshire "thereby sinking their labor and not enriching the State," as he explained to the earl of Shelburne.[26] That waste was bad not only for the province but for England as well. It made payment for English manufactured goods difficult, subsequently lessened the demand for those items, and made the colonists begin to think about developing their own manufactures, a situation completely antithetical to theorists' views of the proper role of the colonies in the mercantile system.

Wentworth felt he had the answer to this problem, that he knew the way to bring New Hampshire back into line with the expectations from Britain and at the same time return prosperity to the inhabitants of the province. "The Land will produce plentifull Corn, Hemp, Flax, Cattle, and Horses which if encouraged," he wrote to Shelburne, "may be the means to revive, extend and render . . . [New Hampshire's] Commerce beneficial to Great Britain, which is now of little Value, and tends directly to impoverish the Province." Agricultural production, according to Wentworth, had to be fostered so that New Hampshire not only would at last be able to feed itself but would accumulate a substantial amount of produce for export. He believed that the current unprofitable trade situation would thus be "totally changed, our Export being more natural and more valuable. The demand from England would be augmented and paid for, the Inhabitants be enriched, contented, orderly and industrious."[27]

From the perspective of more than two hundred years, it is difficult to see the large advantage John Wentworth envisioned in a change from a timber to an agricultural exporting economy in New Hampshire. There would be no demand for agrarian products in England. As with lumber, agricultural goods would in all likelihood find their outlet in the West Indies, to be exchanged, like wood products, for molasses and sugar. The effect would seem to be merely the substitution of one commodity for another, providing little, if any, improvement in the overall efficiency of the empire. In New Hampshire, though, Wentworth probably did see that such a change would stop the outflow of money paid to other colonies for foodstuffs. He had made that point about all of New England to Rockingham in his report of 1765. This self-sufficiency would be an important means of keeping valuable currency in New Hampshire, thus improving purchasing capability for British manufactures.

Something else Wentworth may have had in mind was the slow but persistent recession of forest land away from Portsmouth. Although Portsmouth was still the largest exporter of lumber in the colonies, the best timber lands were becoming increasingly distant from the port. By 1772, Falmouth in Maine had replaced the New Hampshire capital as the number one mast shipping center. As surveyor general of the woods, Wentworth was well aware of that development. Most of his forest surveys were conducted outside his own province, in Canada and Maine, and on the far side of the Connecticut River. As in so many instances, Wentworth may have been looking to the future when another export would be needed to replace the lumber that had for so long been New Hampshire's mainstay.[28]

Whatever his reasons, Wentworth believed that extensive agrarian development was the key to internal prosperity and harmony within the British trade system. It would also, and he added this important point especially for the edification of those in London, preclude the people in New Hampshire from "forming an Idea or conceiving a practicability of manufacturing even to the remotest periods of futurity."[29] On this point John Wentworth remained consistent throughout his entire term as governor. He knew the British government's disapproval of manufacturing in the colonies, and he repeatedly discouraged it in New Hampshire. This policy was alien to his natural inclination. In fact, it must have been difficult for him to separate agricultural from manufacturing interests. The two went hand in hand in the eyes of enlightened, farseeing men who were concerned with the prosperity and progress of their country. John Wentworth had a good example in the marquis of Rockingham's efforts in his home county in England, and all of Wentworth's own interests and propensities— curiosity about the environment, enthusiasm for new discoveries and developments, desire for efficient use of resources, and not least his abiding affection for New Hampshire and desire to see it prosper—indicate that, had there been no official restrictions on manufacturing in America, he would have advanced it as vigorously as possible.

Shortly after arriving in New Hampshire, Wentworth took the time to write to Edward Bridgen in London thanking him and the Society of Arts for a number of pamphlets on the production of potash. Because potash was one of the few manufactures of America that were encouraged from Britain, Wentworth had been happy to distribute the literature to producers in his province. A short time later he wrote enthusiastically to Bridgen about the discoveries of one potash maker in New Hampshire, who had improved both the quantity and quality but with no added expense. Wentworth believed the man deserved a reward from the government and was writing the Lords of Trade to that effect. His duty, nevertheless, as he fully realized, was to discourage the manufacture of goods that might in any way compete with those of the mother country. In 1768 the only product of any consequence that he could find produced in New Hampshire was linen made from homegrown flax. He assured his superiors in England, however, that the native cloth sold at a higher price than the imported one and thus was not competitive. A small amount of ironwork was also carried on for the necessities of shipbuilding and husbandry; but it, too, was more expensive, and the delays and problems were interminable. As for the production of wool, an item so jealously guarded by the English industry that every governor's instructions included a separate article forbidding its export from any colony, by any conveyance, "to any other Place whatsoever," Wentworth reported, "there is scarce the appearance of it." Over his years as governor, he was consistently able to reassure Whitehall that New Hampshire, in large part because of his vigilance and commitment to the British system of empire, had developed no industry of note. His success stemmed from what he believed to be "the surest and possibly the most eligible mode of discouraging manufacturers," namely, the encouragement of people entering into agriculture.[30]

People were entering New Hampshire at a fast enough rate that Wentworth did not have to promote migration to his province; nevertheless, he was always eager to do what he could to augment the flow of eager husbandmen bent on transforming New Hampshire's backcountry wilderness into productive farmland. He did his best to fulfill new requests for land and, in at least one instance, had a friend in another province recruiting settlers. He was even willing to offer cash bounties, as in 1771 when he told Joseph Trumbull of Connecticut that he would give four hundred pounds to thirty families who would settle on the Connecticut River.[31] Neither did he have any prejudice against Indians coming to New Hampshire, as long as they conformed to acceptable sedentary agrarian roles. All were welcome who would help the province meet the goal set out for it by the new governor: to make New Hampshire into an economically sound, contributing member of the British Empire. The way to success was through increased agricultural production, for as John Wentworth believed of his fellow inhabitants, "the produce of Agriculture exported enlarges their ability to pay for British Goods in much greater quantity and perfection than they can acquire in any other mode of employ." The beneficial effect of settlement for British industry was especially true in a wilderness area like New Hampshire, because according to Wentworth it could be twenty years before these people would approach self-sufficiency. In the meantime, he predicted, every new family would "consume at least Six pounds Sterling p an^m. in British Manufactures."[32]

The sustaining feature of that relationship, though, and the main purpose of the new settlement, certainly in John Wentworth's mind, was increased agricultural production for export. Export from New Hampshire, however, meant that those goods would have to find their way to Portsmouth, the colony's only port. The cheapest and easiest transportation to the seacoast was always by water. Sending goods through Portsmouth thus presented a definite problem because, although the town was situated on a deep tidal river—the Piscataqua—that river extended only a few miles into the hinterland before it dissolved into several insignificant streams. On the other hand, the major rivers that served the interior of New Hampshire, such as the Merrimack, the Connecticut, and the Saco, all had their mouths outside the province. As a result, any surplus trade that developed upcountry was carried beyond New Hampshire's borders for sale and export. The beneficiaries were the merchants in towns such as Newburyport, Boston, and Springfield in Massachusetts or Hartford in Connecticut. Not only did those men make the profits on any export of these goods, but the New Hampshire traders turned around and exchanged their newly acquired cash with the same dealers for needed manufactured items. This money thus was not recirculated in New Hampshire, and the province's persistently serious shortage of cash was made even worse. New Hampshire was paying dearly for the various boundary decisions made over the previous 150 years that had left it somewhat of a geographical oddity with only eighteen miles of coastline. Most of the province, as Jeremy Belknap noted, was "by nature cut off from any commercial intercourse with the only port." Because of this, Wentworth found it impossible to provide the home government with an accurate report of New Hampshire's imports and exports. He had no way of determining the value of the many goods carried out of the province from the interior.[33]

Wentworth was determined to do something about this peculiar trade problem. He was not encouraging families to put their roots down in New Hampshire only to have the fruits of their labor accrue in neighboring provinces. The only answer, he realized, was to build several major roads connecting Portsmouth and the tidewater region of Great Bay with the most important new areas of settlement in the west and north. Wentworth was not the first to conceive of this plan. One of his uncle Benning's main concerns was to make sure that Portsmouth remained the major entrepot of the province. To that end, he had seen the need for a highway linking the Piscataqua with the Connecticut River. In 1763 several proprietors of the Coos region on the upper Connecticut petitioned the assembly for a road to be cut from Haverhill to Dover or Durham, both of which had access to Great Bay and the Piscataqua. A year later, Jacob Bayley again urged the legislature to subsidize such an enterprise for the sake of efficiency of trade in New Hampshire. The abundance of productive lands in the area created a large market for English manufactures, but, Bayley complained, the settlers had to get those goods from Boston, "cart them to Northfield, (which is as far from Boston as we are from Portsmouth) and then we have a long Water Carriage." Accordingly, the assembly voted to have a route marked out between Durham and the new town of Haverhill.[34]

For some reason beyond that of the rigors and hazards of surveying in a wilderness in the eighteenth century, the task was not completed until four years later in 1768. By that time, however, migration to New Hampshire was moving at a rapid rate. More communities on the upper Connecticut were asking for roads to the older part of the province, and a younger, more energetic governor had arrived with a belief that good roads were a necessity if New Hampshire were to play a role in helping the British mercantile system succeed.[35]

Within less than a year after returning to New Hampshire, Wentworth had had time to survey the situation and write to the earl of Shelburne in England, "Some principle Roads thro' the interior part of the province . . . wou'd exceedingly facilitate the population and cultivation of the Lands [and] be an immense relief and advantage to some thousand poor and faithful peasant Subjects of his Majesty, now struggling against every hardship and Misery of settling a remote, wild, and almost pathless Wilderness." A short time later he told his cousin Hugh Hall Wentworth that the new roads he was encouraging would obviate the need for inhabitants of New Hampshire to trade any longer at Boston, a practice he was "bitter against." Wentworth was confident that vessels out of Portsmouth would soon be carrying goods of much greater value, and he even went so far as to predict that New Hampshire's seaport "cannot fail soon to be the first provision Market in N[ew] England."[36]

Within a few months of those words, early in 1769, acts were passed in the assembly for two more roads linking the Connecticut River with the seacoast. One would pass from Charlestown, the site of old Fort Number Four, an important garrison during the French and Indian War, to Boscawen on the Merrimack River, where it would join the road to Durham coming down from Haverhill. The other was to be built from Stonington, in the fertile intervales of the big bend of the Connecticut north of Haverhill, through the White Mountains and down to Wolfeboro. Because of the governor's own land in Wolfeboro and his efforts, already begun, to build a sumptuous country estate overlooking the scenic lakes and mountains of that region, he was at that very time putting pressure on proprietors and inhabitants of towns lying between his property and Portsmouth to complete their part of a road between those two points.[37] The proprietors of Stonington could be confident that the governor would keep that part of the road from Portsmouth to the upper Coos open.

Few in New Hampshire disagreed with their young governor on the need for new highways in the province. The roads would be an advantage to the settlers in the west if their distance to market was cut. The established merchants of Portsmouth would benefit from the increased trade. The prosperity of the entire colony would grow by the retention and recirculation of scarce specie. But with money already in short supply in a poor colony, it was difficult to convince people to part with more of what little cash they had in hand in hopes of a promised increase in a none-too-certain future.

Here Wentworth's road program ran into problems. The assembly was willing to approve acts for building roads; the question was, who would pay for them? Despite the governor's repeated requests for a grant for this purpose, the assembly refused to appropriate province tax money to pay for the road construction. Money was too short and debts too great, it was argued. Wentworth reminded the representatives that the province's economy would never prosper "until Roads are made Thro' the Province by which the Produce of the interior Districts can be consum'd or exported by this Government, and their Imports provided in the same Circuit." It was up to the legislators to take the first step. As he told them, "thereon depends the very being of our commerce, The support and Encouragement of your People, and every reasonable prospect of acquiring any Currency."[38]

The House agreed that there was a great need for roads but answered that the cost should not be borne by the entire province. Instead, payment should be made by those through whose lands the roads would pass, because they would receive all the direct benefits. It was the job of the selectmen of each town through which a road was to be built to see that all land within the town was taxed equally to pay for the town's share of the road. If a road traversed any ungranted lands, the cost incurred was to be paid by the proprietors of nearby towns, who would be reimbursed by levys on future grantees of the land.[39] The inadequacy of this method of financing a road building program must have been readily apparent to Wentworth. If one body of men chosen by the people as their representatives could not be persuaded that a province-wide tax was necessary for the project, why would numerous proprietors and inhabitants in dozens of different towns, many themselves struggling for subsistence, have the foresight

willingly to lay out part of their paltry, hard-earned cash for the future benefits of a road? Resistance, delays, out and out opposition, were inevitable.[40] But
although the assembly was recalcitrant, Wentworth did not give up his hope for
the provincial unity and prosperity that would result from roads. He had an idea   113
about another possible source of funds that could be put to the purpose.

When he wrote to Secretary of State Shelburne in 1768 to recommend the
construction of roads in his province, Wentworth suggested that this purpose
might be a prudent use of quitrents, and that the application of these unpopular fees to such a good cause would "secure a ready and chearful payment." The
quitrent, a small yearly fee owed by all who held land from the Crown in recognition of royal sovereignty, was a remnant from England's medieval past.[41] In
America in the eighteenth century, it was resented and if possible avoided. As
with so many of his other instructions that promised to be troublesome, Benning Wentworth had exerted little effort to carry out this one. As a result, the
collection of quitrents during his term as governor had been haphazard at best.
This lack of enforcement created a problem for his nephew, who took his instructions seriously. Wentworth not only wanted to put payment of quitrents
back on a systematic basis but had hopes of collecting those that were in arrears.
The way to accomplish this goal, he believed, was to convince the people that
their money was being put to use in a way that would benefit them.

In July 1768, the earl of Hillsborough, who in January had been placed at
the head of the newly created American Department, wrote to Wentworth that
the plan to use quitrent receipts for building roads seemed to have merit and
that he was going to lay it before the Board of Trade for further consideration.
In August the board recommended to the king in council that Governor Wentworth's proposal be approved. That was what Wentworth wanted to hear. He
could now proceed with his plan to build the roads that would eventually turn
New Hampshire into an integrated economic community. Within three years
considerable progress had been made toward that goal. He reported to Hillsborough that not only had people willingly complied in the payment of quitrents but that five hundred pounds in back quitrents had been collected and
used to open more than two hundred miles of roads between the Connecticut
River and the seacoast. There was still much to be done, but a sound beginning had been made. The assembly had been unwilling to grant any money,
but Wentworth had found other funds for the project. And he did not abandon
the hope that the legislature might yet see its way to providing a tax-supported
grant for roads. As he suspected, there was opposition by individuals in towns,
but the assembly continued to show its support for the goals of the program by
passing acts for new roads, paying for surveys, and warning those who refused

to contribute their share that their property would be confiscated and sold for taxes.[42] Thus, despite some inevitable difficulties, Wentworth's design for tying the newer parts of New Hampshire to the old through a system of major roads got off to a promising start during the first years of his administration.

John Wentworth's efforts to improve New Hampshire's internal economic situation had their roots in the three years he had spent in England and the role he had played in the Stamp Act controversy. There Wentworth was directly confronted with the problems facing the British Empire and was asked his opinion on how they could best be solved. His own thinking about what should constitute a properly functioning colonial system and the consequent resolution of the immediate crisis by the Rockingham administration had led him, on being appointed governor, to resolve on a plan to make the province of New Hampshire a strongly contributing, loyal member of the empire, an empire that would work to the benefit of all of its various parts.

In general Wentworth had made a good beginning. Encouraged by the governor, new settlers were entering New Hampshire in large number. This migration pointed to increasing agricultural production and a surplus for export, which would bring the specie needed to purchase British manufactured goods. Wentworth's shrewd plan to use quitrent receipts for financing roads that would link the developing Connecticut River valley with Portsmouth would ensure that New Hampshire and not other colonies benefited from the export of its own agrarian surplus.

Persuading settlers to stake a claim in New Hampshire was one challenge; keeping them there was another. Their own hard work would produce their food and the currency they needed to buy English goods. John Wentworth was aware, however, that people required more than material necessities. He had, in fact, begun work on plans to bring education, religion, and the legal system to the new residents of interior New Hampshire.

»7«
MAN OF
THE INTERIOR

Developing the Frontier,
1767–1770

F or John Wentworth, immigration and transportation were the key elements in making New Hampshire agriculturally prosperous and in bringing it into line with the ideas of Britain's mercantile theorists. But such
an extensive development of the interior as he envisioned produced other problems. Principal among those and something that he recognized early was the
need to extend provincial government, especially the judicial system, to outlying
areas. Since the founding of the colony, all courts had been held in Portsmouth.
For many years that caused no problem because the province was small and most
of the population lived within twenty miles of the capital. By the middle of the
eighteenth century, however, complaints arose about the necessity of traveling
to Portsmouth for all judicial proceedings, no matter how small.

During Benning Wentworth's term as governor, the assembly attempted to
divide New Hampshire into two counties for the purpose of creating courts in
other towns. The governor and council were not opposed to a division of the
province into counties but absolutely refused to consider calling any courts outside of Portsmouth. Their excuses were that the king had earlier disallowed such
an attempt and that, in cases of timber violations, local juries in the interior
would never vote for conviction.[1] What Benning Wentworth and his council
were most worried about, however, was a dilution of the power they wielded
in New Hampshire through a total centralization of authority in Portsmouth.
Benning Wentworth would never compromise on this issue, but the assembly, as
late as July 1766, was still looking for a way to divide the province into counties.[2]

By 1767 new growth in New Hampshire was apparent, and with settlement
growing rapidly along the Connecticut River more than one hundred miles

from Portsmouth, it was becoming increasingly difficult to deny the need for a county system and an expanded court structure. Some of the newcomers from other provinces feared that "a swarm of pettifoggers" from Portsmouth would

116 be unleashed on them by such a plan, but more no doubt sympathized with the farmer from Charlestown who complained that he missed nine days at the height of the planting season when he was ordered to transport a prisoner to the jail in Portsmouth.[3] Such occurrences could be prevented by an adequate county court system in the west. The assembly was well aware of this fact, and now, with a new governor who might be more receptive, the question was raised again.

On 21 August 1767, a committee appointed by the House recommended the division of New Hampshire into four counties. Five days later, the council replied that any more than two counties at this time would be "inexpedient." The Merrimack River, they added, would be a proper dividing line. The House, showing its willingness to compromise, stated that it would be satisfied with three counties provided that both the superior and inferior courts were held where they would "best Accomodate the Inhabitants." In September the two bodies agreed on three counties and the general lines that should divide them. The House then proposed when and where each court should meet in each county. The council replied that it could not agree to their proposal, because the right of setting the times and places for courts, the councillors claimed, lay with the prerogative of the Crown. Governor Wentworth must therefore be consulted. There the matter stood at the assembly's adjournment early in October.[4]

It now looked as though New Hampshire was going to get the division into counties and expansion of the court system it had long needed. But in February 1768 when the legislators returned, they immediately made it clear that they were not going to ignore what they considered a challenge by the council. The assembly agreed that the power to "Erect, Constitute and Establish" courts was given to the governor in his commission. They argued, however, that this right was left over from the time of the first settlement in New Hampshire when the original courts were created. Since then the courts had always met in Portsmouth, and there had been no need for the governor to use this power, which in any case applied only in the original instance. Now there were many people living in the areas where the new courts were to be established, and as a matter of right, they were entitled to participate in the choice of times and places for the meeting of the courts. The House denied any intention of encroaching on the prerogative of the Crown and hoped that the council was equally as opposed to "a Design or Desire to extend the Prerogative beyond the Legal Limitations . . . to Diminish the Just liberties and Privileges of the People, or to introduce any approaches toward the appearance of . . . superseding the Laws of the Province."

Neither the assembly nor the council would yield the point; the situation was a standoff. Early in March, in a gesture designed to indicate that they had already compromised more than could reasonably be expected and that they would not be bullied by the council, the members of the assembly voted to return to their original demand for four counties. The council registered a unanimous veto.[5]

Although there is no indication that Governor Wentworth expressed his views on the point in dispute, the House no doubt assumed that he stood with the council, as governors had in the past, especially since the question revolved around the pregrogative of the Crown. The representatives must thus have been surprised when on 24 March, in dissolving the assembly, Wentworth praised the representatives for their "repeated and mature consultations" that had thrown such important light on the "advantageous measure" of creating counties, that the question could not but soon result in a "more Extensive and more effectual conclusion . . . than has hitherto appeared Probable to the most sanguine."[6] It was nearly two more months, however, before he made his official position known.

Shortly after the new assembly convened in May, Wentworth sent down a message along with a portion of a letter he had written in March to Secretary Shelburne. In that letter he had recommended that New Hampshire be divided not into three, nor even four, but into "at least five Counties." With more foresight than the council, Wentworth was looking fifty years ahead, by which time he was certain the entire province would be populated. A division into five counties now would take care of many of the administrative and judicial problems of the future. He went on to describe to Shelburne how the current court system served as a source of great inconvenience and expense for the inhabitants of New Hampshire. He also emphasized the need for extension of the law into the far reaches of the province to prevent people from degenerating into a "wild, loose, ungovernable state."[7]

Here then was a man after the assembly's own heart, a young new governor who seemed to have an interest in all the people of the province, not just those within a fifteen-mile radius of Portsmouth. Benning Wentworth would never have made such a proposal. But times had changed. Different conditions now required imaginative new policies. The council, still predominantly made up of Wentworth relations, clung to the long ingrained rule of the old governor, that all the affairs of the province must be controlled from Portsmouth. These men were reluctantly jolted into the present by Benning's nephew and successor. With the growth of population in the newer parts of the province, John Wentworth realized that the complete centralization of government instituted by his uncle was no longer workable. In fact, the maintenance of some control and order throughout New Hampshire was now dependent on establishing counties with their own judicial systems.

Wentworth did not propose this program because he had no other choice. He conceived it, rather, as a positive part of his plan to develop the interior and transform New Hampshire into a productive, unified whole. If people in the west continued to suffer the inconveniences of a lack of government and law, their complaints would discourage others from coming to the province. New Hampshire's wilderness landscape could never be turned into a cultivated pastoral scene without the sweat of many settlers; and lacking extensive cultivation, Wentworth's vision of his province as a prosperous, agricultural exporting unit of the British Empire would never become reality. As he told Shelburne, the growth of New Hampshire would be "incredibly accelerated by a permission to form these Counties." In addition, Wentworth knew that, besides advancing his own long range plan for the province, the county proposal would be a wise political move. It was bound to gain him support in the assembly; the representatives had been willing to settle for three counties, and he proposed five. At the same time, the appointment of judges in the counties would be a welcome addition to his patronage, the lack of which he decried as a dangerous detriment to his success as governor. These judges would also be important in helping him maintain control throughout the province. From every perspective the plan appeared advantageous.[8]

The reply from the representatives, then, must have surprised and disturbed Wentworth. Although their message opened by praising the proposal and the governor's "perfect benevolence of mind towards the Inhabitants" of New Hampshire, the remainder of the text was devoted to disputing the last sentence of Wentworth's letter to Shelburne. Wentworth had asked the secretary the proper way to proceed on the division of New Hampshire into counties— "Whether by an Act of the General Assembly, or by the Governor and Council." That question struck a sensitive nerve in the assembly. If Wentworth had realized the reaction it would bring, he probably would have struck the query from the copy of the letter he had sent down to the House. The reply to Wentworth was adamant that the creation of new counties and thus courts could be done in no other way than by acts of assembly, "which Acts can in no wise consistent with the Constitution of his Majesty's Government here, be repealed, annulled, or altered by the Governor and Council."[9] As it had admonished the council in February, the assembly was now in May making clear to the governor that it would tolerate no interference with what it considered to be the legislative body's constitutional rights. Even though the governor's five-county plan was highly favorable to their interests, the representatives would never accept it if it were created by executive order. The precedent would be too dangerous; the encroachment of royal prerogative too great.

In late spring 1768, John Wentworth was getting his baptism in practical politics. He had been close to political maneuvering and power struggles before, especially in England, but only as an observer. Now he was a central player. His enlightened ideas, his popularity, his "benevolent" programs, all counted for nothing when power was at stake, for in colonial politics, possibly even more than in English politics in the eighteenth century, the maintenance of power while attempting to advance on that of others was the cardinal rule. No prerogative or principle was ever surrendered easily. Wentworth became even more aware of this fact when a few days later, in early June, the assembly declined to vote the annual supply for the maintenance of government on the basis that the people, suffering under the hardship of not having counties, could not afford it.[10] The assembly was telling the governor that, instead of originally referring the matter to England for a possibly lengthy deliberation, he should have proposed it first to the provincial legislature so that a suitable bill could have been drawn up. The act would need to be suspended for royal approval in any case. In the eyes of many, the governor's action to have the idea previewed in England first was an extra step that only added to the length of time that would have to pass before the needed counties became a reality.

Wentworth was using caution. He was a new governor, he was young, and he had recently been at Whitehall, where he had seen the scrutiny to which colonial governors were subjected. He knew what dissatisfaction with his performance could mean—his own uncle was his best reminder. He also had a strong desire to please his English superiors because his patron, the marquis of Rockingham, had recommended him to the post. He did not want to let Rockingham down. Any extensive plan, such as dividing his province into counties and expanding the court system, he felt obligated to clear first with England. It probably did not cross his mind that the assembly might object to this move.

After several days consideration, Wentworth replied with a long, self-justifying message to the House. Even if what they complained of as a "grievance" was legitimate, he wrote, no good could be gained by laying another on top of it, which was what the representatives had done. But his actions, he assured them, far from being a grievance, were in the best interests of the province. It was much better to have the proposal for division into counties preliminarily screened than to go to the trouble of drawing up an act and submitting it to England only to have it disallowed. In such a case, which was all too likely according to Wentworth, an extra year would be required to pass another act, resubmit it to England, and have it approved. His method, which he predicted would take "probably but a few months," would help the people of New Hampshire achieve their goal of a convenient court system much more quickly. Taking personal offense at what he considered the impertinence of the House, Wentworth stated that he could not comprehend the reasons for "applying the epithets of grievance, Burthens, Hardships and oppression in answer to the Speech from the Chair which recommended attention to the most interesting and Honorable concerns of the Province, and I am fully satisfied that neither my words or conduct can have any such intention, appearance, or tendency." This confrontation with the assembly had been unexpected and unsettling for Wentworth. Nevertheless, nothing more could be done until word arrived from England, and in early July he adjourned the legislators.[11]

On 3 August the Board of Trade recommended that Governor Wentworth be allowed to "give his Assent to an Act of the General Assembly for dividing the said Province into five counties." On the thirteenth, Lord Hillsborough wrote to Wentworth notifying him of the decision. When the assembly reconvened in October, however, the governor had not yet received Hillsborough's letter. Nevertheless, he sent down a note urging an immediate grant of supply for the province and, probably as an inducement, a portion of a letter from Hillsborough written in July that was vaguely optimistic about the chances of approval for the county proposal. That may have had some effect, because two days later the House voted 2,200 pounds to supply the province treasury for the current year. Unfortunately, the act never went into effect because the council and the assembly could not agree on the details of the excise to fund it. When Wentworth prorogued the assembly at the end of October, there had still been no provision made to meet public expenses.[12]

It was not surprising, then, that when the assembly met again in February 1769 Wentworth's first consideration in addressing the members was for "the allowances Due for the respective services of Government," which money he complained was "now two years in arrear." When that action had been taken, he continued, he would be ready to join with the council and the assembly to form a proper bill that would divide New Hampshire into five counties. The implication was clear—that his cooperation was needed to pass such a bill and that he would not join with them until the supply was voted. Wentworth was playing the assembly's game; he was as unwilling to sacrifice any of his power as they were theirs. Even though the county bill was an eventual certainty, he did not want them to think that their tactic of withholding money until it was done could be used as a precedent. As a matter of principle, the supply must come first. For that reason he made no mention of Hillsborough's letter, which he had received the previous November, in which the colonial secretary sent the king's "Royal Permission to assent to an Act of the General Assembly" for dividing New Hampshire into five counties.[13] If the assembly saw this letter he would have no grounds for not approving such an act, even if the supply had not been granted. If they knew he had received instructions from England specifically calling for an act of assembly to create counties in New Hampshire, he would lose any leverage he might have had.

The assembly, however, realized what the governor was doing and was not to be deterred. No mention was made of a bill for supply, but within several days a committee was appointed to meet with a body similarly chosen by the council to draw up a plan to divide New Hampshire into counties. The members of the assembly suspected, from Wentworth's offer to join with them in this plan after they had passed a supply bill, that he must have received assent from England to do so. One week later, on 7 March, they called the governor's bluff by asking him exactly what instructions he had received from Whitehall regarding the matter. He could no longer keep the information from them. It is not difficult to imagine his chagrin as he tersely told William Parker, John Sherburne, and John Goffe, the committee sent up from the House, that "all he had Relative to the subject" was that he had been given permission to consent to an act of assembly for dividing the province into five counties.[14]

Having found out what they needed to know, the assembly proceeded to the long-awaited business of dividing New Hampshire into counties. Two weeks were spent dueling with the council over boundaries. The main intention of the House seemed to be to keep the area, and thus jurisdiction, of the easternmost county, the one that would include Portsmouth, as small as possible. The council, still reluctant to give up centralized control over the province, was working for just the opposite. The councillors wanted included in the eastern county most of the larger towns in the province, which naturally were also in the east. A compromise was finally worked out whereby Dover and Rochester were left out of the county that included Portsmouth. On 23 March agreement was reached on the boundaries of the five counties. In accordance with the governor's original plan, three were to become immediately active while the other two, those to the north, would gain full county privileges when their populations warranted it. The long sought division of New Hampshire into counties was at last completed.[15]

On 27 April, following a brief adjournment, an act establishing five counties with their courts passed both bodies of the legislature. It included the required suspending clause and could not go into effect until approval arrived from England; nevertheless, the hardest part was over. The names given to the counties showed the influence of the governor. The first, the easternmost and most populous one that had been so much the center of contention, was called Rockingham after Wentworth's patron and friend. The province, too, owed the marquis a debt, for as Wentworth stressed even before he became governor, it was through Rockingham's unswerving effort that the Stamp Act had been repealed. New Hampshire had been too niggardly to commission a statue or even a portrait of the former first minister. Now they found a cheaper way to immortalize him. The county just to the north, one that was to be inactive but which included Dover, the town that Wentworth believed, because of its proximity to the interior, would eventually become the metropolis of New Hampshire, was given the name of Strafford, another title associated with the Wentworth family. Sir Thomas Wentworth, the first earl of Strafford, who had sacrificed his head in the ill-fated service of Charles I in the seventeenth century, was the most notable of that name. More recent to hold the earldom was William Wentworth, a cousin of Rockingham whom John Wentworth had come to know in England. Naming the middle county Hillsborough was wise politically because of the current secretary of state for America, Wills Hill, the earl of Hillsborough. Cheshire, the name of the westernmost county, seems to have been derived from the English county of that name, but the reason for choosing it is not certain. Grafton, the name given the other inactive county in the northwest, can be traced to the duke of Grafton, one of the secretaries of state in Rockingham's administration and now himself first lord of the Treasury.[16]

With the county division complete, a supply of three thousand pounds for the province was finally approved.[17] The assembly's goals had been accomplished; there was no longer any need to withhold the money. The representatives had been stubborn; they had made their point. They had aptly demonstrated their power to the new governor. Wentworth had no means to coerce them, and he had been forced to accept that fact. Nevertheless, he was pleased when the county act was completed. This division was an important part of his broad program to invigorate New Hampshire's agrarian economy and make the province a self-sustaining component of the British Empire. The increased convenience for the people and the renewed sense of justice and order imparted by the county system could not help but be an encouragement for others to settle New Hampshire's wilderness lands. Wentworth must also have realized that it did much for his own image and that of royal government generally in the province, for the plan had originated with him. John Wentworth was a different kind of governor from his uncle. He professed to have a genuine interest in the interior of his province, in areas other than Portsmouth and the seacoast. Now the division of New Hampshire into counties proved that this interest was real.

Two other developments during his early years as governor served to separate Wentworth in the public mind from the political and mercantile aristocracy long identified with Portsmouth and to establish him as a man of the interior. Those were the building of his country home in Wolfeboro near Lake Winnipesaukee and the establishment of the first college in New Hampshire in the wilds along the Connecticut River. Wentworth had maintained his interest as one of Wolfeboro's proprietors while he was in England. When he returned, he found that the town still had no settlers, so, to speed up the process, the proprietors had divided the land into twenty-four approximately equal lots drawn at random among themselves. Wentworth had received lot number seven, 642 acres on the east side of Smith's Pond, a lake nearly four miles long and three miles wide connected by Smith's River to the much larger Lake Winnipesaukee. Within the next few years he had added to his original plot adjacent land from Wolfeboro and nearby Middleton and New Durham, creating an estate of some six thousand acres. Wentworth's desire for a fashionable country home, spawned by his experience at Wentworth-Woodhouse and encouraged by his dissatisfaction with the house allotted him in Portsmouth, was now spurred on by his accumulating property. Wolfeboro was an ideal location. It was fifty miles inland from the capital, and the magnificent view of blue lakes and rugged, pine-covered mountains made even the lush Yorkshire countryside pale by comparison.[18]

During the first spring after his return to New Hampshire, Wentworth sent two men to "clear a few acres and build an humble habitation" for him on his land. The building probably served as a temporary shelter while he surveyed his property and made plans to erect a permanent home. Within a year, in the spring of 1769, the foundation was under construction. In April his friend from Boston, Joseph Harrison, with his brother Peter, visited him in Portsmouth. Peter Harrison was collector of customs at New Haven, but, more important, he was the finest architect in the American colonies. Among the buildings to his credit were the Redwood Library in Newport and King's Chapel in Boston. Wentworth solicited Harrison's advice for his Wolfeboro house and promised to send him the dimensions. During the summer of 1769 Wentworth spent as much time as he could at Wolfeboro and, when a minister was available, even held Sunday services at his home for the new settlers of the region. By autumn, however, the house was still far from finished. In September Wentworth sent the measurements to Joseph Harrison for his brother's perusal. Only two rooms had been completed as far as plaster, and those, he offered, "I had rather undo than spoil the House," which "may be divided any way the Architect shall design." Wentworth's only requirement was for one room forty feet in length.[19]

This measurement gives an indication of the size of the dwelling, for this room was not to run along the front or the back but through the depth of the house. Upon completion, John Wentworth's Wolfeboro home measured one hundred feet by forty, and it was unquestionably one of the largest mansions in New England. To the right of the main hall upon entering lay the forty-foot drawing room. This area was probably where he held Sunday church services for his neighbors. A room of such size would be adequate for almost any official function the governor might need to conduct while away from Portsmouth. The council could easily meet here and, eventually, some of the new courts for Strafford County if necessary. Above, on the second floor, was a room of the same dimensions designated as the ballroom. Across the hall on both floors were six more rooms that in themselves would have composed a large house.[20]

As with construction, no efforts were spared in decorating and furnishing. Wallpaper in an oriental fashion was ordered for one of the upper rooms, which was to be known as the "East India Chamber." Wentworth seemed to have a predilection for the oriental style, which was common in England. His Portsmouth home contained an unusual set of Chinese-style chairs and settees, which still survive. Damask paper and curtains were used in other rooms. Marble fireplaces were found throughout the house. In spite of the great size of the dwelling and the difficulty of transportation, every room had a full complement of furniture including maple, mahogany, and walnut tables, chairs, sofas, chests, and beds. Carpets covered the floors. Wentworth likewise did not skimp on his library for the new house, which contained upwards of 450 volumes, including works on architecture, navigation, and drama, along with various magazines, pamphlets, and official papers.[21]

Apart from the mansion itself, Wentworth built a number of other structures, including a large barn for cattle, sheep, and other livestock; two stables with coach houses; a dairy; and a building that housed shops for a blacksmith, carpenters, and cabinetmakers. An elm-lined mall stretched from the house to the lakeshore where the two-masted *Rockingham* and other watercraft waited to transport people, supplies, or building materials. A six-hundred-acre wild animal enclosure for moose and deer was bordered by a wide ditch and a high embankment topped with felled trees. This was a country estate in the grand English tradition and certainly one of the most elaborate in the American colonies.[22]

It was obvious that Wentworth did not intend Wolfeboro as a place for only an occasional summer visit. In fact, he told Daniel Rindge that he planned to live there "from May 'till November, exept any Provincial Business shou'd call me a few days to Town." Thus he would spend half the year, perhaps more, away from Portsmouth. Despite the magnificent house, his reasons for doing so were not merely for personal enjoyment or for the prestige of living like a landed English nobleman. As much a motivating factor was his desire to turn the wilderness

A detail from Samuel Holland's map of New Hampshire,
showing the Wolfboro estate of Governor John Wentworth.
(New Hampshire Historical Society)

into a garden, to develop his land to its greatest agricultural potential. Like the marquis of Rockingham in Yorkshire, he would provide an example for others to follow. It is no coincidence that in 1768, the year Wentworth began to clear his land, the first families finally began to settle in Wolfeboro.

Wolfeboro gave John Wentworth a chance to be personally involved in his own large plan to develop New Hampshire as a strong agricultural exporting province of the British Empire. He had a vision that, through his leadership, Wolfeboro within ten years would be populated "more usefully than is seen from this town [Portsmouth] to Florida." Where Wolfeboro went, could the rest of New Hampshire be far behind? Wentworth believed not. But his efforts at Wolfeboro were not merely the manifestation of an abstract plan, strictly utilitarian in concept. His goals both for his own farm and for the province emanated also from a personal love of nature and agrarian improvement. As he wrote to a friend in the fall of 1769, he was "assiduously attending Mr. Cushmans practical Lectures on Agriculture, cutting down a Tree here, and planting another there, clearing, building, and plowing with equal Avidity."[23] Here, then, as settlers could see, was a governor not so unlike themselves, clearing the wilderness as they were (though on a grander scale), a man not afraid to dirty his hands in the soil. Here was a man they could identify with and place their trust in.

The other occurrence during Wentworth's first years as governor that established him in the minds of the new inhabitants of the interior as sympathetic to their interests was the relocation of Eleazar Wheelock's Indian school from Connecticut to New Hampshire's Connecticut River valley. By 1767 Wheelock was anxious to carry out his proposed move to a site closer to the Indians. He had several locations in mind, one of which was the upper Connecticut River in New Hampshire, not far from several tribes of Canadian Indians and convenient to water transportation to the Iroquois nations in the west. He had not forgotten John Wentworth's promise, while in England, of a township for the school. Another major inducement for Wheelock's serious consideration of New Hampshire as a site was that it was one of the few places where the possibility existed of obtaining a charter for his school. He had long sought a charter, but now it was especially crucial for the independence it would give him from an English Board of Trustees that administered the funds his representatives had raised in England, and who were beginning to insist on greater control over the school. He felt the time had come to bring the school to John Wentworth's attention again.[24]

Late in the year, Wheelock traveled to Portsmouth to collect some needed money that had been willed to the school. He took the opportunity to pay a brief visit to the governor and personally introduce himself. Wheelock did not then spell out his ideas, but a short time later, at the end of December, he wrote to Wentworth that their visit had encouraged him to again consider the possibility of moving his school to New Hampshire. In particular, he had in mind the upper Connecticut River where many of his friends and acquaintances from Connecticut had settled, people who were eager to have the school there. Desiring to know the governor's attitude toward the school without appearing over eager, Wheelock added, "[I] shall leave it wholly with you to determine whether I suggest anything worthy your notice."[25]

127

Wentworth did think it worth his notice. In March 1768 he wrote back with a renewal of his offer of a town for the school. He would charge no fee for the grant, and, other than the normal terms for all new townships, his only requirement was that he be made a permanent trustee. Wentworth promised "every personal assistance" in his power, and, true to his word, when Wheelock sent Ebenezer Cleaveland to New Hampshire in August to search for a suitable site, the governor assigned one of his deputy surveyors to accompany and assist Cleaveland.[26]

Wentworth was going out of his way to insure the location of the Indian school in his province. Much of his reason lay in Wheelock's mention of the enthusiasm of the settlers in the upper Connecticut valley for the school. Those people, many of whom had emigrated from the area of Lebanon, Connecticut, were aware that Eleazar Wheelock's new school would not be exclusively for Indians. Discouraged with the high rate of failure among his Indian missionaries, Wheelock had become intent on educating white youths to serve the natives, possibly with certain selected Indian students. The people in New Hampshire's new Connecticut River towns, however, saw other possibilities for Wheelock's white trainees. Ministers and teachers were badly needed in the towns. The school, they reasoned, might provide them without interfering with its missionary activities. Wentworth knew of Wheelock's intentions and the settlers' hopes and saw the school as an important inducement in getting more people into this relatively unpopulated region, one of his primary goals for the province.[27]

But a school for only natives would have been enough reason for Wentworth's enthusiastic response. The prospect of bringing the Indians adjacent to New Hampshire's borders under the civilizing influences of education, Christianity, and the king's government would be a strong encouragement to potential settlers contemplating a move to the rich intervale lands of the upper Connecticut but reluctant because of vivid memories of the savage frontier raids of the last war. Wentworth realized that Eleazar Wheelock's school would do much to erase those fears, improve relations between Indians and Europeans, and productively populate the province. Moreover, Wentworth felt a moral commitment to Indians that was unusual for his time. To a later request from Wheelock for land for an unfortunate band of Indians, he replied: "I most sincerely pity these poor people and shall heartily rejoice to have them under my protection, to have an opportunity of rendering them the benevolence due to Humanity, which I fear has been too much neglected toward Indians in general wherever Europeans have come."[28]

There were few in New Hampshire who did not see advantages in the school. Members of the Portsmouth gentry contributed generous quantities of land to the school in the belief that its existence would increase the value of their other landholdings. Similar reasoning prompted most of the river towns and even others to the east, such as Plymouth and Campton, to compete strongly for the school.[29] Thus, not only would landing Eleazar Wheelock and his school be an important boost for Wentworth's long-range plan for New Hampshire, but such a success, as he must have realized, could not help but increase his own popularity.

Ebenezer Cleaveland, on returning from his exploratory expedition, which included sections of Massachusetts and New York as well as New Hampshire, reported to Eleazar Wheelock that he could "without partiality say that all the purposes of the design may be as well answered in western parts of the Province of New Hampshire as any other places." In particular, he recommended Haverhill and Orford for their fertile soil and large amount of cultivated land. Wheelock wrote to Wentworth that he was leaving the choice of the site to the English trust but that he would make clear his preference for the Coos region of New Hampshire and especially the towns of Haverhill and Orford. This he did in his report to England of 23 December 1768.[30] With the selection of the site relatively certain, Wheelock turned his attention to his next difficult task—approaching the governor about a charter.

This was a delicate situation. If Wentworth was informed of the English trustees' likely opposition to incorporation for the school, he would not grant the charter. If he was not informed but questioned his own right to grant such a charter, he might write to England for a legal opinion and discover that Wheelock had not told him the whole truth about the trustees' position. Either way Wheelock knew his hopes for a charter would be dashed. His most prudent move, he finally decided, would be to have two friends in Portsmouth, Congregational ministers Samuel Langdon and Samuel Haven, first sound out the governor on the idea.

Wheelock shortly was relieved to find out that John Wentworth harbored no qualms about granting the school a charter, and he swiftly set to work drawing up the document. With the draft completed in late August 1769, he sent it off to Portsmouth with his son, Ralph, and Nathaniel Whitaker for the governor's approval. The report they brought on their return came as something of a shock. Wentworth had not objected, in fact, was probably highly pleased with Wheelock's suggestion to him that the school might be chartered as a "college" instead of an "academy," as written in the draft. Neither was he bothered by Wheelock's major innovation in the charter, the creation of a second trust. A new American trust would control the school, while the English body was left with virtually no power. What the governor was concerned with was the composition of those trusts. To the American board, which was headed by himself and Wheelock and completed with Wheelock's close family and Congregationalist friends from Connecticut, Wentworth wanted the addition of at least three provincial officers from New Hampshire. Most disturbing to the head of the school, though, was his understanding that the governor insisted on the addition of the bishop of London to both trusts, as the most powerful member in England and ex-officio in America.[31]

This proviso suggests another reason for Wentworth's desire to have the school in New Hampshire, especially as it was now to be a college with degree-granting rights. He was an Anglican who, throughout his term in office, promoted the expansion of the English church in his predominantly Congregational province. Did his main interest in the college derive from a desire to turn it into an Anglican institution, one that by supplying ministers to new towns would play a key role in his religious designs for New Hampshire? Evidence can be found that would support that conclusion. In a letter to the bishop of London little more than a year later, Wentworth praised the college as so "perfectly liberal" that it would "unavoidably spread and promote" the establishment of the Church of England in America. He went on to claim that it would be "so great an acquisition to the Church" that it was drawing fire from many Congregationalists in New England. Several years later, an Anglican missionary in New Hampshire, Ranna Cossit, asserted in a letter to England that "Governor W[entwor]th is fully perswaded in time he shall bring [the college] about . . . to be of the Establishment."[32]

These letters indicate that Wentworth saw a connection between Eleazar Wheelock's school and the Church of England. They do not, however, suggest that his main reason for wanting the school in New Hampshire was to advance Anglicanism. Because of the circumstances under which it was written, the letter to the bishop of London can not be taken at face value. Wentworth was faced with the task of convincing an Anglican bishop to sit on the board of a school in America that was run by Congregationalists. He naturally had to play down the dissenting aspects of the college and at the same time emphasize what it

129

could do for the Church of England. Had anyone in New Hampshire read the letter, they would have realized how far the governor was stretching the truth, evidenced by his inference that Congregationalists were against the school on the grounds that it would be a boon to Anglicanism. This was pure propaganda designed solely for the eyes of the bishop of London. The statement by the missionary Ranna Cossit doubtless did contain some truth, but it was made more than three years after the college was actually chartered in New Hampshire, and it should not be assigned more importance than it deserves.

Wentworth's thinking, he claimed, in assigning the bishop to serve as a trustee was guided only by his wish to avoid Anglican objections to the college and thus to insure continued support for it in England. As he told Wheelock, "As many insinuations have been and are yet frequently transmitting to England to depreciate the reputation of the intended College, insinuating that the benevolent Charities will be applied merely and exclusively to the advancement of sectaries and particular opinions, with a fixed view to discourage the Established Church of England, it is not only important, but essential that such ideas should be exterminated." His proposal would aid the school and in no way compromise its religious position. Wentworth went on to explain that there had been a misunderstanding of his intentions. He wanted the bishop of London on just the English trust, and then as a member with no more influence than any other. Further, for the "security" of the college he was only recommending, not insisting on, the addition of three provincial officers to the American trust.[33]

Wheelock's alarm at the prospect of an Anglican bishop connected with his school is entirely understandable. There had been fear for some time by dissenters in all the colonies that the Church of England was making plans to subvert their faith by sending bishops to America. Adding to this apprehension was the likelihood that such a project would be financed by colonial taxation. This fear was an underlying factor in the deteriorating relations between Great Britain and her colonies that had erupted into open violence at the time of the Stamp Act. Wheelock himself made the sensitivity of this issue clear to the governor when, in responding, he spoke of the "formidable idea our country in general have of a Bishop, and how jealous people are of their religious rights and privileges, and of everything that has the least look of infringement upon them." Wheelock was so upset, in fact, that he was determined to move his school to another location. Thus Wentworth's success in persuading him to accept the terms and come to New Hampshire after all was a major achievement. Wentworth's ability to convince a shrewd, doubting dissenter such as Wheelock is good evidence for the sincerity of his explanation.[34]

But there is even more reason to believe that Wentworth's interest in the school was not mainly religious. He knew that the college was Congregational and would be sending dissenting ministers out to New Hampshire's towns. If his greatest concern was with the spread of Anglicanism, he would never have allowed the school to move into his province from Connecticut. Wentworth remained strongly committed to Anglicanism in New Hampshire, and he undoubtedly did hope that the college could eventually be turned to that persuasion. That hope was only natural and over the years, whenever opportunities arose, he sought in small ways to promote that end.[35] Yet he never did anything to antagonize Wheelock and the others who ran the college or to cause them to have misgivings about having moved to New Hampshire. On the contrary, throughout his term as governor he uttered nothing but praise for the school and time and time again went out of his way to secure support for it.[36] His strong commitment to the college was evidenced by personal visits and the interest he took in the students and in specific programs and problems.[37] The nonpartisan enthusiasm Wentworth expressed for the school over the years is the best proof that his Anglican faith was not a major factor in his original efforts to entice Dr. Wheelock to New Hampshire. Rather he was motivated by his desire to populate and develop the province frontier and by his belief that a school in the interior would greatly facilitate that goal. Fittingly, one of the major roads he proposed for the province was to lead from his new home at Wolfeboro to the college on the Connecticut River.[38]

With his fears assuaged and the decision to move to New Hampshire made, Eleazar Wheelock returned to more practical matters. One of the first considerations was the name to be given the college. At the end of his letter of 25 October 1769, in which he agreed to the governor's terms, Wheelock offered to christen the college for Wentworth. This was a politic move but not one he was sincere about, for on the same day he wrote to his emissary in Portsmouth, Alexander Phelps, that more advantages could be gained by naming it after the earl of Dartmouth, head of the English trust.[39] The implication was clear. Phelps was to agree to name the college for the governor only if that seemed necessary. Fortunately for Wheelock, it was not. Wentworth declined the honor in the best interest of the school, for he was as aware as Wheelock that they needed all the help they could get from the other side of the Atlantic. Anger on the part of the trust in England was fully expected. They had not wanted any charter; now they were going to be confronted with one that not only went beyond the original intention of the school to educate Indians but that transferred most of their assumed powers to a trust in America. The name of Dartmouth College in the charter might help soften the blow and, after the initial shock wore off, insure the continuation of the English benevolence that was so important for the school's success.

In August, Wheelock had received the English trust's approval of New Hampshire's upper Connecticut valley as the new site for his school. The choice between Haverhill and Orford would be left to him. In December the governor signed the charter, bringing the college officially into existence. The following month, according to his promise, he granted the unsettled town of Landaff as an endowment. He also viewed it as the best potential site for the school. Because Landaff had no proprietors or settlers, he explained, the college could control the government of the town as was done "usefully in England" at Oxford and Cambridge. Wentworth listed Bath and Haverhill as two alternatives, however, because of their proximity to the river. Hanover seems to have been mentioned as a possibility as early as January 1770, and by February and March other towns were renewing their offers of land and raising substantial subscriptions of money as inducements for the college.[40]

The choice of a location, which had appeared relatively settled only a short time before, was now an open question again. Eleazar Wheelock decided that the only solution was to view the various sites and make the selection himself. He set out for New Hampshire's Coos region in April and, following several side trips, arrived there early in June. He found the towns quarrelling among themselves and asked the governor to join him to help resolve the problem, but Wentworth could not get away from Portsmouth. Bearing the burden himself, Wheelock and his party traveled up and down the river for sixty miles. He then moved east to look again at Plymouth, Campton, and Rumney, which, though not on the Connecticut, he found "very inviting." On 26 June, with Moses Little and Colonel Jacob Bayley, he headed for Portsmouth to meet with Wentworth and the other New Hampshire trustees. On 5 July 1770, after a week's discussion, the president of the school, the governor, and the other trustees present selected Hanover as the site for Dartmouth College.[41]

It is no wonder that this choice came as a surprise to many, for Hanover had scarcely been mentioned and had not seemed to be in serious contention. Haverhill had appeared the most likely site. Wheelock called Hanover "most central on the river" and said that it was near the only convenient place for a bridge. Other than that, it is difficult to tell why it was chosen over Haverhill. A number of people, especially from other competing towns, understandably were upset. Some accused Wheelock of owning land in the town and choosing it for his own personal gain. Even George Whitefield, the famed evangelist who supported the school in England, said that, from that side of the ocean,

Wheelock gave the appearance of using the trust money to his own advantage. There was no evidence for these charges, however, and Wentworth, who had originally hoped for another town, stood resolutely behind the choice. As he wrote to Wheelock, "It was our Duty to judge and determine, without any other view than to promote the College as benevolently instituted."[42] To Wentworth the exact site was not that important. What was significant was that at last the college was securely situated in New Hampshire. In the long run, it could not help but be a highly valuable asset in his larger plans to populate the province, tap the agricultural potential of the area, and thus make New Hampshire itself a valuable asset to Britain's system of empire. In addition, notwithstanding the partisan carping that accompanied the choice of Hanover, Wentworth's success in establishing Dartmouth College in New Hampshire could do nothing but heighten his popular image as an actively concerned, resourceful governor who kept the best interest of his province and its people foremost in his mind.

John Wentworth had emphatically proved to be a significant change from his uncle. His entrenchment among the seacoast commercial aristocracy was not nearly as obvious as that of Benning, and he clearly showed more interest in the interior of the province than in Portsmouth. Much of that concern stemmed from his own natural inclination. Equally important was his desire to make New Hampshire a stonger member of the British mercantile system. With the end of the French and Indian War, settlers from outside the province had begun moving into New Hampshire's undeveloped lands. Viewing those people as the key to increasing agricultural production, first to subsistance level, then to the all-important point of surplus needed for export, Wentworth guaranteed the continuance of that migration by encouragements to landholding, the creation of a convenient judicial system, and the founding of a college in the new area of settlement that would help fill the newcomers' religious and educational needs.

Wentworth did encounter problems, probably more than he originally expected. New Hampshire's relative poverty and the assembly's understandable reluctance to grant money had hit him personally in the form of what he considered substandard living accommodations and an inadequate salary. More important for his long-range goals for New Hampshire, though, was the assembly's refusal to tax the province for the roads that even they agreed needed to be built. And Wentworth also discovered that, regardless of how much he or his programs were liked, a certain inevitable barrier existed between him and the provincial legislature simply from the fact that he was the representative of royal authority. The change in British policy at the end of the French and Indian War and the resulting Stamp Act controversy had created in all of the colonies a heightened awareness of consitutional questions in general and renewed sensitivity to boundaries of power in particular. New Hampshire was no exception, as Wentworth found out when the assembly refused to grant the annual supply until an act for the creation of counties had been approved to send to England.

134   But though Wentworth may have been disappointed, he did not press the assembly on any of these points. He built his own palatial estate in the country, and he was confident that an adequate permanent salary would soon be forthcoming from England. Funds for the road building program were found in previously untapped quitrent receipts. Wentworth sparred briefly with the assembly over the supply question, but he found he had no power to coerce that body. He did not want to give up any power to the assembly, but even less did he wish to antagonize its members since to do so would interfere with his major objective for the province. He was intent on making New Hampshire a strong member of the British Empire, and he felt he must at the same time minimize potential political friction between his province and England. For John Wentworth, those two goals were related. As he wrote to the earl of Hillsborough concerning the division of New Hampshire into counties, not only would such an act be beneficial to the internal development of the province, it would also "augment a spirit of reverence and obedience to Government, toward which great end every measure shou'd urge."[43]

»8«
MAN IN THE
MIDDLE

Keeping the Peace,
1767–1768

lmost immediately on arriving in New Hampshire in 1767 Wentworth plunged eagerly into the work awaiting him as governor. In
line with his instructions, he set about drawing up an exact account
of the sources of funds for the government in New Hampshire, including the
fees taken for granting land and a report on the current state of quitrents in
his province. Concerned with military readiness, he inspected Fort William and
Mary at the harbor's mouth in Newcastle, the province's only defense against
attack from the sea, and within several months made a tour to review the various regiments of provincial militia.[1] Made aware in July of some settlers near
New Hampshire's eastern boundary being kept off their land by claimants from
eastern Massachusetts (Maine), Wentworth did not hesitate to involve himself
in the controversy. He was convinced that his own people were right and wrote
to Governor Bernard of Massachusetts making clear his determination to stand
by the boundary as originally drawn.[2]

Much of Wentworth's energies went into his duties as surveyor general of the
woods. Early in July he informed Peter Randolph, surveyor general of customs
for the southern district in Williamsburg, that he had "private Intelligence" of
masts, yards, and bowsprits being clandestinely shipped out of Virginia and the
Carolinas for Havana, where they were used in masting Spanish men-of-war. As
surveyor general he was determined to halt the treasonous traffic and asked for
Randolph's help. Wentworth's concern ranged over all the colonies but focused
mostly near home. He found that people in the backcountry of New England,
especially in Maine, had broken the law by cutting Crown timber for so long
that they no longer respected royal authority. He was determined to change this

situation. He sent out a deputy surveyor, Joshua Loring, to seize illegally cut logs, and he badgered Governor Bernard for a proclamation warning against further depredations on the king's woods. In August he prosecuted and won his first timber case in the Boston vice-admiralty court. Although the logs, which were sold at auction, did not bring enough to pay court costs, Wentworth was convinced that the case would serve as an example of his determination to stop illegal cutting and thus act as a deterrent in the future. By September he could write to Whitehall with optimism about British forest policy in America.[3]

136

Wentworth took all his responsibilities seriously, yet one concern took precedence over others—the maintenance of peace and respect for royal authority in New Hampshire. In England during the Stamp Act episode, Wentworth had become acutely aware of the seriousness with which high British officials viewed acts of violence and disrespect perpetrated against officers of the Crown in America. Many had considered the colonial actions a direct threat to the English constitution, and Wentworth had been in the Commons himself when George Grenville warned of "open rebellion," even "revolution," in America. In the words of Horace Walpole, "The insult to Parliament was unparalleled and accompanied by every kind of aggravating circumstance." In the House of Lords, the earl of Hardwicke had called the consideration on America "the greatest in its extent and consequences, that ever came before parliament," while the earl of Sandwich accused the Americans of simply wanting "to get loose from the Act of Navigation."

Grenville's answer to what he considered this colonial outrage was to enforce the Stamp Act. But cooler heads had prevailed. The moderate, conciliatory policy of the Rockingham administration eventually resulted in repeal. The decision was far from unanimous, however, and the many strong feelings raised against the colonies were not easily assuaged. Following the passage of the repeal bill, thirty-three peers signed a written denunciation of the Rockingham ministry for its weakness in dealing with the American problem. Even a friend of America, Lord Camden, stated that on the next such occurrence, "Force must be used." The earl of Northington pointed out that the Declaratory Act now provided the basis for introducing a police force into the colonies.[4]

Wentworth had returned to New Hampshire with those threats still ringing in his ears. If the British system of empire were to be given a chance to work, there could be no more outbursts in the colonies such as those that marked the opposition to the Stamp Act. The next time it happened, as he well knew, retaliation was likely. The consequences of any such punishment might easily be disaster. To minimize potential reactions to any new British policy, Wentworth knew he would need the earliest possible intelligence from England. Not willing to rely on Whitehall for the most rapid or complete information, he instructed Alexander Yeats, a London stationer, to forward "papers of the latest Date by every Vessell . . . Especially if any thing of Consequence Occurs." On receiving a vote of the House of Commons from Yeats a short time later, Wentworth asked him to continue "to inquire prudently and write me frequently." To Stephen Apthorp in Bristol he wrote of his desire to know everything that occurred in England relative to America. He also wanted to be informed of what was happening in other colonies, and when Joshua Loring, his deputy surveyor, set out for Canada in July, Wentworth told him to send back "frequent Advice of all Matters Local, Political, Commercial, etc. . . . as I am desirous to form a just Idea of British America."[5]

Wentworth could not control the situation in other provinces, but he would do his utmost to maintain an obedient climate in New Hampshire. From the moment he arrived he was sensitive to the general political atmosphere in his province, taking steps to make it as favorable to his position as possible. One of his few means of direct influence was patronage, the offices and appointments that were his as governor to distribute. Although he lamented the severe limitations placed on his patronage, Wentworth was intent on using the power to his best possible advantage. Ten days after his commission was read, he nominated Peter Gilman, John Sherburne, and Thomas Westbrook Waldron for a vacant position on the council. These three men represented families long inveterate enemies of the Wentworths and their interests in New Hampshire. Out of personal inclination and for obvious political reasons, Wentworth felt it was time to mend broken fences and eliminate another source of divisiveness in the province. He also turned his attention to influential members of the assembly such as Doctor Josiah Bartlett of Kingston, whom he appointed justice of the peace in September. Two years later he made Bartlett a lieutenant colonel in the militia.[6]

Wentworth's appointments during his first few months in office reflected more a commitment to a long-range plan than a reaction to any immediate threat, for the political situation he found in New Hampshire in 1767 was largely pleasing to him. It was natural for the governor in his official correspondence to want to put the best face on conditions in his colony; thus he wrote to the Lords of Trade and Plantations, "The Inhabitants of this Province are remarkably quiet and happy, and as far as I can discover, universally, indeed I believe without exception, are disposed to the justest and most ready obedience and dependence on the British Government." It is obvious from his personal letters that Wentworth really believed this. He told Stephen Apthorp, "Whatever Surmises may have Arisen or disgust taken place against the other Provinces, New Hampshire is not in the least involv'd in it. They are obedient faithful Subjects and ready to exert their utmost Power to support and defend the British Government." And he singled out for praise the assembly, which he found "disposed to the most cheerful observance of Every recommendation and to pursue the Business before them with such temper and respect as may obtain an Approbation of their prudence and Loyalty."[7]

138

New Hampshire would certainly present a happy prospect for any royal governor, and Wentworth had every right to be optimistic. But at the time New Hampshire was not particularly exceptional, for since the repeal of the Stamp Act, all of the colonies had been relatively peaceful. Some new British measures, however, were about to change all that. Strong dissent would soon be forthcoming in larger provinces such as Massachusetts and Virginia, and Wentworth could not expect to keep New Hampshire isolated from that reaction.

When Wentworth left England, the Pitt administration, which had succeeded that of Rockingham, was in control. Pitt had earlier refused to join the Rockinghamites, but his sympathy for America was well known and produced optimism that moderate policies would emanate from Whitehall. By 1767, however, it was apparent that the new administration was not living up to expectations on either side of the Atlantic. The main reason lay in Pitt's decline; he was no longer the man he had once been. Old, physically and mentally ill, once known affectionately as the Great Commoner but now become the earl of Chatham by grant of the king, Pitt was incapable of providing leadership. As a result, the ministry was divided and weak, and the only member who spoke forcefully and carried weight in Parliament, Chancellor of the Exchequer Charles Townshend, was more often in agreement with the opposition than with his fellow cabinet members. The failure to muzzle Townshend or to oust him was itself a sign of the administration's weakness.[8]

Charles Townshend, at one time head of the Board of Trade, knew his way around American affairs and, since the early days of the last French war, had talked of the need to raise a revenue in the colonies. He voted to repeal the Stamp Act, but only because the act was obviously inexpedient and not worth going to war over. In May 1767 he presented Parliament with a new set of plans by which the colonies would again be expected to contribute substantially to the support of their own defense. His ideas were so well received that early in June, at the same time John Wentworth arrived in New Hampshire, the House of Commons passed several new American trade and revenue acts.

The major bill of these Townshend acts called for import duties on lead, glass, paper, paint, and tea coming into the colonies. The preamble to the Revenue Act of 1767 stated that the revenue raised was to be used in America "for making a more certain and adequate Provision for . . . the Administration of

Justice, and the Support of Civil Government, in such Provinces where it shall be found necessary; and toward further defraying the Expences of defending, protecting, and securing the said Dominions." The colonists had opposed the Stamp Act because it had called for an internal tax. Why not, then, reasoned Townshend, raise the money by import duties, something the Americans had always accepted as part of the trade system of the British Empire? To enforce this trade system more rigidly than in the past and thus insure that the revenue was raised, another bill was passed creating a new Board of Customs Commissioners to be resident in America.[9]

If Charles Townshend thought those measures would be easily accepted in the colonies, he was wrong.[10] At the end of August, the *Boston Evening-Post* published news of Townshend's revenue measures. This opened up a running debate in the Boston newspapers between those who saw the taxation plan as "an open and daring attack upon the natural and constitutional rights" of the colonists, and others who termed such opposition the work of "vile incendiaries" attempting to "alienate the minds of truly loyal and affectionate people from their dependence on the Mother Country." In October arguments raged back and forth over proposals made to stop the importation of all British manufactured goods. At the Boston town meeting on 28 October, resolutions were adopted listing more than fifty items that should not be imported after 31 December and encouraging colonials to increase their own manufacturing. No mention was made in these resolutions of rights, liberties, or any other constitutional issues. The argument was based solely on the economic hardship the British measures would cause the town. Not wanting to be isolated in their opposition to the Crown, Boston's selectmen sent copies of their vote to other communities in Massachusetts and to major towns in the other colonies.[11]

John Wentworth was well aware of what was happening in Massachusetts, just the sort of thing he had hoped would not occur. When he wrote to Peter Gilman in Exeter about the matter late in November, he made no attempt to conceal his contempt for the actions taken in Boston. "I am not a little sur-pris'd," he stated caustically, "that any people of Common Modesty only, should assume to themselves such a Shapeless Importance; or should presume to diminish the Consequences of others by supposing themselves an infallible Rule to N. England and that every Town will receive politicks from them, or follow their Example because said and Done by the great and wise ones of Boston Town meeting. . . . I expect shortly to hear These powerful Stile themselves the *Elect* of all the *Select* in British America."[12]

Responding to the Boston call for more self-sufficiency and less reliance on luxury goods from England, Wentworth asserted that he had no objection to hard work and economizing but could not see that those goals would any more result from "Noisy Declamations, Subscriptions, and Epistolary Circulations, than that Cucumbers and Cabbages will be best produc'd by the Rays . . .

140 from the Moon, which has as much living Heat as these Clamorous professions have of true Operating dispassioned Virtue." Wentworth was confident that the people in his province would not be mindlessly led by what he considered mere rhetoric. Portsmouth would provide Boston with no support and, he hoped, with Gilman's help, neither would Exeter.[13]

In fact, Boston's own merchants were not enthusiastic about the nonimportation plan, a scheme that would clearly have a negative effect on their business. Nevertheless, support for the boycott began to grow in other Massachusetts towns, in Rhode Island, Connecticut, New York, and further south in other colonies. In early December the first of a series of twelve letters appeared in Philadelphia newspapers from "A Farmer in Pennsylvania" strongly championing nonimportation, but from a constitutional standpoint. The farmer, John Dickinson, an influential lawyer and member of the Pennsylvania gentry, admitted that Parliament did have the right to regulate colonial trade but no authority whatsoever to lay taxes on America, either internal such as the stamp tax, or external, which the new British acts represented. Though the tax was on trade, its purpose was not regulation but to raise a revenue. Americans were not represented in Parliament, thus their property was being taken from them without their permission, an act patently in violation of the English constitution. To Dickinson, the Townshend acts marked another dangerous step in a long parliamentary program to subvert the rights and liberties of Englishmen in America. The *Letters from a Farmer in Pennsylvania* embodied the most cogent statement yet made concerning constitutional rights of colonial Americans, and they were soon reprinted in nearly every colonial newspaper.[14]

John Dickinson's writings caused little reaction in conservative Pennsylvania. They did, however, provide more radical Massachusetts with an important impetus to increase the tempo of opposition to the Townshend acts. On 20 January 1768, the Massachusetts House of Representatives petitioned the king for repeal of the Townshend legislation. Of more importance, the House on 11 February approved a circular letter to be sent to all of the other North American assemblies urging them to follow suit. A few days later, the New Hampshire House of Representatives received its copy. Because it was near the end of the session, the only action taken was to send Massachusetts a response of general approval. The first province actively to join the Massachusetts campaign was Virginia, which on 14 April agreed on petitions to the king and Parliament and on a letter to the other colonies informing them of their action. By that time, news of the Massachusetts letter had reached London, where it drew an angry response from the secretary of state for the colonies, Lord Hillsborough. In a circular letter of his own dated 21 April, Hillsborough called on all of the colonial governors "to defeat this flagitious Attempt to disturb the public Peace by prevailing upon the Assembly of your Province to take no Notice of it." That was a tall order, as the secretary must have realized, for he added that, if any "Countenance" was given "this seditious Paper," governors were under orders to dissolve their assemblies.[15]

In the meantime, resistance to the Townshend acts continued to mount, especially in Massachusetts. In March a renewed interest in nonimportation was shown by Boston's merchants. Meeting at the British Coffee-House they agreed not to import any English goods for twelve months if merchants in other provinces would do the same. Accordingly, they sent their resolution to other port cities. At the same time, a potentially explosive situation was building between Boston radicals and the new Board of Customs Commissioners, which had been created by the Townshend measures and headquartered in the city the previous November. The existence of the board was visible proof of Britain's determination to enforce its laws in the colonies, and especially in New England. Antagonism was inevitable.[16]

During the months after the board's establishment, minor customs employees were harassed, both verbally and physically. In March when a mob formed outside the home of William Burch, a member of the board, the commissioners began to be uneasy about their own safety. Two weeks later, another commissioner, Charles Paxton, was hung in effigy on the anniversary of the Stamp Act repeal. Open violence finally broke out on 10 June when the sloop *Liberty*, owned by wealthy merchant John Hancock, was seized on order of the commissioners for allegedly smuggling wine. The collector of customs for the port, the officer charged with confiscation of the ship, was John Wentworth's old friend from England, Joseph Harrison. Upon completion of his duty, Harrison found himself face to face with an enraged mob. He and Benjamin Hallowell, the comptroller, who had gone with him, were stoned, beaten, and chased through the streets, and Harrison's eighteen-year-old son, who had accompanied them, was dragged by the hair. Later that evening the mob broke the windows in the collector's house and then burned his prize sailboat. Harrison received such a beating that he was forced to stay in bed for two days. On the thirteenth he fled to the protection of Castle William in the harbor. Four of the five commissioners had already taken refuge on board the man-of-war *Romney*.[17]

During the spring of 1768 Wentworth watched the developments in Massachusetts and elsewhere but remained confident that the trouble would not

141

spread to New Hampshire. In March he wrote Shelburne that, in spite of repeated solicitations from Boston, there was not the slightest inclination in his province to take part in any protest. The people of New Hampshire would continue their trade as usual with England, and they had no intention of pursuing manufacturing on their own. Wentworth gave much credit to the assembly for this atmosphere of moderation. But neither did he fail to mention his own efforts, which, he claimed, had "prevented a Single Instance of Opposition, disrespect, or even discontent, taking place and succeeded in unculcating and confirming . . . effectual principles of Loyalty and Obedience to His Majesty and the Parliament." [18]

In May Wentworth wrote to Rockingham to try to explain what this latest trouble was all about. He told his patron that the reaction was similar to that against the Stamp Act. He had opposed that act, but he made it clear that he did not view the Townshend acts in the same light. Their removal he called the "senseless object" of a few "factious minds" propagating "groundless Fears and anxietys" among the people. Nevertheless, he assured Rockingham, there was no need to worry because the people cherished their ties with the mother country and could not long be fooled. Wentworth praised New Hampshire for opposing the various schemes against trade. He also admitted that by taking pains to receive early knowledge of these plans, he had been able to plant the seeds of resistance that guaranteed their rejection in New Hampshire before they ever arrived. [19]

Thus the news in June of the open violence connected with the *Liberty* incident must have been highly disturbing to Wentworth. It struck especially close to home because of the involvement of two personal friends, Joseph Harrison and John Temple. Temple, who lived in Boston and whom Wentworth had known since his college days, had from 1761 held the office of lieutenant governor of New Hampshire as an honorary title. Retaining that position, he was in 1767 also appointed as one of the five commissioners to sit on the new American customs board. It is not surprising that on receiving word of flight of the commissioners from Boston for their safety, Wentworth invited them to New Hampshire. The peaceful atmosphere and goodwill of the people in his province, he told them, would guarantee their welcome. Two days later the commissioners thanked Wentworth but declined his offer. Their refusal was probably for the best. Not long after this, the New Hampshire assembly passed a resolution in unequivocal terms that the customs commissioners were not welcome in the province. [20] Things were now beginning to stir in New Hampshire.

In its brief reply to the Massachusetts circular letter in February, the assembly expressed confidence that, following the upcoming election in New Hampshire, the body would take steps to follow the recommendations of the Massachusetts legislature. The prediction proved correct. On the first of June, the new assembly considered the Massachusetts letter once again. This time the representatives selected a committee to draw up a petition to the king and his ministers. With the customary summer adjournment beginning on 9 July, the committee would have better than two months to word this important document.[21] Wentworth had wanted more than anything to avoid such an eventuality. In late June he received Hillsborough's vehement instructions, which put even more pressure on him for a satisfactory solution to the problem. The House had already replied to Massachusetts, and Wentworth had done nothing about it. He might be excused for that inaction because it had occurred long before the secretary's instructions arrived; now, however, the assembly was considering a petition to the king. When Wentworth sat down with pen and paper to reply to Hillsborough, he faced the difficult necessity of putting the situation in New Hampshire in the best possible light.

Wentworth explained that, when the Massachusetts letter arrived, he "strenuously" urged that it be ignored. The "most sensible and judicious" representatives had argued, however, that to do so would signify tacit approbation. So, although he would have preferred no reply, he told Hillsborough, he finally settled for a negative answer. The governor admitted that the message sent to the Massachusetts House was "express'd in too civil and polite terms," but he claimed that it had the intended effect of discouraging any hopes harbored in that province that New Hampshire might join "any Union or combination." Had Hillsborough seen the actual letter, he would have wondered at Wentworth's interpretation of it. It was true that the New Hampshire assembly made no mention of specifically joining with others and put off taking any direct action at that time. Nevertheless, the letter's contents hardly constituted a discouragement. The Massachusetts measures, the letter read, were "highly approved." In fact, they were so apt that the assembly felt nothing more could be added. Further, there were hopes and assurances that the next assembly would follow the suggestions of the circular letter.[22] Wentworth clearly made the best of New Hampshire's reply.

He then went on to reiterate his earlier claims that there was not the least interest in boycotts in New Hampshire and that the people felt a strong sense of allegiance to Great Britain. Avoiding any mention of the recently proposed petition to the king, he laid claim to having so far prevented any response on the subject from the current assembly. Finally, he assured Hillsborough, "pursuant to His Majesty's comands," if any attempt to answer were made he would prorogue, or dissolve, the legislature.[23] That was a course of action Wentworth wished to avoid if at all possible, for it would likely mean the rapid deterioration of his relationship with the assembly and an almost certain loss of his effectiveness. His only alternative was somehow to prevent the proposed petition to the king in opposition to the Townshend acts. He would have to await the assembly's next move and be prepared for any outcome.

Wentworth's thoughts were distracted from these troubles by personal grief in the middle of July when his younger brother, Thomas, died following a protracted illness. Thomas left a widow and five children, and Wentworth took a personal interest in their welfare.[24] His attention was not long diverted from public affairs, however. On 1 August a special town meeting was called in Portsmouth for the purpose of instructing the town's representatives to the assembly, scheduled to reconvene later in the month. At the meeting the delegates were told they must make every effort to see that a petition for redress of grievances occasioned by the Townshend acts be drafted and forwarded to the king, along with appropriate assurances of loyalty to the Crown. Among those who called for this meeting were some of the governor's closest friends and relatives, including Daniel and John Peirce, Daniel Rindge, Daniel Warner, Theodore Atkinson, Sr., Theodore Atkinson, Jr., and James McDonogh.[25] There now seemed little doubt that the assembly would petition the Crown. Wentworth had hoped to avoid that step, but it was also about that time that he began to sympathize with colonial resistance.

In a letter written not long after the Portsmouth meeting to a friend in England, Dr. Anthony Belham, Wentworth made it clear he disapproved of the actions taking place in the colonies. But he did not place complete blame on the Americans, especially, he noted, when they are "goaded into Excess by either a Deficiency or contempt of conciliatory prudence in those who have to carry a disagreeable Measure into Execution." Wentworth was referring to the customs commissioners in Boston. It seems that his change of opinion about those men was influenced by his friend Joseph Harrison, who worked for them but since his beating during the *Liberty* affair had become increasingly disaffected from his superiors. Wentworth did not see how the rest of the people could be "condemn'd for resentment when every Officer in the department complain and groan under . . . supercilious Austeritys they can scarcely endure." Wentworth had no quarrel with the Townshend acts. He made no mention of the constitutionality of the duties or any such arguments being used against them. They were the law of the British government; he accepted them. As he put it, "they are not for me to consider." Reflecting his own emphasis in governing, his objection was to the manner in which the act was implemented. The "contemptuous positives" and "exclusive Edicts" of the enforcing officers were bound to produce a reaction among the people. Wentworth likened the customs officials to naval officers telling their sailors, "'Obey the Act and be damn'd.' The Answer," he went on, "is readily known from London Bridge thro' all his Majestys Dominions without enquiring what it is. All English Men will huzza out 'We'll be damn'd if we do.'" Had only a little moderation been used, some honesty and conciliation shown, Wentworth was convinced that the Townshend acts would have been readily accepted. Unfortunately, he lamented, "Not one healing Measure has yet appear'd," and he wondered if England, Scotland, or Ireland would put up with the same thing.[26]

Wentworth told Belham that by acting forthrightly he had prevented any violent outbursts in New Hampshire. All that was necessary to gain the people's respect and keep them satisfied was to govern with "Candor and reason." He noted that America was quite capable of the increased manufacturing being urged by the radicals in Massachusetts, and he warned that if the British government did not begin to treat the colonists with more respect, within sixty years they could produce all of their own needs and a surplus for export. It was simply a matter of sound policy. Wentworth hoped the British would back off, let the disturbances and resentments die down, and then begin again in a much more judicious and sensitive manner. A key to success would lie in allowing officers such as himself, men familiar with the needs and subtleties of the situation, to act with more "discretionary power." Britain would then have no more trouble with her colonies. "Otherwise," he exclaimed prophetically, "within a Century she will have the Love and Alliance of a Sister State that sprung from her own Bowells."[27]

If Wentworth retained any hopes of preventing a petition to the king, they were dashed on 24 August when the assembly read a letter from the Virginia House of Burgesses. Following Massachusetts's lead, the burgesses had petitioned the king and sent a remonstrance to Parliament. They hoped that other colonies would do the same so that, through union, their constitutional rights might be protected. New Hampshire now had not one, but two examples to follow. Three days later the House voted to send a letter to the Virginia burgesses, concurring with their sentiments and informing them that New Hampshire was also petitioning the king. The petition, approved on the same day, expressed a fear of loss of constitutional liberties through taxation without consent and asked for relief from the recent acts of Parliament. It was to be signed by the speaker, Peter Gilman, and forwarded to New Hampshire's agent at court, Barlow Trecothick. Wentworth did not dissolve the assembly, but that afternoon, 27 August, he adjourned it until 18 October to allow a committee to consider necessary measures for creating a supply bill.[28]

On 1 September 1768, Wentworth wrote to the earl of Hillsborough. He observed that the people were upset about the Townshend acts but that there had been no trouble in New Hampshire. He made no mention of the petition to the king. On the twenty-seventh, the governor rode out of town for Boston. He was going to see Joseph Harrison, as Harrison later noted, "to encourage and cheer me up a little." Wentworth doubtless also wanted to see for himself the situation in the Massachusetts metropolis. What he gained was confirmation of his beliefs about the customs commissioners. He found Harrison a beaten man, and he attributed it to the commissioners. They were using the collector to do their dirty work and thus bear the brunt of the radical attack. The seizure of John Hancock's *Liberty* provided only the best example. Harrison's friends believed he had been sent out purposely to draw the rage of the mob. An attack on such a worthy customs officer would do much to discredit those opposing the revenue acts.[29]

Wentworth was given even more reason for disliking the customs board when he discovered that they had dismissed his brother-in-law, John Fisher, from his position as collector at Salem. Unfortunately, the actions of the commissioners showed no signs of the moderation that Wentworth felt was needed to calm the situation in America and rebuild faith and trust between the colonies and the mother country. On the contrary, their every action seemed designed to aggravate the trouble. Wentworth had visible evidence of this himself on 28 September, when he looked out on Boston harbor to see more than a dozen warships and transports flying the British flag and carrying two regiments of troops requested by the commissioners of the customs. The soldiers disembarked two days later and "drums beating, fifes playing, and colours flying," marched first to the town house and then to the common. The people remained calm, and there were no incidents, yet the tension and anxiety produced by this major turn of events could not be ignored. Boston had taken on the appearance of an armed camp.[30]

With these burdens on his mind, Wentworth returned to Portsmouth in the middle of October and shortly began to inform his friends in England of the deteriorating circumstances in the colonies and of his apprehensions. Writing to Rockingham, he repeated much of what he had told Anthony Belham and again, though now more vehemently, singled out the customs commissioners as the root of the problem. Their "superciliousness" and little disguised hatred for America, Wentworth reported, gave rise to vitriolic feelings against them, which were eventually transferred to the Revenue Act. Now, he believed, there was little hope of ever collecting the duties. Opposition was rooted too deeply. The potentially workable plans of the British government had been ruined by what he told Paul Wentworth was "the unprecedented Weakness, Pride and fatal interested Designs of my fellow Servants." The one member of the board for whom Wentworth had respect was John Temple. When Temple originally urged that the new measures be instituted with caution and prudence, the others insulted and ignored him. This angered Wentworth, and he exclaimed to Paul Wentworth that "All the paper imported since their arrival wou'd not suffice to record their Arrogance and unavailing Management." When that "management" was known in England, he told Rockingham, there should no longer be any surprise at the failure of the customs service in America.[31]

Wentworth also reported to his patron on the arrival of the soldiers, and in connection with that event made what is perhaps the clearest, most cogent statement of his beliefs on how affairs in America should be handled by the British. He wrote,

> I am at a loss to inform your lordship of any real use or necessity for this armament: it cannot be advantageous to the revenue, which will not suffice to pay half the expense. If it is intended to secure the dependence of the colonies, I fear it will exceedingly operate the other way. Perhaps military power may preserve the subjection of conquests; but I believe it is positively true, that the just dependence of the British colonies on this continent can be ascertained only by a wise, moderate, and well-timed reformation and strengthening of their government, gradually introducing the beneficial regulations necessary, always securing measures to take place before they were proposed publicly, which may always be effected, nay, in many instances, cause them to be solicited, if time and faithful attention were cordially exerted here, upon seasonable direction and independent support from Administration.[32]

Wentworth had opposed the Stamp Act, but he found nothing particularly objectionable about the current Townshend measures that were beginning to provoke as much opposition. It might be asked, What would have been the result had the Townshend acts instead of the Stamp Act been passed and introduced into the colonies in 1765 with all the caution and prudence advocated by John Wentworth? As a tax on trade, which the colonists had long been familiar with and which had not been questioned in regard to parliamentary prerogative, the chances are great the Townshend acts would not have produced opposition nearly as severe as did the Stamp Act. If such had been the case, constitutional arguments against the revenue acts might have remained undeveloped. Wentworth, then, would have been correct in seeing the major source of discontent in the method of implementation and not in any perceived subversion of the English constitution.

What he did not see, though, was that the Stamp Act had made constitu-

147

tional questions a key issue in the continuing dispute between the colonies and England. It had raised the Americans' consciousness of basic liberties and sensitized them to their rights under the English constitution. That fact had combined with the inept handling of the Townshend acts to produce the worsening situation Wentworth saw in the colonies in late 1768. Even if the measures had been applied slowly with caution and tact as he had wished, because they were designed to raise a revenue it was unlikely the duties would have been accepted. The Stamp Act had permanently altered thinking in the colonies. Constitutional considerations could not now be easily set aside or ignored. Wentworth's perception of the situation and its solution was at least partially correct. What he did not realize was that the time had passed when goodwill alone could be effective.

148

Wentworth did not perhaps perceive all of the complexities of the British Empire, but he was a good judge of human nature. The revenue acts would have been accepted, he believed, had they not been thrown in the colonists' face in an arrogant, defiant manner. He could see that people were reacting to this insulting behavior, and he did not blame them. What particularly irked him about the customs commissioners was that they were making his job of keeping the peace in New Hampshire extremely difficult. As he told Paul Wentworth, "all my Art and Assiduity hath been necessarily exerted to keep this Province Steady and right."[33] Wentworth had become particularly sensitive since the recent receipt of a letter from the earl of Hillsborough.

John Wentworth's letter of late June, describing the assembly's brief reply in February to the Massachusetts circular letter, had not gone unnoticed by the colonial secretary. Despite Wentworth's attempts to make the response appear unimportant, Hillsborough rightly suspected there was more to it than the governor let on. Hillsborough wrote back that he hoped he could conclude that the assembly "meant at least to treat that Letter with the Contempt it deserves; but as you have not thought fit to transmit the Proceedings themselves, and as there is (you will pardon my Observation,) an Obscurity in the Manner in which you have expressed yourself on the Subject, that leaves many Parts of the transaction in a State of great Doubt, I am not able to form a Judgment whether His Majesty's Orders of the 21st of April have or have not been duly observed. If the Answer given to the letter from the Province of Massachusett's Bay," the secretary continued, "contains an Approbation of a Petition to his Majesty, which however filled with Expressions of Loyalty and Obedience, does in Effect deny or draw into Question the Power and Authority of Parliament to enact Laws binding upon the Colonies in all cases whatever, it would have been your Duty to have put a Stop to every Proceeding of such a Tendency, and you will be highly blameable if you did not." Not only had the New Hamp-

The Earl of Hillsborough. (Emmet Collection, Miriam and
Ira D. Wallach Division of Art, Prints and Photographs, The New York
Public Library. Astor, Lenox, and Tilden Foundations)

shire Assembly expressed its agreement with the Massachusetts petition, it had now approved one of its own to be sent to England. Further, Wentworth had ignored his orders to dissolve the House. The pressure was on. He had received a clear warning from the colonial secretary. Further, as an added inducement for Wentworth to forward a complete and punctual report of the assembly's proceedings, Hillsborough had included a copy of the four-year-old charges against Benning Wentworth for the same deficiency.[34]

Wentworth had desperately wanted to keep New Hampshire the model of a dutiful and peaceful province. He prided himself that so far there had been no suggestion of violence, but he had not been able to prevent the assembly from considering and taking action on the Massachusetts circular letter. He now knew he would no longer be able to hide that fact from England. Faced again with describing a bad situation in the best possible terms, Wentworth penned a reply to Hillsborough on 7 November. He stated that the assembly had drawn up a petition to the king for relief from the Townshend duties. He then went on to explain, "A Committee was chosen to prepare and send the Petition, who are not yet determin'd to forward any. Whenever they do determine I am assured . . . that it is intended to pray for Relief solely upon their utter inability without any reliance on any other matter whatever." This last statement was not true. Wentworth unquestionably had read the petition approved by the House late in August. Though couched in repeated phrases of respectful loyalty, the document made clear the assembly's denial of any parliamentary right to tax the colonists, exactly what Hillsborough had warned the petition must not do.[35] By asserting that the New Hampshire petition did not call parliamentary authority into question, Wentworth absolved himself from any neglect of duty in not dissolving the assembly. To do this, he had had to lie. He now had to make sure that the petition was not sent.

Wentworth had stated that the committee designated "to prepare and send" the petition had not yet decided to forward it to agent Trecothick for presentation at court. It was true that the petition had not yet been sent. The man whose responsibility that was and whose signature was needed to make the document official was speaker of the House, Peter Gilman. The committee that had prepared the petition, William Parker, Samuel Livermore, and Jacob Sheafe, may also have still been involved. What is apparent is that Wentworth succeeded in putting pressure on Gilman, and possibly on these other men, not to send the petition. Certainly in Gilman's case, this persuasion was not difficult, for he was against such a radical step and considered himself a friend of the governor. There are indications that other representatives knew the petition had not been sent; the assembly was later accused of being "cold in the Cause and . . . indifferent."[36]

A logical reason for their reticence can be found in the fear of the legislature that the arrival of the petition in England would lead to certain rejection of the governor's pending proposal for dividing the province into counties.

Wentworth did his best to point out to the representatives a relationship be-
tween the calm, loyal atmosphere in New Hampshire and the province's chances for having the proposal approved. In October, on sending to the assembly Hillsborough's slightly encouraging remark concerning the counties, he included with it one other paragraph from the secretary's letter stating that the "steady Resolution" of the province's inhabitants "in refusing to accede to the measures and Proposals that have been urged with so much indecent warmth in other Colonies cannot fail to recommend them" to the Crown.[37] The message was clear, and apparently well taken, for no dissenting voices were raised questioning the fate of the petition. Wentworth saved himself from a severe reprimand and possibly worse by preventing New Hampshire from following Massachusetts, Virginia, and other colonies in petitioning the Crown for redress from the Townshend acts. He thus secured his image in England as one of the few governors in North America who had managed to maintain complete loyalty in his province. At the same time, by not dissolving the assembly, he had not jeopardized the all-important but fragile positive relationship that existed between him and the representatives.

One advantage Wentworth enjoyed in keeping New Hampshire quiet through this difficult period was the reluctance of Portsmouth's merchants to join in the boycott of British goods. That did not indicate a lack of resentment against the recent revenue acts. On 28 September a group of merchants met at the home of John Stavers and voted unanimously not to import any tea, glass, paper, or paint after 1 January 1769 until the acts were repealed and not to consume any tea on which the duty had been paid. A committee was chosen to present these decisions to the other traders in town. Two days later, "Americanus," writing in the *New Hampshire Gazette*, disavowed the use of violence but said that the way to gain redress from the oppressive acts was to quit consuming tea and all other imported products. He admitted that such a step would require "Resolution" in the beginning. Apparently, there was not enough of this resolve, especially among the commercial class, for a boycott was not instituted in the New Hampshire port for more than a year and a half, and then only half-heartedly. Most of the wealthy and influential merchants in Portsmouth were relatives or friends of the governor, and many of them sat on the council. These men wielded their power among their lesser colleagues in trade and, much to John Wentworth's relief, kept New Hampshire out of the boycott movement longer than any other colony. There were some important merchants outside of the Wentworth circle, such as Woodbury Langdon, Samuel Cutts, and George Boyd, who opposed the Townshend acts and had pushed for the petition to the Crown. Even they, however, were not willing to risk their profits by joining the boycott.[38]

152

By late November, things had again settled down, and Wentworth wrote to Rockingham that "nothing hath lately occur'd to disturb the general quiet." One hindrance to activities in general was the extremely severe winter that set in. It was so cold that the tidal Piscataqua froze and people walked between Portsmouth and Newcastle over the ice. Wentworth complained that New Hampshire's weather would "give comparative comfort to a Siberian Winter." The bitter cold, nevertheless, was not enough to discourage the morbid curiosity of a mob that swarmed to the south side of town on 30 December to see Ruth Blay hanged. She had been convicted of the "Burial and concealment of her Bastard Child." Concealment alone was enough to demand the death sentence, but a jury called to view the infant's body concluded that it "came to its death by violence." Wentworth did issue the woman reprieves on three different occasions, but the court records do not support a nineteenth-century story that he granted another on the thirtieth, only to have it arrive too late because Sheriff Thomas Packer had not wanted to miss his dinner.[39]

The cold in December kept Wentworth close to home, and he wisely spent some of the time trying to shore up his standing in England. He had maintained regular contact with Rockingham, but the marquis and his associates were still out of power and there was little he could do for his friend in America. The able Barlow Trecothick was the province agent in London, but he was finding it increasingly difficult to carry New Hampshire's interest at court against those who now wielded more political influence. In turn, as a merchant, his own ties to New Hampshire began to weaken when economic opportunities moved elsewhere. Wentworth would rather have had as agent someone he was close to, someone he could entrust with confidential information and count on to handle with delicacy the many sensitive situations arising during these difficult times. Thus, when Hillsborough wrote that New Hampshire "should have, as formerly, an Agent here" and directed him to take appropriate measures, instead of questioning the order Wentworth saw it as an opportunity to appoint a co-agent with Trecothick. Hillsborough had some specific names in mind, but so did the governor. The man he wanted for the job was Paul Wentworth.[40]

Paul Wentworth's background has never been completely clear. Another distant Wentworth relation, he apparently came from Barbados to New England, spent time in Boston and perhaps Portsmouth, and went to England about the same time as John Wentworth in the early 1760s. There he became, possibly with the exception of Rockingham, Wentworth's closest confidant. The two men lived not far from each other in London, and Wentworth was responsible for introducing Paul to the marquis.[41] Both acquaintances were important to Paul Wentworth, for lacking the connections of John Wentworth, he was a man on the make, seeking money, position, and titles.

153

By the middle of December, the governor had sounded out leaders of the House and reported confidently that in the spring Paul Wentworth would be a unanimous choice to serve as agent with Barlow Trecothick. Unfortunately for Wentworth, he misjudged the sentiment in the assembly. When the matter was raised, it was pointed out that New Hampshire already had an agent and, as far as the representatives could see, he was perfectly adequate. Wentworth was disappointed, but he at least was able to use the decision to his advantage in England. When he told Hillsborough of the assembly's determination to continue with a single agent, he let on that he had *prevented* the House from appointing Paul Wentworth as co-agent so that the colonial secretary's friends might have a better chance for the position in the future.[42]

Hillsborough in the meantime had discovered that his directive was out of order. He informed Wentworth that he had erroneously assumed New Hampshire had no agent because Trecothick had failed to register his appointment with the Board of Trade. One agent, he told the governor, was sufficient; his order should be ignored. Wentworth realized that he had lost his chance for a new agent who might be able to do more for him at Whitehall. He would have to continue to rely on Barlow Trecothick and make the best of the situation. To renew the agent's flagging interest in the fate of New Hampshire, Wentworth in May chartered a new town to be called Trecothick and made its namesake one of the new proprietors. To Paul Wentworth he promised a council seat as soon as one became available. He had greater hopes, however, that if John Temple could be persuaded to resign as lieutenant governor of New Hampshire, Paul Wentworth might have that post. That eventuality, the governor wrote to Paul Wentworth, combined with the return of the Rockingham Whigs to power, would give him complete happiness.[43]

And no wonder. By that time John Wentworth had learned through firsthand experience the imperative of having a British administration that was sensitive to the volatile political conditions in the colonies and was also aware of the difficulties and needs of royal officials there. Wentworth knew that Rockingham and his ministers had been unsurpassed on both counts. If he could not now expect to place Paul Wentworth in the New Hampshire agency, he harbored strong hopes that the Rockinghamites would be reinstated at the head of government in England.[44]

It was the inept British handling of the Townshend acts, Wentworth believed, that had forced him to walk a tightrope between the New Hampshire assembly and the home government. Hillsborough's instructions had put him in the position of either alienating the representatives—his base of support in New Hampshire—on the one hand, or disobeying an official directive—a move that carried the possibility of a severe reprimand or even dismissal—on the other. Rather than commit political suicide by confronting the assembly head-on, Wentworth chose to work behind the scenes to prevent a petition to the king denouncing the Townshend revenue measures. But that course led him, in an attempt to avoid official censure, to risk lying to Secretary Hillsborough about what was actually taking place in New Hampshire.

Wentworth was convinced he would never have found himself in such a difficult situation if Rockingham was still in office. The return of a Rockingham ministry was what he hoped for. More than that, if the situation in the colonies did not improve, it was what he believed must and would take place.

»9«
A TIGHT
ENGLISH REIN

John Wentworth and
the British Ministry,
1769–1770

D uring 1769 Wentworth found no respite from the tension of trying to reconcile the interests of the British government and those of his fellow colonists. His attempts to make his position in England as strong as possible did in fact prove to be wise, because over the course of the year he became more frustrated by British policies and reactions to his efforts than by anything that took place in the colonies. In February he was still complaining about the customs commissioners. Not only had they dismissed another able Crown servant, their secretary Samuel Venner, but their "positive Menaces and injudicious Hauteur," he told Rockingham, were beginning to solidify opposition to royal authority. People were starting to believe that Britain was actually out to oppress them. The prevailing peace in New Hampshire Wentworth attributed to what he termed his own "open disinterested Steadiness." This only provided additional evidence to support his belief that there were no basic objections to the revenue acts, only to the way in which they were implemented. As he phrased it, "Men and Manner and not measures are most obnoxious." Eight months later his opinion had not changed when he declared, "God knows they [the commissioners] richly merit" dissolution.[1]

In March Wentworth lost his struggle with the assembly over the supply bill. He was first forced to allow the representatives to draw up an act for dividing the province into counties. The following month he received another rebuff from the legislature. Resolving to get to the bottom of the controversy with Massachusetts over New Hampshire's northeast boundary and receiving little satisfaction from Governor Bernard, Wentworth ordered that the line be resurveyed. He designated Isaac Rindge, surveyor general of the province, to carry out the job. Contrary to the Massachusetts charge that the original line of 1741 was in error, Rindge's survey of one hundred miles proved that the land claimed by Massachusetts, including part of the town of Rochester, was clearly in New Hampshire. In April, Wentworth reported this good news to the House and requested a grant to pay Rindge for his services. The representatives voted it down. The governor made no angry reply. He chose, as with the supply issue, to accept the assembly's decision with no comment.[2] His reticence may have been linked to the assembly's dormant petition to the Crown. After his hard work to suppress the petition, he wanted to do nothing now that might provoke renewed interest in sending it. The petition was on his mind at this time. Only a few days later, with the supply bill finally enacted and the assembly safely prorogued, Wentworth at last felt confident enough to inform Hillsborough of the fate of the petition. Agreement could not be reached on it, he told the secretary, so at his suggestion that none be sent, "the House readily approved that the Whole Measure should subside."[3]

In June 1769 Wentworth again traveled to Boston. This time he was beckoned by official rather than private business, although the trip did give him a chance to renew his friendship with Harvard classmate John Adams. The governor of New Hampshire, along with several other provincial officials including councillors George Jaffrey, Daniel Rindge, and Jonathan Warner, and the comptroller of the customs for the Piscataqua, Robert Trail, had been asked to sit on a special court of admiralty in a case involving the impressment of seamen. Governor Bernard headed the court, which also included Chief Justice Thomas Hutchinson and Secretary Andrew Oliver of Massachusetts, Boston admiralty judge Robert Auchmuty, Commodore Samuel Hood (commanding officer of the British fleet in America), collectors Joseph Harrison of Boston and John Nutting of Salem, and several officials from Rhode Island. The trial, which involved the killing of a British naval officer, was of potentially serious consequence, for not only was Bernard coming under increasing attack by the Boston radicals but resentment of British military presence, fed by a constant flow of opposition propaganda, was growing day by day.[4]

The case stemmed from an incident on Saturday morning, 22 April, when the frigate *Rose*, under impressment orders from Commodore Hood, stopped the brig *Pitt Packet* making for Marblehead with a load of salt from Cadiz for its owner, wealthy merchant Robert Hooper. A press gang led by Lieutenant Henry Panton, second in command on the *Rose*, was sent on board. Convinced that not all the brig's hands were accounted for, Panton ordered a search of the ship, which, as he expected, turned up four more men. Hiding in the forepeak and armed variously with a musket, hatchet, fish gig, and harpoon, the four swore they would cut off the limbs of the first man who tried to take them. When several attempts at persuasion failed, a member of the boarding party fired a pistol and wounded one of the resisters. Then, in the words of John Adams who served as defense counsel for the four *Pitt Packet* sailors, one Michael Corbett drew a line in the cargo of salt and warned: "If you step over that mark again I shall take it as a proof of your determination to impress me and by the eternal God of Heaven, you are a dead man. Ay, my lad says Panton, I have seen a brave fellow before now, took his snuff box out of his pocket, and snuffing up a pinch, resolutely stepped over the line. Corbett instantly threw an harpoon iron, which cutt off the carrottid artery and jugular vein. Panton cry'd the rascall has killed me, and fell dead in a few minutes."[5] Reinforcements from the *Rose* finally subdued the four men who were brought to Boston for trial.

Several factors gave the case significance within Boston's highly charged political atmosphere. The first was the probability that the trial would not be by jury. A parliamentary act of 1700 stated that decisions by this infrequently called court for crimes committed at sea would, when taking place in the colonies, be made by special commissioners. Such a trial by selected royal officials would provide the radical whigs with but yet another prime example for their argument that the colonies were being methodically subverted by a growing British despotism.

Adding fuel to the fire was the fact that none of the Massachusetts council had been included among the commissioners. In Massachusetts, unlike other royal provinces including New Hampshire, councillors were chosen by the assembly and thus were not the governor's men. The House, in fact, was at this very time accusing the governor of trying to have the council made appointive. It came as no surprise that Bernard named none of the council to the special court, but the opposition was not about to let such a valuable piece of propaganda go unused. The radical newspaper column "Journal of the Times," composed by Sam Adams and his associates, reported, "the inhabitants [of Boston] had the mortification to perceive, that the whole of his Majesty's Council of this province, who had been included in all former commissions, was excluded from the present; while, not only the Council of a neighbouring colony, but even pro. temp. collectors, helped to constitute this court. For such an indignity thrown upon this ancient and loyal province, it is known we are obliged to the generosity and prudence of G[overno]r B[ernar]d." The men Bernard had chosen from his own province to sit on the court, Hutchinson, Oliver, and Auchmuty, were derisively known as his "Cabinet Council."[6] Highlighting the importance of the case was the fact that the three best lawyers in Massachusetts were taking part, John Adams and James Otis for the defense, and Jonathan Sewall as advocate-general for the Crown.

John Adams's first move was to push for a trial by jury, and he nearly succeeded. Adams based his argument on a 1717 parliamentary statute that persons accused under the act of 1700 "may be tried and judged" according to the original statute of Henry VIII, which had created this special court for sea crimes.[7] That law called for trial by jury. Bernard and the rest of the court had accepted this argument and were making plans for calling a jury when Chief Justice Hutchinson, who had been ruminating on the matter, countered with an argument of his own. All the statutes, according to Hutchinson, referred only to English juries. Furthermore, he pointed out, the word "may" in the statute of 1717 could as easily be interpreted to mean permitting but not requiring a trial by jury as "shall," as held by Adams. Accepting Hutchinson's reasoning, the court set aside the idea of calling a jury. This pretrial maneuvering took place in May; the court then adjourned until 14 June to take up the actual case. John Wentworth and his retinue arrived in town on Tuesday, the thirteenth, and the trial started promptly the next day.[8]

With soldiers in their streets and warships in their harbor, the people of Boston showed a zealous interest in a trial stemming from an incident of apparent British military provocation. The courtroom was packed with onlookers. The telling question was the intent of Lieutenant Panton and his boarding party. The prosecution, hoping to prove that the sailors had had nothing to fear from Panton and thus were guilty of murder, attempted to show that the boarders were acting only as customs officers searching for illegal goods. On the other side, John Adams mounted evidence that Panton was in fact attempting to impress Michael Corbet and his three compatriots. If this was so, Adams argued, the men had a right to protect their freedom by resisting, even to the point of taking another man's life if necessary. They had that right, the lawyer stated, whether impressment was legal or not. But to seal his case for acquittal of the sailors, Adams was prepared to prove that the impressment mission of the HMS *Rose* was a violation of the law.

John Adams owned a complete set of the British Statutes at Large, the only such copy in all the colonies he believed. In one of those volumes, lying on the table in front of him in the courtroom, was a parliamentary statute of Queen Anne forbidding impressment in American waters. As he began to make his argument, however, his earlier nemesis, Thomas Hutchinson, abruptly interrupted and moved for adjournment to the following day, 17 June. Hutchinson, Wentworth, Bernard, and the other commissioners filed out of the room and remained out until one o'clock the next afternoon. At that time they returned and, to the anxious defendants and audience, Bernard read the verdict: acquittal on the basis of justifiable homocide. No further reason for the decision was given. Hutchinson later wrote that acquittal resulted because no special authorization for impressment had been granted from the Admiralty. Adams believed that Hutchinson's hasty move to cut off his argument, as well as the trial's favorable result, stemmed from a determination by the chief justice and the other judges, who included Commodore Hood, not to publicize the question of the legality of impressment until they could get the nonimpressment statute of Queen Anne repealed.[9] Whatever the mixture of reasons for the decision, one overriding consideration could not have helped but influence Bernard, Hutchinson, and the other commissioners: A vote to convict might easily have been the spark to ignite a highly volatile political situation.

What the commissioners discussed as they came to their verdict can only be conjectured. Because the immediate crisis affected Massachusetts and not his own colony, John Wentworth doubtless listened, asked some questions, and willingly adhered to the decision of those most closely involved. One thing is sure; in this short time, Wentworth was made aware of the pressure that Bernard, Hutchinson, and other royal officials in Masachusetts were operating under. New Hampshire, although not many miles distant, basked in a vastly different political climate. Wentworth now saw and heard for himself just how critical the situation was in Boston. And he was exposed not just to the viewpoint of the Crown, for he had a chance to talk with John Adams.

Fourteen years had passed since the two good friends had graduated from Harvard, and there was much to discuss—old acquaintances, activities, accomplishments, perhaps most of all, recent events.[10] As they conversed, it must have become painfully apparent that occurrences beyond their personal control were driving them to opposite sides of a political barrier that both wished was not there. As a royal governor, Wentworth was bound to uphold the decisions of the British government whether he agreed with them or not. His friend, now one of the most prominent attorneys in Massachusetts and an ardent student of English law, felt compelled to oppose the recent acts of Parliament that he believed violated the constitutional principles he had so painstakingly learned. Wentworth may not have agreed with John Adams's interpretation of the developments taking place in England and the colonies, but he would not have doubted his friend's sincerity of belief. Adams had a first-rate mind, and on all sides he was considered a man of learning and reason. Wentworth doubtless came away from this meeting with a broader perspective on the conflict between England and the colonies.

John Adams, 1766, by Benjamin Blyth
(Courtesy Massachusetts Historical Society)

Although Wentworth did not particularly like Francis Bernard, he would never have done anything to undermine the authority of another royal governor. Nevertheless, during his sojourn in Boston he was unwittingly used by Bernard's opponents in their continuing propaganda war against the Massachusetts governor. On Thursday, 22 June, Wentworth was invited to an elegant dinner held in his honor in Cambridge at the home of William Brattle, a member of the Massachusetts council. There he was greeted by other members of the council and various professors and tutors from Harvard College. From Brattle's house, the entire group trooped over to the college, ostensibly for a tour of the new library built by subscriptions raised after the old building and its books were destroyed by fire in 1764. The fact that the Massachusetts House was meeting at that time in the chapel of Harvard Hall certainly was no coincidence. On his arrival, Wentworth was met by a committee of the assembly headed by James Otis, who expressed the wish of the individual members that they might have the honor of personally meeting the governor of New Hampshire. For the next two hours, Wentworth shook hands and chatted with the Massachusetts representatives as Thomas Cushing, the speaker of the House, introduced them in small groups. When the last greeting had finally been made, Wentworth did get his tour of the library, and Professor John Winthrop even performed some experiments for his former student.

As he rode back into Boston that evening in his coach, Wentworth must have felt good about the day's events and perhaps wondered how such a rift could have developed between the council and assembly, on the one hand, and the governor and other royal officials, on the other. He may even have wondered if the situation in Massachusetts need have deteriorated to its present state had he been governor. Bernard, however, on hearing of the activities in Cambridge, doubtless saw the affair as only another incident in the opposition's well-planned campaign to discredit him. The newspapers of the following week bore testimony to that opinion. The radical *Boston Gazette*, in reporting the event, noted that "Mr. Wentworth, like a Governor, and like the Representative of the greatest and best of Kings, . . . is much respected by all Ranks, and caressed by those who his affairs will admit to the Honour of his Company." Bernard's antagonists were holding up a royal governor for praise, showing that their opposition was not to royal authority or to the Crown but only to individuals who abused their power. The comparison to be drawn was obvious. The *Evening Post* was even more direct. The courtesy and respect shown to Governor Wentworth in Cambridge, it concluded, proved that "however the People of this Province may have been represented, as inimical to any who may chance to wear his Majesty's Commission, the World in this instance may be clearly convinced that the Spirit of Disgust, arises not from the Commission with which our most gracious Sovereign thinks fit to honor any of his subjects, but from a dislike to those whose Deportment is unworthy the royal Favour."[11]

162 It is possible that John Wentworth was gaining a reputation among the opponents of royal government in Massachusetts as the kind of royal governor they would like to see in office. After all, there had been little disturbance in New Hampshire and no complaints against the governor. And, too, it was easy to bestow praise on a governor from another province who posed no threat. But the situation in Massachusetts was far different and more complex than that of its neighbor to the north, a fact that was easily recognizable. The main purpose of the Massachusetts council and assembly in going to such great lengths to honor John Wentworth was to stage a highly public dramatization of the point they wanted most to make: that they were loyal subjects of the Crown and opposed only royal officials who threatened their basic liberties, namely Francis Bernard.

As Wentworth headed for home at the end of June, he certainly had a deeper understanding of the situation in Boston. As a result of his visit, he probably viewed the prospects for peace in Massachusetts and the rest of the colonies with mixed feelings. The sailors' case had been resolved without causing any further trouble, and the Massachusetts legislators, at least in their dealings with him, had appeared sensible, moderate men with a healthy respect for the authority of the Crown. At the same time, his conversations with royal officials such as Bernard and Hutchinson, on the one hand, and with John Adams, on the other, had doubtless made him aware that what had started out as a difference of opinion over the British revenue acts was hardening into principle. But he had no control over Massachusetts. His concern was with New Hampshire, and at the moment the outlook was optimistic. He thus could focus his attention on matters other than his colony's relations with Britain.

The acts passed by the last assembly, including the one dividing the province into counties, still had to be submitted to England for approval. With that task completed, Wentworth turned to his responsibilities as surveyor general of the woods. In late July he boarded the sloop *Beaver*, put at his disposal by Commodore Hood, and sailed east from Portsmouth to inspect timberland in Maine and Nova Scotia. The fact that his father had recently been replaced as mast agent in America because of a change in contractors in England did not dampen Wentworth's enthusiasm for enforcing the timber laws.[12] This job was important to him not only for saving valuable masts for the Royal Navy but because he tended to see the lawlessness in the forests as part of the general breakdown of respect for authority in the colonies. Moreover, as surveyor general it was a problem that he had some control over.

As early as April, Wentworth had become aware of large-scale violations in the woods in the vicinity of Brunswick in Maine, and he had vowed, if need be, to put a stop to it himself.[13] He was now on his way to do that. The second day out of Portsmouth he reached the Androscoggin River and the site of the saw-mills that were cutting up the illegally felled logs. The governor quickly notified the people of his identity and his business there and requested that as many of them as possible, with a justice of the peace, meet him at the mills. When they arrived, Wentworth read them the act of Parliament reserving the pines for the British navy. He made a special effort to impress on these country people the strength of the law, and the serious consequences of breaking it. To empha-size the power of parliamentary law Wentworth went unarmed and ordered his deputy, another aide, and the boatmen who rowed them to the mills to do like-wise.

When he had finished, an older man stepped forward and, speaking for the rest, said that the people were poor and depended on the timber for their living. They had assumed that since it was on their land it belonged to them. They now, however, could see their error; they would not oppose Wentworth in his duty and would protect him as long as he was there. Then, in Wentworth's words, he "singled out one man who had been the most zealous and warm in the scheme of making their Country too hot for Officers . . . and required him to aid and carry me off in his canoe upon the River . . . and there help me seize and mark about 500 logs, which belonged to him and the rest who waited on the Banks of the River within 30 yds, which he directly performed." The local magistrate was put in charge of the logs and Wentworth and his men stayed overnight at the local inn to consider any claims people wanted to make against the seized tim-ber the next day. No claims were lodged, and the inhabitants reaffirmed their vow to adhere to the law.[14]

How long they kept this promise is a matter of conjecture. The rough folk on the Androscoggin River were startled when a royal governor suddenly appeared in their midst reading to them from the statutes of Parliament. They probably had known they were doing something wrong, but nothing serious enough to provoke a visit by such an important official. This encounter undoubtedly made an impression on them, along with Wentworth's sincerity and forthright man-ner. For a time the woodsmen may have been cowed by this event and by the fear that the surveyor general and his party would momentarily return. But as the memory faded, it no doubt was replaced by a vision of the profits that could be had from the tall pines. The law may have seemed awesome to these people when John Wentworth read it to them, but as time passed, their allegiance to authority was supplanted by their practical need for these trees—trees on their land, trees that the government might never make use of. The moratorium on cutting was bound to be only temporary.

Wentworth realized that fact, as well as the truth that the wooded areas of New England were too vast for him and his four deputies to patrol effectively. To facilitate his enforcement of the forest laws, he requested the detachment of a small schooner from the British fleet, with from fourteen to twenty men, to carry the inspectors along the coast and up the rivers where the illegal logging operations were prevalent. The ship never materialized, but he continued to press for funds to pay badly needed additional deputies. Yet Wentworth knew these measures were only makeshift, made necessary by an unrealistic policy laid down by Parliament in the 1720s that forbade the cutting of any white pine trees not within a township or on private land granted before 1691.[15] In a frontier area such as Maine, nearly all the pines were covered by that law. It was thus difficult to clear and cultivate land, and the use of much of the timber from settlers' own property, timber that was valuable to them but worthless to the navy, was declared illegal. The law clearly was inequitable, and it was unrealistic to think that people would not break it.

As Wentworth sailed east to Nova Scotia, where he reserved a two hundred thousand-acre tract of pitch, Norway, and white pine for the navy, he likely considered and reconsidered various alternatives to Britain's present timber policy in America. In fact, it would not be long before he was provided additional impetus to formulate a viable plan of his own. In October he was threatened with court action by a group of wealthy Massachusetts landowners who claimed that mastcutters, with authorization from Wentworth, were infringing on their private property rights by taking trees in a large tract of land along the Kennebec River. Wentworth believed that under existing law the trees belonged to the Crown, and to prove it, he initiated action himself in the admiralty court. The case was eventually decided in favor of the Kennebec proprietors on the basis of ownership of the land prior to 1691, but before it was over, Wentworth had devised and proposed new timber regulations that he believed would be more beneficial to all parts of the British Empire. Instead of a blanket reservation of white pines or setting aside large tracts of woods such as that in Nova Scotia, Wentworth called for a small reservation of forest lands in every new town and inducements for individuals to preserve for the Crown the best trees on their own land. This plan would save the best trees for masts, make them less isolated and thus easier to get out, and allow settlers the use of the timber growing on their own property. Nevertheless, there was no guarantee that his ideas would be accepted, and until any changes were made, John Wentworth, as in all cases involving royal authority, was dedicated to upholding existing law. To that purpose, he felt his trip to Maine and Nova Scotia had been a success. After eight days of sailing from Halifax, he was back in New Hampshire before the first of September.[16]

On his return, Wentworth found two disconcerting letters waiting for him, one from Hillsborough and the other from Rockingham. Both involved criticism from Whitehall, and in particular, by the American secretary. Hillsborough's letter, dated 15 July, was in reaction to the New Hampshire governor's attempt to ease his province's currency problems. An act of assembly setting the value of silver and gold coins circulating in the province had been disallowed in England because it contradicted a similar act of Parliament devised by Sir Isaac Newton and passed in 1704 during the reign of Queen Anne. On learning of the action taken by the home government, the assembly complained that the parliamentary act did not cover the coins that were known in New Hampshire, many of which were Spanish and Portuguese, and thus was useless in the colony. Monetary transactions were in confusion because no one knew what money was worth. In the spring of 1769, the House had declared that this matter was another one that would have to be cleared up before a supply bill could be granted. As a temporary expedient, until a more permanent answer could be found, Wentworth had agreed to issue a proclamation setting the value of the foreign coins in English shillings. He signed the proclamation in March and in May informed the secretary of state of his action.[17]

As John Wentworth read Hillsborough's July letter, there was no mistaking the secretary's opinion of the proclamation. It was, he informed the governor, "a matter of as much consequence as has come before me, not only since I have been Secretary of State, but since my first coming to the Board of Trade." Hillsborough saw the proclamation as a clear contravention of the act of Parliament of 1704, and, as he told Wentworth, it was not justified "by your Instructions as Governor, by the Arguments you make use of in your Letter, or by the Interests of the Colony." He was referring the matter to the Privy Council.[18]

Wentworth was furious. He had gone to great lengths to preserve peace in his colony, and he had hoped his efforts would stand him in good stead with the British government. The relative tranquility in New Hampshire had been commented on favorably, but now he found himself in trouble anyway, merely, he believed, for doing something that was good for the colony and that in no way could be harmful to England. Possibly worse than his own immediate trouble with England was the added difficulty this rebuke might cause him in keeping the peace at home. To many New Hampshire colonists, this action could give validity to the cries of arbitrary and unjust authority that were continuously repeated in neighboring Massachusetts. With great reserve, Wentworth wrote

165

Hillsborough that everyone had agreed the proclamation was "the only prudent expedient that cou'd preserve the Province from immediate dissolution." The disallowance of recent acts of assembly, he went on as a way of warning, had already "exceedingly alarmed the minds of the People" and made them more susceptible to arguments being raised against government.[19]

In a letter to Rockingham on the same day, Wentworth was more open about his frustration. Other provinces had passed bills identical to New Hampshire's, he told the marquis, yet none of them had been disallowed. The rejection of this act had left the people of the province not knowing the equivalents of shillings, pounds, or pence. Taxes could not be collected, thus the supply could not be granted. Because Whitehall had not provided "the lest instruction, what to Substitute in lieu of money," Wentworth explained, the only alternative to total chaos was the proclamation. "The Country already inflamed almost beyond human power to restrain," he continued,

> it surely was my duty to embrace the only method that cou'd preserve the King's province from direct Ruin—which has kept all things just as they were. Our Judges have no Salaries and wou'd have resign'd directly, neither would have any others taken their Seats in such a circumstance. Creditors wou'd have been ruin'd and Debtors skreen'd from justice. This is absolutely the Fact; And whatever may be its other consequences, I rejoice that it has accomplish'd the preservation of a good Province from confusion, bloodshed and total distruction. I can therefore so far join with his Lordship [Hillsborough] in its being a matter of importance That I verily think That I shou'd have richly deserv'd to have lost my head, had I not prevented the threatned evils by this the only possible means that was left to me.[20]

The governor allowed his resentment and indignation even freer rein in a letter to Paul Wentworth. He was incredulous that New Hampshire, among the most obedient of provinces, should be "the first to feel the hand of ministerial Resentment." If objections were voiced by the government to measures such as his proclamation, there was no telling what kind of opposition Britain would arouse against its policies in the colonies. "Good God," Wentworth exclaimed to his relative, "what Governor will not rather throw this Province into Confusion rather than risque any Measure not verbatim instructed. I believe it would cost Government more than 6000 Guineas p an[m] not very importantly employed if we take all as it is literally written." Hillsborough's criticism he found "ludicrous."[21]

As if Hillsborough's letter was not enough to spoil Wentworth's return from

his profitable trip into the woods, the second letter awaiting him, from Rockingham, contained a reminder of another instance of Hillsborough's displeasure
with his conduct. This missive concerned an admiralty case involving his uncle,
Daniel Rindge. In May 1767, one of Ringe's ships, purportedly on a trading
voyage to Newfoundland, was forced by bad weather into the harbor of the
French island of Micquelon. Detected by the British navy, the ship was seized
and condemned without trial in a court of admiralty. Rindge believed he had
been treated unjustly and sent a memorial for redress of his grievance to agent
Trecothick for presentation in England. In October 1767, he also sent a petition
to the governor and to his fellow members of the council seeking support for
his claim.[22]

Wentworth took an active interest in the case. While it was still under consideration by the admiralty court, he wrote to the judge in support of his uncle.
The following spring (1768), in his report to the secretary of state, Wentworth
enclosed Rindge's petition to the governor and council and offered his opinion of the proceedings against the Portsmouth merchant. It was apparent, he
urged, that Rindge was innocent because the goods carried by his ship were the
same as those used by the people on the French island for payment in trade.
The people of Micquelon would not want the same items coming in that were
going out. Wentworth felt it was unfortunate that the proof for Rindge's innocence had not been considered in the trial, especially since the ramifications of
the decision went beyond just one merchant. As he explained to Hillsborough,
the case "has alarm'd the Trade here with unusual apprehensions for the Safety
of all their foreign Navigation, which is their Dependence." That kind of arbitrary and unjustified action would hurt fair trade, slow the demand for British
goods, and diminish respect for the trade laws. It was particularly unfortunate
that it had happened to a New Hampshire merchant, Wentworth pointed out,
because there had been no opposition in the province to the regulation of trade
and because it was especially important at this time for prudence to prevail in
relations between the colonies and England.[23]

A year later, in March 1769, Hillsborough wrote back that, as far as he could
see, the case had been properly prosecuted and any appeal should have gone to
the admiralty court. Further, he felt the council had overstepped its jurisdiction
in giving an opinion on the verdict. Now, in September, Wentworth received
news from Rockingham that Hillsborough was irritated that the governor had
involved himself in the case at all. Sympathizing with Wentworth's position,
the marquis offered some advice. "Tho' I know you would not brook any little
sharpness, if any there should be," he wrote, "Let your Answer be quite Calm."
Wentworth should explain, continued Rockingham, that he had felt it "a point

167

of duty to send any information which might be of use and which might point out any real hardship under which anyone in N[orth] America might labour."[24]

168

In fact, that was what Wentworth had thought he was doing, and he did not understand this criticism from Hillsborough. He had been especially careful, he wrote back to Rockingham, not to comment on the merits of the case but only to point out how it might affect the province in a general way. The mild appeal for redress and the concurrence in it by the governor and council had, he claimed, headed off trouble for the English government. He explained that handling the matter in this way "prevented an universal petition from all the Continent against all Courts of Admiralty and a positive determination not to appear at or be impleaded in them." Otherwise, the Rindge case "wou'd have been the wish'd for instance on which to ground their utter refusal of Admiralty Jurisdiction in America." "I was much surprised," Wentworth went on, "that this part of my duty had not given satisfaction." Hillsborough's entire "manner," he wrote with discouragement, "almost precludes me any use in answering."[25]

These two instances of chastisement by the home government—for his proclamation setting the value of coins in New Hampshire and for his interest in Daniel Rindge's admiralty case—were frustrating and disheartening for Wentworth. He was doing his best to keep a difficult situation under control in the interests of royal authority, yet the British ministry seemed set on undermining all of his efforts. Rejection of the coin proclamation would add burdens to New Hampshire's already difficult financial situation, cause resentment of British colonial policy, and make Wentworth's task of preventing disorder in these tenuous times more difficult. The kind of arbitrary and unjust decision involved in the Rindge case served as a hindrance instead of a help to trade and the mercantile system. And Hillsborough's reaction was yet another example of the ministerial insensitivity that was promoting obstruction of British policy rather than attempting to facilitate its acceptance. This situation was exactly opposite to what Wentworth had hoped for when he left England. Key elements in his vision of a successful system of empire were an enlightened administration at home and strong, knowledgeable governors in the colonies with enough independence to do what was necessary to insure the workability of Britain's colonial policy. Unfortunately, from Wentworth's point of view, the present ministers were not farsighted enough to let governors take needed steps for restoring faith and tranquility in the provinces. Instead, with its arbitrary, uninformed pronouncements, Whitehall was defeating its own purposes and putting the colonial governor in an extremely difficult position. It is not surprising that Wentworth in the fall of 1769 was especially desirous that the Rockingham Whigs should return to power in Westminster.[26]

The customs board in Boston had foolishly provoked trouble for itself, for other royal officials, and for British policy in general. Now the ministers in London were exhibiting a similar lack of wisdom. Those developments had much to do with Wentworth's deepening pessimism about the prospects for improved relations between the colonies and Great Britain. He may also have been reflecting on the strong convictions he had heard on both sides of the dispute in Boston in June when he wrote to Rockingham in September that, though the trouble in the colonies was "first impell'd by vexation and passion into Excess, it now seems subsiding into principle and System, infinitely more likely to get rooted than all the former Noise and Clamor." He wished, he told the marquis, that he could believe that conditions in the colonies were returning to their previous state, but he could not. If something was not done soon to allay colonial "apprehensions and jealousies," he warned, the American colonies would "be forever the cause of difficulty and trouble to Gr[eat] Britain."[27]

To be forced to this conclusion was especially discouraging for Wentworth because he had done so much himself to bolster royal authority in America. His greatest accomplishment, he believed, lay in preventing any open protest from his province against the trade laws, but his efforts had not ended there. The energies he expended tramping the woods were not solely for the practical purpose of preserving masts for the navy. Just as important, and in Wentworth's mind related to the overall problem of respect for royal government in America, was the need to demonstrate the strength and immediacy of parliamentary law. Although he was not in favor of the British troops in Boston, he willingly cooperated with General Gage when called upon. On hearing in March that some of Gage's men had deserted and were being concealed in the vicinity of Londonderry, New Hampshire, the governor issued a proclamation against harboring such soldiers.[28] At that very time he was also devising a plan to advance the Anglican church in New Hampshire, a development he strongly believed would do much to promote close ties between the people of his province and the mother country and encourage reverence for British authority in general.

The Anglican church owed its beginnings in New Hampshire to the efforts of Benning Wentworth and his friends, who in the 1730s were looking for a means of political leverage that would be of use in England against the designs of Massachusetts.[29] The Portsmouth parish was founded then, and after becoming governor, Benning continued his support by setting aside one lot in every township he granted for the use of the Society for the Propagation of the Gospel (SPG), the missionary arm of the Church of England. The church had not taken advantage of this bequest, however, and no new parishes were established during his term. John Wentworth now wanted to build on his uncle's groundwork and advance the church, for he saw Anglicanism as a potentially important ally within his province.

Wentworth had a definite plan in mind, which he disclosed to Joseph Harrison in late September 1769. He wanted to see one Anglican minister established each year in New Hampshire. His method called for the SPG to place several missionaries in towns at fifty pounds a year each. With the ministers living and working on the society's reserved lots in the towns, the property would increase rapidly in value and soon be capable of providing support for more missionaries, each of whom would repeat the process. In this way the church could be expanded dramatically with little initial investment. Wentworth envisioned forty new parishes within the first ten years. Now was the time to start, he told Harrison, for schism was fracturing all churches in the province, and the Anglicans could take advantage of the situation by serving the many new settlers who were eager for religion but too poor to support it. Wentworth hoped to begin by having a chaplain appointed to himself who would form a parish in Wolfeboro and neighboring towns.

Wentworth realized that the expansion of the Church of England was a sensitive issue in all of the colonies, including New Hampshire. It had become especially so as resentment grew against British policy in America. He thus warned that his program would have to be implemented slowly, the new missionaries not to make open attempts to proselytize. He stressed that the greatest "Caution, Prudence, and Secrecy" would need to be exercised in order not to provoke a backlash. Certainly there were risks involved, but there was no question for Wentworth that they were worth taking. The Anglican church would be given a great boost in New Hampshire by this plan, and, probably most important during these difficult times, it would be a significant aid in securing and spreading allegiance to royal authority. Religion, the governor explained to Harrison, "is part of a Man's political Character," and a more vigorous Anglican establishment in New Hampshire, he believed, "wou'd produce very desirable effects in the Administration of civil Government."[30]

Joseph Harrison, a beaten man by this time, was leaving America for England. Wentworth was providing him this information to carry to the bishop of London. "I cordially venerate the Church of England," he told Harrison, "and hope to see it universal in this Province." The following spring, he repeated and expanded on his program in a letter to the bishop of London himself. Unfortunately for Wentworth, little came of the plan. During his years as governor, only one additional parish was established in New Hampshire, that at Claremont on the Connecticut River by SPG missionary Ranna Cossit. One itinerant minister was also sent, but he proved inadequate to the job. Even the Portsmouth church found itself in trouble. Following the death of the Reverend Arthur Browne in 1773, the church wardens and even Wentworth himself encountered great difficulty in getting support from the society for another clergyman to take his place.[31]

The SPG was guarding its resources closely and apparently did not feel that the expenditure of funds required by Governor Wentworth's program could be justified in one small province such as New Hampshire. The major reason, though, that the SPG did not follow up on Wentworth's plan to promote the church was the uncertain political situation in the colonies. The activities of the society in America were slowed significantly during this period, because of Whitehall's reluctance to approve a church policy that might additionally antagonize the colonists. Another reason for the society's stinginess with New Hampshire may have lain in the failure of Barlow Trecothick to lobby for Wentworth, as the governor had wished, at SPG headquarters in London. In the long run, it may have been just as well for Wentworth, because the Congregationalists, who made up the vast majority of the inhabitants of the province, became apprehensive about the little progress that was made by the Church of England.[32] Greater success in Anglican expansion, in contrast to Wentworth's belief, might have adversely affected his political position in the province, especially had his detailed instigation of it ever been discovered. That was one development, however, that he never had to worry about.

The criticism from Hillsborough awaiting Wentworth on his return from the forest had depressed him and seemed to magnify the problems between the colonies and England. In fact, in the fall of 1769, tension did remain high in many of the colonies, especially in Massachusetts, where resentment of the British soldiers stationed in Boston grew daily. Conditions in New Hampshire, though, returned to nearly normal, allowing Wentworth to turn his attention to matters other than politics. During the first week in November, he sat for John Singleton Copley, who came to Portsmouth to paint his portrait. Like the one done in London for Rockingham, this likeness was also intended for a close friend in England, Paul Wentworth.[33] Copley's painting shows a man considerably more mature and self-confident than the youthful governor-to-be of the English portrait three years earlier. Wentworth had gained experience rapidly in the office where British policy and provincial politics converged. A few days later occurred the most notable event in New Hampshire that autumn, a very personal one for the governor. At the age of thirty-two, he was married.

John Wentworth's marriage was made possible by the death, on 28 October, of Theodore Atkinson, Jr. A member of the council and since March successor to his aging father as secretary of the province, Atkinson died after a long battle

John Wentworth, 1769, by John Singleton Copley
(Hood Museum of Art, Dartmouth College,
Hanover, New Hampshire)

with tuberculosis, the same disease that had claimed Wentworth's brother the previous year.[34] His passing was thus no surprise. What must have been a shock, at least to some, was the marriage of his widow, Frances, to the governor of the province on 11 November, just ten days after her husband was buried. Frances   173
Wentworth Atkinson, John Wentworth's cousin, was only twenty-three at the time, although she had been married since she was sixteen. Wentworth had known her since his college days when he had visited his uncle Samuel Wentworth's house in Boston and she was only a child. Portsmouth lore has long fostered a story that the two carried on a heated romance behind her husband's back.[35] That legend may be true but by itself does not account for such a hasty wedding, an obvious breach of social decorum.

Wentworth later felt compelled to explain the circumstances in a long, defensive letter to Rockingham. Although he had proposed waiting, he told his patron, the marriage took place soon after the funeral on the insistence of his parents, who had long desired that he be married, and of old Benning Wentworth, who before he died wished to see his nephew take a wife. Even Colonel Atkinson, who was relieved that his son was out of his misery and who loved Frances like a daughter, gave the match his blessing and wished the ceremony to take place as soon as possible. Wentworth's aunt, Mrs. Atkinson, was equally in agreement, Wentworth claimed, because she herself felt she had not long to live. This account might have some validity, but a simpler, more accurate assessment of the circumstances within which the wedding took place probably can be found in another event—the birth of a son to John and Frances Wentworth less than seven months later. The child apparently did not live long, for no further mention of him can be found. Nevertheless, the fact that he was given a name, John, and was baptized seems to belie Wentworth's attempt to mask the event as a miscarriage, "Sustain'd from Mrs. Wentworth's being frighted by an attack of a large dog." [36]

Regardless of the circumstances, the wedding was a gala affair. It was performed by the Reverend Arthur Browne on the morning of Saturday, 11 November, "before thousands," as Wentworth later remembered. The governor was dressed in white silk stocking breeches, white coat, and blue silk waistcoat, all accented with gold buttons and lace. The attire of his bride must have contrasted sharply with the mourning she had worn in Queen's Chapel only days before. Ships flew their flags in the harbor, cannons were fired, and all the town bells were rung. Everyone seemed to enjoy the occasion, and if there was any impropriety, no one seemed to care.[37]

As winter set in, time passed uneventfully, doubtless to Wentworth's relief. In a February letter to Hillsborough, he reported that the "quiet peaceable and orderly State of the Province" left "Nothing of Importance to communicate." A

Frances Deering Wentworth, 1765, by John Singleton Copley
(Collection of the New York Public Library. Astor,
Lenox, and Tilden Foundations)

highly visible sign of the tranquility that prevailed in Portsmouth through the winter of 1769–1770 was the frigate HMS *Beaver* anchored in the harbor. Relations between her captain and crew and the townspeople remained exceedingly cordial. Early in January, Speaker Gilman laid before the assembly a set of resolves communicated by the Virginia Burgesses denouncing as unconstitutional a parliamentary proposal to have persons accused of treason in the colonies transferred to England for trial. The New Hampshire assembly took no further note of the resolutions before it adjourned at the end of the month. Neither was any heed being paid to the nonimportation agreements. John Wentworth happily told the colonial secretary that "Some Scott Merchants have to import their European Goods hither where [they] sell without the least Molestation." There was little sentiment of defiance in New Hampshire. This mood of accommodation could only have been encouraged by a circular letter from the colonial secretary to John Wentworth and his fellow governors. In his message, the earl of Hillsborough announced that the ministry, at the next session of Parliament, intended to propose the removal of all of the Townshend duties except the one on tea.[38]

Whatever his reasons, Wentworth was thankful for the peace in his province. It gave him not only hope for the future but also time to consider what he had accomplished in his nearly three years as governor. Great strides had been made toward his goals of improving New Hampshire internally and making it a productive part of the British Empire. His other aim and by this time his primary concern, that of keeping New Hampshire quiet and loyal, had been more difficult, largely because much of the situation was beyond his control. Nevertheless, he had expended all his efforts and here, too, had been successful. No nonimportation movement had taken hold in New Hampshire, and he had prevented any open protestation to the Crown against the revenue acts. Nevertheless, by late 1769 Wentworth was despairing for the general colonial situation because of the intemperance of radicals in the colonies, mainly in Massachusetts, but even more because of the lack of prudence and foresight exhibited by not only the customs commissioners in Boston but the ministry at Whitehall as well. He himself had felt the frustation of the arbitrary, unwise, actually destructive directives coming out of the colonial office. Rather than helping him maintain royal authority in his province, the policymakers in London were undermining his efforts.

By early 1770, however, there was some reason for optimism. Perhaps the news of the imminent repeal of most of the Townshend duties would cool colonial tempers and bring a return to reason and goodwill. Moreover, for beleaguered royal officials in the colonies such as John Wentworth, that development provided evidence for renewed faith in the wisdom and motives of the men who were running the British government.

»IO«
PRESERVING A
FRAGILE ORDER,
1770-1771

The delicate tranquility that John Wentworth was nurturing in New Hampshire was smashed by events in Boston on 5 March 1770. The slowly building bomb of human emotion, the hate and resentment growing between the townspeople and the British troops, finally exploded. A confrontation between a cursing, snowball-throwing mob, by now a common sight in Boston, and a party of grenadiers resulted in disaster. Goaded by insults, threats, and a barrage of missiles, the soldiers fired their muskets into the crowd killing five men. Although a tragic incident, this "massacre," as it was termed by Boston's radical press, served the purpose of Sam Adams and other leaders of the liberal party in arousing anti-British feeling to a new high.[1] As Governor Wentworth soon found out, that feeling was not confined by the boundaries of Massachusetts.

Two weeks after the shooting, the town of New Ipswich in New Hampshire agreed to join Boston's program of nonconsumption and boycott. At a town meeting on 26 March, Exeter voted to discourage the importation and consumption of British goods, to stop consuming tea, and to promote manufacturing in the colonies. Although not going that far, Portsmouth on 11 April banned further purchases from one McMasters, apparently the Scottish merchant who Wentworth had reported earlier was operating so successfully in town. Circumventing the Boston boycott, McMasters had been importing and selling British goods through Portsmouth with little trouble. Now anyone found dealing with him was to be branded "unfriendly to the Interest of his Country." Tavern keepers selling his goods would lose their licenses.[2]

Those were the first overt actions taken in New Hampshire in sympathy with the colonial boycott of British goods. But for John Wentworth, that was not the worst result of the Boston Massacre. More serious was an investigation by a committee in Exeter of the petition for redress of grievances that had been voted by the assembly in 1768 to be sent to the Crown. At the town meeting, it was reported that the petition had in November 1768 been sent to Speaker Gilman in Exeter for his signature, thence to be forwarded to New Hampshire's agent in London. It was discovered, however, that the petition was never sent because Gilman would not sign it unless he could add a postscript expressing his disagreement with its contents. The town hoped that this inaction would not be interpreted in England "as a Submission to the unconstitutional Revenue Acts." Exeter then voted that the petition be sent immediately and that expressions of New Hampshire's concurrence in the united cause against the British measures be forwarded to the other colonies.[3]

A writer in the *New Hampshire Gazette* wondered how such a lapse could have gone undetected all that time and raised questions concerning the assembly's role in the affair. On 14 April the assembly, offering no explanations, voted that "the Address to his Majesty which was prepared some time past . . . should now be forwarded." Hardly the firebrands of Massachusetts or Virginia, the New Hampshire representatives in a separate letter instructed Barlow Trecothick not to present the petition if the Townshend duties had been repealed. Making clear their intention in taking this action now, they told their agent, "If it has no other effect, . . . it may serve as a Remembrancer that we acted in Concert with our neighbors." To that end, the letter and resolves from Virginia that had been laid before the House in January were brought out again. This time an answer was prepared expressing concurrence with the burgesses' stand against Parliament's revival of the treason act that would send colonists accused of that crime to England for trial. Similar resolves from Maryland were also affirmatively answered. In addition, to ensure further that New Hampshire's failure to petition the Crown until now was not seen as weakness in the cause, a duplicate of the assembly's letter of 1768 expressing agreement with Virginia's petition of that year was made and sent along with the answer to the more recent letter.[4]

Wentworth watched helplessly as the flurry of anti-British activity swept through his province. Although the actions taken were mild and left intact New Hampshire's image as one of the more, if not the most, conservative of the colonies, for Wentworth they spoiled his record of having kept the province almost entirely free of opposition to Britain. This time there was no way he could prevent the petition from being sent. The assembly may have been cooperative at first, but now that the representatives' failure to follow up on the petition had been made public, he realized that for reasons of saving face they had no choice but to send it. Unfortunately for Wentworth, he had to report that fact and the other recent occurrences in New Hampshire to the earl of Hillsborough. He nevertheless made clear in his letter that his province was not alone. As he explained it, the killing of civilians by soldiers in Boston had "spread a flame like wildfire thro' all the Continent." Had it not been for that, he went on, the assembly's petition, "which has laid on their Table neglected for two years," would "have slept for ever."

For Hillsborough, the governor naturally wanted to put the situation in the best possible light. He assured the secretary that the petition was "much more moderate than any other that has been sent" and, stretching the truth, asserted that the instructions to New Hampshire's agent directed him not to present it if its "Contents should render it inexpedient." In fact, the assembly's instructions said nothing about the petition's contents; the only condition under which suppression was approved was the repeal of the Townshend duties. Wentworth also emphasized that largely because of his own unstinting efforts, peace had been maintained in New Hampshire. And he pointed out that, although the merchant McMasters was being boycotted, it had been voted that he should suffer no abuse.[5]

Wentworth nevertheless did not try to hide the fact that feelings were running high against Great Britain. "I never saw such an exasperated spirit in this Province," he told Hillsborough. Everyone was convinced, he continued, that the customs commissioners and the revenue acts were designed to "absorb the property and destroy the Lives of the people." Reason was of no use to dissuade them. Adding to Wentworth's miseries at this time were "a violent Rheumatic Complaint" and the ironic fact that, when he wrote to Hillsborough on 12 April, he had been playing host for nearly three weeks to William Burch and Henry Hulton, two members of the customs board in Boston. Following the massacre, the eruption of feeling against British officials in Boston had compelled all of the commissioners except John Temple to flee the city. Governor Wentworth was not far away, and his reputation for keeping the peace and maintaining loyalty to the Crown made Portsmouth a logical place for Burch and Hulton to seek asylum until tempers had cooled. They undoubtedly did not know of Wentworth's strong feelings against the customs board and its activities, and one can only speculate on the degree of cordiality extended to the men by the governor during their stay. As a fellow royal official, he was of course obligated to be of assistance, but they did not make his job any easier. When it was known the commissioners were in town, attempts were made to start a riot against them.

Wentworth was able to quell the incipient uprising but warned that if Charles Paxton, another member of the board, showed up in Portsmouth he would not be able to guarantee the safety of any of them.[6]

Prospects looked bleak to John Wentworth in mid-April 1770. But things were not as bad as they seemed, and conditions in New Hampshire gradually began to improve again. By the end of the month, one potential source of trouble evaporated when Hulton and Burch departed for Brookline, near Boston, where Hulton lived.[7] Neither did the disclosure that the petition to the Crown had not been sent prove to be a problem for Wentworth. It was common knowledge that he had been against it, and, as the king's representative, it must have been expected that he would try to discourage the assembly from sending it. Any fault for not forwarding the petition after it had been voted to do so lay with the speaker and, seemingly, other members of the assembly who did not speak up. Peter Gilman lost his seat at the next election, but the popularity of the governor did not appear to suffer as a result of this incident.

The nascent boycott movement in New Hampshire never got off the ground. In July the town of Portsmouth appointed a committee to draw up resolutions on nonimportation. There was sentiment for the movement when the committee reported back, but Woodbury Langdon, a committee member, prevented any resolves from being adopted. Boston threatened to cut off trade with the recalcitrant merchants of Portsmouth if they did not take some positive action, but by that time it was too late. By May, word had arrived in America of the repeal of all the Townshend duties except the one on tea, which Parliament insisted be retained as a symbol of its right to tax the colonies. With that news, the impetus to continue the boycott of British goods disappeared. One by one the major ports, New York, Philadelphia, even Boston, diluted their nonimportation agreements so that by the fall of 1770 the movement was virtually dead.[8]

In October Wentworth could report to the secretary of state that a mood of peace was solidly entrenched in New Hampshire. Again he took the credit for removing the people's doubts and fears and explained that he had kept the peace by announcing he would oppose in person any unlawful action. But the citizens of his province had been cooperative. Attempts by the "Hydra headed demagogues at Boston" to stir up trouble in Portsmouth, he told Hillsborough, had been of no avail. Neither had Boston's scheme "to Starve and compel" New Hampshire into its "Combination" disaffected the people. In fact, it was only the maintenance of the rule of law in New Hampshire that had prevented an emissary of the Massachusetts radicals from being tarred and feathered and run out of town. Wentworth was obviously pleased to be able to tell the colonial secretary that the crisis of the Boston Massacre had passed and that reason and loyalty to government had returned to New Hampshire with, as he believed, "a degree of Success, that is Singular in the Provinces of America."[9]

In New Hampshire, as in most of the other colonies for the next several years following the demise of the nonimportation movement, there was no serious trouble. Although the tax on tea had been retained, the repeal of the remaining Townshend duties pushed the dispute between the colonies and England into the background. Under this prevailing calm, the governor, assembly, and people alike were able to concentrate on and enjoy more positive developments within the province. In March 1771 Wentworth was finally able to announce to the assembly that the act for dividing the province into counties had been approved by the king in council. It had been over two years since the measure was passed, and everyone, not least the governor, was relieved and pleased with the news. The following week, in an uncharacteristic act of generosity, the assembly voted Wentworth one hundred pounds "for sundry Extra services Render'd the Province."[10] This reward no doubt related directly to the governor's effort in securing the much desired county division.

In April, Barlow Trecothick forwarded equally exciting news. By vote of the Commons, New Hampshire was at last to receive its claim for expenses for the last war, more than six thousand pounds. Wentworth had worked on this project himself when he was in England, and many no doubt had given up any hope of ever seeing the money. Such a sum, nearly three times the annual supply, meant a great deal to a small province like New Hampshire. In December, Wentworth informed the assembly that the payment had been made. At the same time, he put in a personal plea for reimbursement for expenses incurred while serving in England in what he termed the "unavoidably expensive and peculiarly laborious agency for this Province." He told the representatives that he had not previously wanted to burden the taxpayers with this request. Undoubtedly, the real reason for the delay had been his realization that he had no chance of collecting. It was hard enough just to talk the assembly out of a meager salary. Now, however, his instincts were right. In January 1772, the assembly, feeling generous with its newfound wealth, voted Wentworth five hundred pounds for "extraordinary services."[11]

At the same time they honored another request by the governor. Samuel Holland, his majesty's surveyor for the northern district of North America, had offered his services during the winter to carry out a detailed survey of New Hampshire. Because Wentworth's instructions called for such an assessment of the province bounds, he was anxious to take advantage of Holland's offer. Although the House had refused a similar request before, it now approved the sum required for the survey.[12]

The lower portion of a map of New Hampshire
surveyed by Samuel Holland in the 1770s.
(New Hampshire Historical Society)

Relations between the governor and the assembly in New Hampshire were obviously good. But Wentworth was not lulled by this new surge of internal harmony into believing that the cleavage between the colonies and Great Britain was mended. There was ample evidence that, although the immediate crisis had abated, the root problems had not been solved. In November 1770, Wentworth's hopes that the ministry had become more sensitive to the situation in America were dealt another blow when John Temple was removed from the customs board in Boston. Temple, who had married into the Bowdoin family, was closely linked with Boston's whig element. Governor Bernard and the other commissioners considered him an obstructionist in the way of their policy, and Bernard requested his removal. Wentworth, however, felt John Temple was the only competent member of the American customs commission. When Bernard's request was granted, New Hampshire's governor readily wrote recommendations for Temple to carry to England in his attempt to vindicate his conduct and, if possible, secure a better position. For Wentworth, this dismissal was yet another example of Whitehall aggravating rather than improving the situation in America.[13]

Signs were abundant, too, that the colonists had not forgotten the dispute. In March 1771, on the first anniversary of the Boston Massacre, a contributor to the *New Hampshire Gazette* recommended an annual commemoration of the event as a warning to the people to remain alert against their enslavement by tyrants.[14] More serious was an incident the following October when mob action against the customs service surfaced in Portsmouth for the first time. On the twenty-sixth, the brig *Resolution*, owned principally by Portsmouth merchant Samuel Cutts, entered its cargo without problem at the Piscataqua Customs House.[15] Two days later, however, the collector of the port, suspecting that the *Resolution*'s master had not reported all of the dutiable molasses on board, seized the ship and part of its cargo. The collector, new at his post, was George Meserve, the former stamp distributor who had been threatened and forced to give up that position at the time of the Stamp Act.

Meserve had only two tidewaiters to guard the vessel until trial could be held in the vice-admiralty court, and he asked Wentworth for help. The governor responded by ordering Captain Cochran and four of his men from Fort William and Mary to board the *Resolution*. The armed guard not withstanding, at midnight on 29 October 1771 fifty armed and disguised men suddenly "appeard on Deck." They locked the waiters in the cabin and ordered the captain and his men off the ship. Refusing to be cowed, Cochran and the soldiers held their position on the quarterdeck but were helpless to prevent the removal of forty to fifty hogsheads of molasses that had not been legally entered. By the time the collector could call out the sheriff and the magistrates, the men and molasses had disappeared, and the town was quiet.

One week later the molasses on which the duty had been paid was also forcibly removed from the ship. The rest of the *Resolution*'s cargo was condemned when trial was held in admiralty court on the fourteenth of November. At that time, tidewaiter Jesse Saville, who was known to be an informer for the customs service in Massachusetts, was called to testify. Word soon spread, and when Saville emerged from the trial at dusk, he found a crowd of about five hundred "Sailors, Labourers and Boys" waiting for him. He was chased through the streets, caught, and was being knocked around when several "Gentlemen" happened by who rescued him and broke up the mob. Hearing the noise and confusion, Wentworth himself headed out into the streets and, as he told Hillsborough, "walk'd unattended and publickly thro' the midst of those remaining."

What he found was a residue of some three hundred people from the mob loitering about in small "knots" of six to twelve. Expecting trouble, Wentworth was ready to call out every law officer in New Hampshire if necessary. Fortunately it was not. Although both he and the customs officials were in the street, no noise or sign of disrespect was raised against any of them, "as is evident," he reported to Hillsborough, "for my Chariot pass'd uninterruptedly thro' them four times." Nevertheless, he had seen in his own province what could happen when the revenue laws were rigidly enforced. Wentworth admitted that Meserve's methods were new to New Hampshire. He felt, however, that it had been the right thing to do and that the *Resolution*'s owner, Samuel Cutts, deserved to lose his cargo. The whole episode of the *Resolution*, occurring in an overwhelmingly loyal province such as his own and at a time when peace and tranquility had seemed to return to all of the colonies, was just more evidence to support Wentworth's by now pessimistic belief that the differences between the colonies and England had become deep-seated and would not disappear with superficial solutions.

In spite of the repeal of the Townshend duties and the demise of nonimportation, Wentworth became increasingly negative about the situation in America. His somber outlook stemmed largely from what he detected as a very subtle yet definite hardening of attitude on the part of the colonists. Late in 1770, just as conditions were returning to a semblance of normality, he wrote to Rockingham, "The change of manners and sentiment . . . are so gradual, and marked with such imperceptible effects, that time only can discover them." Violence could be suppressed, but, he went on, "I verily think a far more dangerous spirit is thereby rooting in the minds of the people—who begin to think Gr[eat] Britain intends to enslave and destroy them by mere force—whence it is easy to see a settled gloom and inquietude take place every where." This deepening belief by the people that Britain was now determined to oppress them was, in Wentworth's opinion, "much more important than all the noise and reprehensible violences that have preceded this time." As he told Rockingham, "This is such a marking period in American affairs, that I dare not omit mentioning it."[16]

What Wentworth seemed to be saying was that the disturbances in the colonies had been fomented by only a small group of people. Britain's reaction, however, was having the effect of turning many more colonists against the mother country. That mistake was a fatal one from which there might be no turning back. By July 1771 Wentworth's viewpoint had not changed. The "present calm" he attributed to "Supression" rather than "eradication." Although he was not overtly critical of the government at Whitehall, he made clear to Rockingham his belief that the ministry could and should embark on a more enlightened policy if ultimate disaster were to be averted. "Alienation," he wrote, "takes deeper Root in these quieter times than when much evaporated in passion: And I do verily believe America is lost to England unless some conciliatory means of mutual use and safety are adopted. There is no doubt but that Gr[eat] Britain can subdue and Subordinate America; but it may be apprehended that such a vast extended Continent of disgusted Subjects wou'd be extremely useless if not finally detrimental."[17]

To Wentworth, force was not the answer; rather, the only viable solution lay in the same theme that he had advocated to Rockingham at the time of the Stamp Act and which he now repeated. The only realistic expectation for continued harmony between England and her colonies, he wrote, lay in "the reciprocal benefit of both." America and Britain should "be inviolably cemented by mutual interest—the only sufficient bond of durable connection between countries or even Members of the Same country."[18] Wentworth perceptively realized that a continued preoccupation in Britain with the right of Parliament to legislate for the colonies in all cases, as evidenced by the retention of the duty on tea, would serve only to drive America further into opposition. What was needed in England were some moderate, prudent, and, most of all, practical minds in the government who realized that the most effective, and in the long run profitable, policy was one that maximized advantages for all parts of the empire by minimizing restrictions on trade. Wentworth more than ever wished the Rockingham Whigs back in power.

Although attitudes seemed to be changing for the worse, the general calm that had settled over America was welcome. It not only gave Rockingham, Burke, and other friends of the colonies in England a chance to try to improve the situation there, it allowed Wentworth to devote some time to the particular interest of New Hampshire.[19] One concern especially occupied the governor's mind until nearly the end of 1771—his desire to regain jurisdiction over the land west of the Connecticut River, that area decreed part of New York by the Order in Council of 1764.

Wentworth's interest in this region is easily understood. Bounded by the Connecticut on the east, and in the west by Lake Champlain and a line roughly twenty miles east of the Hudson, this area, which would later become the state of Vermont, would have doubled the size of New Hampshire. Abounding in tall pine forests and fertile river valleys, it had been too great a temptation to Benning Wentworth, who had granted townships covering half the area.[20] It also loomed large in the eyes of his successor, who was making a concerted effort to improve the fortunes of his province through a program of settling and developing the interior. With fewer and fewer lands left to grant east of the Connecticut, it was only natural that New Hampshire's governor should begin to look longingly at the millions of acres of virtually virgin soil to the west. This land was an obvious place for the expansion of New Hampshire settlement, especially in the Connecticut River valley, a region with a natural unity of its own. Although a large number of towns had been granted, not many had actually been settled. In 1765 an estimated 225 families on each side of the Green Mountains were scattered thinly throughout a few towns.[21] Here, then, was a great expanse of valuable land just waiting to yield its riches to the woodsman's ax and the farmer's spade. New Hampshire might profit enormously from the resources of this region.

Another source of encouragement for Wentworth's interest west of the Connecticut lay in the number of important New Hampshire residents who owned land there. Thanks to Benning Wentworth, many leading merchants of Portsmouth, councillors, and members of the assembly had received grants in the area. Daniel Warner was made an original proprietor in fifty-one different townships; Theodore Atkinson, Sr. and Jr., held seventy-three proprietorships between them; and John Wentworth's father, Mark Hunking Wentworth, between 1760 and 1764 received shares in thirty-seven towns west of the Connecticut River. Those proprietors, as well as the majority of grantees from other provinces such as New York and Connecticut, were holding their shares for speculative purposes. They, too, had high hopes for the development of the region and would welcome New Hampshire's control over it. Yet New Hampshire, despite Benning Wentworth's boldness, had never had clear title to the land, and the decision in England in 1764 had seemingly decided jurisdiction once and for all in favor of New York.[22] Subsequent events, however, generated renewed hope for New Hampshire's claim.

In 1765 settlers occupying New Hampshire grants west of the Green Moun-

187

tains became alarmed when they encountered Isaac Vrooman, a surveyor working for James Duane and several other New York speculators who claimed the land they were living on under a patent issued by Lieutenant Governor Cadwallader Colden of New York. The inhabitants were informed that they might either buy or lease the land, land that they assumed they already owned. An order was shortly issued by the New York council that no actual settler should be dispossessed of his property. Soon, however, both settlers and the vastly larger numbers of nonresident proprietors were disturbed by the realization that, to maintain possession of their land, they would have to pay relatively high fees for confirmatory patents from New York. For both settlers living at subsistence level and proprietors owning large tracts of land, that exaction would be disastrous. In addition, they would be subject to New York quitrents, which were considerably higher than those of New Hampshire. The New Hampshire grantees were finally goaded into action by Governor Henry Moore and the New York council. In June 1766 an order was issued that all those holding New Hampshire titles must have them confirmed by New York within three months or face the loss of their land.[23]

In the fall of 1766, several meetings of settlers and nonresident proprietors held in Massachusetts and New York resulted in a decision to petition the king. Arguing that the high fees and quitrents demanded by New York were an intolerable burden, the petitioners asked that their original titles be confirmed and that jurisdiction over land west of the Connecticut River be vested in New Hampshire. Appointed to present the petitions and work for their acceptance in England were Samuel Robinson, a resident of Bennington, the oldest town in the grants and named for John Wentworth's uncle, and William Samuel Johnson, a lawyer and special agent for Connecticut who had a reputation as a very able man. The agents presented their case in March 1767 and, at the same time, enlisted a powerful ally, the Society for the Propagation of the Gospel. In all of Benning Wentworth's grants, shares had been set aside for the Church of England and for the SPG. Now, in a petition to the king drawn up by Johnson for the SPG, New York was charged with regranting those lands without reserving the customary shares for the church and the society. The SPG claimed it thus was being divested of what rightfully belonged to it. The efforts of Johnson and Robinson appeared to be paying off when the king in council, on 24 July 1767, ordered the governor of New York to cease making grants in the area "until his Majesty's further Pleasure shall be known."[24] The restraining order on New York promised nothing to the New Hampshire grantees, but, significantly, it gave them hope.

Up to this time, New Hampshire had taken no part in the controversy between the grantees and New York. It was not long before that situation changed. Given a new lease on life by the order in council, the proprietors of the New Hampshire grants were determined to press on for victory. Looking for help wherever they could find it, they were persuaded that their case would be greatly enhanced if the governor and legislature of New Hampshire could be enlisted as allies in the cause. Accordingly, on 18 October 1768, John Wendell of Portsmouth, who had been appointed American agent by the proprietors petitioning the king, presented a memorial to Governor John Wentworth, the council, and the assembly, on behalf of more than one thousand grantees of lands west of the Connecticut River explaining their desire to have the area "re-annexed" to New Hampshire. Wendell also included an extract of a letter from William Samuel Johnson "from which may be deduced," he pointed out, "that if the legislature of this Province would join with the said Grantees in their application to his Majesty in Council, the one for the Jurisdiction, and the other for the Property of said Lands, there is a great Probability of success to both." Johnson had written to Wendell proclaiming his surprise that New Hampshire had not taken a more active part in attempting to get the lands back and suggesting that, had the province been more aggressive, jurisdiction would probably have been regained by now.

The legislature took no immediate action on the memorial. Wendell's plea, however, stimulated the interest of Governor Wentworth, whose thoughts now turned to the enticing prospect of a New Hampshire doubled in size by the addition of land west of the Connecticut. The matter was put before him again at the end of November when Wendell, upon hearing of the death of Samuel Robinson in England, sent him another petition on behalf of the proprietors. This time, two additional reasons were presented to support the case for New Hampshire jurisdiction. The grantees complained that under New York they had to travel great distances for the administration of justice and that the organization of local government was not of the constitutional type they were familiar with. New York made no provision for representative government as exercised in the New England town meeting.[25] Very shortly, another problem emerged that provided John Wentworth the opportunity to take action on his own.

In December 1768 Wentworth was visited in Portsmouth by one William Dean, an inhabitant of Windsor on the far side of the Connecticut River. Dean told the governor that he had been trying to get the trees on his land surveyed so that he might know which ones he could legally cut. He claimed that Benjamin Whiting, a resident of Newbury upriver from Windsor and one of Wentworth's deputy surveyors, had not responded to his requests. Dean then asked that he be appointed a deputy surveyor himself. Wentworth did not want to make any

189

more appointments, but while Dean was still in the governor's office, Whiting and another deputy, Captain John Peters, came in and promised that they would do the job. With that assurance, Dean returned home.[26]

Early in January 1769, however, Wentworth received information from Israel Curtis, another Windsor resident, that William Dean was illegally cutting mast trees. Wentworth determined to go himself and put a stop to this brazen depredation by a man who, less than a month earlier, had met with him and asked to become a deputy surveyor. Despite what he described as a "painful Rheumatic Complaint in my Breast, which extends to my Neck and throat," Wentworth, in the middle of January during one of the bitterest winters in years, set off on horseback for the Connecticut River.[27] He traveled, as he later explained, "three hundred miles in excessive Cold and Snow, thro' a Wilderness, almost uninhabited." The effort, however, proved worthwhile. Crossing the ice on the Connecticut, Wentworth caught the unsuspecting Deans—William and his sons William, Jr., and Willard—red-handed in the act of cutting mast pines. Over five hundred logs lay on the frozen river waiting for the spring thaw to float them to sawmills in Massachusetts. Three trees were still on the ground that measured from thirty-two to forty-four inches in diameter, well over the legal cutting limit of twenty-four inches. Wentworth, in addition, had three witnesses willing to testify to seventeen logs cut by the Deans in December that measured between twenty-eight and forty inches.[28]

Among those with the governor in his confrontation with the Deans was a mastliner who for many years had worked the yards in Portsmouth. He described the seized logs as among "the best and prettyest Timber he had ever seen." According to another witness, Elijah Granger, with whom William Dean had contracted for the lumber, Wentworth told Dean: "Mr. Dean, you have been guilty of a very ungodly trick. You are the person who applyed to me at Portsmouth for a Deputation to be a Surveyor. You would have made fine havock by being a Surveyor." Also present was Benjamin Wait, one of Dean's neighbors, who pointed out that most of the cutting had not even taken place on Dean's land.[29] With all the evidence he needed, Wentworth did not tarry. He hurried back to Portsmouth to institute proceedings against the Deans in the admiralty court.

Wentworth was concerned about this flagrant violation of the pine laws. Shortly after returning from his trek across New Hampshire, he wrote to Jared Ingersoll, the one-time enemy of the Wentworth family who now was judge of vice admiralty at New Haven, requesting that process be initiated against the Deans. But devotion to his duty as surveyor general of the woods had not been the only reason driving Wentworth three hundred miles through the wilderness in the forbidding elements of a frigid New Hampshire January. He also had been thinking about the possibility of regaining jurisdiction west of the Connecticut River. His interest in that project rekindled, probably by John Wendell's petitions of late 1768, Wentworth, while he was in Windsor, seems to have met with Nathan Stone, a political leader of the town and a fierce opponent of New York authority. Not surprisingly, on the second Tuesday in March, the traditional New Hampshire day for holding town meetings, Windsor held a meeting to organize its town government, proceeding in accordance with New Hampshire rather than New York practice.³⁰

There is little question of Wentworth's feeling at that time. He told William Bayard that the 1764 boundary decision in England had been made "upon false, absurd and iniquitous Misinformation." Neither was the governor the only one who was concerned, for as he explained to Bayard, "Many Gentlemen of respect and property" in Portsmouth had become worried about the security of their holdings under the New York government and were considering petitions to the king and Parliament. Wentworth noted that he had written nothing on the affair himself but confidently predicted that the region west of the Connecticut "will very shortly be reannex'd to New Hampshire." News of John Wentworth's enlistment in the cause of the New Hampshire grantees (against New York) traveled fast. In early May, William Samuel Johnson in England wrote to a friend: "I am glad that Govr. Wentworth appears at length disposed to give the Propr[ietor]s his assistance, had he embarked on it heartily when his friends [the Rockingham ministry] were in power three years ago, I doubt not the matter might have been set right with great ease."³¹

On 19 October 1769, a serious confrontation occurred at the farm of New Hampshire grantee, James Breakenridge, in Bennington. Surveyors working for the owners of a New York grant that conflicted with the Bennington patent were stopped by Breakenridge and a group of armed friends and, according to the surveyors, threatened with violence. New York considered the incident grave enough to swear out arrest warrants for the members of what it considered a disorderly mob. At the same time, nearly five hundred settlers of Bennington and five other nearby towns signed a petition addressed to Governor John Wentworth. This petition proclaimed the hardships endured by the settlers as a result of being placed under New York jurisdiction and mentioned ejectment suits against them that were pending in the New York courts. These suits were related to the proceedings in the Dean case.³²

Wentworth had found that Ingersoll did not have jurisdiction in the case and that it had been transferred to the vice-admiralty court of Judge Richard Morris in New York. Even with that done, processes moved slowly, and in the meantime, Wentworth discovered that William Dean had conveyed his property to another party and left the area. Wentworth saw little chance of catching Dean but held out hope of at least making him forfeit his land. With that in mind, in July he wrote to John Tabor Kempe, who as attorney general for New York had been assigned by Judge Morris to prosecute the case, to "try at least the validity of his [Dean's] Conveyances."[33] Wentworth's reluctance to give up on the case, and especially his determination to get at Dean's land, was of great significance to the prosecutor.

John Tabor Kempe, along with James Duane, who served as defense counsel for the Deans, was one of the largest holders of New York grants within the disputed region. It can hardly be coincidental that Kempe and Duane, who were serving on opposite sides in the Dean case, at that very time chose to pool their efforts in beginning ejectment proceedings in the New York courts against persons occupying land under New Hampshire grants that conflicted with their own claims. Kempe and Duane doubtless realized that, regardless of what happened to the Deans personally, if Wentworth succeeded in having their land forfeited in payment for their crimes against the king's woods, a dangerous precedent would be set favoring the title of the New Hampshire grantees. The reason lay in the township grants made by Benning Wentworth.

Under the New Hampshire town charters, anyone found guilty of violating the forest laws was to lose his land. This penalty was over and above that prescribed by parliamentary law and applied only to those holding New Hampshire grants. If Dean could be forced to forfeit his land, it would mean that Benning Wentworth's grants, in the eyes of the court, were valid and that Kempe and Duane had no claim to their twenty-six thousand acres that overlay New Hampshire grants.[34] From John Wentworth's point of view, it might also be a large step toward getting that land back for New Hampshire. The suits filed in New York by Kempe and Duane, aimed at ejecting New Hampshire grantees from their land, were an attempt to counteract Wentworth's move by setting a precedent that would confirm New York titles.

John Wentworth's wholehearted commitment to an effort to regain control over the disputed region became evident in December 1769 when petitions were circulated in New York's Cumberland County, reportedly at the governor's instigation, asking for a return to New Hampshire jurisdiction.[35] In February he was anxiously awaiting the petitions so that he could send them to his kinsman, Paul Wentworth, whom he had recommended to the grantees as their agent in England. On the eighteenth, Wentworth wrote to Hillsborough informing him of the forthcoming petition to the king from settlers west of the Connecticut desiring reannexation to New Hampshire. He explained that these people were "objects of real Compassion. Already many of them fill our Streets, and should they finally be ousted, Some Many Hundreds will inevitably perish by famine, and Despair urge Multitudes to fall Victims to the Laws." Affecting an objective pose, Wentworth told Hillsborough that he would make no judgment on the matter. He had, however, as he well knew, thoroughly condemned New York with his description of "Confusion," "wretchedness," and "Devastation" visited on residents of the New Hampshire grants under New York rule. The council, he noted, was drawing up a full report on the situation. Wentworth fully expected New Hampshire to regain its lost territory, for in the spring he recommended the uninhabited town of Landaff, close to the Connecticut River, as the home of Dartmouth College on the grounds that it would be near the center of the province.[36]

In the meantime, the Deans, in spite of help from friends, had been apprehended and brought to trial. When the case opened in October 1769, testimony was taken against the defendants charging them with the illegal destruction of seventeen white pine trees. The penalty involved was fifty pounds sterling per tree. The Deans apparently produced no witnesses on their behalf, and in December Wentworth got his much desired conviction. The Deans were fined for sixteen trees amounting to eight hundred pounds sterling. The satisfaction Wentworth must have felt on receipt of this news was, nevertheless, of short duration. He soon learned that during the proceedings the Deans had been visited in jail in New York by one Samuel Wells, a justice of the Court of Common Pleas in Cumberland County. William Dean, who had conveyed his estate earlier in the year and then taken repossession of it, now conveyed it again, this time to Judge Wells. Wells placed Dean's personal property in the possession of John Grout, a local attorney, for safekeeping in an unknown location. The Deans thus possessed nothing that could be seized for payment of their fine. In lieu of this payment, Judge Morris, on 25 January 1770, sentenced William Dean to four months in prison and his sons to three. To the Deans that must have seemed fair justice indeed, at least in the face of the astronomical sum of eight hundred pounds.[37]

Wentworth was enraged. Not only had the Deans suffered little, but court costs from the lengthy proceeding now fell on the Crown. Worst of all, his design on the Deans' lands as part of the attempt to secure the validity of New Hampshire titles had been foiled. He had learned during the fall that men of property in New York were apprehensive that the Dean case posed a threat to their interests in the region. He had not, however, expected this result. Nevertheless, he was not willing to give up easily. Early in February, Wentworth sent a letter and a memorial to Lieutenant Governor Colden of New York castigating Wells for his obstruction of the service of the king and requesting that the Deans' land be escheated to the Crown "according to the Express Tenor of that Grant by which they held"—a New Hampshire grant—on the grounds that conveyances such as that made by Dean to Wells were not valid.[38]

194

If Wentworth was angry with Wells and his abettors, New York officials were just as displeased with Wentworth. They knew of his interference and even attributed the trouble on the west side of the Green Mountains, where Wentworth had never ventured, to his encouragement. In December, Cadwallader Colden had written to Wentworth desiring a public statement by the governor that would discourage further resistance to New York by settlers in the Bennington area who, Colden noted, "seem to flatter themselves . . . will be favoured with the weight of your Authority." Wentworth replied that he had always discountenanced unlawful resistance to authority, and he told Colden, "I am at a loss, by what means it can be more publickly testify'd." In return, when Wentworth complained about the activities of Judge Wells, Colden responded that the conveyance of property had been taken by the justice merely to provide money for the hard-pressed Deans to live on while in jail. It was, asserted Colden, "an Act of Humanity and not criminal in Mr. Wells." As for the escheatment of the Deans' land, that matter was being referred to the New York council for consideration.[39] It would be some time before Wentworth received an official reply to his request. New York officials and landholders had called Wentworth's bluff, and now they were waiting to play their own trump. This advantage they hoped to find in the ejectment suits.

In May 1770 Wentworth was paid a visit in Portsmouth by one Ethan Allen. Allen, who along with his brothers had speculated heavily in the New Hampshire grants, had been chosen in Bennington by the New Hampshire proprietors to represent them in the ejectment suits. He came to procure from Wentworth copies of the original grants made by Benning Wentworth west of the Connecticut and the royal instructions under which those grants were made. Eager to help in any way, Wentworth readily produced the desired documents and recommended as legal counsel Jared Ingersoll of New Haven. Allen proceeded to New Haven, from where he and Ingersoll went to Albany where the ejectment proceedings opened in June. It became apparent almost immediately that the New Hampshire title holders had little chance of winning. When the judge refused to admit as evidence the documents Wentworth had provided, Ingersoll, as Ethan Allen's brother Ira later wrote, "saw the cause was already prejudged, and did not attempt to defend it." It was charged that no proof had been produced that New Hampshire ever had any claim to land west of the Connecticut River or that Benning Wentworth had any right to grant it. A precedent had

now been set for the removal of New Hampshire grantees who failed to conform to New York regulations and pay the requisite fees. Moreover, John Wentworth's hope for a precedent of his own that might go far toward establishing
New Hampshire's rightful claim to the disputed territory was shortly squelched.   195
On 25 September 1770, the New York council finally submitted its report on
his request for the escheatment of the Deans' land under the terms of the New
Hampshire charter. Such reversion was not warranted, according to the council,
"because we consider the Grant which his Excellency refers to, as merely void
for want of authority in the Government of New Hampshire, to issue Patents
for Lands . . . on the West side of Connecticut River."[40] Thus by the fall of 1770,
New York appeared to have successfully thwarted John Wentworth's efforts to
build a case for the restoration of the disputed territory to New Hampshire.

But Wentworth had not given up, and he believed he could count on the
continued support of many people west of the Connecticut River. In May and
June there had been serious riots against New York authority in Windsor, and
if Ethan Allen could be believed, settlers west of the Green Mountains would
not meekly submit either. During the course of the ejectment proceedings when
Allen was visited by Duane and Kempe urging him to persuade the New Hampshire grantees to make the best possible terms with their New York landlords,
he retorted, "The Gods of the valleys are not Gods of the hills," and if they did
not understand they could come up to Bennington to see what he meant! Allen's
promise was soon made good when new attempts by New York patentees to
survey their land were met by armed resistance. As time went on, violence became increasingly commonplace on the grants. Wentworth continued to urge
these people not to accept New York jurisdiction and to help him work for reversion to New Hampshire.[41]

In October 1770 he wrote to Hillsborough referring to the "deplorable State"
of the settlers on the far side of the Connecticut and pointing out that much of
their trouble could never be remedied because of their great distance from the
New York capital. Portsmouth was of course much closer. Wentworth sent his
views to England in November with John Temple, who was then departing to
vindicate himself with the home government. Temple was to assure authorities
that the restoration of the disputed region to New Hampshire "will be a public
charity to a distressed people and will also promote the King's service."[42]

In January 1771 Wentworth was busy soliciting more petitions from west of
the river because, as he said of the people living there, "As much might they
hope for a Crop, without planting—as for redress without timely setting forth
the Calamities they endure." He had also fixed on a survey of the Connecticut River in February as an important part of his mounting effort to retrieve

New Hampshire's lost land. His reasons for commissioning this survey he disclosed to Eleazar Wheelock: "I am well inform'd that your River is laid down, trending to the Westward, and heading in Lake Champlain in a Map transmitted from N[ew] York, upon which it was tho't proper to annex the district in consideration to N[ew] York. I therefore imagine, that the true course of said River being proved by this Survey, will exceedingly discover the practiced impositions . . . and promote a restoration." Wentworth was confident enough to assure Wheelock: "There is not the [least] doubt but that these Lands on the West [side of] the river will be immediately reannex'd to [this] Province."[43]

The New Yorkers, however, had other ideas, and by this time they had learned to play Wentworth's game. Shortly after the arrival of John Dunmore as the new governor in October 1770, New York began to circulate petitions of its own complaining of interference from New Hampshire designed "to aggrandize the family of the late Governour Wentworth" and asking for New York confirmation of New Hampshire titles for "moderate fees." In March 1771, Dunmore sent these petitions to Hillsborough with an account of the difficulties in the New Hampshire grants and affidavits providing evidence that "the disorders above mentioned are promoted by people of the greatest power in the Province of New Hampshire." The affidavits mentioned John Wentworth by name. The increased militance on the part of New York gave some residents west of the river second thoughts about signing John Wentworth's petitions. Eleazar Wheelock reported to the governor in January that the people of Norwich across from Hanover had been placed under a "destroying fear" by New York agents. In the meantime in England, the Board of Trade was delaying its decision on the dispute in anticipation of the report of the New Hampshire council that Wentworth had promised a year earlier. Hillsborough wrote repeatedly to remind him of the need for this report.[44]

In August the council finally completed its evaluation of the problem. Expectedly, the report consisted of a series of reasons, including historical precedents, why New Hampshire's boundary should extend to within twenty miles of the Hudson River. Wentworth forwarded the document to Hillsborough on the twentieth with the pointedly neutral comment that, because the matter had originated before his governorship, he had little to say about it. His only interest, he claimed, was that those holding New Hampshire titles should be justly treated. Wentworth noted, however, that the people had petitioned to be returned to New Hampshire jurisdiction "without which," he went on to add, "a confirmation of property cannot fully relieve the inhabitants who in every instance of manners, interest, situation and interior police, are and must ever be strongly connected with and bound to this Province." He then explained why this region, which could produce large quantities of corn for export, was much more valuable to New Hampshire than it could ever be for New York.[45]

It thus is clear that in the late summer of 1771 John Wentworth was as ardent as ever for his project of regaining jurisdiction over the New Hampshire grants. That is why his actions over the next few months became puzzling to others, especially to Jacob Bayley. Bayley had received a grant west of the Connecticut from Benning Wentworth in 1763 and had been one of the founders of Newbury just across the river from Haverhill. He had helped Eleazar Wheelock in his search for a site for Dartmouth College and, though himself supporting Haverhill, had aquiesced in the choice of Hanover. As a holder of a New Hampshire title west of the river, Bayley understandably was disturbed by the building controversy over the grants. In January 1771 he told Wheelock that he was writing to Governor Wentworth but admitted that he was uncertain about which side it would be best to support. Wentworth persuaded him that his best interests lay with New Hampshire, and within a few months, Bayley was circulating a petition in the Connecticut valley that asked for reinstatement to the jurisdiction of Wentworth's province. Late in August, shortly after sending the council's report to Hillsborough, Wentworth and a small party traveled to the Connecticut for the first commencement of Dartmouth College. The governor took this opportunity to call on Bayley at his home in Newbury again to urge his assistance and to assure him of his own unremitting effort to regain the grants for New Hampshire. Thus Bayley was shocked when several months later he received a letter from Wentworth announcing his withdrawal of support for efforts to regain New Hampshire jurisdiction over the region in dispute and recommending that Bayley make the best possible terms with New York.[46]

Not willing to accept such a sudden reversal without any explanation, Bayley rode to Portsmouth where, he later recounted, Governor Wentworth "rather seemed to put me off, and discover a good deal of coldness and indifference, the reason of which I could not learn." Bayley thought he had learned, though, after traveling to New York. There he was shown a letter that John Wentworth had written to William Tryon, governor of New York since the previous July. In the letter Wentworth explained how his uncle Benning, who had died in October 1770, had reserved for himself five hundred acres in every town that he granted. Because that action was deemed improper, it was not believed that the former governor had any rightful title to the lots. Wentworth then asked Governor Tryon the favor of granting to him those lots reserved by Benning west of the Connecticut River that had not yet been regranted. Here then, in front of Bayley's own eyes, was the answer. Wentworth had sold out the proprietors and settlers west of the river, people who were counting on New Hampshire's leadership, in order to further his own personal interests. Incensed at what seemed to be Wentworth's callous opportunism, Bayley traveled up and down the river telling the story to others.[47]

198   It is not surprising that the letter caused suspicion, especially because Wentworth had bothered to inform Tryon that, upon his uncle's death, he had received no inheritance. He later defended his action by noting special precautions he had taken not to yield any jurisdictional claims to New York.[48] That much was true. There was no reference in Wentworth's letter to Tryon about which province had rights to the land west of the Connecticut River. But implicit in Wentworth's application to Tryon was an admission that, at least at that time, New York had the upper hand in the area. That situation might yet be reversed in England, and there is reason to think Wentworth still held some faint hope of that possibility. Nevertheless, if the governor of New Hampshire was willing to take conveyance of land under New York authority, how could anyone else reasonably argue against New York jurisdiction? His request was of potential damage to the New Hampshire cause, and Wentworth must have known that. It seems clear that he had changed his position regarding the question of jurisdiction over the land west of the Connecticut.

Bayley's interpretation of the governor's shift, however, probably was not accurate. For one thing, nearly a year after Benning Wentworth's death, his nephew was still pushing hard for renewed control over the New Hampshire grants. More to the point, it seems highly unlikely that Wentworth would have given up the huge advantage to be gained by the addition to New Hampshire of that large and valuable area of land merely for the personal acquisition of an uncertain number of widely scattered five-hundred-acre lots. The reason for his about-face more likely lies in a report from the Board of Trade to the Privy Council dated 6 June 1771, which Wentworth probably received sometime in early autumn. Not willing to wait any longer for the promised report from the New Hampshire council and desiring to answer New York's request to grant lands to soldiers under the Parliamentary Act of 1763, the board was proceeding with its recommendations for settling the dispute. The news was good for those actually settled under a New Hampshire grant. They were to have full title to their land with no further payments to be required by New York. The news for speculative holders of unimproved New Hampshire grants and for New Hampshire itself was not as favorable. Those persons, it was suggested, should be given a date by which they must obtain a title from New York or lose claim to their land, which in no individual case should exceed five hundred acres. That decision meant that there was no inclination in England to change jurisdiction from New York to New Hampshire. Wentworth doubtless realized there was little hope left for that eventuality and that it would behoove everyone, including himself, to make the best deal they could with New York.[49]

A question that needs to be asked is why Wentworth did not inform Bayley of this news when he urged him to seek confirmation from New York. It appears now that though Wentworth no longer expected to gain reversion of jurisdiction to New Hampshire, he believed there still was a chance that it might happen. The Board of Trade only recommended; the Privy Council made the final decision. And perhaps the belated report of the New Hampshire council might yet have some influence. He would not want word to get to England that he had abandoned hope of regaining jurisdiction, for that might easily kill what little chance remained.

199

Wentworth was not totally resigned to defeat. Although he seems to have given up active participation in the dispute by late 1771, he still refused New York's requests for a public statement renouncing his interest west of the Connecticut, and his letters to England continued to reflect hope that New Hampshire might yet be awarded jurisdiction over that area. There seems little reason to doubt the spirit of his statement to Wheelock in the spring of 1773—that he had always favored reannexation of the area, and "my endeavors are not now wanting to that point." He admitted, though, that he had told Bayley that he "saw no prospect of success." A short time later he learned that his assessment of the situation had been correct. An order in council of 5 March 1773, in reference to charges made against the conduct of New York by the New Hampshire council, stated that those charges, serious as they might be, should not "weigh in the scale of Consideration against those principles of true policy and sound Wisdom, which appear to have dictated the proposition of Making the River Connecticut the boundary Line between the two Colonies, and therefore the said Lords Commissioners cannot advise any alteration to be made in the measure."[50]

For John Wentworth and for New Hampshire, the issue of jurisdiction over the lands west of the Connecticut River was closed.[51] Unfortunately for New York, the sentiment of Ethan Allan, his cousin Remember Baker, and other speculators in New Hampshire grants was not similar. The requirement of paying fees to New York for their huge accumulations of land meant ruin to these men, thus their continued violent resistance to New York authority was not surprising. Within only a few years, the contest between New Hampshire and New York for the area would be looked on by both provinces as an exercise in futility. Exemplifying the independent spirit of the other colonies, the frontiersmen between the Connecticut and Hudson rivers successfully struggled to create a state of their own.

The episode of the disputed New Hampshire grants was another aspect of John Wentworth's dedication to the development of his province, at the expense of another province if need be. His assertion that the acquisition of the region would in the long run mean much more to New Hampshire than New York was unquestionably true, and he showed himself a hardheaded and shrewd politician in attempting to gain that end. He clearly was working against New York authority, New York knew it, and he knew that New York knew it. Yet he never let down his guise of detached innocence and never provided New York authorities with anything substantive that could be used against him. His seeming shift of position in order to obtain New York lands for himself and his family came only when he discovered there was almost no likelihood New Hampshire would succeed in the dispute. Even then he continued to support the cause to get the entire region back for New Hampshire.[52]

Although his quest was ultimately unsuccessful, Wentworth's efforts in this affair were important for himself and for his province. It was believed in the colony that New Hampshire's general tranquility and loyalty to the Crown during the recent troubles over the revenue acts might be an inducement in England to return the land west of the Connecticut.[53] With such a prize at stake, there was little incentive for antagonizing the home government. Wentworth's well-known advocacy of reinstatement of New Hampshire jurisdiction over the region complemented his efforts to suppress overt objections in the province to British policy. The quest for the grants west of the Connecticut River must be seen as a factor in the continuing harmony of New Hampshire.

»II«
TROUBLE AT HOME

The Case of Peter Livius,
1772–1773

Fortunately for John Wentworth, no new tensions arose between Britain and the colonies to disturb the peace in New Hampshire, and the calm that had settled over North America following the repeal of the Townshend duties continued on into 1772. By that time, Wentworth House at Wolfeboro was substantially completed, and the governor and his new wife were spending more and more time there. Although she attempted to make the best of the situation, Frances Wentworth was not well suited to the rigors and isolation of life in the country. She dreaded the trips between Portsmouth and Wolfeboro; her fragile constitution, she was sure, would not stand the strain. When finally at the new house, Frances was left alone for long periods of time to entertain herself. "I get but very little of my Governor's company," she wrote from Wolfeboro to a friend. "He loves to be going about, and sometimes (except at meales) I don't see him an hour in a day."

Wentworth seemed to thrive on the outdoor life and the continuous activity demanded by his estate. If he was not busy inspecting his property or directing workmen in various projects of construction or cultivation, he was pursuing one of his favorite pastimes—collecting unusual specimens of North American fauna and flora to send to Rockingham in England. In February 1772 he shipped the marquis a buck moose, which he hoped would eventually mate with the doe he had sent to Wentworth-Woodhouse the summer before. He had had a pair that summer, but his gamekeeper, much to Wentworth's chagrin, had tied the male to a tree with a rope around its neck. As he explained to Rockingham, the moose, "sprung with such violence that it stove in his Skull and he dropped dead instantly." With the moose he also sent some sugar made from maple sap; to

Lady Rockingham, Frances gave two pairs of wild birds. Similar to a pheasant but slightly smaller, they had been captured in a remote section of New Hampshire, "the only part of America they are known in," Wentworth claimed. He was confident that they, too, could be bred on Rockingham's Yorkshire estate.[1]

The year 1772 was good for an extended stay at Wolfeboro because, until early fall, Wentworth had little else to be concerned with but routine matters of government. But then trouble loomed up again, not as a result of precipitating events from the outside as before but rather from within New Hampshire and aimed directly at the governor himself. On 7 August the earl of Hillsborough wrote to Wentworth enclosing a notice from the Board of Trade that notified the governor of serious charges lodged against him in England by a member of his own council, Peter Livius. Wentworth was instructed to respond to each of the accusations, collect official documents and depositions to defend his case, and, because Livius was in England, see to it that the councillor's supporters in New Hampshire were encouraged to do the same. Though distressing, the news did not come as a complete surprise to Wentworth. Peter Livius had for some time been troublesome for those in power in New Hampshire, and when he left the province the previous spring without giving notice, Wentworth had written to Hillsborough asking that Livius be replaced on the council. The governor described Livius as a man who would be a "perpetual Source of Confusion, Disorder and Disobedience in any Part of North America."[2]

Peter Livius, two years younger than John Wentworth, had been born in Portugal, the son of a German father and an Irish mother. Schooled in England, he there married a daughter of John Tufton Mason, hereditary claimant to the Mason grant in New Hampshire until he sold it in the 1740s. Anna Elizabeth Mason had grown up in Portsmouth, and in the early sixties Livius took her back there with the apparent intention of overseeing the remaining Mason holdings, making his own fortune, and joining the local aristocracy. His eye immediately fell on the royal mast trade, which he correctly perceived as the most lucrative business in New Hampshire. When he discovered that the Wentworths had an impenetrable lock on masting in New England, his resentment of the family and its associates grew. When Benning Wentworth came under scrutiny by the home government, Livius tried to persuade his father-in-law, John Tufton Mason, to seek the governorship. In 1765, after first expressing his support of George Meserve, the appointed stamp distributor, Livius turned completely around upon the arrival of Meserve's commission and joined the popular clamor, writing a pamphlet opposing the Stamp Act. That same year, bypassing the governor completely, he managed through his connections in England to procure an appointment to the New Hampshire council, where, he had earlier claimed, he would "oppose the Conduct of the Gov[erno]r and Council in Generall."[3]

Livius was true to his word. In 1768 in a dispute between the assembly and the council over powder money collected on foreign shipping, he sided with the assembly, expressing his dissent from the decision of the council. In 1771, however, a more serious break with the governor and council occurred. Benning Wentworth had died the previous fall, and in March, John Wentworth asked the council to consider the validity of the old governor's numerous five-hundred-acre grants to himself and the advisability of resuming and regranting those lands. The council returned that it did not believe the conveyances by Benning Wentworth to himself carried rightful titles and that the governor should regrant the lots. The only dissenting vote was that of Peter Livius. One week later, he produced a detailed list of reasons for his action, among which were his claims that Benning's grants were indeed valid and that many purchasers of those lands who had made substantial improvements would be wrongfully dispossessed. The crux of the matter, though, lay in Livius's charge that John Wentworth wanted the lands for himself.[4]

Other recent developments seemed to support Livius's accusation. During Benning Wentworth's last years, it was generally believed that his estate would go to his family, in particular to his brothers, but with his nephew and successor, John Wentworth, receiving a major share. When Benning's will was disclosed following his death, however, it was discovered that all had been left to his young wife, Martha Wentworth. The people of Portsmouth were shocked. John Hurd reported to a friend, "It engages the conversation of everybody—and doubtless chagrins many—I won't say who—but our good little governor, who best merited, bears all like a hero."[5]

John Wentworth had, in fact, been anticipating a substantial portion of his uncle's estate, but his and others' expectations had been thwarted, he confided to Rockingham, by a mutual relation, Michael Wentworth. Colonel Michael Wentworth, a retired army officer, had come to New Hampshire in 1767, the same year that John Wentworth returned as governor. Bachelors and friends, it was only natural that the two men should share accommodations. John Wentworth had a large house with more than enough rooms for himself, and Michael lived there with him until a few months before the governor's marriage. When Michael moved out, Wentworth worried that he had "attached himself to some very wretched low people," but the governor need not have been concerned on that account for Michael Wentworth had also ingratiated himself with some very substantial people, namely Martha and Benning Wentworth. As Wentworth was later to recount, Michael "grew more and more attach'd and assiduous about the poor infirm old Gent. and his young Wife." He moved in with them, "took charge of all the Keys and was shortly the Man of the house." His purpose soon became apparent to John Wentworth when Benning Wentworth, "worn out with Age and domestic vexation," after viewing the destruction of his original will, was prevailed on to draw up a new one that completely disinherited all of his family and named his wife, Martha Wentworth, as sole beneficiary. Shortly after Benning's death, Michael Wentworth took out a license to marry the former governor's widow.[6]

Peter Livius prefaced his dissent from the council in March 1771 with the statement that the governor had "desird the advice and consent of Council for the granting to his own use thro' the intervention of other Persons, all those Lands that were granted or reserved to the late Governor." Livius later claimed that he suggested the impropriety of this request to the governor, who quickly brushed such a notion aside, and that his dissent was never entered in the council journal and not placed on file for over a year. John Wentworth responded that he had asked the council "about granting these lands to such of his Majesty's subjects as would improve and settle" them, and that "no question was ever put to the Council, about granting these lands to" himself. The council vigorously corroborated the governor's rebuttal, claimed that Livius's dissent was placed on file on 26 March, the day he produced it, and explained that it was not copied into the journal because "no Reasons of Dissent had ever been so recorded at length" and that "the Council would not have acted inconsistent with their Duty in rejecting it intirely because the Allegations contained therein were not True." Secretary Theodore Atkinson provided separate testimony vouching for the veracity of John Wentworth's interpretation of what had transpired between himself and the council.[7]

In all likelihood there was some truth to both Livius's charge and Wentworth's rebuttal. Wentworth probably hoped to obtain some of Benning's lands for himself. He knew better than to reserve lots in his own name in each of his township grants. His uncle had done so for years and eventually lost his job because of it. It was easy enough, though, for Wentworth to make grants to friends and family who could then deed them back over to him.[8] This path he could conveniently follow with Benning's resumed lands.

Far more important to Wentworth, however, than obtaining personal title to these lands was his desperate need to reassert Crown control over them to bolster his suffering patronage. Benning Wentworth had maintained a grip on New Hampshire's political system through the liberal dispensation of land to family, friends, and especially political enemies. John Wentworth attempted to do the same. A survey of grants made during his administration discloses the same names again and again, such as uncles Daniel Peirce and Daniel Rindge, brothers-in-law John Fisher and Benning Wentworth, cousins George and Joshua Wentworth, and of course his father, Mark Hunking Wentworth. This method was the one means John Wentworth possessed to repay the money he borrowed from his father for his material needs, among them his elaborate Wolfeboro home. Members of Portsmouth's merchant elite—Atkinson, Whipple, Cutts, Moffatt, Jaffrey, Warner, Boyd—were kept closely within the Wentworth fold with repeated gifts of land. John Wentworth rewarded old friends and close associates—people such as Joseph and Peter Harrison, Ammi R. Cutter, Thomas Macdonogh—with rights in new township grants. Very much an Anglican, Wentworth curried Portsmouth's Congregational ministers, Samuel Langdon and Samuel Haven, by repeatedly making them grantees. Perhaps most important to his well-being, he saw to it that potential opponents were not left out of the land granting process. Among them, the Gilmans, the Waldrons, Woodbury Langdon, John Sullivan, and Hall Jackson all received their share.[9]

In spite of his many grants, however, John Wentworth found it much more difficult to reward people with property than his uncle had. The reason was the increasing scarcity of desirable land. In the 1740s, the Masonian proprietors appropriated much of the most valuable land in the province, everything within a sixty-mile radius of the coast. After Benning Wentworth became governor, he doled out the remaining choice lands between the Merrimack and Connecticut rivers. When that area was exhausted, he set his sights west of the Connecticut, a region the governor had a dubious claim to, but a claim he hoped his grants would reinforce. He was mistaken. By late in his term, he was ordered to make no more grants in that area. By the time John Wentworth was in a position to make land grants, most of New Hampshire's prime land was already accounted for. As a result, most of his grants were far upcountry, along the northern reaches of the Connecticut or in the White Mountains, many of them consisting of inaccessible, untillable land. If he could gain jurisdiction over Benning's own reserved plots, however, most of them in prime locations in rapidly developing towns, the governor saw the prospect of a new supply of land guaranteed to please friend or foe.

It is not known if Livius at this time fixed on the idea of raising serious charges in England against the governor. Wentworth's activities concerning the resumption and regranting of his uncle's and, by implication, other lands, were central to those charges, but Livius did not file them for more than a year, in July 1772. During that year he did publicly circulate copies of his dissent "in a manner," as Secretary Atkinson later complained, "Injurious and Derogatory to the Honor of the Governor and Council." That dissemination may have been preparation for prosecuting his case. If Livius had not yet determined on such action, another incident that occurred in the interim was probably a deciding factor in persuading him to pursue it. As an inferior court justice, Peter Livius was known for his blatant partisanship in cases involving friends, whether plaintiffs, defendants, or attorneys. In 1771, when word was received of the approval of the act to divide the province into counties and it became necessary to issue new commissions for positions on the bench, Livius found that the governor had not renewed his judgeship. That slight was all the impetus he needed. Livius sailed for England in the spring of 1772 and on 9 July filed his charges with the Board of Trade.[10]

In addition to the complaints that the governor and council had prematurely and without due process resumed and regranted lands and that Wentworth had attempted to obtain Benning Wentworth's lands for himself, both actions allegedly involving the dispossession of rightful holders of those lands, Peter Livius made other accusations. Harking back to the powder money dispute between assembly and council in 1768, he stated that the council refused to provide an account of those presumably public funds and denied him the right of entering his dissent. Livius accused the governor of attempting to obtain a desired judicial opinion by repeatedly changing judges in a court case in which he, Wentworth, had a special interest. Pointing out that the New Hampshire council was composed almost entirely of Wentworth's relations, Livius charged that body and the governor with collusion in a conspiracy against justice. As proof of Wentworth's attempt to hide these unseemly actions, Livius drew attention to the fact that the journals of the council had never been forwarded to Whitehall by the governor as his instructions required. The disgruntled councillor even complained that he had been subjected to personal abuse by Wentworth.[11]

Late in October, John Wentworth informed the earl of Dartmouth, president of the Board of Trade, that he had received the board's notification of the charges against him and was, with all requisite haste, collecting the necessary information to clear himself of these unjust accusations. He indicated to Dartmouth that he felt the earl of Hillsborough, by so easily accepting the complaints of such a disreputable figure as Peter Livius, was again treating him with an unnecessarily heavy hand and, in the process, only further undermining the authority of royal governors in America. In mid-December, Wentworth expressed his frustration over Hillsborough's conduct more directly to Rockingham. It seemed, he wrote, that Hillsborough "preferred the unsupported Complaint of a discontented single Man, ruin'd by his own folly and absconding that instant

from his Creditors, to the representations of a Provincial Gov[erno]r who but
a few weeks before was honor'd with the Royal approbation." Wentworth was
in fact placing much of his hope for vindication on his laudable record of keeping opposition to royal government at a minimum in New Hampshire. He also
expressed confidence in obtaining fair treatment from Dartmouth, who in the
mid-1760s had been close to the Rockingham Whigs and who had now replaced
Hillsborough as colonial secretary.[12]

Wentworth told Rockingham that he had completed his defense and was
sending his private secretary, Thomas Macdonogh, to England to present his
case. Macdonogh, long a member of the English customs service, had come
over with the American commissioners to Boston. For nearly a year, however,
he had been serving Wentworth as personal secretary. On 18 December, Wentworth wrote letters to Dartmouth and to the Board of Trade introducing Macdonogh, who would present his replies to the charges and the numerous depositions collected in his behalf. He had made every effort to give the supporters of
Peter Livius an opportunity also to obtain depositions, he explained, but none
had been forthcoming. On 20 December 1772, Macdonogh, documents in hand,
boarded the *Dolphin* and set sail for England. Several days later, the council drew
up its own memorial to the Board of Trade refuting Livius's claims. Theodore
Atkinson forwarded it to Barlow Trecothick for presentation at the board.[13]

Although Wentworth had heard a rumor that he was to be removed from
office, he gave it no credit and was confident of his complete exoneration from
charges he believed to be "groundless and of no import." He had good reason
to be optimistic. In addition to his own strong denials and those of the council,
Wentworth had sent copies of a number of letters from the Crown expressing
approbation of his conduct, especially in regard to his successful peacekeeping
endeavors in New Hampshire and his strenuous efforts to enforce British forest
laws. Also forwarded were copies of the missing council records with an explanation by Secretary Atkinson that, because they had not customarily been sent
during the tenure of Benning Wentworth, the practice was merely continued
under the new governor. Most important, though, were the numerous depositions collected by Wentworth from some forty people he termed "the first char-
acters in this part of the Province."[14]

These written statements included attestations by members of the council
that no land had ever been regranted on which improvements had been made
and that due process had always been followed in the resumption of any lands.
A number of new grantees of Benning Wentworth's resumed lots declared that
John Wentworth had no interest whatsoever in their lands. In response to the
charge that the governor changed judges in a case in order to obtain a desired

verdict, New Hampshire's attorney general, Samuel Livermore, and several of the judges who were involved asserted that the appointment of special judges was a common practice, that the reason they were appointed in this instance stemmed from another case pending at the same time, and that Governor Wentworth had never mentioned the case to them at all. Adding weight to this part of Wentworth's defense was the testimony of Hunking Wentworth, the governor's uncle but representing the opposing side in the court case, who swore that he knew of no attempt to influence the judges and added that he had been completely satisfied with the administration of justice in this instance. In addition, there were depositions attesting to Livius's unethical business activities and his unworthiness as a judge. The foundation of support Wentworth had built with his land granting policy now paid off. Congregational ministers Samuel Langdon and Samuel Haven wrote in defense of their Anglican governor, and John Sullivan of Durham and Meshech Weare of Hampton Falls, soon to be leaders in the revolt against royal authority in New Hampshire, signed depositions on behalf of Wentworth. Numerous unsolicited declarations of confidence in the administration of John Wentworth were also sent to England by individuals, towns, and at least one county.[15]

In the face of this mass of evidence, Peter Livius could do little, for he had few supporters in New Hampshire. Among his few friends were the Langdon brothers, Woodbury and John, successful merchants but outside the Wentworth circle; however, when Woodbury Langdon and Michael Wentworth, supposedly Livius's agents in the province, were informed by the attorney general that they were to collect depositions for him, "they declared that they had nothing to do with the affair" and left their friend to rely primarily on his own rebuttal of the governor's defense. Thus there was much reason for Wentworth to be encouraged about his prospects in the case, even more so when he considered who was helping him in England. Thomas Macdonogh possessed qualities he admired—"an excellent understanding, most inflexible probity and inviolable . . . prudence"—and he had complete confidence in his secretary to coordinate the measures necessary for a successful defense. The marquis of Rockingham, though out of power, was a man of considerable influence, and Wentworth knew that he could be counted on to do what he could to help. Barlow Trecothick was still New Hampshire's agent and could be expected to bring his extensive political skill to the aid of the governor. Paul Wentworth, for whom John Wentworth had finally obtained a seat on the New Hampshire council, although he had never returned to America, was also engaged in the battle against Livius.[16]

On the first day of February 1773, Barlow Trecothick wrote to Dartmouth and to John Pownall, undersecretary for the American department, introducing

Thomas Macdonogh, who "I think," he told Pownall, carries "conclusive Refutation of the several Charges preferred against" John Wentworth. "The General Esteem Governor Wentworth has acquired by the Rectitude of his Conduct, during the course of his Administration, and the frequent Expressions of Approbation from his superiors here," Trecothick went on to tell Dartmouth, "are strongly in his favour." New Hampshire's agent expressed his intention to attend the hearings because, as he exclaimed, "the Governor seems to Me to have been very greatly traduced."[17]

Macdonogh in the meantime was arranging the depositions and other materials to make the best possible case, while keeping Rockingham apprised of his progress. In April the marquis busied himself obtaining a copy of a legal opinion presented in 1752 by Sir Dudley Rider and William Murray (now Lord Mansfield), respectively attorney general and solicitor general, expressing conditions under which land might be resumed and regranted and seemingly supporting the activities of Governor Wentworth. By the time Macdonogh presented the materials in defense of Wentworth to Dartmouth at the end of April, the governor could confidently state that Livius's charges against him were in England "now known to be Calumny only."[18]

It is not difficult, then, to imagine the shock of Wentworth and his friends on learning of the Board of Trade's opinion of 10 May 1773. Although acknowledging the continued "peace and prosperity" fostered in New Hampshire under the governorship of John Wentworth, the board went on to proclaim, "the instances of the maladministration with which he has been charged" make him not a "fit person to be entrusted with your Majesty's interests in the important station he now holds." This was a recommendation for dismissal! The substantive considerations of the decision were that Wentworth had resumed and regranted lands without proper notice, due process, or presentation of evidence, that there was not justification for reclaiming the lands Benning Wentworth had left to his widow, and that the governor had repeatedly changed judges in a court case in which he had an interest. The opinion of Sir Dudley Rider and William Murray of 1752 was dismissed as not applicable in the present case.[19]

John Wentworth later blamed Barlow Trecothick for not adequately supporting him at this crucial time. There probably was little more the agent could have done, however, and Wentworth's criticism appears unjustified. Nevertheless, the decision of the Board of Trade—accepting the word of one man against that of a popular and successful governor, his council and numerous supporters—is difficult to explain, especially in light of the fact that there were no complaints from any victims of Wentworth's alleged land-grabbing operations. Livius's claim that these people were too poor to draw up depositions was certainly weak. Important influencing factors in the board's pronouncement seem to have been the preponderance of Wentworth relations sitting on the provincial council, and the fact that the council records had not been forwarded while Wentworth had been in office. These circumstances made Livius's otherwise unsubstantiated charges look suspiciously true. One cannot escape the conclusion, however, that those facts should not have been enough to overturn the mass of evidence in Wentworth's favor. The earl of Dartmouth, president of the board, apparently felt that way, which probably explains his absence when the opinion was given.[20] He could not support the decision but, likewise, could not come out openly for Wentworth since it would associate him too closely with the Rockinghamites who were in opposition to the government.

As disturbing and disheartening as the board's report was, Wentworth's friends in England knew they must not give up. A month later, early in June, Macdonogh, Paul Wentworth, and Sir Thomas Wentworth of Bretton Hall in Yorkshire, an influential relation and Wentworth's acquaintance from his sojourn in England, petitioned George III for a review of the decision by the Privy Council. On 24 June, John Pownall informed the three that their appeal had been granted, and six days later, the matter was referred to a committee of the Privy Council. No stone was to be left unturned this time. Rockingham was especially zealous in his efforts, obtaining the services of John Lee, a man of strong whig principles who recently had served as counsel for those who had sent John Wilkes to the Commons. Lee joined John Skynner, member of Parliament and the original counsel in the case. Skynner and Lee were two of the most prominent and able lawyers in the kingdom.[21]

Early in July, Macdonogh met with the lawyers in Skynner's chambers at Lincoln's Inn to provide the necessary documents and to help coordinate the effort for the governor. Rockingham himself remained in the background, for he knew that, rather than a help, his obvious presence would be detrimental to the case. The Rockingham faction was in opposition to the ministry, and the marquis realized that John Wentworth could not be exonerated without the approbation of the ministers. He was particularly intent on having Wentworth cleared because he had recommended his appointment as governor. Moreover, he believed that the Board of Trade had made a mistake and that John Wentworth had been wronged. "The more I look into the matter," he remarked determinedly, "the eagerer I grow in Gov[erno]r Wentworth's conduct, and stamping it as illegal—arbitrary etc. etc. are deep wounds to a man's private character." Rockingham was interested enough in Wentworth's vindication to put off a remonstrance against a bill before the Irish Parliament, a bill already approved by the Privy Council, until after a decision was made in the governor's case.[22]

Counsel was set to be heard for Wentworth on 22 July, and for Livius, one week later. Interest in the hearings ran high in London among not only visiting colonists but also English observers. The Lords postponed their summer recess, and it was reported that the presentation on the twenty-second for the gover- nor was attended by a "crowded Audience; among them many of the principal Gentry from all the American Provinces, and from the West Indies." Attorneys Skynner and Lee presented John Wentworth's case with voluminous documents, depositions, and witnesses. Among those ready to testify on the governor's be- half were Daniel Sherburne, recently arrived from New Hampshire; Commo- dore Hood, with whom Wentworth had served on the special admiralty court in Boston in 1769; and John Williams, Inspector General of the Customs in North America.[23] The great Pitt himself favored Wentworth's cause but could not be prevailed upon to present his opinion to the Privy Council. On the twenty- ninth, Livius had his turn. Rockingham later wrote to Wentworth, "It made great Impression on the Privy Council that no one joined Mr. Livius in giving Evidence ag[ains]t You." Livius did produce three depositions, but they were of questionable value. The rhetorical powers of one of his attorneys, however, impressed one observer enough to compare him with Pitt.[24]

The case was extensively discussed in the London newspapers.[25] One com- mentator filled three entire columns in support of Livius's position. An aspect that seemed particularly to fascinate the English was the degree of Wentworth family control in New Hampshire. In the *Public Advertiser* of 29 July 1773, one "Americus" was stimulated to parody the situation in the form of a conversa- tion between a "Virginian" and a "New Hampshire Man" supposedly seen in an American paper. "I think your Province is very little mentioned. I suppose you have very few People," began the Virginian. "Far otherwise I assure you," re- plied the New Hampshire Man. "Our Members are not much short of 100,000 white People."

Virginian. Indeed! you surprise me. Pray what is the Reason you are so
little talked of?
New Hamp. We are generally an orderly, quiet, well-disposed People; and
yet we labour under Inconveniences and Oppressions that
are peculiar to us.
Virginian. Pray what do they proceed from?
New Hamp. They proceed from the strong Family Combination which
is in Possession of our Government.
Virginian. Pray who is your Governor?
New Hamp. John Wentworth, Esq.

Virginian. Wentworth! Is he any relation of Lord Rockingham?

New Hamp. The Governor says he is; but we know better.

Virginian. Pray who is your Secretary?

New Hamp. Theodore Atkinson, Esq; the Governor's Uncle and Father-in-law.

Virginian. Pray who is your Chief Justice?

New Hamp. Theodore Atkinson, Esq; the Governor's Uncle and Father-in-law.

Virginian. Who is President of your Council?

New Hamp. Theodore Atkinson, Esq; the Governor's Uncle and Father-in-law.

Virginian. Good now! And who is Clerk of your Council?

New Hamp. Theodore Atkinson, Esq; the Governor's Uncle and Father-in-law.

Virginian. Who is the Governor's Deputy Surveyor?

New Hamp. Theodore Atkinson, Esq; the Governor's Uncle and Father-in-law.

Virginian. Who is Colonel of your First Regiment?

New Hamp. Theodore Atkinson, Esq; the Governor's Uncle and Father-in-law.

Virginian. Truly this Theodore Atkinson, Esq; the Governor's Uncle and Father-in-law is well provided. Pray is he your Speaker too?

New Hamp. O! no: They say that is incompatible with the Presidentship of the Council; and so John Wentworth is Speaker.

Virginian. Why I thought John Wentworth was your Governor.

New Hamp. So he is.

Virginian. And Speaker too?

New Hamp. Yes indeed.

Virginian. Why sure you are not in earnest?

New Hamp. Indeed I am. John Wentworth is our Governor, and his Cousin J. Wentworth is our Speaker.

Virginian. Is that the Case? And how many of these Wentworths have you?

New Hamp. With us they are very prolific. We have even another John Wentworth, Uncle of the Governor, and Judge of our Common Pleas.

Virginian. Pray have you any more of these Wentworths?

New Hamp. Ad Infinitum. A John Wentworth is also our Judge of Probate.

Virginian. Good Lord! John Wentworth Judges! John Wentworth Governor! John Wentworth Speaker! I hope your Council is not to be Wentworth'd.

New Hamp. Pretty much so. First there is our President Theodore Atkinson, Esq; whom I have already told you of; then comes Daniel Warner, Esq; He is not the Governor's Relation; But all his three Sons married the Governor's First Cousins. The next is Mark Hunking Wentworth, Esq; the Governor's Father.

Virginian. What! His own Father!

New Hamp. Yes, then comes Peter Livius, Esq; He is not the Governor's Relation; then is Geo. Jaffrey, Esq; our Treasurer, whose Father married the Governor's Aunt; then comes Daniel Warner's Son Jonathan, who married two of the Governor's First Cousins; then Daniel Rindge, Esq; the Governor's Uncle; then Daniel Rogers, Esq; the Governor's Uncle; then Daniel Pierce, Esq; the Governor's Uncle and Keeper of our Provincial Records.

Virginian. Are these all your Council?

New Hamp. Yes, for there are just now some Vacancies.

Virginian. Who has the Governor recommended to fill them?

New Hamp. Why there has been some Difficulty about it. There are Wentworths in Abundance; but as they do not all look like Gentlemen, the Governor, I have been told, has been obliged to recommend a Mr. Paul Wentworth, a Relation of his now in England, who has been out of the Province so long that he can know very little of its Concerns.

This shrewd description of nepotism and Wentworth family dominance in New Hampshire, carefully separated from the context in which that hegemony had developed, by implication pronounced the governor guilty of connivance against anyone outside the family circle such as Peter Livius. Much of the situation, however, was the legacy of Benning Wentworth. Theodore Atkinson, who sat on the council before John Wentworth was born, had been collecting offices for years. Many members of the council, too, had not been chosen by the present governor. Neither had he had anything to do with the selection of his cousin, whom he was not close to, as speaker of the House. Nevertheless, there was little exaggeration in the facts as stated, and the point was well made, undoubtedly by a friend of Peter Livius, or possibly by Livius himself. Fortunately for the governor, it was not one of the central points in the case against him.

Following the hearing on Thursday, the twenty-ninth of July, Rockingham set out for Wentworth-Woodhouse in Yorkshire, where he would await the decision. Thomas Macdonogh no doubt remained close by in London to receive the first possible word. John Wentworth in the meantime, forced to leave his fate in the hands of a few friends three thousand miles across the ocean, could only busy himself nervously with local matters and be content with an occasional encouraging report from England. On 26 August the committee presented its report to the Privy Council, stating "that there is no foundation for any censure upon the said John Wentworth, Esq. Your Majesty's Governor of New Hampshire, for any of the charges contained in Mr. Livius's complaint against him."[26] This judgment, however, was not the final decision. That had to come from the Privy Council as a whole.

It should have been perfunctory, but as time passed and the decision did not appear, Wentworth's supporters became apprehensive. On 21 September Edmund Burke wrote Rockingham: "The Lords of the Council by their delay are laying up much disapprobation and unpopularity for their decision whenever it shall appear. Supposing it to be such as they gave your Lordship reason to expect . . . from the Character of some of them and even from this delay I begin a little to doubt." Rockingham thought he knew who was responsible. The Privy Council's "unanimous opinion is well known," he told the duke of Portland at the end of September, "but by Manoeuvres of Sir Fletcher Norton, who does not avow that he differs—the Report is kept back, he pretending that he must have Time to more fully consider it." The marquis was indeed worried, for he had heard a rumor that the decision had been delayed to allow another charge to be made against the governor, a legal machination that, he complained to Portland, "would not have been Suffered at the Old Baily."[27]

Rockingham's fears were dispelled, however, on 8 October when the king in council upheld the committee's report and dismissed Peter Livius's charges against John Wentworth. The deciding factor turned out to be the lack of evidence to support the complaint. Only slight censure of the governor was implied by the pronouncement that the provincial council was in error in concluding that Benning Wentworth's grants to himself did not actually convey title to the land. Wentworth also was ordered from that point on punctually to forward official copies of the council journal. On the twelfth of October, the marquis informed Lady Rockingham, the "Governor is *most honourably* acquitted," and added with a touch of pride, "I own I feel a degree of triumph in it."[28]

At the end of the month, Dartmouth sent Wentworth official notification of the decision, but of course by that time word of the acquittal was well on its way across the ocean. The sweet news of victory was soured somewhat by the accompanying rumor, which proved to be true, that Livius had persuaded Dartmouth to appoint him chief justice of the province in place of Theodore Atkinson. An unwise move that could only have resulted in more dissension and increased turmoil in New Hampshire, it was swiftly blocked by John Wentworth's counterattack. Early in 1774 Macdonogh organized a memorial to the king that resulted in the transfer of Livius's appointment to Quebec. There Livius returned, where within several years he became embroiled in a controversy with Sir Guy Carlton, governor of that province. For Wentworth nothing could have completely spoiled his relief at this happy ending of the ordeal of uncertainty and frustration that had haunted him for a year and a half. Beyond that was the sense of justification and restored honor that came with his vindication. Wentworth's friends and supporters were so pleased that they gave a ball in his honor at the end of January 1774, which the local paper asserted "did in Brilliancy and Elegance, far exceed any Thing of the Kind ever seen before in this Province."[29]

The Livius affair could be interpreted as a sign of John Wentworth's weakness and vulnerability as governor. On the contrary, however, it appears to have proved his strength and support in New Hampshire. It is true that enemies did come forth, some for the first time, but no organized opposition appeared that was willing or able to mount a concerted attack on the governor. No strong, well-coordinated faction developed with the aim of removing Wentworth from office. That fact is particularly remarkable given the relative ease with which that end could have been accomplished. With his friends out of power, Wentworth's position in England was tenuous, a fact confirmed by the original recommendation of the Board of Trade that he not be continued as governor. Had there been a general desire to force him out, this would have been the ideal time. A limited campaign to collect depositions against Wentworth might have been all that was needed. Yet the best Livius could get was affidavits from three uninfluential people. Rockingham later told Wentworth that his enemies had done him a favor by not writing in support of Livius.[30] There were a few people of note who opposed Wentworth and his family's entrenched dominance, but they were not organized, had no specific goals, had no idea of someone to replace Wentworth, and were not willing to give evidence against him. Not only did Wentworth have the support of the preponderance of the province's commercial class, but his popularity at the grassroots level left little adverse sentiment to be turned against him.

Three factors would be at work from this time on, though, that would make John Wentworth's position in New Hampshire increasingly difficult and drive him and the people of his province apart. First was the effect of the Livius case on his general outlook. The criticisms and admonitions of Hillsborough and the colonial office had irritated Wentworth before, and he had expressed his displeasure to Rockingham and others over what he considered this unjustified interference. Now, however, he had come face to face with the full power of Whitehall and within a whisker of losing his office. That experience deeply impressed him, and he realized that he could not afford to make any mistakes. Right or wrong, the power was in London, and that fact he could not afford to take lightly. Also, he felt a debt to those who had helped him in England, especially to Rockingham who had appointed him and who had just spent so much effort to justify that appointment. Wentworth knew that he could not let Rockingham down or embarrass him in any way. He knew that he must do exactly what Whitehall expected of him. If the Livius affair did not make Wentworth fearful, it could not have helped but make him more careful—careful not to do anything that might antagonize the British government. He would be increasingly cautious and less willing to take an objective middle ground in any further dispute between England and the colonies. He would take a harder line on opposition to royal authority and would provide any necessary assistance to ensure that authority. John Wentworth would leave no reason to doubt that he was a worthy and loyal servant of the king.[31]

A second factor affecting Wentworth's relations with the people of his province served to accentuate his attitude of caution. As a result of the Livius episode, the governor now perceived enemies within New Hampshire. He first saw potential trouble among a group of unscrupulous land speculators in the vicinity of the Merrimack River. Those men, he believed, thought they would profit from a general breakdown of authority in the province. As a result they were eager to help Livius in his attempts to unseat the governor, and they sought support among, as Wentworth termed them, the "poor, ignorant peasants." Describing this movement as "replete with disobedience, mischief and levelling principles," Wentworth believed the common people were being enticed with greater political participation, and, significantly, he linked it to the troubles that had been plaguing Massachusetts since the time of the Stamp Act.[32] Fortunately for the governor, his apprehensions were not borne out. If there was such a threat from this quarter, it never developed, and Peter Livius did not receive any support from the Merrimack River region.

More serious, because it was more real, was the enmity that surfaced nearer home. Hoping that the Livius case would draw any enemies into the open, Wentworth remained away from town and at his Wolfeboro estate during the summer of 1773 and discreetly suppressed all news from England of his prob-
able success. The scheme worked. At the end of August, he confided to a friend: "Many have unexpectedly declared both for and against me." Among those he discovered against him were Dr. Hall Jackson, who was a local physician, and Woodbury Langdon. Wentworth told Thomas Waldron that not only had he been the focus of a "torrent of obloquy," but that it had overflowed onto his servants and even his wife, who bore it, he remarked, "with that resolution becoming her rank and name." The purported insults may have been related to a later accusation by Langdon that the governor had been cuckolded.[33]

Whatever the case, Wentworth felt threatened. The situation was made worse when he discovered that a number of important letters to him had been "clandestinely intercepted." Even after receiving word of his vindication by the Privy Council, Wentworth seems to have kept the decision quiet, probably to give his enemies hope and to expose as many of them as possible. The assembly finally had to send a committee to the governor to request information about the official determination of the case.[34] Thus, for the first time, Wentworth felt a sense of unease and estrangement within his province. He was confident that the great majority of people were on his side, but his realization now that there were persons, both known and unknown, who desired his removal put him instinctively in a defensive attitude, ready to stand firm behind the authority of the Crown.

Nevertheless, Wentworth's popularity was such that this trouble would have eventually receded into the background and become insignificant had it not been for a third, and most important, element affecting the relationship between him and the people of New Hampshire. That development was the changing situation between the colonies and Great Britain. Since the repeal of the Townshend duties in 1770, resistance to British authority had been minimal, tranquility prevailing generally throughout the colonies. The only trouble in New Hampshire had resulted from the seizure of the brig *Resolution* in the fall of 1771, but that disturbance had been short-lived. In May 1773 in response to a request from the Virginia House of Burgesses, the New Hampshire assembly created a standing committee of correspondence to exchange information with the other colonies. The burgesses were concerned with what seemed another violation of constitutional rights in a British proposal that offenders arrested for the destruction of a revenue cutter in Rhode Island be sent to England for trial. At the end of May, though, Wentworth prorogued the assembly to January 1774. After that, nothing further was heard on the matter, and peaceful conditions were not disturbed.

This pattern of harmony and accord seemed seriously threatened in November, however, when Wentworth received disturbing news from his friend Henry Caner of "tumultuous riots mobs and Town Meetings" in Boston.[35] Caner referred to actions taken by Boston's radicals in resistance to a new piece of British legislation.

In May 1773, in an effort to aid the ailing East India Company, Parliament had granted the company the right to reship its tea to America with a full rebate of the duty it had paid upon bringing the tea into Britain. That rebate would allow the tea to be sold cheaply in America with the hope that volume would help the company make up some of its losses. The plan was based on the presumption that the colonists would not object to paying the three-pence-per-pound duty, the only one of the Townshend duties that had not been repealed, in order to buy cheap tea. Some in Parliament disagreed, including Barlow Trecothick, who offered that the only way to guarantee consumption in the colonies was to remove the duty. Lord North's ministry, however, was not willing to give up this last assertion of Parliament's right to tax the American colonies. The result was the Tea Act of 1773.[36]

Understandably, there was little immediate reaction in the colonies. Nothing was blatantly obnoxious about the Tea Act, in fact, it was not aimed directly at the colonies. It was an attempt to bail the East India Company out of its financial difficulties, and, on the surface, it looked as though it would be advantageous for America, providing the colonies with cheaper tea. On 29 September, however, a letter in a Philadelphia newspaper pointed out that, contrary to what some people seemed to believe, the Townshend tea duty had not been repealed by the Tea Act, and if the tea was landed and sold, no matter how low the price, a precedent would be set for unconstitutional parliamentary taxation of the colonies. The writer, a colonist in London, urged Americans to "convince Lord North that they are not *yet ready* to have the yoke of slavery riveted about their necks and send back the tea whence it came." This warning was not ignored, and the cry for resistance soon spread throughout the colonies. In Boston the popular leaders vowed not to allow any East India tea to be sold in that town and threatened violence to the consignees if they did not resign.[37]

Henry Caner reported this negative turn to Wentworth, but New Hampshire's governor soon had troubles of his own, for his province was not isolated from the rising sentiment against the Tea Act. On 12 December a notice appeared in Portsmouth of a town meeting to be held on the sixteenth to consider necessary measures concerning the importation of East India tea. At that meeting on 16 December, eleven resolves were approved proclaiming the unconstitutionality of the Townshend tea duty and the determination of the people of Portsmouth not to allow any tea to be landed or sold. A local committee of correspondence was created, and the resolves were forwarded to the other major towns in the province. Within a short time, Dover, Newcastle, Haverhill, Exeter, and other towns issued resolves of their own, and by early 1774, opposition to British policy was more widespread in New Hampshire than it had ever been before.[38]

    John Wentworth was disturbed. He wrote Dartmouth, "It was utterly impossible to prevent the people from these measures. The unwearied applications from Boston communicated the Flame here . . . which had before run thro' all the other Colonies." He was certain, though, that this new problem would not have arisen if Peter Livius had not "spread reports and publications against the stability of the Governor and Council." Wentworth was under the illusion that the trouble in New Hampshire was related principally to the ferment Livius had raised against him. Woodbury Langdon, however, one of Livius's most influential backers, had voted against the Porstmouth tea resolves. The governor was mistaken in believing that, if the Livius episode had not taken place, his province could have remained isolated from these new disturbances. He did not realize that the current difficulties for royal government in New Hampshire were not primarily the making of his enemies from the Livius affair. They were, rather, the result of a much larger problem. Wentworth was soon made aware of that fact, for on 16 December 1773, an event took place in another colony that proved to be of far greater consequence for him than the resolves passed that day in Portsmouth. That evening, a mob numbering close to a thousand, some fitted out in Indian clothing complete with blankets and tomahawks, descended on Griffin's Wharf in Boston, boarded the ship *Dartmouth*, and heaved East India tea worth nearly ten thousand pounds into the harbor.[39]

219

»12«
REVOLUTION
COMES TO NEW
HAMPSHIRE,
1774

When the provincial assembly reconvened in January 1774 after more than a seven-month hiatus, the representatives were greeted with a charge from Governor Wentworth "to render effective the Laws for preventing Infectious and Pestilential disorders being spread among the Inhabitants Especially of Portsmouth, a calamity too Dreadful and Distressing and (without some more coercive Laws) I am certain is too likely to happen."[1] Wentworth ostensibly was referring to an outbreak of smallpox menacing Portsmouth, but equally on his mind was the dangerous political plague he saw creeping over the American colonies.

John Wentworth was once again deeply concerned about the spread of unrest to New Hampshire. He wrote to the earl of Dartmouth that he wished the House members "were in as pacific a disposition as formerly," but, unfortunately, he had to report, "The insidious Arts of discontented Men . . . have infused such jealousys and popular schemes into their minds, That my utmost attention and influence is employed, and scarce enough, to prevent their entering upon any measures they find pursued in the neighboring colonies."[2] Wentworth found his endeavors not enough and his fears borne out. His long prorogation of the assembly following its adoption of a standing committee of correspondence in May 1773 had served no purpose. The Tea Act and now the Boston Tea Party again raised the seemingly dormant dispute between America and Great Britain into the immediate consciousness of the colonies.

New Hampshire proved no exception. On the fifth of February 1774, the House moved to have a committee send replies to letters received since the previous May from Massachusetts, Connecticut, and Maryland. All of the correspondence reflected concern over threats to colonists' rights under the English constitution, and all included resolves expressing strong concurrence with the Virginia burgesses' call for intercolonial solidarity. Each of the provinces had appointed a committee of correspondence and had urged New Hampshire to do likewise. The responses agreed to by the assembly on 11 February stated New Hampshire's unequivocal desire to cooperate with the other colonies and indicated that the province had already followed Virginia's example and chosen a committee to correspond with the other legislatures. The seriousness with which the representatives now considered the situation was expressed in their letter to Massachusetts. "By the best Intelligence we can obtain," they wrote, "it appears that the British ministry are Resolved in a great Degree if not fully to Enslave the Inhabitants of the Colonies in America subject to the Crown of Great Britain if by any means they can effect it, which much concern the Americans to withstand and Prevent."[3]

This spirited feeling was not restricted to the assembly or to Portsmouth. Following Portsmouth's example, by March at least nine other towns in New Hampshire had passed resolutions condemning the Tea Act as subversive of the constitutional rights of colonists and pledging not to consume English tea. In Kingston a tea peddler by the name of Graham was pushing his wares by passing out free samples to the women of the town. When their husbands found out, Graham was forced to flee through a window of the tavern where he was staying and hide in a nearby swamp. Then, to the joy of a large crowd of onlookers, his tea was dumped at the foot of a "Liberty tree" and set on fire to the "repeated hurra's of Liberty and no taxes."[4]

Despite this flurry of activity, sentiment in the province was far from unanimous against tea or British policy. Among a series of resolves passed in March, the town of Hinsdale, in derogatory reference to the anti-tea declarations of other communities, asserted: "It is the Opinion of this Town that under the disguise of Patriotism, . . . Factive Self-Interest and private Ambition are frequently Concealed and that many Persons who Pretend to be Patriots and declaim Loudly in Defence of the Rights of their Country are bound by no Ties but those of Partial Passion and private Interest." In the *New Hampshire Gazette*, "Susanna Spindle" charged "That the Merchants under a pretence of Guarding our Liberties, prevented the Landing of the East India Company's TEA; and at the same Time sell their own at such an extravagant Price, make it evident it is not our Interest; but their own private Gain they are pursuing." Such responses must have encouraged Wentworth, and though Henry Caner kept him regularly informed of the continuing troubles encountered by Governor Hutchinson in

Boston, he remained optimistic that he could maintain peace in New Hampshire.[5]

Wentworth's main concern was with the assembly. On 12 February, following what he considered the representatives' precipitate action of joining in league with the other colonies to oppose British policy and fearing even more inflammatory measures "relating to the supremacy of Parliament," he adjourned them. After considering the situation for several weeks, the governor, early in March, dissolved the assembly with the hope that new elections would produce a House more congenial to the exercise of royal authority. At this juncture a cry went up for a broader, more equitable representation in New Hampshire's legislature. Given the state of representation in the assembly and the popular arguments currently enjoying wide circulation in the colonies, this development should not have surprised Wentworth. One "Publicus" argued in the *Gazette* that, if the issue of "no taxation without representation" were to be taken seriously, one of the first places to be considered for reform should be the provincial assembly. He pointed out that Nottingham, one of New Hampshire's major towns, had never been granted representation and that all of Grafton County, which was taxed and supported two militia regiments, remained unrepresented in the legislature.[6]

Publicus had hit on a sensitive point for the leaders of government in Portsmouth. In 1773 only 46 of the province's 147 towns were represented; nearly 40 percent of New Hampshire's taxes were collected in towns that had no voice in the assembly.[7] Although John Wentworth had been eager to extend the judicial system to remote parts of the province, his plans for development of the west had not included an expansion of representation. The reason is easy enough to see. Judgeships were the governor's to fill and gave him a direct means of control in distant, newly settled areas. Elected seats in the assembly, however, were not within his purview. Wentworth already felt that his patronage power was well below what was necessary to maintain an adequate influence of royal government in New Hampshire. Any significant broadening of representation would have made the House almost impossible to control.

Now, though, there were impelling reasons to take that long-avoided step. For the first time, there was widespread unrest in the province. Moreover, Wentworth found that inflammatory arguments that had been used broadly in the colonies against Great Britain now were cropping up at home and being turned on his own administration. He wisely recognized that the seriousness of the situation demanded the elimination of all possible sources of discontent. Accordingly, when a petition was sent to the governor and council requesting more equitable representation in the assembly, Wentworth, as one observer reported, "recommended it for his Majesty's Service, and Peace and Quiet of the Government." That he took this step under pressure in order to head off further trouble is clear. Open to question, though, is whether he intended to grant representation to towns on the basis of population, or if he was planning to apportion election writs selectively in order to pack the assembly with "friends" who could be counted on for support. Judging from the towns that gained representation a year later, the latter motivation appears more nearly correct. It made no difference in the spring of 1774, however, for the council opposed Wentworth and rejected the petition.[8]

The new assembly was no larger than the old one when it met on 7 April, but the turnover in personnel was considerable. The governor was uncertain what the temper of the new body would be, especially, he explained to Lord Dartmouth, because "the present popular commotions in the Colonies, renders it impossible to form any rational conjectures of their future Conduct." The representatives' request for a month's adjournment thus happily provided him an opportunity for more studied consideration of the new makeup of the House.[9]

Wentworth was worried mainly about the Portsmouth members, who, he was afraid, would spread that town's "spirit of opposition" to the rest of the assembly. His concern stemmed in part from the written instructions Portsmouth had provided its representatives. Among those directives were calls for annually elected assemblies, open galleries in the House, and investigation of the expenditure of all public money, all demands strongly reflective of the English opposition political ideology—by 1774 resounding stridently throughout all the colonies—that was so vitally concerned with threats to the liberty of the people by an overpowerful government. Wentworth could see suspicion of his own prerogative and the council's in the calls for trial by jury in the court of appeals, for superior and inferior court justices who would sit on good behavior rather than at the will of the Crown, and for adequate public salaries for judges to place them above influence. Worst of all from Wentworth's point of view, though, was the first instruction to the Portsmouth assemblymen proclaiming a determination to join with the other provinces to resist current British policy.[10]

It was not just the instructions that bothered Wentworth; it was the representatives themselves. Two out of the three members of Portsmouth's delegation were new. In the place of William Parker, who had never opposed the governor, and John Sherburne, whose tendency to support the anti-British cause had been subdued with judiciously proffered political appointments, the town had returned Samuel Cutts and Woodbury Langdon. Cutts, like Langdon a successful merchant outside the Wentworth sphere, had since the time of the Stamp Act been an unswerving and active opponent of all English efforts to enforce trade laws. For his smuggling activities he had suffered more than once at the hands of the vice-admiralty court, including the loss of his ship, the *Resolution*, in 1771. Samuel Cutts clearly had no love for royal authority. Woodbury Langdon, of course, had been John Wentworth's avowed personal enemy since the Livius af- 225 fair. It thus is not surprising that Wentworth expected nothing but trouble from those two men.[11] Moreover, Woodbury Langdon's emergence onto the political scene heightened the governor's sensitivity to the threat he believed had arisen from the activities of Peter Livius.

As during the previous December, Wentworth in April was still linking the atmosphere of dissent in Portsmouth to Livius's efforts to unseat him. Late that month he wrote to Dartmouth that peace and harmony would undoubtedly still have prevailed among the people of his province had not "Mr. Livius unhappily disseminated other principles among them" and raised in some the "hopes of succeeding into the offices of Government, thro' his influence."[12] The Livius affair had indeed encouraged certain longtime opponents of the dominance of the Wentworth family, in particular Woodbury Langdon, to declare openly against the governor. Others who would have liked to do the same but were still hesitant may have finally seen the opportunity to attack John Wentworth in the unrest generated against the authority of the Crown by the Tea Act and the dumping of the tea in Boston. In that sense, Wentworth's troubles of 1773 were related to the deteriorating political situation he saw in New Hampshire in the spring of 1774.

Yet the specter of Peter Livius tended to obscure pertinent issues for John Wentworth. He did not yet comprehend the depth of the conviction behind the anti-British sentiment that was sweeping America, nor did he seem to take into account its nonlocalized nature. Samuel Cutts may long have harbored a resentment of the Wentworths, but he also had been energetically opposing what he considered unjustly restrictive and unconstitutional English laws for nearly a decade. It would be difficult to assign his attitude toward the Wentworths as the main motive for his political activities of 1774. Despite abundant evidence to the contrary, Wentworth continued to place major blame for the current discontent on Peter Livius. From hindsight, his view seems myopic. Yet until now there had been little serious trouble in New Hampshire, and nothing the governor was unable to control. For him to continue looking nervously in the direction from which the only real threat to his administration had emerged was a natural reflex. In any case, as he told Dartmouth, he believed that the situation in New Hampshire could be turned around by the application of "prudent firmness and perseverance."[13] Had he known what was taking place in England, he would have had little cause for such optimism.

From the time news arrived in London in January of the destruction of the

East India tea, the cabinet of Lord North was determined that Boston should be punished and restitution made. The ministry was convinced that the only alternative was complete loss of control over all the colonies. Britain must this time stand resolute; there could be no backing down. By February a plan was resolved upon that would take away Boston's port privileges until a proper indemnity had been paid to the East India Company. Lord North introduced the bill into the Commons on 18 March; it passed on the twenty-fifth, over pleas for more moderate measures by a few Rockinghamites, and was signed into law by the king five days later.

The Boston Port Act stated that, as of 1 June 1774, Boston would be closed to all maritime commerce except for military supplies for the forces of the Crown and food and fuel needed for the sustenance of the town's inhabitants. This ban would be lifted only when "full satisfaction" had been made to the English East India merchants, when "reasonable satisfaction" had been offered to customs officers in Boston, and when the Privy Council had decided that restoration of "peace and obedience" was advanced enough to warrant reopening the port. The terms were decidedly vague. Showing a willingness to use force if necessary, the government named General Thomas Gage to replace Thomas Hutchinson as governor of Massachusetts and sent him out with four regiments of British soldiers.[14]

The New Hampshire assembly convened as scheduled on 10 May. That same day, news of the Boston Port Act reached Massachusetts. Reaction was swift. Within two days a letter signed by Samuel Adams for the Boston committee of correspondence was on its way to Portsmouth. Calling the closing of Boston harbor a "stroke of Vengeance," the letter made a plea for all colonists to stand together to "frustrate" this abominable measure. Just as Wentworth had feared, the Portsmouth delegation led the way in the opposition to British authority by reading this communication in the assembly. The governor was probably relieved and possibly hopeful when the issue was set aside by the House for the consideration of more traditional business, but his respite was not long. On 27 May the assembly approved the appointment of a provincial committee of correspondence that included Samuel Cutts and others, such as Josiah Bartlett of Kingston, known to be strongly anti-British. The following morning a resolution was approved for the speaker to answer all letters from other colonies to assure them of New Hampshire's willingness "to join in all salutary measures . . . for saving the Rights and Privileges of the Americans." The defiant mood of the assembly was made clear to Wentworth when those actions were followed by a vote for an annual supply of one thousand pounds. Such a small sum had never before been proposed during his governorship, and he considered it less than half of the minimum amount needed to run the province adequately.[15]

Wentworth may have received some comfort from the fact that the House was almost evenly divided over the vote for the committee of correspondence. Nevertheless, he could take no chances on further radical actions, a realization reinforced by the arrival of a letter from Dartmouth expressing the king's displeasure at news of the Portsmouth tea resolves and warning the governor to be on his guard. Accordingly, on Monday, 30 May, he adjourned the assembly and spent the next week attempting to get the votes for the "extra Provincial measures" rescinded. Because of the close division in the House, Wentworth doubtless considered this effort not too difficult a task. A little influence applied on a few key representatives would certainly remedy the situation. Before he could accomplish his goal, though, he received more disturbing news. A movement was afoot for a meeting of all the colonies in a general congress.[16]

227

In Virginia, upon the arrival of the news that the port of Boston had been closed by the British, the House of Burgesses without hesitation moved that 1 June be set aside as a day of fasting and prayer "to implore the divine interposition for averting . . . destruction of our Civil Rights and the Evils of civil War, [and] to give us one heart and one Mind firmly to oppose, by all just and proper means, every injury to American Rights." Understandably taking offense at this strong statement, Governor Dunmore dissolved the House. Spurred on, the burgesses met extralegally the following day at the Raleigh Tavern and sent out a call for an intercolonial congress. Other colonies soon followed Virginia's lead, including Connecticut on 3 June. Communications from those two provinces concerning a congress of the combined colonies probably were the ones that John Wentworth learned that his cousin, Speaker John Wentworth, had in his possession at the end of the first week in June. Here was an even greater threat than the measures already adopted by the assembly. Wentworth may have recognized the inefficacy of the Boston Port Act, but his first concern had to be the maintenance of royal authority in New Hampshire. He realized he could not allow his province to join the others in such a blatantly inflammatory action, and on 8 June, rather than continue to work for a reversal of the earlier votes, he dissolved the assembly. He hoped that a cooling-off period of a few weeks would convince prospective members of the next assembly "of the imprudence and error of measures that tend to weaken or subvert the subordination of the Colonies."[17]

John Wentworth faced the unending sequence of unsettling events with great equanimity. He even seems to have contemplated a normal, leisurely summer at

Wolfeboro, for he invited Henry Caner to spend the season with him in New Hampshire. Unfortunately for the governor, no opportunity was provided for tempers to subside. The day after he dissolved the assembly, word arrived in New Hampshire of further measures by the British government that could only exacerbate the anger, resentment, and fear already raised by the Boston Port Act. In a move obviously designed to augment royal control, Parliament had passed a bill significantly altering the Massachusetts Charter of 1691. The most radical provision of the Massachusetts Regulatory Act changed the Massachusetts council from a body elected by the assembly to one now appointed by the Crown. The act also took away a number of other longtime political functions of the people and vested them in the royal governor. If that action were not enough to convince many colonists of a determined effort in England to subvert their constitutional rights, another act passed Parliament allowing any magistrate in Massachusetts accused of murder or other capital crimes in the suppression of disorderly riots to be removed to Great Britain or to another colony supposedly to insure a fair trial. To many in the colonies, however, it looked like a license for the unlimited use of physical force against them by the British, and, not surprisingly, in America it became commonly known as "the Murdering Act." [18]

News of these additional English measures only fed the flames ignited in Boston by the Port Act. When Henry Caner wrote in the middle of June reluctantly to decline the governor's invitation, he noted disparagingly that the "Sons of Violence," in spite of the presence of two new British regiments, were keeping up their pressure against royal authority. Wentworth did not have to be reminded of the trouble in Boston, for he continued to see its effects in New Hampshire. On 5 June the Boston committee of correspondence adopted what it termed the "Solemn League and Covenant," an agreement to cease all trade with Great Britain as of 1 October if the so-called Intolerable Acts had not been repealed by that time. Any merchant refusing to conform was to be "boycotted forever." [19] The covenant was then circulated for adoption by other towns. Portsmouth picked it up and, later in the month, sent a similar covenant of its own to the other New Hampshire towns along with a cover letter signed by Samuel Cutts for the local committee of correspondence.

The Portsmouth covenant, a printed form with a blank for each town to fill in its own name, expressed sympathy for the oppressed people of Boston, spoke of the need to "preserve and recover the much injured Constitution of our Country," and called for a halt to trade with Britain and a boycott of British goods. Most of the rest of the province, however, was not ready to take such drastic action. In Dover the governor's friend, Jeremy Belknap, though strong in the colonial cause, contended that this unilateral command on the part of

Jeremy Belknap. (Courtesy Massachusetts Historical Society)

the Portsmouth committee could hurt many innocent merchants and had no grounding in popular will. "Tyranny in one shape," asserted Belknap, "is as odious to me as Tyranny in another." Taking the minister's statement to heart, the town of Dover set the covenant aside. So did most of the other towns in New Hampshire. Wentworth knew, though, that his immediate trouble lay not in the interior but in Portsmouth. He thus was prepared when in June another potentially volatile problem arose close to home.[20]

230

The merchant Edward Parry, despite his claims to the contrary, had apparently been expecting a shipment of East India tea.[21] John Wentworth was informed, and on Saturday, 25 June, when the mast ship *Grosvenor* arrived at the mouth of the harbor with Parry's tea aboard, the governor had the consignee send the ship's master procedural instructions via Fort William and Mary. After the example of the Boston Tea Party, after the determination expressed by Portsmouth not to let any tea enter New Hampshire, and with the still rising intensity of feeling in the town against the British, Wentworth realized that special precautions would be needed to avoid violence without compromising the operation of royal law. During the weekend, the governor made a point of openly leaving town for Dover. He did not return Monday morning, and at noon the twenty-seven chests of tea stowed on the *Grosvenor* were loaded into boats, rowed to the wharf, and carted to the customhouse without incident. Wentworth's ruse worked. Not expecting the tea to be landed during the governor's absence, those intent on keeping "that pernicious, destructive, troublesome commodity" out of New Hampshire were caught off guard.

They did not take long to recover, though, and a town meeting was hurriedly called for that afternoon. There a committee was chosen to wait on Parry and inform him that the tea must be shipped out of the province as soon as possible. The town also voted to post a watch on the tea, no doubt as much to prevent the authorities from trying to move it as to avoid any incidents repetitious of the Boston Tea Party. The next day, Tuesday, 28 June, upon confrontation by the committee, Parry wisely cooperated and agreed to reship the tea. He was then allowed to pay the duty.

This event clearly was a victory for John Wentworth. East India tea had entered New Hampshire peacefully, and the duty had been paid. There had been no breach of the law. Wentworth did not care if the tea was reshipped; that could not be considered an offense by the authorities in England. This fact no doubt galled some, especially his enemies like Woodbury Langdon and those strongly anti-British such as Samuel Cutts, but their voices were not strong enough to prevail. The majority seemed not to mind that the duty had been paid, probably because they realized that, with the tea gone, the tax could not be passed on to the inhabitants of New Hampshire. With the agreement made, the twenty-seven chests of tea were loaded on board the sloop *Molly* to be shipped out by noon the following day. All Parry had to do was to find a destination for it.

Trouble, however, was not over. About nine o'clock that evening, "three overheated mariners," as Wentworth described them, attempted to raise a mob to destroy the tea and the *Molly*. The governor responded by calling on Colonel John Fenton, a recent acquaintance but a man he knew he could rely on. Fenton in turn "gathered a few gentlemen" and stood guard during the night, preserving both ship and cargo from further danger. On Wednesday morning, the *Molly* weighed anchor and began to fall downriver. But the crisis still had not ended. Parry sent the governor a message asking that the ship be "detained at the Fort, untill I shall have proper time to Consider and find out where to send the Tea, that it may be secure from being destroyed which, by the present juncture of affairs, perplexes me very much to know." Still apprehensive that violence would overtake the *Molly* before she reached the open sea, Parry requested a guard for the ship at the fort.

Parry's fear was not a product of his imagination. Drums were beating in the town to raise volunteers for one last effort to destroy the tea before the chance was missed. Taking immediate action, Wentworth sent out a call for all members of the council and every available magistrate to meet him at the wharf. He was determined to intervene personally if necessary to counteract the threatened riot. He also ordered Captain Cochran and his men to board and defend the ship until it was ready to leave port. In Cochran's absence, Sheriff John Parker would command the fort. But to Wentworth's relief, he was informed shortly that several magistrates and councillors Warner and Rindge had confronted the crowd and persuaded the people to disperse.[22] In the meantime, Parry, having decided that the only safe port for tea in America was Halifax, sent instructions to Benjamin Partridge, master of the *Molly*, to set his sails and proceed to the northeast immediately. Partridge was more than willing to oblige but, on clearing the fort, found the sloop becalmed and was forced to return to port for another tension-filled night. Finally, on Thursday, 30 June, the ship set sail, and the controversial East India herb left New Hampshire for good.

Wentworth had weathered another storm. He had acted resolutely, even boldly. But he had taken a chance by having the tea brought in and entered at the customhouse. His scheme could have backfired and produced a reaction as serious as that in Boston.[23] Wentworth had not moved unwittingly to uphold royal authority regardless of all costs, however; he acted rather on the basis of a keen perception of the circumstances peculiar to New Hampshire. A few days after the episode, he wrote to Dartmouth that he had been "confident the magistrates and freeholders would not desert me." He had gauged the situation correctly. Even though there was evidence of strong anti-British sentiment in the colony, and especially in Portsmouth, the predominant attitude was still one of mod-

eration. There was a growing determination to stand firm against arbitrary and unjust enactments of Parliament, but there was an equal desire to avoid unnecessary violent or provocative acts. The governor noted that when he returned to town from Dover in the midst of the controversy he was treated with the "usual kindness and respect." The town itself had placed a guard on the tea, and the committee chosen to deal with the consignee, Wentworth related, was made up of "many principal gentlemen, discreet men, who I knew detested every idea of violating property: Men disposed to prevent mischief." There was not a controlling radical party in Portsmouth as in Boston. The town was operating under the influence of concerned but still basically conservative men. Thus Wentworth had again been able to avoid a serious incident in his province. Nevertheless, when only a few days later he saw the rise of a less violent but in the long run more serious threat to royal authority, he found he had no control at all.

The general appeals for an intercolonial congress that had reached New Hampshire early in June took a more definite form upon the arrival on 17 June of an invitation from the Massachusetts House of Representatives to send delegates to a congress at Philadelphia on the first of September. Here was something concrete that the assembly could act on, except that the governor had dissolved it on 8 June precisely out of a fear that this situation might arise. Now was a chance, though, for the provincial committee of correspondence, chosen before the assembly's dissolution, to show its effectiveness. It did not prove lacking. The committee notified all representatives to convene in Portsmouth on 6 July for the purpose of choosing New Hampshire's delegates to the proposed Philadelphia congress.[24]

Under existing law, this meeting clearly was illegal, and, when the assemblymen convened in the House chamber on the sixth, Wentworth was ready for them. When they had barely settled into their seats, the governor marched in with Sheriff John Parker close at his heels. This "illegal" and "unwarrantable" summoning of the provincial assembly, Wentworth declared to the representatives, by "wresting out of the King's hands his sole prerogative of calling Assembly's, in open opposition to and defiance of the Laws of his Majesty's authority," was a dangerous step toward "the utter subversion of the Constitution of this Province." Wentworth then ordered them to disperse and directed Sheriff Parker to see that his command was carried out. Force would have been of little avail to the governor in this instance, and fortunately for him, it was not necessary. Acceding to his wishes, the members left the room in orderly fashion. Wentworth headed home to write Lord Dartmouth, confident that he had again succeeded in preventing the consummation of openly illegal measures in New Hampshire.[25]

As he shortly found out, however, his optimism was premature. As the Virginia burgesses had done in May in Williamsburg following dissolution by the governor, the New Hampshire representatives repaired to a local tavern and proceeded with their business. They decided there to call on each town in the colony to send delegates to a provincial congress to be held in Exeter on 21 July for the purpose of selecting representatives to the intercolonial congress slated for 1 September in Philadelphia. Two weeks later, the first provincial congress convened in Exeter, eighty-five members present. They lost no time in voting to send John Sullivan of Durham and Nathaniel Folsom of Exeter as New Hampshire's delegates to Philadelphia. A committee was created to draw up instructions for the men, and before disbanding, a unanimous vote was taken to recommend that each town in the province contribute something toward the relief of Boston.[26]

The events of mid-July 1774 marked a significant turning point for John Wentworth. Up to that time he had been successful in controlling anti-British dissidence in his colony, probably as successful as any governor in America. Through the turmoil that had been shaking the British Empire since he had taken office, Wentworth had maintained unusually good relations with the assembly. In the winter and spring of 1774, when it became apparent that he could no longer suppress dissent within that body, he retained control of provincial affairs by exercising his royal prerogative and twice dissolving the assembly.

The unauthorized meeting of the legislature on 6 July was significant because it marked the first openly antagonistic confrontation between the governor and the assembly in New Hampshire. Of even more importance was the now apparent fact, as a result of the representatives' actions in the Portsmouth tavern and the congress in Exeter, that John Wentworth's prerogative no longer carried any effective power. His order to the assemblymen in the name of the Crown to desist from their unconstitutional activities had simply been ignored. Moreover, the first step had been taken since the earliest settlement of Englishmen in New Hampshire, a momentous step, toward the creation of a government based on the sovereignty of the people of the province rather than on the king in Parliament. Wentworth had no coercive power, military or otherwise; he was politically impotent. Although he kept up the illusion of authority, he knew from this point on that he had lost control of not only New Hampshire but his own future, and that his fate was tied directly to the broad problem of the deteriorating relations between Britain and the colonies.

Wentworth was not optimistic about this situation. A week after the call for

John Sullivan. (State of New Hampshire, State House)

the congress in Exeter, he wrote Dartmouth: "I am apt to believe the spirit of enthusiasm, which generally prevails through the colonies, will create an obedience that reason or religion would fail to procure." Yet Wentworth was enough impressed by that "enthusiasm" to give brief consideration, rare for him, to the arguments the colonials were now so stridently trumpeting against the British. The word *liberty,* which had become such a stock part of patriot rhetoric, was a term that gave him pause. In a revealing letter of 22 July, the day after the meeting of the Exeter congress, Wentworth expressed his thoughts to William Williams, a friend in Connecticut. "The Cause of Liberty," he wrote, "is undoubtedly, the great Duty of all good Men; and under the English Constitution must be more essentially the interest of those intrusted with the administration of Government, seeing their power, emoluments—honor and usefulness are rooted in the Laws," laws that, he went on, "may be well denominated Rules for the enjoyment of liberty."[27]

Liberty was everyone's concern, but for Wentworth it was especially the concern of those whose job it was to uphold the law, that is, of government officials. Under the English constitution, the law was the guarantee of liberty, and Wentworth clearly implied that liberty could not exist over and above the law. In fact, there could be no hope for liberty unless the law was obeyed. Government was the protector, not oppressor, of basic liberties. Thus the colonists' argument for preserving liberty by defying British law was, to Wentworth, completely fallacious and subversive of the constitution. Like Thomas Hutchinson, his fellow governor in Massachusetts whose conventional and rigid perception of government had already forced him out of his seat, and unlike many colonials who were increasingly searching the writings of John Locke and other political philosophers for answers to the growing conflict between Britain and the colonies, John Wentworth could not conceive of a law higher than British law.

But Wentworth did not linger long in considering the ideas of the heightening constitutional debate. Those notions were, for him, only manifestations of much more practical problems that stemmed from the fact that leaders on both sides had temporarily lost sight of their mutual interests. Wentworth's belief, which in the first instance had been so influenced by Rockingham, in the necessity of a moderate approach to the British-American relationship that took into account the needs and welfare of both sides was at this time reinforced by the marquis. "If the competition," he wrote Wentworth, "is now between this Country and North America which shall be Wildest and Rashest I can hardly guess at present wh[ich] of the two will go the greatest lengths." Critical of the ministry, Rockingham decried the most recent British measures as not "form'd on principles of justice and policy." He "equally disapprove[d]" the actions taken in America. Rockingham expressed what Wentworth believed: that the problem lay in the unwise formulation and administration of policy.[28]

But as bad as the current difficulties were, Wentworth felt that the fundamental ties between England and the American colonies were too strong to be permanently sundered. "Certain I am," he told William Williams, "that Britain and America have a reciprocal affection, which neither can give up." That former "harmony, which of late seems to be obscured," he continued, "I am convinc'd cannot be eradicated. Time will allay the dispositions that now operate powerfully." It may have been wishful thinking on Wentworth's part, but more than that, it was the conviction of a man in whom sentiment for America and England mingled equally and inseparably. John Wentworth's attachment to both was so deep that he had genuine difficulty perceiving them as separate entities. Wentworth has been called "the most English of Americans." Just as accurately, he might be described as the most profoundly American of British officials in the colonies. Indeed, at this time of worsening relations, he thought of himself as one who might "render essential services to both Countrys" in moving toward reconciliation. But he also realized that he was in no position to do so. His influence was "so small," he lamented, "that like the Widows mite, it's merit consists chiefly in the sincere integrity of it's Intention."[29] Like Rockingham in England, he could only watch helplessly as extremists on both sides made the situation worse.

There was little for Wentworth to do now but await the results of the Philadelphia congress and hope that moderate minds would prevail. In the meantime, he would have to stay as close as possible to Portsmouth and use what influence he did have to maintain peace, or at least try to prevent the kinds of outrages that had been perpetrated against royal authority in other provinces. Periodic correspondence from Lord Dartmouth let him know that Whitehall, even with the greatest trouble concentrated in other colonies, was not ignoring the situation in New Hampshire. As the end of August approached, Wentworth, for the first time since the founding of Dartmouth College, called off his annual commencement trip to Hanover. At that time, he saw potential trouble in the presence in Portsmouth of Boston's town clerk, who, he believed, was soliciting donations for the relief of that town's inhabitants. More than that, however, Wentworth was concerned about the imminent arrival of another shipment of tea, which he had known about since July.[30]

Much had transpired since the tea incident in June, and Wentworth expected trouble.[31] The situation was aggravated early in September by the arrival of a tea ship in Salem, which aroused tempers in Portsmouth in anticipation of tea destined for the Piscataqua. On 8 September, the mast ship *Fox* anchored in the river with thirty chests of East India Bohea tea aboard, consigned once again to Edward Parry. The town remained quiet until late that evening, but a little after ten the governor received an urgent note from Parry explaining that rowdies were smashing his windows "with such Violence as to force Open the Inside Window Shutters" of his house. Wentworth had doubtless been enjoying his conversation with Thomas Macdonogh, who had arrived that very day on board the *Fox*. He had not seen his secretary since Macdonogh's departure for England in December 1772 to organize the defense for the Livius case. There was much for the two men to discuss. This was Wentworth's first opportunity to hear a firsthand account of the trial. It was also a chance to gain crucial information about the political situation in Great Britain, not only on policies and attitudes towards the colonies but on the condition and prospects for change in the current ministry. Now all that was thrust into the background on the immediate alarm of fifes and drums calling out the mob.

When Parry's message arrived, Wentworth dispatched Macdonogh and his brother-in-law, young Benning Wentworth, who was also at his home, to see how serious the trouble was. By the time they reached Parry's house, the violence had subsided, but the following morning the merchant petitioned the governor and council for protection. The council responded by calling in the town magistrates and charging them to keep the peace and protect Parry. Significantly, though, the governor and council also sent for Parry and Zacharia Norman, captain of the *Fox*, and informed them that, because the ship was anchored on the far side of the river and was thus within the jurisdiction of Massachusetts rather than New Hampshire, they could not be responsible for any violence perpetrated against the vessel or its cargo. Wentworth was willing to seize on this technicality to avoid a potentially dangerous confrontation over the tea. He in fact found the situation in Portsmouth "more precarious" than that of the previous June, and he later wrote that it was overcome only after "the utmost Peril and Difficulty." Wentworth was so concerned that he requested the sheriff and the attorney general to return from Exeter where the superior court was meeting. He then called in Peter Gilman and Thomas Westbrook Waldron to bring the council to full strength and held it in session until two o'clock in the morning.

In the meantime, Parry had been meeting with representatives from the town. They were apparently willing to accept his claim that the tea had been shipped without his consent or knowledge, for they agreed, as before, to allow the tea to be entered and the duty paid if Parry would immediately reship it. Accordingly, on Saturday, the tenth, the tea was brought in, and on Sunday it left Portsmouth for Halifax. The episode indicated the moderation still prevalent in Portsmouth, especially in light of Wentworth's almost open invitation to destroy the tea by declaring it out of his protection. Wentworth was relieved that his predicament had been resolved peacefully, but he was not optimistic. Two days after the departure of the tea, he wrote to Dartmouth that sentiment in New Hampshire was now wholly unified in support of the colonial position. On that, though, he was not entirely correct.

On 5 September 1774 the First Continental Congress convened at Carpenter's Hall in Philadelphia. Recent news of the Quebec Act, which among other things established a government in that northern province without a representative legislature, gave a sense of urgency to the proceedings. The delegates did not flinch in the face of what now seemed a consciously concerted British effort at total subjugation of colonial rights. Making their position clear, they voted on the seventeenth to approve the radical resolves of Suffolk County, Massachusetts, which not only denounced "the attempts of a wicked administration to enslave America" but called for defiance of the recent British acts and exhorted the people of the province to prepare themselves militarily. Late in the month, the congress made a substantive decision of its own when it resolved that the colonies should boycott all British goods as of 1 December. The boycott took concrete form in the specific enumerations of a plan called the Continental Association, adopted on the eighteenth of October. Putting teeth into this commercial coercion, the Association called on all towns in the colonies to establish committees of inspection to insure enforcement of the boycott movement. Before it dissolved itself on 26 October, the Philadelphia congress also adopted a formal Statement of Rights and Grievances, approved a petition to King George asking for redress of the wrongs done the colonies, and set 10 May 1775 for the meeting of a second congress in case no action had been taken on the petition by that date.[32]

Although John Wentworth assumed that all New Hampshire had unquestioningly joined the radical cause, in October several interior towns declared their support for established authority and warned that they would not meekly follow the dictates of self-appointed protectors of the English constitution. The residents of Francestown, though affirming their deep concern for the preservation of basic rights, resolved to "show our disapprobation of all unlawful proceedings of unjust men congregating together as they pretend to maintain their liberties." The town of New Boston adopted similar resolutions on the same day.[33] But if Wentworth was cheered still to find pockets of what he considered rationality within his province, he nevertheless realized it meant little against the prevailing atmosphere of increasing bitterness toward Britain, especially in the older part of New Hampshire.

In mid-September the town of Kingston sent its sympathies and one hundred sheep to Boston. On the nineteenth, Portsmouth appointed a committee to receive donations for the Massachusetts port. Three weeks later, on 10 October, the town went even further and voted two hundred pounds for Boston's relief, "near four times their Province tax," exclaimed an incredulous John Wentworth. At that same meeting, a committee of ways and means, consisting of forty-five members, was chosen to meet regularly to consider anything "unfriendly to the Interest of the Community." The formation of that body fit very well with the call from the Continental Congress for local committees of inspection. The governor, however, was not pleased, and he soon became disgusted with what he considered the Portsmouth committee's foolish pettiness. When it was discovered that three barrels of pineapples and oranges en route from the West Indies to General Gage's wife in Boston were aboard a ship in the Piscataqua, Wentworth was forced to rescue the fruit from zealous committee members and take it to his own house for safekeeping. "Such Follys," he remarked to a friend, "dishonor a country."[34]

239

John Wentworth's comment was born out of disappointment, not bitterness. Early in October, Henry Caner had guided to Wentworth's care an Anglican minister, Samuel Peters, who was fleeing back to London from anti-English furies in Connecticut. The governor entertained Peters in his home but then, fearing for his safety, sent him off to Fort William and Mary to await the sailing of the next mast ship. Before the minister departed, Wentworth advised him not to be vindictive on his arrival in England but to tell his story with moderation and not to treat harshly even "those who have most cruelly treated him."[35] This entreaty was a tribute not only to Wentworth's benevolent nature but also to his enduring belief that a solution, though not necessarily immediate, would eventually be found in the dispute between the colonies and Great Britain. Regardless of the current bleak prospects, reconciliation was a certainty in his mind. Unfortunately, Wentworth took a step at this time that not only made the situation worse but cost him whatever small bit of authority and sympathy he still commanded in New Hampshire. Although he could not know it at the time, his action would mean lifelong alienation from his province.

»13«
FALL FROM
AN "HONORABLE
PRECIPICE,"
1774-1775

G eneral Gage needed barracks for his soldiers. With Boston verging on open rebellion, he knew there was little chance of obtaining enough local artisans to construct the buildings. When the general turned to the governors of other provinces for help, John Wentworth responded. Realizing that the situation in Portsmouth was now little better than in Massachusetts, Wentworth contacted Nicholas Austin, a friend from Middleton, asking that he gather as many carpenters as possible in the Wolfeboro vicinity. When the craftsmen arrived in the capital, Wentworth informed them that General Gage would pay their wages, and then he packed them off to Boston. The governor kept his action as quiet as possible, hesitating to disclose even to Austin the destination of the carpenters. But Nicholas Austin suspected the purpose Wentworth had in mind for the workers, and soon others knew too.

On 28 October a notice from the Portsmouth committee of ways and means in the *New Hampshire Gazette* reported, "Some Person or Persons under the Crown" had been procuring carpenters in the area of Wolfeboro. Because the purpose of the men was to aid General Gage in constructing barracks and thus "give every Assistance to the present despotick Measures," declared the committee, the "cruel and unmanly" person responsible for this outrage should be deemed "an Enemy . . . to the Community." There was no question who that person was. If anyone needed concrete proof, they got it on 8 November when the Rochester committee of correspondence called Nicholas Austin before them and forced him to confess that he had been working for the governor.[1]

Why did John Wentworth make such a provocative move? First of all, he viewed it as a badly needed bolster to royal authority in the face of growing anarchy. He could see that if the current trend continued with no countervailing force, the colonies might soon slip into chaos. As a Crown official, Wentworth felt a responsibility to prevent the complete subversion of established order and authority. By the fall of 1774 he realized that, to keep order, military force might be necessary. "Popular torrents," he remarked to Thomas Waldron, "cannot safely be check't, without irresistable power." Moreover, Wentworth was convinced he had done the right thing. "Be assured my friend," he wrote Waldron concerning the carpenters two days before his censure by the Portsmouth committee, "it is a happy circumstance to the province; it will help a reconciliation, infinitely promote it! Small circumstances often produce great events, or at least lead to them." The governor at this time was also encouraging the return of deserters to Gage's army and was securing blankets for the general.[2]

Second, although Wentworth realized that colonial opposition had been widely adopted in New Hampshire, he underestimated the depth and conviction of the sentiment. Thus in November 1774 he was still ascribing a large share of his immediate trouble to "Mr. Livius' few adherents." Central among those was Woodbury Langdon, to whom Wentworth attributed the "sole production" of the resolves that had condemned him for recruiting the carpenters. But even though he was willing to explain away the resentment raised against him as the work of a small knot of personal enemies, from the beginning Wentworth had been aware of the serious nature of his undertaking. The fact that he attempted to keep it secret is proof enough of his understanding. When the furor broke, he must have at least partially realized, difficult as it was to admit, his misjudgment. Even such a close friend as Eleazar Wheelock, who was still strongly supportive, could not help injecting a questioning note in a letter to Wentworth concerning the governor's wisdom in the affair.[3] It was unfortunate, but he had been discovered. As he found out, the consequences were disastrous. Regardless of whose work it was, John Wentworth had been branded an enemy of his province. His authority and influence were smashed beyond redemption.

For the first time John Wentworth felt uncomfortable in New Hampshire, the province of his birth, the province he had known and loved all his life. Surrounded by hostile forces, Wentworth began to feel a sense of isolation, alienation, even fear. Early in November he wrote to Captain Mowat of HMS *Canceaux* in Boston harbor expressing his regret that the ship was sailing for New York instead of Portsmouth. The governor in fact had little reason for optimism. The tide of sentiment in New Hampshire was now running strongly against Great Britain and royal authority. Exeter, like Portsmouth, granted a substantial sum for the relief of Boston. On 8 November a congress was held in Hillsborough County to "excite in the minds of people a due respect to all just measures that may be recommended by the present Grand Congress at Philadelphia." On that same day, New Hampshire's delegates to Philadelphia, John Sullivan and Nathanial Folsom, arrived in Portsmouth, where according to the *New Hampshire Gazette,* they "were joyfully received by the Inhabitants." At midmonth Wentworth was complaining about "reprehensible violences" being carried out under the name of "liberty" in both Hillsborough and Cheshire counties. The committee of ways and means in Portsmouth took steps to enforce the Continental Association by preventing a Captain Chivers from carrying fifty head of sheep to the West Indies. At its town meeting on the twenty-eighth, Durham unanimously approved the proceedings of the Continental Congress and appointed a committee to see that the Association was enforced. Two days later, the provincial committee of correspondence sent notices to all towns urging that they do the same. The committee also called on the towns to meet once again to choose delegates to the congress scheduled for Philadelphia in May. John Wentworth found government in New Hampshire "totally prostrated" by "popular Tyranny."[4]

Wentworth's repeated expressions of optimism during this period thus come as a surprise. On 9 September he reported to Rockingham, New Hampshire "has caught the infection; but I think it has passed the crisis." Nine days later he informed Eleazar Wheelock that the clamor over the carpenters had abated in Portsmouth and that peace even seemed to be returning to Boston. Further, Wentworth expected this mood to "spread thro' all the country, as did all the disquiet that has disturbed the people for six years past." On the same day he told Jeremy Belknap he believed the worst was over and that conditions would now begin to improve.[5] His statements appear anomalous within the political situation of November 1774, especially given Wentworth's perception of his own difficulties. They might be dismissed as wishful thinking, as the normal reaction of anyone in the midst of crisis who seeks to reassure himself that all is not as bad as it seems and that conditions soon will get better. But his remarks represent more than that.

John Wentworth apparently saw at hand at least the possibility of a solution to the conflict between America and Britain. On 18 November he declared to Belknap, "there is some prospect of a civil creation soon emerging out of the present chaotic jumble of discordant political elements." Wentworth did not elaborate on this "civil creation," but a letter written to Thomas Waldron a week later provides a further clue to his thinking. "Whenever the period is arrived," offered the governor, "that the Colonies can expect to be invited to send an agent to negotiate their more than important concerns at the Court of Gr[eat] Br[itain], it will be truly glorious to the elected if happily they can be useful in

243

obliterating those disquietudes which will shake the political elements of both countries into confusion and certain ruin, unless some American constitution is fixed."[6]

244   Even though John Wentworth strongly opposed what he considered the inflammatory actions pursued in the colonies, he showed himself sympathetic to colonial grievances. Moreover, although Wentworth had not been inclined to consider constitutional issues, he was now convinced of the necessity of some kind of constitutional readjustment for the colonies. What he meant by an "American constitution" can only be surmised. It may be assumed, however, that he saw at least the need for a formal definition of the colonies' position within the British Empire, an unambiguous statement of colonial rights, privileges, and responsibilities drawn up with an eye to resolving the differences that had estranged America from the mother country. Wentworth may have been influenced by a proposal put forth at the Philadelphia congress by Joseph Galloway, a delegate from Pennsylvania. Attempting to salvage the ties between the colonies and Great Britain, Galloway's plan of union called for a separate American legislature, a grand council, that would deal exclusively with all policy involving both the colonies and Britain. The approval of that body would be needed, along with that of Parliament, for the passage of any measure. The congress rejected Galloway's plan, but for others such a proposal represented the only possibility for preventing a complete break between England and America.[7]

Among those in Britain supportive of the idea was the colonial secretary, Lord Dartmouth. "The Idea of a Union upon some general constitutional Plan," he declared, "is certainly very just and I have no doubt of its' being yet attainable, thro' some channel of mutual consideration and discussion." As an associate of the Rockingham group at the time of the Stamp Act and a moderate man, Dartmouth's commitment to this kind of solution would not have surprised John Wentworth. Nevertheless, he could not expect Dartmouth, standing alone within a ministry that had shown little willingness to make concessions of any sort to the colonies, to undertake an effective plan of accommodation. What encouraged Wentworth to think that a reasonable settlement might yet be found was his persistent hope that the Rockingham Whigs would again head the government. A parliamentary election had been scheduled for the end of November. Informed by his English sources, Wentworth expected the notorious John Wilkes to win a seat from Middlesex. Wilkes, like other English radicals, was vehemently opposed to the coercive measures that had been instituted against the colonies during 1774. If the election went strongly in favor of that opposition, George III might be compelled to form a new ministry, one more moderate in its approach to the colonies. Thus the prospect of Wilkes sitting in the

Commons led Wentworth to conclude that if there were "many such changes in the new P[arliament] the administration of 1766 will grow again into power."[8]

Clearly Wentworth did not envision the use of force as the answer to the British-colonial crisis. A lasting relationship had to be built on mutual agreement, trust, and, as he had told Rockingham in 1765, common advantage. He realized by late 1774, though, that any agreement would have to include some alteration of the constitutional structure of the empire. He accepted that and had hopes that the Rockingham Whigs, who might provide the initiative for such a move, would be returned to office. In the meantime, however, peace and order had to be maintained so that all chances for a reasonable settlement were not destroyed. To that end Wentworth was willing to provide support for General Gage's army, obviously an unpopular move but the price he believed that one who "loves both countrys so much" had to be willing to pay. His was a precarious position; nevertheless, he stoically advised Thomas Waldron, any man devoted to reconciling the two sides must remain "inconscious of the imminent dangers that hang around the honorable precipice he must tread."[9]

Unfortunately for Wentworth, the parliamentary elections did not provide the results he had hoped for. Wilkes did gain his seat in the Commons and was even elected Lord Mayor of London, but in the rest of the House there was no slackening of support for the colonial policies of George III and Lord North. Wentworth had to concede that "it is very probable the administration are stronger in P[arliament] now than in the last." Since the king and North had by now decided that hostilities were inevitable, there appeared little hope for peace. It was, in fact, a royal directive based on that attitude that very shortly brought New Hampshire, for the first time, to the forefront of the revolutionary movement. On 19 October the king issued a proclamation forbidding the export of arms or munitions from Britain to the colonies. At the same time, he commanded all royal governors to prevent the importation of war materials from any place. News of the orders reached America by early December, causing immediate apprehension among those who most feared British use of force against the colonies. In Rhode Island, the governor, one of only two in the colonies elected in a province, ordered the removal of all armaments from Fort George in Newport to the relative security of Providence.[10] Action taken in New Hampshire was even more drastic.

At four o'clock in the winter dusk of Tuesday, 13 December, Paul Revere arrived in Portsmouth after a hurried ride from Boston with a message from that town's committee of correspondence. Finding Samuel Cutts of the Portsmouth committee walking on the parade near the state house, Revere hustled him into Stoodley's Tavern. There he imparted his urgent news of the royal proclamation

245

forbidding the importation of arms into the colonies, Rhode Island's reaction, and the even more pressing intelligence that on Sunday British troops had surreptitiously boarded ships in Boston. Conjecture was, Revere related, that the ships and soldiers were bound for the Piscataqua to seize the arms and munitions at Fort William and Mary. The news spread quickly, and by noon the following day, Wentworth heard drums reverberating in the streets. He soon learned that volunteers were being summoned to remove the powder and cannon from the fort before the British could do the same. Distressed but not surprised, the governor had already warned Captain Cochran to be on his guard.[11]

Wentworth dispatched Chief Justice Atkinson to the parade to disperse the gathering crowd. On confronting the people, Atkinson could not obtain an answer about their purpose. He then informed them that he knew their intention and warned that any move against the fort would constitute an "Act of High Treason and Rebellion." With that, he ordered them to disband. No one moved. Major John Langdon, Woodbury Langdon's brother, then stepped forward and, after openly ridiculing the old man, led the assembled men off on their mission. Wentworth frantically called in the council but could not persuade them to accompany him to the fort. Determined to go himself, he could find no one to man his barge. Sheriff Parker could not even obtain a messenger to alert Captain Cochran of the approaching mob.[12] Here was proof, if the governor needed it, to justify his assertion of a month earlier that government in New Hampshire was "totally prostrated."

In the meantime, John Cochran had been having his own trouble. Shortly before noon, several residents of Newcastle ambled into the fort to warm themselves, as they said, and visit the commander. When the sentry reported more men approaching from various directions, Cochran told his visitors, "I wonder much at your Coming now, as you have never before been to see Me since my living here almost four Years." Sarah Cochran, astutely suspecting the men had come to overpower her husband and capture the fortress, slipped him a pair of loaded pistols. After ordering the men out of the fort, Cochran hurried his five soldiers to defensive preparations and pressed a sixth man into service, Elijah Locke of Rye, who unhappily had chosen that time to come to the fort on business.[13]

By one o'clock, a great crowd, including the men from Newcastle, those who had marched from Portsmouth, and others from across the river in Kittery, had gathered at the gates of Fort William and Mary. When John Langdon stepped forth as the group's spokesman and demanded the gunpowder stored in the magazine, Cochran snapped back, as he later remembered, that they "must produce the Governor's Orders for it. Langdon replied they had forgot to bring his

John Langdon. (New Hampshire Historical Society)

Orders," Cochran continued, "but the Powder they were determined to have at all Events. I replied they must take it by Violence for that I would defend it to the last Extremity." Moments later a signal was given, and some four hundred men stormed the walls on all sides. Cochran ordered his soldiers to fire, but the cannon balls and musket shot hit no one. Bracing himself against a wall, the captain tried to fend the attackers off, and even his wife, wielding a bayonet, attempted to help. But seven men and a woman were no match for hundreds. The defenders were soon overpowered, "Whereupon," Cochran recalled, the invaders "gave three Huzzas or Cheers and hauled down the King's Colours." They proceeded to break open the magazine and carry off a hundred barrels of gunpowder, leaving one behind.[14]

On receipt of the news of these events from Cochran that evening, John Wentworth frantically dashed off a message to General Gage. He stressed the total ineffectiveness of government in New Hampshire without "some strong ships of war in this harbour." He also reported that a call had gone out to other towns to help remove the cannon and arms that still remained at the fort. The following morning the governor called in his council, the magistrates, and militia officers and ordered that thirty men be raised to go with him to protect the fort in the afternoon. Again, not one man answered the call. "Fear," Wentworth painfully observed, "had possessed those that were out of the rebellion."[15]

At one o'clock he received word that five hundred men were descending on Portsmouth with Major John Sullivan at their head. Wentworth sent for Sullivan, who explained they were operating on the belief that British ships and soldiers were expected momentarily with the intention of seizing the arms and artillery at the fort. Wentworth vehemently denied this report and ordered the major to disperse the crowd. Sullivan conferred with the people and returned to the governor with a committee that included John Langdon. They stated that, since the removal of the powder had been intended as strictly a defensive measure, if the governor would promise pardons to those who had participated on the previous day the people now gathered in town might be convinced to return to their homes. If Wentworth's characteristic prudence had prevailed at that point he might have avoided a second assault on the king's fort, which he had no other power to prevent. By this time, however, frustration had led to anger, and clinging to a sense of duty that was all that remained of his authority as governor, he exploded that "it was the height of absurdity to suppose this little Colony cou'd oppose the vengeance of Great Britain, or escape it's just resentment for an insult upon it's Honor and Government, which all the States of Europe wou'd not offer with impunity." Under no circumstances would he pardon those who had attacked Fort William and Mary. With that, Sullivan and the others went off to Tilton's Tavern to consider their next move.[16]

Wentworth heard nothing more until about seven o'clock when a messenger reported that more than one thousand men were marching into Portsmouth from other New Hampshire towns and that another six hundred were coming from Berwick and Kittery in Maine. That news, he also found out, had encouraged John Sullivan and his party to embark in gundalows for Newcastle. Arriving at the gates of the fort at ten o'clock, Sullivan announced that they had come to take possession of the stores belonging to the province. Cochran realized by this time that he could put up no defense, so he told the major he would let in ten men providing they took only what belonged to the province and not to the king. He hoped to convince the invaders that their share "consisted only of forty or fifty old useless Musquets and some inconsiderable small stores of no value." Sullivan agreed, and the gates swung open. The ten men proceeded inside, but the others followed after them and set about appropriating as much of the fort's ordnance as they could move. Working through the night as John Cochran looked on helplessly, Sullivan's men by eight o'clock the next morning had loaded "Sixteen pieces of Cannon, ten Carriages and about forty two Musquets with shot and other Military stores" onto their gundalows to be carried upriver and distributed through the countryside.[17]

By the time the cannon reached Portsmouth the tide was too low to proceed any further. A large body of armed men on foot and horseback thus remained in the capital during the sixteenth under the direction of Nathaniel Folsom, New Hampshire's other delegate to the Philadelphia Congress, to insure that no attempts were made to recapture the booty from the fort. Wentworth went to meet the council at noon, but while they were inside the state house, eighty armed men were trooped in front of the door. The mood in Portsmouth was no longer merely defiant but was aggressively hostile toward all Crown officers and sympathizers. No longer was there any pretence of respect for the governor or for any royal authority. To Wentworth's order that the men disperse, the retort shot back that the people were "Subjects of King George and not King James." The men refused to move. Wentworth was allowed to proceed through them to his home, but he was concerned for his own safety. He gave credence to a rumor that the mob "propos'd to load with Ball and kill all the Torys— meaning the Governor and Council." Only "some unknown caprice or other," he believed, prevented this from happening. That evening on the high tide, the guns were sent up the river, and the crowd evacuated the town. The following night, much to John Wentworth's relief, the armed British ship *Canceaux* arrived at the harbor mouth and hove to just off the fort. Now the threats to carry off the remaining heavy cannon and raid the province treasury could not easily be carried out. Two days later, Monday, 19 December, the man-of-war *Scarborough* joined the *Canceaux* in its vigil on the Piscataqua.[18]

Peace had finally returned to New Hampshire, but for John Wentworth, that was small consolation. For the first time in the colonies, the British flag had been ignominiously assaulted by the king's own subjects, and it had occurred in New Hampshire! This "insult" to the Crown, Wentworth told a friend, "grieves me to my soul." Making matters worse was the fact that this outrage against royal authority could not be attributed to the unthinking zealousness of a motley rabble. The leaders of the raids were all men of substance. Naturally attempting to minimize the significance of these events for Lord Dartmouth, Wentworth described the New Hampshire radicals as people of "no considerable Rank in the Community." In his heart he knew that claim was not true. John Langdon was an influential Portsmouth merchant. John Sullivan of Durham and Nathaniel Folsom of Exeter enjoyed enough prestige in the province to have been elected delegates to the Philadelphia Congress. Josiah Bartlett of Kingston—physician, colonel in the militia, and member of the assembly—had been ready to march to the fort at a moment's notice. Stephen Batson, who pried open the powder magazine with a crowbar on the night of the fourteenth, was the brother-in-law of George Meserve, the collector of the port. One contemporary observer was probably only slightly exaggerating when he described the participants as men "of the best property and note in the Province."[19]

John Wentworth's frustration was even greater because he realized there was little prospect of bringing the offenders to justice. Although he issued a proclamation the day after Christmas calling for the arrest and punishment of those who took part in the raids, Wentworth told Dartmouth that they could never be kept in jail, and, even if they could be detained, no jury would convict them. His words reflected his realization that sentiment in New Hampshire was now overwhelmingly against Great Britain. That resentment, of course, also carried over to all Crown officers, including himself. As a result he felt extremely isolated and vulnerable. The people he could still count on for support he could number on one hand—councillors Rindge and Jaffrey; his secretary, Thomas Macdonogh; Colonel John Fenton; and his brother-in-law, Benning Wentworth. In describing the assaults on the fort, he complained that "Not even the Revenue officers" came forth to help. "All chose to shrink in safety from the storm and suffered me to remain exposed to the folly and madness of an enraged multitude."[20]

The arrival of the two British warships did nothing to diminish Wentworth's fear for his own safety and for that of his few supporters. He believed that a plan

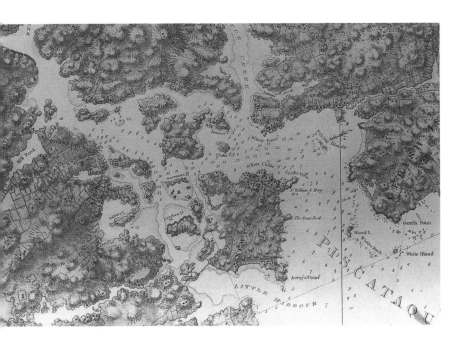

A chart of Portsmouth harbor by J. W. A. DesBarres,
dated 1779, from *The Atlantic Neptune*.
(New Hampshire Historical Society)

had been devised by "our Junto," in case of open warfare, "to secure . . . and to expose us for a cover in their battle, or to destroy in revenge." The *Scarborough* and *Canceaux*, lying three miles downriver opposite the fort, would afford little protection against this kind of attack. Wentworth thus wrote to both General Gage and Admiral Samuel Graves, commander of the British squadron at Boston, asking for an additional sloop-of-war with a contingent of forty to fifty marines. Such a vessel, the governor explained, could "lay over to the Island opposite to our Church where there is a fine place in deep water, an Eddy out of the tide, Ice or other harm." Without this commitment, he continued, "I am convinc'd . . . That very deplorable mischiefs may be reasonably expected in this Town and Province." Unfortunately for Wentworth, Admiral Graves believed his naval forces already too thinly dispersed and could not seriously consider the New Hampshire governor's request.[21]

Wentworth feared not only for his own safety but even more for that of his wife, Frances, who was expecting the birth of a child at any moment. Hard as she tried, Frances could not keep from crying, and her emotional state visibly affected him. He found that "the starting tears often . . . made me fly from their powerful influence." Wentworth had good reason to be despondent, so it is not surprising to find a fatalistic note in his thoughts at this time. Preparing to send four hogsheads of rum and molasses to his Wolfeboro estate, he declared to Thomas Waldron: "I shall not delay sending stores to W[entworth] House, notwithstanding all the menaces. If it is destroy'd, let all go together."[22]

Yet Wentworth had not abandoned hope for a resolution of his difficult situation. He had an unremitting faith in the durability and necessity of British-American ties. "All accounts agree," he stated as the eventful year drew to a close, "that America must be seriously considered and establish'd in connection to Britain." Wentworth continued to believe that somehow a practical, reasonable solution could be worked out. Aware that the current ministry was determined to use force if necessary, he was not sure Parliament would support that policy.[23] The government might thus be induced to offer a constitutional compromise that the colonies could accept, an offer he hoped the Rockingham Whigs would be in a position to make.

Wentworth meanwhile was determined to maintain his composure and not be forced into unwise or precipitate actions. "My mind," he told Waldron, "ought in such times to have no feelings of its own, and I think had not very many except those [brought by Frances's] tears." The balance of the man can be seen in his declared determination to "act with firmness, inflexible, equally distant from temerity and timidity." He was relaxed enough to take the time to read with a critic's eye the second manuscript chapter of his friend Jeremy Belknap's *History of New Hampshire*. Wentworth was even able to summon enough good cheer to offer General Gage and his family "best wishes for many happy Returns of the Season."[24]

The winter months of the new year, however, brought no relief for Wentworth's pervading sense of gloom. By the middle of January 1775, he was convinced that to have any hope of arresting the men who attacked the fort and to protect himself and other royal officers he would need two regiments of British regulars. With the utmost secrecy, he sent Thomas Macdonogh off to request troops from General Gage. In the meantime he endeavored to organize a group of followers bound to his and each other's support in case of attack. On 17 January a mutual protection association was formed by fifty-nine men. Despite the fact that many of them were Crown officers, local officials, close friends, and relatives, all of whom Wentworth could have expected to join, he must have been pleased with the relatively large number who finally signed the agreement. Nevertheless, he had no illusion that sentiment in Portsmouth was becoming more favorable toward Britain and royal government. The next day, he reported to Gage, a mob broke into a small shopkeeper's house and, discovering seventy pounds of tea, forced the man to burn it publicly in the center of town.[25]

One week later, on 25 January, a second provincial congress met in Exeter. In an obvious affront to royal authority, the members chose John Langdon and John Sullivan, respective leaders of the two raids on the fort, as New Hampshire's delegates to the Second Continental Congress, scheduled for Philadelphia on 10 May. The Exeter congress also prepared an address to the people of the province expressing regret that they had been deprived of a representative assembly for the previous ten months. As the only person legally empowered to summon an assembly, John Wentworth was clearly implicated in what the congress warned the people was a concerted plan "adopted by the British Ministry for enslaving you." The congress's exhortation to the provincial militia, which Wentworth had been totally helpless to raise in December, provided evidence that the reins of effective government in New Hampshire had passed wholly out of the hands of the governor, council, and assembly and into those of the ad hoc body meeting in Exeter.[26]

Wentworth received a report that during the congress John Sullivan, "the Durham *hero*," as he called him, had moved to petition the governor to call a new assembly, one that this time would not be dissolved. Responding to Sullivan's challenge, probably in hopes of regaining some of his lost credibility, Wentworth on 28 January issued election writs for an assembly to convene on 23 February. Encouraging this move was word he had received two days earlier that General Gage was sending an officer, in civilian clothing, to confer with him about quartering the troops he had requested. With soldiers behind him, the governor would be able to control any difficult situation that might arise out of the meeting of the assembly. Wentworth had hopes, though, that the new House would be moderate in its makeup. He was, in fact, so concerned with that end that he took special measures to achieve it. To the list of towns designated to receive election writs, he added the names of three small communities in the northwest part of the province, Plymouth, Orford, and Lyme. Hoping that observers would overlook the fact that he had bypassed many older, larger, and more deserving towns, Wentworth believed this extension of writs would lessen the grounds for complaints about lack of representativeness in New Hampshire's assembly. More important for his immediate purposes, however, these towns were likely to support him, and in at least one, Plymouth, he was assured of a favorable delegate.[27]

On 17 February the freeholders of Plymouth elected John Fenton to represent them in the General Assembly. Fenton, although judge of probate, clerk of the inferior court, and colonel of the 11th regiment of militia in Grafton County, preferred the more cosmopolitan atmosphere of Portsmouth, where he spent much of his time. In recent months, serving as a magistrate in the capital, he had become one of John Wentworth's closest friends and strongest supporters. Wentworth told Gage after the raids on the fort that he would fear nothing if he had "two hundred such men" as Colonel Fenton.[28] By his outspoken manner, however, Fenton had created a multitude of enemies in Portsmouth. His choice by Plymouth, moreover, was for Wentworth the only cheering note to emerge from the elections.

Instead of a reasonable group that he might deal with, Wentworth found that one-third of the new House was composed of "the Principal Instigators and Ringleaders in the Attack on the Fort." Making matters worse, his extension of election writs backfired. "A Spectator" in the *New Hampshire Gazette* accused Wentworth of favoring only those towns where he had "plenty of Placemen," new areas that were "chiefly dependent on the Province for their Sustenance." That was especially true of Grafton County, which had received all its "Lands and Grants," Spectator slyly observed, "you know where and how." But even there, he caustically continued in mock address to the governor, "Be sure not to send any [writs] to Haverhill, Hanover, or Lebanon; whereas they are the oldest, strongest, and most independent, . . . but send them to Plymouth, Orford, and Lyme." Considering the composition of the new assembly and the prevailing attitude of strong distrust and antagonism toward himself, Wentworth realized that it would be folly to allow the House to sit. On 22 February, the day before the assembly's scheduled opening, he postponed it until the fourth of May. He hoped that in the intervening period, with the help of troops dispatched by General Gage, he could arrest those newly elected members who had participated in the assaults on Fort William and Mary. Several days later, however, he received another blow when Gage, who had originally thought Wentworth wanted soldiers only temporarily, informed him that he would be unable to provide any troops in the near future.[29]

One bright spot did appear for Wentworth amidst the depressing developments of those dreary winter months. On 20 January Frances Wentworth gave birth to a baby boy. Frances had a difficult delivery, seventeen hours of the "severest natural labor" that the attending physician, Dr. Hall Jackson, could remember. Once mother and child were safe, though, the governor exulted in the "joyful event." Ship guns were fired in the harbor and for a week friends, relatives, and officers from the *Scarborough* and *Canceaux* came to the house to extend congratulations and to celebrate with "cake and caudle wine." "The Governor's happiness seems to be complete," observed Elizabeth Wentworth, Frances's mother, who was living with them in Portsmouth, "and had a young Prince been born, there could not have been more rejoicing." But even this happy occasion could not escape the taint of the province's deteriorating political situation. Wentworth had pegged the doctor, Hall Jackson, as his enemy since the Livius controversy. Although he respected Jackson's skill as a physician, he was sure that he was operating as a spy for John Sullivan. The antipathy between the two men was scarcely veiled while Jackson attended Frances's labor. In a deliberate slight, the doctor spent his waiting time in the servants' quarters rather than in the parlor with the governor. Wentworth accepted this but later remarked disparagingly about the "Obstetric anecdotes, surgery, military instruction, and political phantoms" that Jackson had entertained his staff with. Such "evacuations of . . . mental dysentary" Wentworth was convinced would only hurt Sullivan's cause.[30]

In spite of the terrible strain, Wentworth did not retreat into bitterness. He did not blame the majority of the people, most of whom he felt had been misled or coerced. There had been moderate men at Exeter, but they had been silenced by "an uncontrouled dictatorial power." Many he believed to be "innocently wicked," unaware of the enormity of their actions. Characteristically, too, John Wentworth did not place all the blame on the colonial side. He ruminated on the probability that, had Parliament been satisfied merely to pass the Declaratory Act without attempting to demonstrate its legislative right over the colonies, "the present difficultys [might have] never arisen." That approach had been the moderate, practical position of the Rockingham Whigs in 1766, and though Wentworth doubtless realized the clock could not be turned back, he still clung to a desperate hope that there might yet be "ground for an amnesty."[31]

It was appropriate that Wentworth named his newborn son Charles Mary, after Lord and Lady Rockingham, for in England the Rockinghamites, still pursuing the kinds of policies he admired and which had formed so much of his own thinking, were working feverishly for an accommodation with the colonies in an effort to avoid war. In the Commons in March, Edmund Burke presented a brilliant speech with a detailed plan for conciliation based on repeal of the laws obnoxious to the Americans and the admittance of *"the people of our colonies into an interest in the constitution."* Of this effort Lady Rockingham wrote Frances Wentworth: "I beleive the Wise, and Moderate, deem'd those propositions offer'd by Mr. Burke to approach as nearly to [an acceptable conciliation on both sides] as the sad difficulty of the Case admitted." John and Frances Wentworth, however, were not the only ones facing arbitrary belligerence. Opinions had hardened in England as well as in America, and Burke's propositions were resoundingly voted down. It appeared too late for compromise, and events in the colonies were soon to bear this out.[32]

Conditions were bad in New Hampshire, but in Massachusetts, where the most radical colonial opponents of Britain stood face to face with the king's troops, things were much worse. By early April a revolutionary military government had completely supplanted regular government in the Bay Colony. General Gage concluded that a show of force must be made. He was encouraged in his decision by a letter from Dartmouth highly critical of his failure to take some decisive action. Thus, after nightfall on 18 April, seven hundred British infantry and grenadiers set out from Boston to seize a cache of colonial military supplies known to be located at Concord, some twenty miles to the west.

On the morning of the nineteenth as they marched into the town of Lexington, the soldiers saw ahead of them on the green a large number of colonials all carrying arms. These Massachusetts minutemen had been warned of the British advance and were determined, ill equipped as they were, to stop it. When they refused to disperse, shots were fired, and eight colonists were killed and more wounded. The troops moved on to Concord, but Lexington marked the beginning of an all-day running battle in which the British took heavy losses from enraged but determined Americans who fired on them along the entire route back to Boston. Of far greater significance, the shots fired at Lexington proved to be the first in a long and costly war between Great Britain and her colonies, a conflict that culminated in the creation of an independent American nation.

News of the fighting traveled fast, and in New Hampshire it brought immediate action. On the twentieth, Portsmouth voted to form two military companies of fifty men each, ready to march at a moment's notice. The following day an emergency provincial congress met at Exeter. Working in secrecy, the delegates chose Nathaniel Folsom to lead volunteers from New Hampshire, many of whom had already left to join the colonial army forming at Cambridge. They also appointed a committee to consult with the Massachusetts congress on the number of men that would be required from New Hampshire and on other measures that might be deemed necessary. Feeling ran high throughout the province. On the Connecticut River, John Hurd declared that the people of Haverhill "burn . . . to revenge the innocent blood" shed at Lexington and Concord. Even John Wentworth's friend, the usually reserved Eleazar Wheelock, denounced the events in Massachusetts as "horrid murders and savage butcheries . . . inhumanly committed under pretence of reducing rebels to obedience." Wentworth could only watch as the situation grew progressively "more violent." [33]

Wentworth had gained nothing by postponing the assembly. No troops had been sent, and when the House convened on 4 May, conditions were decidedly worse than they had been in February. Almost immediately a question was raised as to the legality of the governor's issuance of election writs to the three new towns. A committee was chosen to look into the matter, and Wentworth, though reluctant, had no choice but to accede to the assembly's wish for an adjournment until early June.[34] In the meantime all semblance of the old order in Portsmouth totally disintegrated. By the middle of May, the town resembled an armed camp. Those with even remote ties to royal government lived, with some justification, in constant fear.

On the evening of Saturday, 13 May, a heavily armed crowd of about sixty men strode into Portsmouth from the country. They roamed the streets avowedly in search of "Obnoxious Tories." Finding several men who they believed fit that description, they detained them and forced them to recant all allegiances to the Crown. The principal officers and friends of royal government, some twenty in all, soon got word of what was happening and fled to the governor's house. They remained there and kept a watch throughout the night. In the morning the outsiders finally left town, some to join the colonial forces at Cambridge, others to harrass supposed "tories" in the countryside.[35]

Wentworth later learned that their ultimate goal had been to capture the *Scarborough*. One plan, he discovered, was to make prisoners of himself and Andrew Barkley, captain of the *Scarborough*, who dined regularly at his home. The two were to be used as hostages, each at the head of a boat full of men intent on seizing the ship. According to Joseph Cilley of Nottingham, whose scheme it was, if the governor and captain refused to order the sailors to surrender the vessel, their captors "would blow their brains out." The design failed, so Wentworth understood, because of the mob's failure to recruit more volunteers in town. The immediate danger had ended, but fear did not abate. A rotating watch of four men each was maintained at the governor's house. George Meserve and Robert Trail, respectively collector and comptroller of the customs, who had both spent the night of the thirteenth at Wentworth's home, reported to their superiors that "every day . . . brings fresh terrors with it to the friends of Government." John Wentworth characterized the mood in Portsmouth as one of "continual apprehension and alarm." [36]

It is not surprising that on 17 May he informed Dartmouth, "Government is in great measure unhinged, for though the form as yet remains I am exceedingly concerned to acquaint your Lordship that there is not much of the reality." Wentworth, of course, was referring to royal government. On the same day a fourth congress convened at Exeter and, ignoring the governor and the fact that an assembly was officially in session, though adjourned, assumed the functions of governing the province. The congress voted to raise two thousand men and taxes "in the same proportion as was last used in Levying and proportioning the Taxes of this Province." The provincial committee of safety was given executive responsibilities, another committee was authorized to borrow ten thousand pounds on the credit of the colony, and a provincial post office was created.[37]

It was now clear there was going to be war. With that realization came a growing intolerance of any view considered unfavorable to the colonies. On 19 May the provincial congress warned the local committees of safety to watch for "persons who, through inadvertence, wilful malice, or immoderate heat, have thrown out many opprobrious expressions respecting the several Congresses, and the methods of security they have thought proper to adopt." Three days later the congress issued a summons to John Wentworth's friend John Fenton. Fenton was to appear and explain a letter he had written to the people of Grafton County following the events at Lexington and Concord. He had advised his constituents to stay at home and tend their fields and warned them of information he had received that, if they took up arms, they would be attacked by Canadians and Indians. Declining to appear in person, Fenton answered in writing that his statements were based on "opinion only." [38]

Within a few days, Wentworth himself was singled out. Verifying his suspicion that his mail was being intercepted, on 22 May John Sullivan and John Langdon wrote to the provincial congress from Philadelphia that, on their return to New Hampshire, "we shall bring with us Governor Wentworth's Letters to Lord Dartmouth for 12 months past that you may Judge whether he is your friend as he pretends or whether he is not rather your Inveterate Enemy." The congress did not take long to decide. The delegates soon discovered Wentworth's request to General Gage for British soldiers and expressed to him their shock at "your Excellency sending for troops to destroy the lives, liberties, and properties you have solemnly engaged to defend and protect." Within a short time, "Speaking favourable of Governor Wentworth" was considered an act of treason.[39]

As the month of May drew to a close, violence again threatened to erupt in Portsmouth. On the twenty-ninth, two boats from Long Island bearing corn, flour, pork, and other supplies were seized by the *Scarborough* at the mouth of the harbor. A group of town citizens immediately petitioned the governor to have the boats released. The provisions, they argued, were destined for the poor of Portsmouth, who were in great need. Wentworth, backed by several members of the council who feared that the seizure would produce more "violent outrages and Tumults," went out to the *Scarborough* and personally asked Barkley that the boats be freed. The captain, however, was adamant. He had received his orders, and he would follow them. The Restraining Act, passed by Parliament in March, called for the interdiction of all New England trade except that with Britain, which the colonists themselves had cut off. Wentworth doubtless believed, as did his council, that the act could not possibly apply to foodstuffs needed to prevent starvation of the people in the colony. Barkley, however, rightly interpreted the intent of the act to mean *all* trade, and on 30 May, he sent the two boats full of provisions to Boston.[40]

That night some six hundred men went to the battery positioned at Jerry's Point, about a mile from the fort on Newcastle Island, and brought eight of the large cannon there upriver to Portsmouth. Barkley in turn sent a large number of his sailors to the fort to begin tearing it down. The following day, mobs of armed and angry men roamed the streets of Portsmouth in search of guns and powder. They "rummaged several private houses," Wentworth reported, and even came to his own door, "but on being refused admittance they went off." He again believed their purpose was to capture the detested *Scarborough* and her "swaggering scotch Captain," as one inhabitant referred to Barkley. Barkley warned that if any attempt were made to annoy his ship he would fire directly on the town. Moreover, on the same day he made the situation worse himself by impressing twenty local fishermen. Tension was in the air everywhere.[41]

On the night of 1 June, one of the *Scarborough*'s boats, rowed by sailors and commanded by an officer, was making its regular patrol on the river. As it moved in close to the Newcastle shore, a voice rang out in the darkness ordering them to row to the bank and get out. Momentarily surprised, the crew refused, then frantically hauled for open water. With that, some forty men secreted behind a fence stood up and simultaneously fired at the boat. Two sailors were slightly wounded before they were safely out of range. After the crew reached the ship and reported the incident, the *Scarborough*, in protest, fired three of her guns at the island. Open warfare between the town and the *Scarborough* threatened to erupt at any moment. The next day, however, the selectmen of Portsmouth apologized to Wentworth. Discountenancing the unseemly attack on the ship's boat, they promised to attempt to bring the men to justice. Wentworth passed this information on to Barkley, who agreed to release the fishermen.[42] A temporary truce seemed to have been reached, but it clearly was only temporary. John Wentworth by this time was little more than a hostage in his own town.

The assembly convened on the twelfth as scheduled but did not take up any business until the following day. On 13 June the first item considered was the elegibility of the three new members from Plymouth, Orford, and Lyme. Adhering to a committee opinion that the governor had no right under the English constitution to issue new election writs without the consent of the legislature, the representatives voted not to seat the new men. Wentworth ignored this vote and in his message to the assembly, instead concentrated once more on the drastic need for conciliation between the colonies and Great Britain. Moreover, he offered what he believed to be a sound basis for agreement, a resolution passed by the House of Commons on 27 February. Devised by the North ministry, the resolution proposed to rescind all taxes for any colony that raised its proportionate share for defense and provided support for its own government. Wentworth told the representatives that this offer indicated a "great . . . affection, [and] tenderness for your liberties and Readiness to be Reconciled upon Principles, consistent with the just Rights and Dignity of the Parent State and the Priviledges of the Colonies."[43]

That John Wentworth at this point should be desperately grasping at straws is understandable. His advancement and praise of North's resolution, however, indicates an insensitivity to colonial thinking by this time. Much more was now involved than just the question of taxation that had seemed central to the dispute between the colonies and Great Britain in 1765. Ten years of continuing conflict had raised many more issues—the vice-admiralty courts, the prerogative of royal governors, colonial rights of manufacturing and export, and others— that called into question the entire British-American relationship. In spite of his acceptance of the probable necessity of some kind of constitutional realignment, Wentworth seemed not to realize how fundamental a change would be needed now to reconcile the colonies with the mother country. Not only were basic liberties at stake, the long struggle had awakened in the colonists a sense of autonomy. The kind of comprehensive authority exercised by the British government in the past would no longer be acceptable. In 1765 the resolution might have worked; by 1775 it had little chance of success.

Acceptance of the measure was especially unlikely since the Restraining Act made the ministry's offer appear more like coercion than conciliation. It also was obvious that the resolution had been designed to deal with the colonies on an individual basis in an effort to subvert the solidarity they had forged. The opposition in England, including Wentworth's friend Edmund Burke, criticized the resolution as a sham with little sincerity behind it and almost no chance of leading to a settlement. In Parliament, David Hartley called it "not free but compulsory; it is attended with menaces and threats. . . . To say, Give me as much money as I wish, till I say enough, or I will take it from you, and then to call such a proposition conciliatory for peace, is insult added to oppression." Although he was much closer to the American situation, Wentworth was not so perceptive. He was, however, in a much more difficult position than the friends of America in England. The Commons resolution seemed to him the only remaining possibility for avoiding imminent disaster. Accordingly, on the afternoon of 13 June, in order to provide time for "candid consideration" of the proposal by both representatives and their constituents, Wentworth adjourned the assembly until the eleventh of July.[44]

Less time than Wentworth could have expected was given over to consideration of the resolution. That evening as Frances Wentworth sat writing a letter to Lady Rockingham while her husband and John Fenton, who had dined with them, commiserated over recent events, word arrived that the house was about to be attacked. Within moments a mob was heard outside the front door screaming demands that Fenton surrender himself. Already highly unpopular because of his letter to Grafton County warning the residents not to take up arms, Fenton had that day insured popular enmity. In the assembly he had advocated acceptance of Lord North's resolution. Worse, he roundly castigated the representatives after they voted to exclude the three new members, including himself. Wentworth opened the door and courageously asserted that he would not give Colonel Fenton up. This refusal only enraged those outside. They pounded on the house with clubs and, after hauling up a large cannon and aiming it at the front door, announced that no one would escape alive, including the governor's wife and baby, if resistance continued. That was too much for Fenton. He walked out the door and turned himself over to the mob. That night he was forced to march the fifteen miles to Exeter, where he was to be confined until the provincial congress could sit in judgment on his activities.[45]

This violent experience deeply affected John Wentworth. With his family's safety in jeopardy as well as his own, "finding every Idea of the Respect due to His Majesty's Commission . . . lost in the frantic Rage and Fury of the People," he no longer believed he could stay in Portsmouth. No sooner had Fenton been hurried away than Wentworth led Frances with their five-month-old son out the back door and down to the pond. They boarded Captain Barkley's boat, which had come to town, and pushed off for Fort William and Mary three miles downriver where they would be safe under the protective guns of the HMS *Scar-*

borough. Shortly after their departure, the mob returned and ransacked the governor's house. Frances later repeated rumors that the rabble was disappointed the family had fled, and she believed alleged claims by the rioters that "if they cou'd get The Governor's fat Child they wou'd split him down the Back and broil him."[46]

Forced to take refuge at Fort William and Mary, John Wentworth was now clearly an outcast from New Hampshire. He had been deemed an enemy by his own people. Yet he refused to believe that this feeling constituted a majority opinion. His friends, of whom he felt there were many, had been cowed by the rash actions of a few hotheaded radicals. He was confident that, with some British soldiers behind him, the people would not hesitate to speak out in his favor. He seemed not to take into account that the militia, his normal source of armed support, had refused to come to his aid. Wentworth was now misleading himself about the general sentiment of the province. No doubt there were people who were saddened to see what was happening to the governor, who had been a good friend to many as well as an energetic leader, but as royal governor, John Wentworth served as a lightning rod for all the hatred and animosity generated in the province, especially over the previous six months, by the imperious threatening and oppressive British measures. By dint of his office, Wentworth had become party to a plan more coercive than any ever seen during the history of the American colonies.

Wentworth still had hopes Gage would send troops. He would then be able to return to town and maintain control of New Hampshire until the difficulties were settled, either by force or negotiation. On 23 June Admiral Graves encouraged him to think that an armed schooner would soon be on its way to the Piscataqua to back up the *Scarborough*. But four days later, when Captain Barkley informed him of orders he had received to dismantle the fort, Wentworth must have had a haunting suspicion that the British were abandoning New Hampshire. He was reluctant to agree but had no choice. Within the next two days, all of the remaining cannon and military stores were loaded on a sloop-of-war and carried to Boston.[47]

With his own defenses being pulled from around him, Wentworth could only watch helplessly as events in the province began to look more and more like revolution. Early in July he received word that a large body of people had ransacked his house at Wolfeboro and had barely been dissuaded from putting a torch to it. John Fenton had been declared an enemy and sent to Connecticut for confinement. Others were threatened with the same. Even more alarming was the rapid rate at which the provincial congress was moving into the vacuum left by the absence of royal government. On 1 July a committee from the congress visited George Jaffrey, councillor and province treasurer, and forced him to turn over all the money in the treasury. They left a receipt for 516 pounds. Within the next week, similar committees of the congress called on other officials and collected all the provincial records.⁴⁸ John Wentworth was sensitive to this blatant usurpation of authority. When the assembly reconvened just before the middle of July with scarcely enough members present to conduct business, Wentworth sent them a message from the fort asking that they withdraw their exclusion of the three new members from Grafton County. Upon the representatives' refusal, he pointedly adjourned rather than dissolved them so that the congress would not be left as the only governing body in the province.⁴⁹

Wentworth still feared that attempts would be made to take him captive. Nevertheless, because of the cramped living quarters within the fort, he declined Barkley's offer of a detachment of marines. The governor's party, including family, servants, friends, and six men employed to stand guard, numbered about twenty in all. He complained about the "inconvenience of being crowded in this miserable house, confined for room and neither wind or water tight." An observer informed Eleazar Wheelock that "the poor Governor's situation at the sham Fort is truly deplorable." Given his political and physical situation, Wentworth had every reason to be bitter. That attitude was not, however, consistent with the character of the man. On the last day of July he wrote to Tristram Dalton: "I will not complain because it wou'd be a poignant censure on a people I love and forgive." ⁵⁰

By the end of the first week in August, Wentworth despaired of receiving any soldiers from Gage. The general's forces were rapidly being cordoned off in Boston by a mounting colonial army. At almost the same time, a series of incidents shattered the truce that had been grudgingly worked out between the people of Portsmouth and the HMS *Scarborough*. The town had agreed to supply the ship with beef in return for freedom to carry on fishing activities. This compromise seemed to be working until one evening when, after the ship's boat had come to town, one of the sailors deserted. The next morning Captain Barkley seized a man from a passing canoe and notified the town that he would not be released until the sailor was returned. Anger swept through the people; no one, they retorted, had encouraged Barkley's man to run away. The captain did release his captive a few days later, but feeling remained high against him.⁵¹

On the afternoon of 10 August, as the ship's boat again touched the wharf, a group of armed men seized the coxswain and ordered the crew out. The sailors

263

declined, and shots were fired at them. They returned the fire and shoved off. No one had been hurt, but the town was in an uproar. A boat that Wentworth used to ferry supplies from Portsmouth to the fort was dragged out of the water by the mob at the wharf and carried through the streets. Their intention was to burn it, but they were persuaded by some "Principal Inhabitants" to dispose of it in a creek behind the town. Other groups roamed the streets in search of "tories." Order finally was restored, and that evening a town meeting declared the attack on the sailors a "rash and unwarrantable" action. This statement was sent, together with the coxswain, to the *Scarborough*'s captain, but Barkley was not appeased. He asked Wentworth if the attack was meant "as a Declaration of War against the King—and if so that immediate satisfaction would be demanded and the Consequence most likely would be fatal" to Portsmouth.[52]

On the eleventh, Wentworth solicited a disavowal of the townsmen's actions from the council and the next day sent it along with his own apologies to Barkley. But even that did not satisfy the captain. He told Wentworth that, if the men who had fired on his boat were not delivered to him, he would take the *Scarborough* upriver and have "Vengeance" on the town. The situation worsened on 12 August when, about midnight, a party of sailors from the *Scarborough* attacked a group of men keeping watch in Newcastle. One man was wounded, and another, whom town selectmen complained was poor and had a pregnant wife and six children to care for, was carried off to the ship. No longer able to abide the insolence of the "swaggering scotch Captain," the Portsmouth committee of safety on the following day, 13 August, declared an end to all communications with the *Scarborough*, including boatloads of provisions. John Wentworth was the loser in this battle of wills, for Fort William and Mary was included in the ban.[53]

Wentworth was upset with the actions of the town, but he was equally frustrated by Barkley's intransigence. Time and again he had advocated reason and had tried to reconcile the two sides, even from his tenuous residence at the fort. But both sides ignored him. At least one astute bystander, Eleazar Wheelock's friend David McClure, expressed sympathy for the governor's difficult position "as it were, between two fires."[54] Since Barkley in retaliation had cut off all shipping in and out of the port, it now became a question of which, the town or the ship, could outlast the other. Unless a provision boat appeared, the odds definitely were in favor of the town.

By the seventeenth, Wentworth and the others at the fort were beginning to feel the shortage of food. He asked the Newcastle selectmen for supplies, but they replied that they themselves were short of provisions and could not possibly help. The HMS *Scarborough* was faring just as badly, and on the twenty-second,

Barkley informed Wentworth that the ship would have to go to Boston to be reprovisioned. The governor and his party were welcome to go if they wished. What choice did they have? None that Wentworth could see, for he was sure he would be taken prisoner without the support of the ship. On 23 August he sent a brief note to old Theodore Atkinson, in his absence the senior royal official in the province. "I find it necessary to go to sea for a few days, and must desire that in the mean time you will use your best endeavors to preserve peace and quietness as much as possible." The next morning John Wentworth boarded the *Scarborough* with his family and that afternoon sailed out of the Piscataqua.[55]

Wentworth considered his departure only temporary. On reaching Boston, however, he found that Admiral Graves had no ships to spare for New Hampshire waters. He was nevertheless determined to maintain his official position, hollow as it was, as chief executive of the province. Nearly a month after he had left, he embarked on a British schooner in Boston. On 21 September Wentworth landed at Gosport on the Isles of Shoals, a few miles off Portsmouth harbor. That evening he sent a boat into town with a message for Atkinson and a proclamation adjourning the assembly, scheduled to meet on the twenty-eighth, until 24 April 1776. The ship carried only a small force and, after receiving Atkinson's reply the next day, Wentworth again set sail from New Hampshire. He intended to return, he told Dartmouth, as soon as it was at all practical to do so.[56] Certainly by the time the assembly met the following spring, order and royal authority would have been restored. But the New Hampshire assembly never reconvened. John Wentworth never saw his native province again.

EPILOGUE

From the perspective of more than two hundred years and all that is known about the American Revolution and John Wentworth, the first question that many will still ask is why he chose loyalty to England rather than to his native land and fellow colonists. The question, however, is inappropriate. For John Wentworth, it was not a matter of making a choice. When he left New Hampshire in August 1775, he was not choosing England over America. In his mind the two could not be separated. The current trouble, severe as it was, was only temporary. Unfortunately, it finally appeared that force would have to be used to quell the incipient rebellion. There was no question that British might would prevail. Once it had, however, and order and authority had been restored, both sides mutually chastened by the experience could set to the task of creating a more equitable system of empire, one of mutual trust and advantage. That system was the one Wentworth had been working to achieve since he left England for New Hampshire in 1766.

John Wentworth knew there were reasonable, prudent people on both sides. The inhabitants of America would turn to moderate leaders to replace the reckless radicals who had led them into a disastrous civil war, and Wentworth was ready to play a part. On the other side, the British could not fail to see that much of the trouble had been created by an obstinate, uncompromising attitude at Whitehall. Wentworth knew from his own special connection with England that that shortsighted approach was not necessary. In 1765–1766 he had observed and worked with the Rockingham ministry, which through reason and foresight had obtained the repeal of the Stamp Act, a decision in the best interests of the entire British Empire. Had the Rockinghamites remained in power, they would never have attempted to enforce the Declaratory Act, which they had been obliged to accept along with the repeal. That alone, Wentworth believed, would have prevented all the turmoil and grief that had ensued since.

268   But it was too late to think about that now. The crisis had arrived and had to be dealt with. Once it was settled, however, the Rockingham Whigs, or those with similar views, would be brought back to power. Work could then begin on building a strong, closely knit, productive British Empire, one, Wentworth told the marquis of Rockingham in December 1775, "cemented by justice and reciprocation of interest with an evident attention to mutual rights."[1] John Wentworth could not then know that his vision of an integrated empire was not to be, that England and America were destined to become separate nations. He could not know that he would never return to New Hampshire.

* * *

On 9 August 1775, John Wentworth observed his thirty-eighth birthday at Fort William and Mary. When he sailed away from New Hampshire in September, more than half of his life still lay ahead of him. Early in 1776 he sent Frances and their baby son to England. He nevertheless was confident that the British would shortly reassert their authority over the colonies, and he remained in America for more than two years, devoting himself to that end and waiting for a chance to return home. The governor spent most of that time in New York close to the British army. A body of loyalist troops formed under his patronage was known as Wentworth's Volunteers. By 1778 Wentworth realized that the revolution in America would not be easily ended, and in February he sailed for England.[2]

Wentworth spent the next five years in Britain, where he served as a spokesman for the American loyalists. He sought information from every possible source, but the news got no better. He learned that late in 1778 his name had been placed at the head of a list of seventy-six persons forbidden upon pain of death ever to return to New Hampshire.[3] Although he did not know it, the defeat of Lord Cornwallis at Yorktown in 1781 insured his permanent exile. It was bitter irony for John Wentworth in 1782, with the colonies irrevocably lost and Lord North finally removed from office, that the marquis of Rockingham was called back to form a government and conclude a peace with the United States. Throughout the war Rockingham had remained at the center of the opposition, had decried British policy, and had defended the colonies. Now he was the only one who commanded enough support in Parliament to head a ministry. But it was too late to save the colonies for the empire.

John Wentworth was nonetheless thrilled at this turn of events, and from his patron he secured a promise of the governorship of Nova Scotia. Regrettably for Wentworth, Rockingham died within three months of taking office, and the earl of Shelburne gave the position to John Parr, a professional soldier. But Wentworth persevered, and he prevailed on Lady Rockingham to approach the duke of Portland, one of the marquis's most steadfast supporters. As a result, in 1783, the same year Great Britain in the Treaty of Paris recognized the United States of America as an independent nation, John Wentworth was made Surveyor General of His Majesty's Woods for the greatly reduced British Empire in North America. In September he arrived in Halifax, Nova Scotia, to take up his new post.[4]

269

Nova Scotia was as close to New Hampshire as John Wentworth could get. It is a testimony to his love for America and his personal identification with the land and the people that Wentworth was willing to return in a lesser position than governor and to expend nearly superhuman physical effort in performing his job. As a former governor, Wentworth might have treated his office as a sinecure and left the real work to others. But as always, he was diligent, energetic, and enthusiastic in carrying out his responsibilities. He personally spent many months of each year ranging the timberlands of Nova Scotia and New Brunswick, providing invaluable service to the Crown in a difficult and thankless task. Although he still encountered resentment of the mast laws, he made many friends in Nova Scotia.[5]

The 1780s were years of great change in Nova Scotia as the population more than doubled with an almost overwhelming influx of loyalist refugees displaced by the American Revolution. This was a diverse group representing a broad social, economic, and geographic cross-section of the American colonies. Immediate needs of food and shelter had to be seen to as well as a means of long-term self-sufficiency in this beautiful but harsh land. Many gave up and either returned to the United States or went to England. But others stayed and eventually prospered despite much tension and conflict with the preloyalists, settlers who had been in Nova Scotia before they came. Probably more than they would like to have thought, the loyalists brought democratic tendencies and a sense of independence from their background in the American colonies. By the 1790s, many had moved into positions of power and influence in trade and government.[6]

Although the loyalists were a heterogeneous group and were as ready to take advantage of each other as anyone, they were also keenly aware of their common interests and invariably presented a united political front. They were particularly pleased to learn in 1792 that one of their own, John Wentworth, was appointed to succeed Governor Parr, who had died. Wentworth was in England at the time and could still call on the patronage of Lady Rockingham and Edmund Burke. Nova Scotia faced many of the same problems that had challenged John Wentworth in New Hampshire a quarter century earlier, and he immediately put his experience and knowledge to work.

New settlements sprang up, and others grew rapidly with the coming of the loyalists, but they remained isolated—separated by rivers, swamps, and vast tracts of virgin pine. Wentworth recognized the need for transportation and trade, and much as in New Hampshire, he aggressively pushed a program of roads and bridges to link the communities, to make the province self-supporting, and to promote commerce with the outside world. As part of his plan for development, Wentworth sponsored a survey of the interior to identify promising agricultural land that would encourage settlement and produce crops such as hemp, which the British needed as a naval store. John Wentworth could take much credit for the prosperity that came to Nova Scotia in the 1790s as the loyalists began to get their feet on the ground and the bleak days of the previous decade receded into memory. In 1795 he was made a baronet by the king, and during these years he became a close friend of the monarch's son, Prince Edward, later duke of Kent, who lived for a time near Halifax.

As economic conditions improved, loyalists and others in Nova Scotia developed stronger ties to the province. John Wentworth's own example played an important role in that process. Just as in New Hampshire, he made himself accessible to people at all levels, and they saw firsthand his determination to make agriculture and trade thrive in Nova Scotia. They could see that he truly cared what happened to the province and to them. Unlike many royal governors of the eighteenth century, John Wentworth felt a need to identify with the land and the people he governed. A commitment to his place of authority was a necessity for Wentworth, and in Nova Scotia he found a worthy substitute, if not a replacement, for the home he had lost, New Hampshire.

But Wentworth also faced problems in Nova Scotia, some of his own making. Following a trend that emerged in New Hampshire, he was plagued by continuing financial difficulties, both public and private. Before coming to Nova Scotia in the early 1780s, Wentworth signed both his salary as surveyor general and the money due him from the treasury for his loyalist claim over to Paul Wentworth for accumulated debts, including living expenses in England during the Revolution. When Paul Wentworth fled his own creditors and England late in the decade, John Wentworth's personal finances were in a shambles, and he was forced to cross the Atlantic and attempt to straighten them out.[7]

Once he became governor of Nova Scotia, John Wentworth got into even greater trouble through overexpenditure of government money and failure to keep proper accounts and vouchers. White settlement of Nova Scotia had doomed the remaining Indians' means of livelihood, and for humanitarian rea-

270

sons as well as for the safety of the province, Wentworth spent over twice the allotted appropriation on food, clothing, and farming implements for them.

Even more drastic were the expenses he incurred for the Jamaican Maroons. Following a rebellion against the Jamaican government in 1795, some six hundred of these warlike descendants of slaves were sent to Halifax the following year, presumably on their way to the British free black colony of Sierra Leone in Africa. When they arrived, Wentworth saw potential in these people as farmers for his province, and he undertook to settle them in Nova Scotia. Despite his considerable efforts and optimism, however, the Maroons would not adapt either socially or economically to this cold northern outpost. When the authorities in England discovered the details of this fiasco, they ordered Wentworth to send the Maroons to Africa, and in 1800 the Jamaicans were shipped out. In the meantime, Wentworth had accumulated a huge bill that was insufficiently documented, and in 1801 the duke of Portland suspended his salary until the accounts were justified.[8]

John Wentworth clearly did not pay adequate attention to the details of spending money on provincial projects. The tendency had begun in New Hampshire and really was a product of his personality. With his positive, at times aggressive, approach to solving problems, Wentworth saw a need and then set about meeting it in the most efficient way possible, usually requiring the expenditure of funds. Most often these projects were for the betterment of the province and thereby the empire. Sometimes their purpose was to allow Wentworth to live and conduct business in a manner he felt requisite for a governor of a British colony. If the government did not undertake them, no one would. Wentworth felt it was his role to get things done; the money would be found somewhere.

Unfortunately, these situations often turned out to be more complex and expensive than Wentworth imagined, and he discovered himself in financial and political trouble at times. An example of the problems that arose can be seen in Government House, an elegant structure Wentworth convinced the assembly he needed to serve as his home and offices and eventually to be part of a new group of buildings for all branches of the government. As costs for the project escalated far beyond the original estimate, the increasingly unhappy assembly members continued to vote additional funds for fear of losing what had already been invested. When the building was finally completed, it had cost three times the amount originally appropriated. Based on a design by the English architect George Richardson, John Wentworth's Government House in Halifax has been described as "an architectural achievement unequalled by any other governor in the history of Canada." But Wentworth paid a high political price for the beautiful building. It played a significant role in the assembly's determination to wrest control of revenue and appropriations from the executive.[9]

Despite such difficulties, Wentworth accomplished a great deal in Nova Scotia. Perhaps most important, while aiding the Indians, organizing and outfitting the militia, building roads, and founding the first life-saving station in North America, he set an important tone in a young and developing province. The years of John Wentworth's administration have been described as the "Golden Age" of Nova Scotia, a period when "life at the provincial capital possessed an exhiliration and a zest hitherto unknown."[10] Much of that energy seemed to emanate from Wentworth himself.

After 1800, however, time, age, and Wentworth's own past began to catch up with him. The American Revolution and his experience in New Hampshire made John Wentworth especially wary of political opposition. In Nova Scotia he responded with excessive secrecy and an unwillingness to tolerate opinions different from his own. Wentworth kept an iron grip on patronage and surrounded himself with officeholders he could trust completely. They naturally were loyalists, and the powerful oligarchy they formed in Halifax, like that of Benning and John Wentworth in an earlier day in New Hampshire, created numerous enemies, especially outside the capital. The situation was exacerbated by the fact that the loyalists now had almost no influence in the assembly and generally had declined in importance as a group.[11]

Wentworth found himself in a continuous struggle with the assembly to maintain control over the expenditure of public money for roads and other provincial projects. He had experienced such encroachment on what he considered his governor's prerogative many years earlier in New Hampshire, with what he could now see only as disastrous results. He was determined not to relinquish a constitutional right. Age may have been a contributing factor in the hardening of Wentworth's attitudes toward an increasingly belligerent assembly, for he was now well into his sixties. Also, in addition to his firsthand experience in the American Revolution, he had now seen the even more frightening republican anarchy of the French Revolution. Ironically, John Wentworth's final political fall began with his refusal to issue an election writ demanded by the assembly.

In 1806, following charges of alleged election fraud, the members refused to seat Thomas Walker, the son-in-law of a prominent loyalist supporter of the governor. After reviewing the case with his council, Wentworth found the allegations against Walker untenable and refused to comply with the legislature's request. The guilt or innocence of Walker was not the key issue; it was whether or not the governor, backed by instructions from the king, had ultimate constitutional authority over the elected representatives of a provincial assembly. Images of John Fenton and the New Hampshire assembly of 1775 must have borne heavily on Wentworth's mind. More than thirty years earlier, that body had refused to honor Wentworth's writ and seat the elected member. Now the Nova Scotia assembly was declining to accept an elected member for different reasons but was telling the governor that he must issue a new writ. The principle in question was the same. Who had the right to call for elections, the representative of royal authority or the people of the province through their elected assembly?

No less determined to guard his executive prerogative than he had been in the 1770s, Wentworth would not be ordered by the assembly to call an election, and he referred the case to England for resolution. Significant historical changes had taken place since 1775, however, and Governor Wentworth was not happy with the decision he received early in 1808. Before the American Revolution, a major constitutional question turned on the rights and powers of the assemblies within the colonies in relation to the powers of Parliament in English government. In the intervening years that question had been decided. The royal prerogative was no longer absolute in England or America. The legal authorities in England, without question, found in favor of the Nova Scotia assembly.[12]

The decision in England underscored the fact that John Wentworth no longer had any friends or influence in the British government. He was now in his seventies. Rockingham had been dead for twenty-five years. Although George III was still king, a new generation held the reins at Whitehall, and few had knowledge of John Wentworth's role in the American Revolution. That era now belonged to history, and British officials were not looking back. John Wentworth, to them, was only an aging and troublesome provincial governor. By his unwillingness to distribute patronage to any but his closest allies, in large part a consequence of his experience in New Hampshire, Wentworth had created strong sources of opposition, not least in the all-important Nova Scotia assembly. Since the turn of the century Wentworth had fought off increasingly serious challenges from men who did have significant ties to England and Ireland, and now he paid the price. His trouble with the assembly and the rising dissension in the province coincided with ominous signs of another armed conflict between Britain and the United States. Lord Castlereigh, the colonial secretary, needed a strong military presence in North America, and he took this opportunity to solve another problem as well. Early in April 1808, General Sir George Prevost arrived unannounced in Halifax to relieve Sir John Wentworth as governor of Nova Scotia.[13]

Wentworth made the best of this difficult situation, but nothing could reverse the humiliation he felt at the hands of the British government. There was little for him to do once he left office, and he and Frances lingered in Nova Scotia only until 1810, when they sailed to England to live out their days with their son, Charles Mary. Sadly, one last tragedy awaited John Wentworth. As governor of Nova Scotia he had given his personal bond for twelve hundred pounds to clothe the Royal Nova Scotia Regiment, an act "he considered merely pro forma." The bond, however, was sold to an unscrupulous collector, and in 1812, Wentworth, who had been living on a meager pension, was informed that he must pay immediately or be arrested. Late in August, at the age of seventy-five and with his wife dying, he was forced to flee at night under an assumed name. From Liverpool he embarked for Halifax, where he intended to sell some property to pay his debts. In February 1813, before Wentworth could return to England, Frances Wentworth died. With no reason to go back, he remained in Nova Scotia. John Wentworth died in Halifax in 1820 at the age of eighty-three.[14]

John Wentworth was one of a large number of loyalists who went to Nova Scotia in the late eighteenth century. He became a strong and effective governor of the province during a formative period of its development, as well as serving as the leader of the loyalists. They looked to him for guidance and support, and he did not fail them. If only for self-preservation and advancement, the loyalists of Nova Scotia worked together for many years under the patronage of Governor Wentworth. It thus is easy, almost automatic, to think of John Wentworth first as a loyalist; the term became a defining label for him. He was, after all, one of the royal governors who were forced by the Revolution to leave the colonies and who never returned. But John Wentworth did not consciously forsake the American colonies in favor of Great Britain. He was never the hard-line advocate of British authority often associated with the term *loyalist* and with other colonists such as Thomas Hutchinson. Wentworth became a loyalist by default. He was first an American colonist. As an appointed royal governor, however, it was his duty to reconcile British policy and law with the politics and economics of his own colony. He thought he could accomplish that, even when conditions became more difficult than anyone had expected. He was less certain about some of the other colonies, but there had been no precedent since their founding in the early seventeenth century to lead him to a different conclusion. There was no reason to think that the British colonial system would fail now.

When Wentworth left New Hampshire in 1775, he did not know that he had made a choice. Over the next few months and for a number of years he expected to go back as governor of New Hampshire, but he was eventually forced to abandon the idea. John Wentworth never embraced loyalism; it was what he was left with. He did not stay in England in the 1780s, which he could have done, but went to the raw colony of Nova Scotia, not even as governor, because it was as close to New Hampshire and New England as he could get. When

Wentworth gained the governorship in 1792, he became the only Revolutionary period royal governor to serve again at the head of a British North American colony. Wentworth was an American by birth and by nature. It was where he wanted to be, where he felt at home. It is easy to think that, had he not been the royal governor of New Hampshire but only a merchant in Portsmouth, he would never have made the deliberate choice to leave the colony in support of the British cause. But that can never be known.

John Wentworth never harbored ill feelings for the United States of America, which he wished "the most extensive, great and permanent blessings," or for New Hampshire, his "still dear native Country," as he called it in 1791.[15] After his departure, he maintained an interest in the province and continued to correspond with old friends such as John Peirce, Jeremy Belknap, and Eleazar Wheelock's son John Wheelock. Through the 1780s he retained the hope of visiting his family and friends in New Hampshire, but the proscription was never lifted. By the end of the decade, after both of his parents had died, he knew he would never return. That realization reaffirmed his belief that the break between Great Britain and her American colonies was a needless tragedy. "I do verily believe," Wentworth wrote Belknap with conviction fifteen years after the signing of the Declaration of Independence, "had the true, wise, and open measures been embraced on both sides, that their union would have been many years established and their prosperity wonderfully increased."[16]

ABBREVIATIONS

AO	Audit Office
CO	Colonial Office
DCA	Dartmouth College Archives
HLRO	House of Lords Record Office
MHS	Massachusetts Historical Society
NEHGR	*New England Historical and Genealogical Register*
NHA	New Hampshire Archives
NHG	*New Hampshire Gazette*
NHHS	New Hampshire Historical Society
NHPP	*New Hampshire Provincial and State Papers*
NHSL	New Hampshire State Library
NYHS	New-York Historical Society
NYPL	New York Public Library
PRO	Public Record Office
SPG	Society for the Propagation of the Gospel
T	Treasury
WWM	Wentworth-Woodhouse Muniments

NOTES

INTRODUCTION

1. Leonard W. Labaree, *Royal Government in America* (1930; reprint, New York: Frederick Ungar, 1958), 93; Bernard Bailyn, *The Origins of American Politics* (New York: Knopf, 1968), 70. On the question of the power of royal governors see Bailyn, chapter two.

2. Bernard Bailyn, *The Ordeal of Thomas Hutchinson* (Cambridge, Mass.: Harvard University Press, 1974), 1–2.

3. For a general description of royal governors just before the Revolution, see Louise Dunbar, "The Royal Governors in the Middle and Southern Colonies on the Eve of the Revolution: A Study in Imperial Personnel," in *The Era of the American Revolution*, ed. Richard B. Morris (New York: Columbia University Press, 1939), 214–68.

4. Mercy Otis Warren, *History of the Rise, Progress and Termination of the American Revolution* (1805; reprint, New York: AMS Press, 1970), 1:79.

5. Jeremy Belknap, *The History of New Hampshire* (1831; reprint, New York: Johnson Reprint, 1970), 1:358.

6. Timothy Dwight, *Travels in New England and New York*, ed. Barbara M. Solomon (Cambridge, Mass.: Harvard University Press, 1969), 4:112.

7. Lorenzo Sabine, *Biographical Sketches of Loyalists of the American Revolution* (Boston: Little, Brown, 1864), 2:411.

8. Robert McCluer Calhoon, *The Loyalists in Revolutionary America, 1760–1781* (New York: Harcourt Brace Jovanovich, 1973), 129.

9. On James Wright, see Calhoon, *Loyalists*, 3–15; W. W. Abbot, *The Royal Governors of Georgia, 1754–1775* (Chapel Hill: University of North Carolina Press, 1959), 84–183; and Edward J. Cashin, "Sowing the Wind: Governor James Wright and the Georgia Backcountry on the Eve of the Revolution," in *Forty Years of Diversity: Essays on Colonial Georgia*, ed. Harvey H. Jackson and Phinzey Spalding (Athens, Georgia: The University of Georgia Press, 1984), 233–50.

10. Sheila L. Skemp, *William Franklin: Son of a Patriot, Servant of a King* (New York: Oxford University Press, 1990), xi. I have drawn almost entirely on Skemp's book for my information on William Franklin but have also consulted Calhoon, *Loyalists*, 120–26.

11. For this information about Hutchinson I have relied largely on Bailyn, *The Ordeal of Thomas Hutchinson*.

12. Gordon J. DiRenzo, *Personality and Politics* (Garden City, N.Y.: Anchor Press/Doubleday, 1974), 157.

I. SERVANTS OF THE KING

1. John Adams, *The Diary and Autobiography of John Adams*, ed. Lyman H. Butterfield (Cambridge, Mass.: Harvard University Press, 1961), 4:85.

2. Ibid.

3. Clifford K. Shipton, *Biographical Sketches of Those Who Attended Harvard College* (hereafter referred to as *Sibley's Harvard Graduates*) (Boston: Massachusetts Historical Society, 1965), 13:512.

4. "Sir John Wentworth," *Dictionary of National Biography*, 20:1169; John Wentworth, *The Wentworth Genealogy* (Boston: Little, Brown, 1878), 1:xv–xvii, 5–9.

5. Wentworth, *Genealogy*, 1:71–82; Charles E. Clark, *The Eastern Frontier: The Settlement of Northern New England, 1610–1763* (New York: Knopf, 1970), 37–39. In 1791 John Wentworth, then living in Nova Scotia, told Lady Rockingham that his family had settled in America in 1628. See Brian C. Cuthbertson, *The Loyalist Governor: Biography of Sir John Wentworth* (Halifax: Patheric Press, 1983), 51. It is difficult to know if Wentworth's information was correct. It was not corroborated in the nineteenth century by the later John Wentworth who wrote *The Wentworth Genealogy*. In 1628 the several settlements in New Hampshire were very primitive, and Boston had not yet been founded. For a good brief survey of the Antinomian controversy, see the introduction in David D. Hall, ed., *The Antinomian Controversy, 1636–1638: A Documentary History* (Middletown, Conn.: Wesleyan University Press, 1968), 3–20. The best full-length treatment of the subject is Emery Battis, *Saints and Sectaries: Anne Hutchinson and the Antinomian Controversy in the Massachusetts Bay Colony* (Chapel Hill: University of North Carolina Press, 1962). On Wheelwright see especially chapters 9 and 13.

6. Wentworth, *Genealogy*, 1:84–89.

7. Wentworth, *Genealogy*, 1:113–18; Clark, *Eastern Frontier*, 93–95. For a description of the house, see *The Bulletin of the Metropolitan Museum of Art in New York* 33 (1938): 21–23.

8. Fourteen of the children survived. See the *New England Historical and Genealogical Register* 4 (1850): 334–38.

9. Clark, *Eastern Frontier*, 95–97; Jeremy Belknap, *The History of New Hampshire* (1831; reprint, New York: Johnson Reprint, 1970), 1:184–87.

10. Clark, *Eastern Frontier*, 299–300. The quotation is from 106.

11. Clark, *Eastern Frontier*, 299–300. Belcher is quoted on 300.

12. Shipton, *Sibley's Harvard Graduates*, 6 (1942):113–17; Clark, *Eastern Frontier*, 300–301; Belknap, *New Hampshire*, 1:262–63.

13. Shipton, *Sibley's Harvard Graduates*, 6:122–25; Jere R. Daniell, "Politics in New Hampshire under Governor Benning Wentworth, 1741–1767," *William and Mary Quarterly* 23 (January 1966): 99–105; Leonard W. Labaree, *Royal Government in America* (1930; reprint, New York: Frederick Ungar, 1958), 180–84.

14. Enemies of Wentworth deeply resented this family control of New Hampshire, and some, such as Richard Waldron, kept close tabs on it. Among Waldron's papers was found a sheet headed "Family Government" with the following: "*George Jaffrey*, brother-in-law, president of the council, treasurer, chief justice and justice of the admiralty. *Jotham Odiorne*, brother married his grand daughter, second judge and justice. *Henry Sherburne*, cousin &c. counsellor, &c. *Theodore Atkinson*, brother-in-law, secretary, chief justice of inferior court, &c. *Richard Wibird*, governor's brother married his sister, a counsellor. *Ellis Huske*, wife's brother married governor's sister, a counsellor. *Samuel Solley*, who married George Jaffrey's daughter, a counsellor. *Thomas Packer*, a brother-in-law, high sheriff. *John Downing* and *Samuel Smith*, counsellors, related by their cash. Friends, *Wiggin*, justice and judge of probate, *Clarkson, Gage, Wallingford, Gilman, Palmer, Roby, Jenness, Odiorne, Walton* and *Stevens*, justice." See Belknap, *New Hampshire*, 1:336n.

15. For the terms of Benning Wentworth's land grants see William H. Fry, *New Hampshire as a Royal Province* (1908; reprint, New York: AMS Press, 1970), 290–92.

16. On Wentworth's house at Little Harbor, see John M. Howells, *The Architectural Heritage of the Piscataqua* (1937; reprint, New York: Architectural Book Publishing Co., 1965), 96–99, and Charles W. Brewster, *Rambles about Portsmouth* (1873; reprint, Somersworth: New Hampshire Publishing Co., 1971), 1:101–2.

17. Bernard Bailyn, *The Origins of American Politics* (New York: Knopf, 1968), 123–24, 160.

18. The account of Benning Wentworth in chapter one draws largely on Jere R. Daniell, *Experiment in Republicanism: New Hampshire Politics and the American Revolution, 1741–1794* (Cambridge, Mass.: Harvard University Press, 1970), 3–40, and Shipton, *Sibley's Harvard Graduates*, 6 (1942):126–33.

2. A VARIED EDUCATION

1. Harvard University Archives, UA 3, 5.5.2, 2:1; John Wentworth, *The Wentworth Genealogy* (Boston: Little, Brown, 1878), 1:536, 321; Charles E. Clark, *The*

Eastern Frontier: The Settlement of Northern New England, 1610–1763 (New York: Knopf, 1970), 295–96.

2. Wentworth, *Genealogy*, 1:320; Clark, *Eastern Frontier*, 294–95, 300–301.

3. Wentworth, *Genealogy*, 1:319–22; Portsmouth Tax Records in New Hampshire Town Records, NHSL, 15:309, 353, 395, 445.

4. Jere R. Daniell, *Experiment in Republicanism: New Hampshire Politics and the American Revolution, 1741–1794* (Cambridge, Mass.: Harvard University Press, 1970), 5; Nathaniel Bouton et al., eds., *Documents and Records Relating to New Hampshire, 1623–1800,* most often called *New Hampshire Provincial and State Papers* and hereafter cited as NHPP, 18:149–90.

5. Joseph J. Malone, *Pine Trees and Politics: The Naval Stores and Forest Policy in Colonial New England, 1691–1775* (Seattle: University of Washington Press, 1964), 124.

6. New Hampshire Town Records, 16:509, 576.

7. Wentworth to John Peirce, 7 Feb. 1795, Peirce Papers, Portsmouth Athenaeum. On Wentworth's filial devotion, see also Wentworth to John Peirce, 9 Mar., 20 May, 10 Nov. 1786, and 21 Jan. 1788, Peirce-Rindge Papers, NHA; Frances Wentworth to John Peirce, 8 Aug. 1786, ibid.

8. On the Peirce family, see the *New England Historical and Genealogical Register* 28 (1874): 369–70. Short sketches of John and Daniel Peirce are found in the Peirce Papers. See also "Daniel Peirce" in Clifford K. Shipton, *Sibley's Harvard Graduates* (Boston: Massachusetts Historical Society, 1951), 8:460–63.

9. Wentworth to Daniel Rindge, 29 Nov. 1765, Masonian Papers, NHA.

10. Shipton, *Sibley's Harvard Graduates*, 14 (1968): 364–65. The Portsmouth tax records indicate that Mark Hunking Wentworth moved between 1740 and 1741. See New Hampshire Town Records, vol. 15.

11. Charles W. Brewster, *Rambles about Portsmouth* (1873; reprint, Somersworth: New Hampshire Publishing Co., 1971), 1:96–97, 140–43.

12. For New Hampshire trade, I have relied largely on William G. Saltonstall, *Ports of Piscataqua* (1941; reprint, New York: Russell and Russell, 1968), 25–54; and Ronald H. Quilici, "A Voyage to Antigua: A Social and Economic Study of the Maritime Activities of Colonial Portsmouth, New Hampshire" (Master's thesis, University of New Hampshire, 1973), 55–67. For destinations and cargoes, see the naval officer shipping lists in Charles E. Clark and Charles W. Eastman, Jr., eds., *The Portsmouth Project* (Somersworth: New Hampshire Publishing Co., 1974), 11–24. On the export of furniture from Portsmouth, see James L. Garvin, "Portsmouth and the Piscataqua: Social History and Material Culture," *Historical New Hampshire* 26 (Summer 1971): 27.

13. Enumerated items were those that under the British Navigation Acts

could be shipped only to England, Ireland, Scotland, or another English colony. Besides masts this list included such products as tobacco, sugar, indigo, molasses, and naval stores. The commerce of Portsmouth, like that of all other colonial ports, was circumscribed by the Acts of Trade of the mother country. That did not mean, however, that the English laws were never broken, which they often were.

14. Jeremy Belknap, *The History of New Hampshire* (1831; reprint, New York: Johnson Reprint, 1970), 1:265–81; Clark, *Eastern Frontier*, 288–92.

15. Quotations are from Clark, *Eastern Frontier*, 291, and Belknap, *New Hampshire*, 1:280.

16. Samuel Lane, *A Journal for the Years 1739–1803 by Samuel Lane of Stratham, New Hampshire*, ed. Charles Lane Hanson (Concord: New Hampshire Historical Society, 1937), 66; Belknap, *New Hampshire*, 1:288.

17. Belknap, *New Hampshire*, 1:290–91.

18. Deposition of the town of Londonderry, N.H., 1773, quoted in Benjamin F. Parker, *History of Wolfeborough* (Wolfeborough, N.H.: by the town, 1901), 68.

19. Brewster, *Rambles about Portsmouth*, 1:79–82.

20. On primary and secondary curriculum in America, see R. Freeman Butts and Lawrence A. Cremin, *A History of Education in American Culture* (New York: Holt, Rinehart, and Winston, 1953), 118–26; Robert Middlekauf, *Ancients and Axioms: Secondary Education in Eighteenth-Century New England* (New Haven: Yale University Press, 1963), 75–102; Lawrence A. Cremin, *American Education: The Colonial Experience, 1607–1783* (New York: Harper and Row, 1970), 499–509. The entrance requirement is quoted in Samuel Eliot Morison, *Three Centuries of Harvard, 1636–1936* (Cambridge, Mass.: Harvard University Press, 1936), 103.

21. Morison, *Three Centuries*, 103, 120–23; Catherine Drinker Bowen, *John Adams and the American Revolution* (1950; reprint, New York: Grosset and Dunlap, 1973), 56; John Adams, *The Diary and Autobiography of John Adams*, ed. Lyman H. Butterfield (Cambridge, Mass.: Harvard University Press, 1961), 3:259–60.

22. Adams, *Diary*, 3:259–60.

23. Bowen, *Adams*, 64; Morison, *Three Centuries*, 102–5.

24. Harvard University Archives, list of scholars by room; Shipton, *Sibley's Harvard Graduates*, 13 (1965): 271; William R. Cutter, *A History of the Cutter Family of New England* (Boston, 1871), 60–61.

25. Morison, *Three Centuries*, 22–23, 29–30, 57–59, 89–90.

26. Shipton, *Sibley's Harvard Graduates*, 8 (1951): 730–34.

27. Shipton, *Sibley's Harvard Graduates*, 5 (1937): 546–53.

28. The chair of divinity was established in 1721 and that of natural philoso-

phy in 1727 with money donated by an Englishman, Thomas Hollis. Hollis, who in addition to those gifts provided funds for scholarships, scientific equipment, and other needs, was one of Harvard's greatest benefactors.

284

29. Shipton, *Sibley's Harvard Graduates*, 9 (1956): 240–63.

30. Morison, *Three Centuries*, 83; Shipton, *Sibley's Harvard Graduates*, 5 (1937): 265–78; ibid., 13 (1965): 513; Clifford K. Shipton, *New England Life in the Eighteenth Century: Representative Biographies from Sibley's Harvard Graduates* (Cambridge, Mass.: Harvard University Press, 1963), xxiv–xxv.

31. Morison, *Three Centuries*, 110; Harvard University Archives, UA 3, 5.5.2, 2:14; Elmer M. Hunt, *New Hampshire Town Names* (Peterborough, N.H.: William L. Baughan, 1970), 153–54; Wentworth to Daniel Rindge, 27 Jan. 1755, Masonian Papers.

32. Adams, *Diary*, 3:260–61; Wentworth to Daniel Rindge, 27 Jan. 1755, Masonian Papers. A list of the books owned by John Wentworth's parents can be found in Jane C. Giffen, ed., "The Estate of Madam Elizabeth Wentworth of Portsmouth," *Historical New Hampshire* 23 (Spring 1968): 44–45.

33. Cutter, *Cutter Family*, 311–12; Shipton, *Sibley's Harvard Graduates*, 13 (1965): 650.

34. Belknap, *New Hampshire*, 1:310–12; Shipton, *Sibley's Harvard Graduates*, 6 (1942): 228.

35. Wentworth to Daniel Rindge, 27 Jan. 1755, Masonian Papers.

36. Wentworth to Daniel Rindge, 4 Apr. 1755, Masonian Papers; Francis Parkman, *Montcalm and Wolfe* (1884; reprint, New York: Collier, 1962), 139–40, 142.

37. Wentworth to Daniel Rindge, 27 Jan., 4 Apr. 1755, Masonian Papers; Cremin, *American Education*, 537–40; Carl Bridenbaugh, *Cities in the Wilderness: The First Century of Urban Life in America, 1625–1742* (1938; reprint, New York: Oxford University Press, 1971), 443–45.

38. Morison, *Three Centuries*, 119–32.

39. Wentworth to Daniel Rindge, 24 June 1755, Masonian Papers; Adams, *Diary*, 3:263.

3. THE MAKING OF A GENTLEMAN MERCHANT

1. Nathaniel Adams, *Annals of Portsmouth* (1825; reprint, Hampton, N.H.: Peter E. Randall, 1971), 255; Wentworth to Daniel Rindge, 18 Dec. 1757, Masonian Papers, NHA. I have assumed that he lived at home since his name is not found in the Portsmouth tax lists for those years. There is a John Wentworth, Esq., listed in a different section of town from that of Mark H. Wentworth, but I believe that is John's uncle, one of his father's brothers. The title *Esq.* in the

eighteenth century was most often associated with court justices. John's uncle John Wentworth served both as judge of the court of common pleas and judge of probate. See New Hampshire Town Records, NHSL, vol. 16; H. L. Mencken, *The American Language*, 4th ed. (New York: Knopf, 1937), 278; John Wentworth, *The Wentworth Genealogy* (Boston: Little, Brown, 1878), 1:305. Also, it would have been unusual for a single man of John Wentworth's age to set up housekeeping by himself in the eighteenth century. His father had a large home and, for that time, a small family; it is probable that John would have lived there until he either married or left Portsmouth.   285

2. John Adams, *Diary and Autobiography of John Adams*, ed. Lyman H. Butterfield (Cambridge, Mass.: Harvard University Press, 1961), 1:1, 4, 19, 115; Adams, *Annals*, 195; NEHGR, 5 (1851): 414[7], 414[6]; John Adams, *The Earliest Diary of John Adams*, ed. Lyman H. Butterfield (Cambridge, Mass.: Harvard University Press, 1966), 64–65.

3. Clifford K. Shipton, *Sibley's Harvard Graduates* (Boston: Massachusetts Historical Society, 1968), 14:364; ibid., 13 (1965): 512, 651; ibid., 4 (1933): 15–16; Samuel Eliot Morison, *Three Centuries of Harvard, 1636–1936* (Cambridge, Mass.: Harvard University Press, 1936), 91.

4. Otis G. Hammond, "The Mason Title and Its Relations to New Hampshire and Massachusetts," *Proceedings of the American Antiquarian Society* 26 (1916): 261. When the border was finally drawn between the two provinces in 1741, Massachusetts gained a line three miles north of the Merrimack. At the time of the Masonian purchase in 1746, New Hampshire's other boundaries were not defined, leading to a dispute with New York over land west of the Connecticut River.

5. John F. Looney, "The King's Representative: Benning Wentworth, Colonial Governor, 1741–1767" (Ph.D. diss., Lehigh University, 1961), 80–81. For information about the Masonian proprietorship, see Hammond, "The Mason Title," 245–63; William H. Fry, *New Hampshire as a Royal Province* (1908; reprint, New York: AMS Press, 1970), 209–320; and Jeremy Belknap, *The History of New Hampshire* (1831; reprint, New York: Johnson Reprint, 1970), 1:251–54, 296–300. Captain John Mason's heirs apparently never did have legal title to the land. See Elwin L. Page, *Judicial Beginnings in New Hampshire, 1640–1700* (Concord: New Hampshire Historical Society, 1959), 188–90. I am indebted to R. Stuart Wallace for this reference.

6. Benjamin F. Parker, *History of Wolfeborough* (Wolfeborough, N.H.: by the town, 1901), 10–18; New Hampshire Town Records, 1:10–11.

7. Belknap, *New Hampshire*, 1:313–16; Adams, *Annals*, 196; William R. Cutter, *A History of the Cutter Family of New England* (Boston, 1871), 60–61.

8. Belknap, *New Hampshire*, 1:317; Cutter, *Cutter Family*, 68; *NEHGR*, 5:414[7].

9. Adams, *Annals*, 200.

10. The following description of Portsmouth is drawn from Charles E. Clark,
286 *The Eastern Frontier: The Settlement of Northern New England, 1610–1763* (New
York: Knopf, 1970), 320–28; *Strawbery Banke: Official Guidebook* (Portsmouth,
N.H.: Strawbery Banke, 1982), 57–59; Adams, *Annals*, 204–5; and Charles W.
Brewster, *Rambles about Portsmouth* (1873; reprint, Somersworth: New Hampshire Publishing Co., 1971), 1:189–91. The declaration of the Library Society
and the statements from the *New Hampshire Gazette* are quoted in Clark,
325–27.

11. *NHPP*, 6:832–33.

12. *NHPP*, 6:833–34, 831; Samuel Lane, *A Journal for the Years 1739–1803, by
Samuel Lane of Stratham, New Hampshire*, ed. Charles Lane Hanson (Concord:
New Hampshire Historical Society, 1937), 73–74. On the development of the
dramatic arts in Portsmouth, see Winslow Suffern, *From Graces to Gargoyles: A
Social Essay on the Theater in Portsmouth, New Hampshire, 1762–1850* (Portsmouth,
N.H.: Seacoast Arts Council, 1972).

13. Wentworth to Daniel Rindge, 18 Dec. 1757, Masonic Papers. On early
Freemasonry in New Hampshire, see Gerald D. Foss, *Three Centuries of Freemasonry in New Hampshire* (Somersworth: New Hampshire Publishing Co.,
1972).

14. John M. Howells, *The Architectural Heritage of the Piscataqua* (1937; reprint, New York: Architectural Book Publishing Co., 1965), 72–85; Hugh Morrison, *Early American Architecture* (New York: Oxford University Press, 1952),
495–96.

15. Brewster, *Rambles*, 1:110. Brewster implies that Frances married Theodore
Atkinson because her first love, John Wentworth, left for England. That story
is repeated by others. See Wentworth, *Wentworth Genealogy*, 1:548, and Shipton, *Sibley's Harvard Graduates*, 14:131. Wentworth, however, did not depart for
England until the autumn of 1763.

16. New Hampshire Town Records, 1:12; Parker, *Wolfeborough*, 19–20.

17. Lawrence Henry Gipson, *American Loyalist: Jared Ingersoll* (1920; reprint,
New Haven: Yale University Press, 1971), 79–110.

18. *NHPP*, 18:543, 549.

19. Jere R. Daniell, *Experiment in Republicanism: New Hampshire Politics and
the American Revolution, 1741–1794* (Cambridge, Mass.: Harvard University Press,
1970), 36–38. The comments about Benning Wentworth's wife are in *NHPP*,
18:544.

20. William L. Sachse, *The Colonial American in Britain* (Madison: University

of Wisconsin Press, 1956), 39–40. We do not know the circumstances surrounding Wentworth's honorary M.A., but Princeton would grant a degree, with the phrase *Honoris causa* inserted, to anyone holding the same degree from another college. See John Maclean, *History of the College of New Jersey* (Philadelphia: J. B. Lippincott, 1877), 1:210. Since Wentworth already held a Harvard M.A., there were no further requirements. I am indebted for this information to Earle E. Coleman, University Archivist, Princeton University.

21. *NHPP*, 18:557–58.

287

4. SIGHTS, SOUNDS, AND A FORTUNATE ACQUAINTANCE

1. William L. Sachse, *The Colonial American in Britain* (Madison: University of Wisconsin Press, 1956), 7–15; Richard Hofstadter, *America at 1750: A Social Portrait* (New York: Knopf, 1971), 40–42.

2. Wentworth was in London by the end of December, and it is unlikely that he arrived before the first of the month. See bill dated 30 Dec. 1763, Peirce Papers, Portsmouth Athenaeum, Portsmouth, N.H.

3. *NHPP*, 7:105; 18:556–57.

4. Frederick A. Pottle, ed., *Boswell's London Journal, 1762–1763* (New York: McGraw-Hill, 1950), 44.

5. A. S. Turberville, ed., *Johnson's England: An Account of the Life and Manners of His Age* (London: Oxford University Press, Clarendon Press, 1933), 1:170.

6. Turberville, *Johnson's England*, 1:177–80; Sachse, *Colonial American*, 17–18; Wentworth to Daniel Peirce, 15 Feb. 1766, Peirce Papers; Bryant Lillywhite, *London Coffee Houses: A Reference Book of Coffee Houses of the Seventeenth, Eighteenth, and Nineteenth Centuries* (London: Allen and Unwin, 1963), 387–91. On the role of London coffeehouses in the mercantile and political discussions of English and colonial merchants in England, see Alison Gilbert Olson, *Anglo-American Politics, 1660–1775: The Relationship Between Parties in England and Colonial America* (New York: Oxford University Press, 1973), 124–28.

7. Turberville, *Johnson's England*, 1:170–71.

8. Ibid., 1:175–76; *NHPP*, 18:557; bill dated 30 Dec. 1763, Peirce Papers.

9. Turberville, *Johnson's England*, 1:182–83.

10. Pottle, *Boswell's London Journal*, 231; Turberville, *Johnson's England*, 1:186.

11. Turberville, *Johnson's England*, 1:188–89. On the theater, see Turberville, 2:160–89.

12. Robert C. Albion, *Forests and Sea Power: The Timber Problem of the Royal Navy, 1652–1862* (Cambridge, Mass.: Harvard University Press, 1926), 55–56; Lawrence Henry Gipson, *American Loyalist: Jared Ingersoll* (1920; reprint, New

Haven: Yale University Press, 1971), 96. The comptroller of the navy board is quoted in Gipson, 109n, Ingersoll's friend on p. 108.

13. Gipson, *American Loyalist*, 106–9. The deposition against Ingersoll is quoted on pp. 106–7.

14. Ibid., 110.

15. J. L. Sibley, Private Journal, Harvard University Archives, vol. 1, 20 Oct. 1846. In his study of John Wentworth, Lawrence Shaw Mayo treats this story as apocryphal on the grounds that "such an account of their meeting is more suggestive of provincial imagination than of the formalities of Wentworth House." See *John Wentworth: Governor of New Hampshire, 1767–1775* (Cambridge, Mass.: Harvard University Press, 1921), 17. According to J. B. Botsford, however, at Newmarket "the wealthy merchant, on horseback, or in gay equipage, could meet on an equal basis the aristocrat. Undoubtedly it was a shock to many, as to Defoe, that here the person of distinction put himself on a level with grooms or riding boys." *English Society in the Eighteenth Century* (1924; reprint, New York: Octagon, 1965), 221. The fact that Mayo's citation is not to the original source of this story may be related to his unwillingness to accept it. See *NEHGR*, 18 (1864): 51–52.

16. Wentworth to Daniel Peirce, 5 July 1764, Peirce Papers; A. E. Richardson, *Georgian England* (1931; reprint, Freeport, N.Y.: Books for Libraries, 1967), 84.

17. John Wentworth and Charles Watson-Wentworth, second marquis of Rockingham, were distantly related—see page 15. Edmund Burke, in a later reference to John Wentworth, stated that "Lord Rockingham always consider'd the Governor as his family, and as a Person who in every part of his Conduct shew'd a just claim to so honorable a Relation." See *The Correspondence of Edmund Burke*, ed. Thomas W. Copeland (Cambridge, England: Cambridge University Press, 1968), 7:7–8.

18. Ross J. S. Hoffman, *The Marquis: A Study of Lord Rockingham* (New York: Fordham University Press, 1973), 20; John N. Summerson, *Architecture in Britain, 1530–1830* (Harmondsworth, Middlesex: Penguin, 1970), 322–25, 362; G. H. Guttridge, *The Early Career of Lord Rockingham, 1730–1765* (Berkeley: University of California Press, 1952), 15. For more on Wentworth-Woodhouse, see Marcus Binney, "Wentworth Woodhouse Revisited—I" and "Wentworth Woodhouse Revisited—II," *Country Life* (17 and 24 March 1983): 624–27, 708–11.

19. Hoffman, *Marquis*, 13; Guttridge, *Early Career*, 15–16. Arthur Young, the commentator, is quoted in both Hoffman and Guttridge.

20. J. Steven Watson, *The Reign of George III, 1760–1815* (Oxford: Oxford University Press, 1960), 78–90; G. H. Guttridge, *English Whiggism and the American Revolution* (1942; reprint, Berkeley: University of California Press, 1966), 19–

20; Guttridge, *Early Career*, 37; Dorothy Marshall, *Eighteenth-Century England* (London: Longman, 1962), 361.

21. Wentworth to Daniel Peirce, 5 July 1764, Peirce Papers.

22. Wentworth to Daniel Peirce, 14 Aug. 1764, Peirce Papers.   289

23. Ibid. Wentworth mentions in later letters that action is being considered against the Masonian proprietorship.

24. Wentworth to Messrs. Lawton and Carlton, Oct. 1767, Transcripts of John Wentworth Letter Book no. 1, NHA, 49–50.

25. E. B. O'Callaghan, *The Documentary History of the State of New York* (Albany: Charles Van Benthuysen, 1851), 4:574–75.

26. Board of Trade to Privy Council, 10 July 1764, PRO, CO5/942.

27. The charges against Benning Wentworth as surveyor general are mentioned in Jeremy Belknap, *The History of New Hampshire* (1831; reprint, New York: Johnson Reprint, 1970), 1:335. On the considerations concerning the Masonian proprietorship by the Board of Trade in 1753, see NHPP, 29:289–99. John Huske, formerly of Portsmouth and by 1766 a member of Parliament, has been identified as a main instigator in the proceedings against Benning Wentworth and the renewed questioning of the Masonian proprietors' claim. See Jere R. Daniell, *Experiment in Republicanism: New Hampshire Politics and the American Revolution, 1741–1794* (Cambridge, Mass.: Harvard University Press, 1970), 37–39. Whatever Huske's role, it did not diminish John Wentworth's opinion of him. During the debate in Parliament over the Stamp Act, he wrote home: "My friend Mr. Huske has great merit in fighting our Cause, which He has constantly done from the first to this Hour, and now with considerable Success. Surely our Country men have been strangely misinformed about him—they are much oblig'd to him and I not only know it but have pleasure in avowing it." See Wentworth to Daniel Peirce, 15 Feb. 1766, Peirce Papers. For a brief sketch of Huske, see Alan Valentine, *The British Establishment, 1760–1784: An Eighteenth-Century Biographical Dictionary* (Norman: University of Oklahoma Press, 1970), 1:483.

28. Massachusetts Historical Society, *Collections*, 6th ser., 4 (1891): 498. John Wentworth's defense, from which the following account is taken, is found in NHPP, 18:560–67.

29. Wentworth to Daniel Peirce, 8 Apr. 1765, Peirce Papers.

30. Wentworth to Daniel Peirce, probably 27 Aug. 1765, Peirce Papers. Brabant was the old duchy of the Netherlands. It included what is now the southern Netherlands and central and northern Belgium.

31. Watson, *George III*, 110–11; Wentworth to Daniel Peirce, probably 27 Aug. 1765, Peirce Papers.

32. Wentworth to Daniel Peirce, probably 27 Aug. 1765, Peirce Papers; Paul

Langford, *The First Rockingham Administration, 1765–1766* (Oxford: Oxford University Press, 1973), 76; Edmund S. and Helen M. Morgan, *The Stamp Act Crisis: Prologue to Revolution* (1953; reprint, New York: Collier, 1963), 123–24, 139. On the origins of the Stamp Act, see John L. Bullion, *A Great and Necessary Measure: George Grenville and the Genesis of the Stamp Act, 1763–1765* (Columbia: University of Missouri Press, 1982).

33. Wentworth to Daniel Peirce, probably 27 Aug. 1765, Peirce Papers.

5. A MODEL FOR THE FUTURE

1. The following is based on Derek H. Watson, "John Wentworth's Description of the American Colonies in 1765," *Historical New Hampshire* 27 (Fall 1972): 141–66.

2. During the fall, it was well known that Rockingham was in favor of relief for America. By December he seems to have been personally committed to repeal. See Paul Langford, *The First Rockingham Administration, 1765–1766* (Oxford: Oxford University Press, 1973), 126–30. Benjamin Franklin, the most influential colonist in England at that time, hoped for repeal when the Rockingham administration came into power, but he did not expect it. Franklin did not meet Rockingham until early November 1765. See P. D. G. Thomas, *British Politics and the Stamp Act Crisis: The First Phase of the American Revolution, 1763–1767* (Oxford: Oxford University Press, Clarendon Press, 1975), 143–44. Following repeal, the Rockingham administration pushed ahead with trade reforms that answered nearly all the complaints of the colonies. See John W. Tyler, *Smugglers and Patriots: Boston Merchants and the Advent of the American Revolution* (Boston: Northeastern University Press, 1986), 92–107; and Jack M. Sosin, *Agents and Merchants: British Colonial Policy and the Origins of the American Revolution, 1763–1775* (Lincoln: University of Nebraska Press, 1965), 81–85.

3. Watson, "John Wentworth's Description," 156–57.

4. Lawrence Henry Gipson, *The British Empire before the American Revolution*, vol. 10, *The Triumphant Empire: Thunder-Clouds Gather in the West, 1763–1766* (New York: Knopf, 1961), 302; George Meserve to Wentworth, 27 Sept. 1765, Wentworth Papers, NHHS.

5. Gipson, vol. 10, *Triumphant Empire: Thunder-Clouds*, 302–3; George Meserve to Wentworth, 27 Sept. 1765, Wentworth Papers, NHHS; Nathaniel Adams, *Annals of Portsmouth* (1825; reprint, Hampton, N.H.: Peter E. Randall, 1971), 212; George Meserve to Secretary of State Conway, 31 July 1766, PRO, CO5/934.

6. Gipson, vol. 10, *Triumphant Empire: Thunder-Clouds*, 303; John F. Looney,

"The King's Representative: Benning Wentworth, Colonial Governor, 1741–1767" (Ph.D. diss., Lehigh University, 1961), 135–36; Jere R. Daniell, *Experiment in Republicanism: New Hampshire Politics and the American Revolution, 1741–1794* (Cambridge, Mass.: Harvard University Press, 1970), 52–53; George Meserve to Wentworth, 27 Sept. 1765, Wentworth Papers, NHHS; George Meserve to Secretary of State Conway, 31 July 1766, PRO, CO5/934.

291

7. George Meserve to Wentworth, 27 Sept. 1765, Wentworth Papers, NHHS; Daniell, *Experiment in Republicanism*, 52.

8. *NHPP*, 7:92.

9. Wentworth to Daniel Rindge, 29 Nov. 1765, Masonian Papers, NHA.

10. Ibid.

11. Ibid.

12. Ibid.

13. Ibid.

14. Gipson, vol. 10, *Triumphant Empire: Thunder-Clouds*, 290–324.

15. The following discussion of politics in England relating to the Stamp Act is based on Langford, *First Rockingham Administration*, 109–48; and Gipson, vol. 10, *Triumphant Empire: Thunder-Clouds*, 371–414.

16. John Adams, *Diary and Autobiography of John Adams*, ed. Lyman H. Butterfield (Cambridge, Mass.: Harvard University Press, 1961), 1:287.

17. Rockingham is quoted in Langford, *First Rockingham Administration*, 111.

18. D. H. Watson, "Barlow Trecothick," *Bulletin of the British Association for American Studies*, new ser., 1 (September 1960): 36–49, (March 1961): 29–39.

19. Quoted in Gipson, vol. 10, *Triumphant Empire: Thunder-Clouds*, 382n. This success of the London merchants went against a general trend of decreasing effectiveness by the London mercantile lobby in remedying colonial trade grievances. See Alison G. Olson, "The London Mercantile Lobby and the Coming of the American Revolution," *The Journal of American History* 69 (June 1982): 21–41.

20. Lawrence Gipson states that "British trade, as a result of the American boycott, was languishing by the fall of 1765." See Gipson, vol. 10, *Triumphant Empire: Thunder-Clouds*, 381. Because the first official boycott of British goods was not announced until 31 October in New York City (Boston did not follow suit until December), however, this movement was not responsible for the "languishing" British-American trade or the decision of Barlow Trecothick and the London merchants in early December to seek support from other towns for the repeal of the Stamp Act. Trade had been slow for more than a year, and that fact, along with threats from American merchants that payment of bills might have to cease, was what moved the London merchants. See Langford, *First Rockingham Administration*, 117–19. As news of the boycotts began to reach

England in December, it undoubtedly did play a role in the encouraging response of the other towns to Trecothick's circular.

21. Wentworth to Daniel Peirce, 15 Feb. 1766, Peirce Papers, Portsmouth Athenaeum, Portsmouth, N.H. Pitt is quoted in Gipson, vol. 10, *Triumphant Empire: Thunder-Clouds*, 79.

22. Wentworth to Daniel Peirce, 15 Feb. 1766, Peirce Papers.

23. Ibid.

24. Quoted in Gipson, vol. 10, *Triumphant Empire: Thunder-Clouds*, 383.

25. *Journals of the House of Commons* 30 (London, 1803): 513.

26. Michael G. Kammen, *A Rope of Sand: The Colonial Agents, British Politics, and the American Revolution* (Ithaca: Cornell Univ. Press, 1968), 121.

27. Wentworth to Daniel Peirce, 15 Feb. 1766, Peirce Papers. Although not called on during the repeal debate, Wentworth did testify late in March before the Commons Committee on American Papers in favor of the suggestion he had made to Rockingham the previous September that the molasses duty be reduced. In keeping with his practical approach to the empire, he argued that such a reduction would allow the colonies to purchase more manufactured goods from Britain. See Thomas, *British Politics and the Stamp Act Crisis*, 258.

28. Wentworth to Daniel Peirce, 15 Feb. 1766, Peirce Papers; Wentworth to Stephen Apthorp, 18 Aug. 1767, Transcripts of John Wentworth Letter Book no. 1, NHA, 27–28. Jeremy Belknap states that New Hampshire's agents "suppressed" the news about Meserve for fear it would interfere with the repeal effort. See Jeremy Belknap, *The History of New Hampshire* (1831; reprint, New York: Johnson Reprint, 1970), 1:332.

29. Wentworth to Daniel Peirce, 15 Feb. 1766, Peirce Papers.

30. Ibid.

31. Ibid. The salary of the New Hampshire agent is given in Kammen, *Rope of Sand*, 47.

32. Wentworth to Daniel Peirce, 15 Feb. 1766, Peirce Papers.

33. Ibid.

34. Conway is quoted in Gipson, vol. 10, *Triumphant Empire: Thunder-Clouds*, 395.

35. Wentworth to Daniel Peirce, 1 Mar. 1766, Peirce Papers.

36. George T. Keppel, Earl of Albemarle, *Memoirs of the Marquis of Rockingham and His Contemporaries* (London: Richard Bently, 1852), 1:320; Wentworth to Daniel Peirce, 15 Feb. 1766, Peirce Papers.

37. Wentworth to Daniel Peirce, 15 Feb. 1766, Peirce Papers. Wentworth's close idealogical proximity to his patron, the marquis of Rockingham, is well

illustrated in a 1767 letter from Rockingham to the speaker of the Massachusetts Assembly. "I shall always consider that this country, as the parent," Rockingham wrote, "ought to be tender and just; and that the colonies, as the children, ought to be dutiful. A system of arbitrary rule over the colonies I would not adopt on this side, nor would I do otherwise than strenuously resist when attempts were made to throw off that dependency to which the colonies ought to submit, not only for the advantage of this country, but for their own real happiness and safety." Quoted in Peter D. G. Thomas, *The Townshend Duties Crisis: The Second Phase of the American Revolution, 1767–1773* (Oxford: Oxford University Press, Clarendon Press, 1987), 1. For a comprehensive discussion of Lockean ideas about the parent-child relationship, their pervasiveness in popular literature of the eighteenth century, and their role in the coming of the American Revolution, see Jay Fliegelman, *Prodigals and Pilgrims: The American Revolution against Patriarchal Authority, 1750–1800* (Cambridge, England: Cambridge University Press, 1982).

293

38. J. Steven Watson, *The Reign of George III, 1760–1815* (Oxford: Oxford University Press, 1960), 113–21; Langford, *First Rockingham Administration*, 258.

39. Wentworth was at this time covering all possible bases. There are indications that in 1766 he successfully solicited a position as deputy post master general in America. That action may have been taken because he had not heard from New Hampshire about the agency, and Benning Wentworth still had not resigned. See Theodore Jervey, "Barlow Trecothick," *South Carolina Historical And Genealogical Magazine* 32 (July 1931): 159.

40. Most accounts of Benning Wentworth state that he resigned his office. I can find no evidence, however, that he did actually resign of his own volition. In February John Wentworth seemed to have lost patience with his uncle because he had not yet given up his office. See Wentworth to Daniel Peirce, 15 Feb. 1766, Peirce Papers. In Benning Wentworth's correspondence with the Board of Trade before his nephew's appointment as governor in July there is no mention of resignation. In his letter to the board, Richmond does declare that John Wentworth is replacing Benning Wentworth, "who has resigned" (PRO, CO5/928). It seems probable this statement was merely for appearances. Writing to Jeremy Belknap years later, John noted that "it appeared" that Benning "resigned in favor of his nephew" (MHS, *Collections*, 6th ser., 4 [1891]: 498). One of the reasons Wentworth did not immediately leave for home may have been to allow time for his uncle to receive word of his "resignation" and make necessary preparations.

41. MHS, *Collections*, 6th ser., 9 (1897): 54; Wentworth to Robert Temple,

29 Jan. 1768, Letter Book no. 1, 74. On John Temple, see Charles W. Akers, "New Hampshire's 'Honorary' Lieutenant Governor: John Temple and the American Revolution," *Historical New Hampshire* 32 (Summer 1975): 79–99.

42. PRO, CO5/942.

43. Wentworth to Hugh Hall Wentworth, 5 Aug. 1766, Wentworth Papers, NHHS; Wentworth to Paul Wentworth, 27 Oct. 1769, Letter Book no. 1, 306; A. S. Turberville, ed., *Johnson's England: An Account of the Life and Manners of His Age* (1933; reprint, London: Oxford University Press, 1952), 2:64–65; Ellis W. Waterhouse, *Painting in Britain, 1530–1790* (Baltimore: Penguin, 1953), 228. I am indebted to John Hayes of the National Portrait Gallery, London, for identifying the likely artist as Benjamin Wilson.

44. Wentworth to Hugh Hall Wentworth, 5 Aug. 1766, Wentworth Papers, NHHS; *Alumni Oxonienses: The Members of the University of Oxford, 1715–1886* (Oxford: James Parker, 1891), 4:1525; Wentworth to Thomas Smith, 17 July 1767, Letter Book no. 1, 16–17; NHG, 31 Oct. 1766. Wentworth already had received a similar honorary degree earlier in his stay in Britain from Aberdeen University.

45. Wentworth to Hugh Hall Wentworth, 26 Aug. 1766, Miscellaneous Manuscripts, MHS; Wentworth to Daniel Peirce, 10 Sept. 1766, Peirce Papers; John Wentworth, *The Wentworth Genealogy* (Boston: Little, Brown, 1878), 1:xxv; NHPP, 7:106–7. Wentworth had earlier informed Peirce that he would never accept the agency as a joint position. His reasoning seems to have lain not in any misgivings about Trecothick but rather in a desire for independence, efficiency, and, though not stated, a larger salary. See Wentworth to Daniel Peirce, 15 Feb. 1766, Peirce Papers.

46. Wentworth to Daniel Peirce, 10 Sept. 1766, Peirce Papers; NHPP, 7:106–7.

47. Henry Caner to Wentworth, 26 Sept. 1766, and 19 Jan. 1767, Caner Letter Book, 248–58, MSS. D.M. 388, University of Bristol Library; *Alumni Oxonienses*, 4:1525. Samuel Wentworth died two years later at Oxford at the age of eighteen.

48. Frederick Chase, *The History of Dartmouth College and the Town of Hanover* (Cambridge, Mass.: John Wilson Son, 1891), 1:9–55; The Papers of Eleazar Wheelock, DCA, 766661.2, 766666.2.

49. On Rockingham and the whig view, see "The Rockingham Whigs," chapter 2 of G. H. Guttridge, *English Whiggism and the American Revolution* (1942; reprint, Berkeley: University of California Press, 1966), 17–57. On the difficulty of defining the terms *whig* and *tory* during this period, see Watson, *George III*, 58.

50. Wentworth to Daniel Peirce, 15 Feb. 1766, Peirce Papers.

51. Watson, *George III*, 112; Dorothy Marshall, *Eighteenth-Century England*

(London: Longman, 1962), 360–61; Ross J. S. Hoffman, *The Marquis: A Study of Lord Rockingham* (New York: Fordham University Press, 1973), 178. Burke is quoted in Marshall, 361n.

52. Hoffman (*Marquis*, ix) stresses Rockingham's foreign policy concerns. 295 Rockingham's interest in commercial affairs and his relationship with the merchants is discussed in detail in Langford, *First Rockingham Administration*, 109–24.

53. Wentworth to Daniel Peirce, 15 Feb. 1766, Peirce Papers.

54. Watson, "John Wentworth's Description," 157.

55. Wentworth to Daniel Peirce, 29 Nov. 1765, 15 Feb. 1766, Peirce Papers.

56. "Power and Wealth" were Wentworth's own words to describe the desirable goals of a successful empire. See Watson, "John Wentworth's Description," 164.

6. MAKING THE THEORY WORK

1. Wentworth to Messrs. Mayne and Co. at Lisbon, 16 Jan. 1768, Transcripts of John Wentworth Letter Book no. 1, NHA, 69–70; Wentworth to the Commissioners of the Navy, Treasury, Admiralty, Board of Trade and Plantations, and the earl of Shelburne, 3 Sept. 1767, ibid., 53; Wentworth to the earl of Shelburne, 16 June 1767, ibid., 1; Wentworth to Richard Willis, 18 Aug. 1767, ibid., 29; Wentworth to Joseph Harrison, 13 Feb. 1768, ibid., 77–78.

2. Wentworth to the Commissioners of the Navy, Treasury, Admiralty, Board of Trade and Plantations, and the earl of Shelburne, 3 Sept. 1767, Letter Book no. 1, 53.

3. Wentworth to Edward Bridgen, 20 July 1767, Letter Book no. 1, 17; Wentworth to William Byrd, 23 June 1767, ibid., 2–3; Wentworth to Peter Randolph, 10 July 1767, ibid., 11; Wentworth to John Clapham, 15 July 1767, ibid., 15–16; William L. Saunders, *The Colonial Records of North Carolina* (Raleigh, 1890), 7:450; William Tryon to Wentworth, 23 Dec. 1771, NHPP, 10:221. I am indebted to Professor Louise Hall of Duke University for several references concerning Wentworth's trip through the southern colonies.

4. Wentworth to Thomas Smith, 17 July 1767, Letter Book no. 1, 16; Wentworth to William Bayard, 3 July 1767, ibid., 6–7; Leonard W. Labaree, et al., eds., *The Papers of Benjamin Franklin* (New Haven: Yale University Press, 1970), 14:178–79; Joseph Harrison to the marquis of Rockingham, 29 July 1767, Rockingham Correspondence, WWM, Sheffield Archives, R63–8; Derek H. Watson, "Barlow Trecothick and Other Associates of Lord Rockingham during the Stamp Act Crisis, 1765–66" (Master's thesis, Sheffield University, 1958), 100–128.

5. NHHS, *Collections* 3 (1832): 282–83; *Massachusetts Gazette and Boston News-Letter*, 25 June 1767; NHPP, 7:8; Nathaniel Adams, *Annals of Portsmouth* (1825; reprint, Hampton, N.H.: Peter E. Randall, 1971), 221–23.

6. NHPP, 7:8; Adams, *Annals*, 222–23; Wentworth to William Bayard, 3 July 1767, Letter Book no. 1, 6–7; *Massachusetts Gazette and Boston News-Letter*, 25 June 1767; NHHS, *Collections* 3:282–83; accounts and receipts of the province committee in charge of the reception of John Wentworth, May and June 1767, Treasury Records, NHA.

7. The Reverend Arthur Browne to the Society for the Propagation of the Gospel, 6 Nov. 1767, SPG Papers, NHHS, 98.

8. Clifford K. Shipton, *Sibley's Harvard Graduates* (Boston: Massachusetts Historical Society, 1965), 13:655.

9. Charles W. Brewster, *Rambles about Portsmouth* (1873; reprint, Somersworth: New Hampshire Publishing Co., 1971), 1:115. Others referring to Wentworth as "little" were John Hurd (quoted in Jere R. Daniell, *Experiment in Republicanism: New Hampshire Politics and the American Revolution, 1741–1794* [Cambridge, Mass.: Harvard University Press, 1970], 68) and Sylvanus Ripley (Ripley to David McClure, 20 Mar. 1774, The Papers of Eleazar Wheelock, DCA, 774228.2).

10. MHS, *Collections*, 6th ser., 4 (1891): 75. For evidence of Wentworth's efforts to help Belknap collect information for his history of New Hampshire, see ibid., 47–49, 54, 64–65; the Reverend Henry Caner to Wentworth, 13 Nov., 6 Dec. 1773, 14 Mar., 19 and 21 Apr., 16 and 30 June, 8 Aug. 1774, Caner Letter Book, MSS. D.M. 388, University of Bristol Library; Shipton, *Sibley's Harvard Graduates*, 15 (1970): 180. See also MHS, *Collections*, 6th ser., 4:564, 619; Benjamin Thompson to the Reverend Samuel Williams, 18 Jan. 1773, Misc. MSS, Moffatt, Whipple, and Mason Papers, NHHS. In 1773 Wentworth gave ten dollars to John Tuft to help develop "an Astronomical instrument which may prove useful in Navigation if perfected." See subscription of John Wentworth to John Tuft, 8 May 1773, Executive Records, NHA.

11. Wentworth borrowed money for a country estate at Wolfeboro and for other acquisitions primarily from his father. Mark Hunking Wentworth's claim against his son at the time John left New Hampshire in 1775 was 13,680 pounds. See statement of Oliver Peabody concerning the accounts of Samuel Gilman, trustee of the confiscated estate of Governor John Wentworth, 16 May 1793, Rockingham County Probate Records, NHA.

12. Wentworth to Hugh Hall Wentworth, 5 Aug. 1766, Wentworth Papers, NHHS.

13. Shipton, *Sibley's Harvard Graduates*, 6 (1942): 328.

14. Jane C. Giffen and Harriet S. Lacy, "The Governor Wentworth House in Portsmouth," *Historical New Hampshire* 23 (Spring 1968): 51; NHPP, 7:130, 264; John Fisher to John Wentworth, 25 July 1770, Executive Records.

15. Giffen and Lacy, "Governor Wentworth House," 50–54; Wentworth to   297
William Bayard, 3 July 1767, Letter Book no. 1, 6–7. The house still stands on Pleasant Street in Portsmouth. After taking up residence there, Wentworth continued to receive horses from England. See NHG, 17 May 1771.

16. Wentworth to J. Winslow, Jr. , early Sept. and 8 Sept. 1767, Letter book no. 1, 35, 37; Wentworth to Robert Blunt, 8 Oct. and 27 Oct. 1767, ibid., 46, 48–49; Wentworth to Messrs. Trecothick and Apthorp, 31 Dec. 1767, 27 Jan. 1768, ibid., 69, 72–73; Wentworth to William Odiorne, 14 Oct. 1767, ibid., 46; Wentworth to Robert Bayard, 19 Oct. 1767, ibid., 46; Wentworth to Benjamin Harris, 28 Sept. 1767, ibid., 41; Wentworth to Lady Rockingham, Dec. 1776, Rockingham Letters, Ramsden Records, Sheepscar Library, Leeds, no. 51.

17. Wentworth to Joseph Harrison, 13 Feb. 1768, Letter Book no. 1, 77–78; Wentworth to William Bayard, 13 July 1767, ibid., 6–7; NHPP, 7:264, 271, 311; John Fisher to Meshech Weare and others of the House committee, 2 Apr. 1771, and vote of the House of Representatives, 19 Jan. 1773, General Court Records (Minutes), NHA.

18. NHPP, 7:126–30; Bernard Bailyn, *The Origins of American Politics* (New York: Knopf, 1968), 134.

19. Lawrence Henry Gipson, *The British Empire before the American Revolution*, vol. 11, *The Triumphant Empire: The Rumbling of the Coming Storm, 1766–1770* (New York: Knopf, 1965), 111n, and vol. 12, *The Triumphant Empire: Britain Sails into the Storm, 1770–1776* (New York: Knopf, 1965), 139; NHPP, 7:130–47; Jeremy Belknap, *The History of New Hampshire* (1831; reprint, New York: Johnson Reprint, 1970), 1:341; Wentworth to the earl of Hillsborough, 1 Mar. 1769, PRO, CO5/930; Wentworth to Paul Wentworth, 27 Oct. 1769, Letter Book no. 1, 306. On salaries of other governors, see Evarts B. Greene, *The Provincial Governor in the English Colonies of North America*, Harvard Historical Studies, vol. 7 (New York, 1898), 60; and Louise Dunbar, "The Royal Governors in the Middle and Southern Colonies on the Eve of the Revolution: A Study in Imperial Personnel," in *The Era of the American Revolution*, ed. Richard B. Morris (New York: Columbia University Press, 1939), 222, 267.

20. NHPP, 7:173–74, 176–77, 179, 182, 185, 187; Records of the Council and Assembly, 25–26 Aug. 1768, PRO, CO5/935; Wentworth to the earl of Shelburne, 25 Mar. 1768, Hammond Transcripts, NHHS.

21. NHPP, 7:227, 257; Wentworth to the earl of Hillsborough, 4 Nov. 1770, Hammond Transcripts. See also Wentworth to John Temple, 18 Nov. 1770, MHS,

Collections, 6th ser., 9 (1897): 237; Wentworth to Daniel Rindge, n.d., Masonian Papers, NHA; Wentworth to the marquis of Rockingham, 23 July 1771, Rockingham Correspondence, WWM, R1–1383. On the payment of governors out of the customs revenue, see O. M. Dickerson, "Use Made of the Revenue from the Tax on Tea," *New England Quarterly* 31 (April 1958): 240.

22. Wentworth to the marquis of Rockingham, 23 July 1771, Rockingham Correspondence, WWM, R1–1383; Wentworth to the earl of Dartmouth, 20 Apr. 1774, PRO, CO5/938; Wentworth to Hector Cramahe, 5 Apr. 1768, Letter Book no. 1, 92; Wentworth to Thomas Smith, 17 July 1767, ibid., 16; NHPP, 7:232, 257; David McClure, *Diary of David McClure*, ed. Franklin B. Dexter (New York: Knickerbocker Press, 1899), 149. On various services rendered for fees by governors, see Greene, *Provincial Governor*, 61–62.

23. Wentworth to Anthony Belham, 9 Aug. 1768, Letter Book no. 1, 131.

24. Belknap, *New Hampshire*, 1:336, 339; Wentworth to Stephen Apthorp, 18 Aug. 1767, Letter Book no. 1, 28. See also Wentworth to William Parker, 26 Aug. 1767, ibid., 32.

25. Charles E. Clark, *The Eastern Frontier: The Settlement of Northern New England, 1610–1763* (New York: Knopf, 1970), 354; NHPP, 7:168–70, and 10:623–36; Wentworth to the earl of Dartmouth, 5 Aug. 1774, PRO, CO5/938.

26. Wentworth to the earl of Shelburne, 25 Mar. 1768, Hammond Transcripts.

27. Ibid.

28. Derek H. Watson, "John Wentworth's Description of the American Colonies in 1765," *Historical New Hampshire* 27 (Fall 1972): 153; Robert G. Albion, *Forests and Sea Power: The Timber Problem of the Royal Navy, 1652–1862* (Cambridge, Mass.: Harvard University Press, 1926), 269–76. Wentworth's designs for New Hampshire in 1768 were very much in line with what he had told Rockingham in 1765 when he stated, the "true interest of both [the colonies and Great Britain] is to promote population and to direct and encourage them to the most proper employments." See Watson, "John Wentworth's Description," 148–49. "Proper Employments" meant agriculture; it would be the job of the governors to implement this plan.

29. Wentworth to the earl of Shelburne, 25 Mar. 1768, Hammond Transcripts.

30. Lawrence Henry Gipson, *The British Empire before the American Revolution*, vol. 3, *The British Isles and the American Colonies: The Northern Plantations, 1748–1754* (Caldwell, Idaho: Caxton Printers, 1936), 298; Wentworth to Edward Bridgen, 20 July, 11 Sept. 1767, Letter Book no. 1, 17, 39–40; John Wentworth to the earl of Shelburne, 25 Mar. 1768, Hammond Transcripts; A. S. Batchellor et al., *The Laws of New Hampshire, 1689–1835* (Manchester, Concord, and Bristol, 1926), 3:466; Wentworth to the earl of Dartmouth, 3 June 1773, PRO, CO5/938.

See also Wentworth to the earl of Hillsborough, 25 May 1768, PRO, CO5/935; to Hillsborough, 18 Feb., 4 Nov. 1770, PRO, CO5/930; to the earl of Dartmouth, 19 Dec. 1772 and 5 Aug. 1774, PRO, CO5/938. In his letter to Shelburne, Wentworth noted: "The people are by no means inclined to any sort of Manufacture—scarcely a Shoemaker, a Joyner or a Silversmith but quits his Trade as soon as he can get able to buy a little Trust of Land, and build a Cottage in the Wilderness—which disposition I am industrious to cultivate and encourage as the most effectual means to prevent any Schemes of Manufacture taking place."

299

31. Because of the Masonian proprietorship, Wentworth was limited to making grants beyond the curved line that encompassed all land within sixty miles of Portsmouth. That was why his interest in new settlement focused on the Connecticut River.

32. Wentworth to Joseph Trumbull, 27 Nov. 1767, Letter Book no. 1, 59; Shipton, *Sibley's Harvard Graduates*, 16 (1972): 430, and 13:661; Eleazar Wheelock to Wentworth, 5 Dec. 1769, Wheelock Papers, 769655; Wentworth to Eleazar Wheelock, 12 Jan. 1770, ibid., 770112; Wentworth to the earl of Dartmouth, 3 June 1773, PRO, CO5/938; Wentworth to the earl of Hillsborough, 23 Sept. 1771, PRO, CO5/930.

33. Belknap, *New Hampshire*, 2:61–62, 153–54. Belknap's description is from some years later when John Wentworth was no longer governor. The problem, nevertheless, was still the same.

34. John F. Looney, "The King's Representative: Benning Wentworth, Colonial Governor, 1741–1767" (Ph.D. diss., Lehigh University, 1961), 26; NHPP, 18:555, 558–59, 584. Coos, the name of a Canadian Indian tribe, meant literally "crooked river." It was applied to the upper region of the Connecticut River and was variously spelled *Cowass, Cohas, Cohos,* and *Kohass.* See Elmer M. Hunt, *New Hampshire Town Names* (Peterborough: William L. Bauhan, 1970), 224.

35. NHPP, 18:584, and 7:151, 195.

36. Wentworth to the earl of Shelburne, 25 Mar. 1768, Hammond Transcripts; Aaron Stores to Eleazar Wheelock, 10 Aug. 1771, Wheelock Papers, 771460; Wentworth to Hugh Hall Wentworth, 23 Dec. 1768, Letter Book no. 1, 188–89.

37. Records of the Assembly, 11 and 16 Mar. 1769, PRO, CO5/936; Petition of inhabitants of Upper Cohass and other towns to John Wentworth, 11 Feb. 1768, NHA; James W. Goldthwaite, "The Governor's Road from Rochester to Wolfeboro," *New Hampshire Highways*, May 1931, 2–5. Wentworth believed these roads would cut forty and one hundred miles respectively from the traveling distance to Charlestown and Stonington. See Wentworth to the earl of Hillsborough, 3 July 1769, Hammond Transcripts.

38. NHPP, 7:232–34, 260, 262, 268, 274–75, 278.

39. Ibid., 275, 278, 284, 306.

40. In 1770 Wentworth had to admonish the Masonian proprietors to be hardnosed and collect the money owed by the Middleton grantees for expenses of a road built through their town. See Wentworth to the proprietors of Mason's patent, 6 Feb. 1770, Executive Records.

41. Wentworth to the earl of Shelburne, 25 Mar. 1768, Hammond Transcripts. During John Wentworth's term as governor the quitrent on Crown lands was one shilling per hundred acres. For any period from one to ten years after the granting of land, the quitrent could be waived in favor of one ear of Indian corn. Wentworth felt that New Hampshire's requirements were much less strict than those of other provinces. See William H. Fry, *New Hampshire as a Royal Province* (1908; reprint, New York: AMS Press, 1970), 293; Batchellor, *Laws of New Hampshire*, 3:441; and Wentworth to John Nelson, 29 Mar. 1770, Letter Book no. 1, 341.

42. The earl of Hillsborough to Wentworth, 9 July 1768, Hammond Transcripts; Board of Trade to the king, 4 Aug. 1768, PRO, CO5/942; Wentworth to the earl of Hillsborough, 23 Sept. 1771, PRO, CO5/930 and T1/493; *NHPP*, 18:652–53, and 7:278, 283–84, 306. Oddly, in 1772 Hillsborough wrote to Wentworth that the Board of Trade approved of his use of the quitrent receipts for roads, but from then on he would like the governor to get the board's approval first. It seems highly unlikely Wentworth would have proceeded to use Crown money in that way without permission. Perhaps the board forgot that they had approved the project in 1768, or the lapse may have lain with Hillsborough, always a stickler for details and ever ready to point out to Wentworth his errors and shortcomings. See Hillsborough to Wentworth, 7 Aug. 1772, PRO, CO5/947. On Wentworth's success in collecting quitrents, see Wentworth to the earl of Dartmouth, 20 Apr. 1774, PRO, CO5/938.

7. MAN OF THE INTERIOR

1. William H. Fry, *New Hampshire as a Royal Province* (1908; reprint, New York: AMS Press, 1970), 459–63; Jere R. Daniell, "Politics in New Hampshire under Governor Benning Wentworth, 1741–1767," *William and Mary Quarterly* 23 (January 1966): 92–93; John F. Looney, "The King's Representative: Benning Wentworth, Colonial Governor, 1741–1767" (Ph.D. diss., Lehigh University, 1961), 157.

2. *NHPP*, 7:108–9.

3. Jere R. Daniell, *Experiment in Republicanism: New Hampshire Politics and the American Revolution, 1741–1794* (Cambridge, Mass.: Harvard University Press,

1970), 50; Leonard W. Labaree, *Royal Government in America* (1930; reprint, New York: Frederick Ungar, 1958), 378n.

4. *NHPP*, 7:129–44.

5. Ibid., 154–55, 160–62.

6. Ibid., 165.

7. Ibid., 174–75.

8. Ibid., 175; Wentworth to Anthony Belham, 9 Aug. 1768, Transcripts of John Wentworth Letter Book no. 1, NHA, 129–37.

9. *NHPP*, 7:175, 178.

10. Ibid., 182.

11. Ibid., 184–86.

12. Board of Trade to the king, 3 Aug. 1768, Hammond Transcripts, NHHS; the earl of Hillsborough to Wentworth, 13 Aug. 1768, ibid.; Wentworth to Hillsborough, 7 Nov. 1768, ibid.; *NHPP*, 7:191–97.

13. *NHPP*, 7:198; Wentworth to Paul Wentworth, 15 Nov. 1768, Letter Book no. 1, 155.

14. *NHPP*, 7:200–202.

15. Ibid., 202–14. On the disposition of the courts within the new counties, see 213–19.

16. Ibid., 228; An Act for Dividing the Province into Counties, 27 Apr. 1769, PRO, CO5/936; Wentworth to the earl of Dartmouth, 20 Apr. 1774, PRO, CO5/938; John Wentworth, *The Wentworth Genealogy* (Boston: Little, Brown, 1878), 1:xix, 18; Elmer M. Hunt, *New Hampshire Town Names* (Peterborough: William L. Bauhan, 1970), 135. Hunt relates that Cheshire County in England was the site of one of the Wentworth family estates.

17. *NHPP*, 7:229.

18. Benjamin F. Parker, *History of Wolfeborough* (Wolfeborough, N.H.: by the town, 1901), 20–22, 54, 32, 82; New Hampshire Town Records, NHSL, 1:20; Inventory of John Wentworth's estate, taken 8 Jan. 1779 by Caleb Hodgdon and John B. Hanson, Executive Records, NHA; Charles W. Brewster, *Rambles about Portsmouth* (1873; reprint, Somersworth: New Hampshire Publishing Co., 1971), 1:113. In his claim for losses as a loyalist, Wentworth listed the estate at 4,387 acres but later said it was closer to 6,000 acres. The latter seems correct, based on the sale of the property in 1780. See "American Loyalists," Transcript of the Manuscript Books and Papers of the Commission of Enquiry into the Losses and Services of the American Loyalists, NYPL, 14:491; Wentworth to Edward Winslow, Mar. 1786, quoted in Frank B. Sanborn, *New Hampshire: An Epitome of Popular Government* (Boston: Houghton Mifflin, 1904), 208; Peter R. Brunette,

"An Historical Overview of the Governor Wentworth Estate," in *America's First Summer Resort: John Wentworth's Eighteenth Century Plantation in Wolfeboro, New Hampshire*, ed. David R. Starbuck, vol. 30, *The New Hampshire Archeologist*, no. 1 (New Hampshire Archeological Society, 1989), 22–23.

19. NHHS, *Collections*, 3:283–84; Carl Bridenbaugh, *Peter Harrison: First American Architect* (Chapel Hill: University of North Carolina Press, 1949), 142–43; Wentworth to the bishop of London, 28 Apr. 1770, The Papers of Eleazar Wheelock, DCA, 770278.1; Wentworth to Joseph Harrison, 24 Sept. 1769, Letter Book no. 1, 286–87.

20. Parker, *Wolfeborough*, 82–84; Robert F. Meader, *The Saga of a Palace: The Story of Wentworth House at Wolfeboro, New Hampshire* (Wolfeboro, N.H.: Wolfeboro Historical Society, 1962). The reconstruction of the Wolfeboro house, which burned in 1820, is speculative. Parker was the first to attempt a description, but Meader's interpretation is better informed and probably more accurate. It is still impossible to know exactly what the house looked like, but recent archaeological investigations sponsored by the state are disclosing new information and interpretations about the mansion and the estate. See Starbuck, ed., *America's First Summer Resort*. Other unpublished papers and materials relating to this project can be seen at the New Hampshire Division of Historical Resources, Concord, N.H.

21. Inventory of John Wentworth's estate, 8 Jan. 1779; Parker, *Wolfeborough*, 83; James L. Garvin, "Wentworth House: Design, Construction, and Furnishings," in Starbuck, ed., *America's First Summer Resort*, 31, 36.

22. Wentworth to Edward Winslow, March 1786, quoted in Sanborn, *New Hampshire*, 208; Parker, *Wolfeborough*, 84, 87; Brunette, "An Historical Overview of the Governor Wentworth Estate," in Starbuck, ed., *America's First Summer Resort*, 12–15.

23. Wentworth to Daniel Rindge, n.d., Masonian Papers, NHA; Parker, *Wolfeborough*, 54; NHHS, *Collections*, 3:283–84; Wentworth to Joseph Trumbull, 24 Sept. 1769, Letter Book no. 1, 285–86.

24. Frederick Chase, *The History of Dartmouth College and the Town of Hanover*, ed. John K. Lord (Cambridge, Mass.: John Wilson Son, University Press, 1891), 1:90–98, 105; Jere R. Daniell, "Eleazar Wheelock and the Dartmouth College Charter," *Historical New Hampshire* 24 (Winter 1969): 5–14.

25. Daniell, "Eleazar Wheelock," 12; Chase, *Dartmouth College*, 1:99. Wheelock is quoted in Chase, p. 99.

26. Chase, *Dartmouth College*, 1:100, 104. Wentworth is quoted on p. 100.

27. Ibid., 105, 126; Daniell, "Eleazar Wheelock," 28. For an interpretation of

Wheelock's declining enthusiasm for the Indians he served, see "Dr. Wheelock's Little Red School," in James Axtell, *The European and the Indian: Essays in the Ethnohistory of Colonial North America* (New York: Oxford University Press, 1981), 87–109. Wheelock's attempts to missionize and educate the Iroquois in New York had largely failed, and most of his Indian missionaries had broken with him by the time he began to negotiate with Wentworth for a school in New Hampshire. See chapter ten, "Indian Schoolmasters among the Iroquois, from the 1760s to the 1770s," in Margaret Connell Szasz, *Indian Education in the American Colonies, 1607–1783* (Albuquerque: University of New Mexico Press, 1988), 233–57.

28. Chase, *Dartmouth College*, 1:100, 126; Daniell, "Eleazar Wheelock," 21; Wentworth to Wheelock, 12 Jan. 1770, Wheelock Papers, 770112.

29. Chase, *Dartmouth College*, 1:104; Daniell, "Eleazar Wheelock," 15–16.

30. Chase, *Dartmouth College*, 1:105, 107, 109. Cleaveland is quoted on p. 107.

31. Daniell, "Eleazar Wheelock," 19–21, 24–25, 29–30; Chase, *Dartmouth College*, 1:114, 117.

32. Wentworth to the bishop of London, 28 Apr. 1770, Wheelock Papers, 770278.1; Ranna Cossit to the Reverend Dr. Hind, 9 Mar. 1773, ibid., 773209.

33. Wentworth is quoted in Chase, *Dartmouth College*, 1:117.

34. Bernhard Knollenberg, *Origin of the American Revolution, 1759–1766* (New York: Free Press, 1960), 1–2, 81–86; Chase, *Dartmouth College*, 1:115–20, Wheelock is quoted on p. 116. The best recent account of the Anglican church in the American colonies is John Frederick Woolverton, *Colonial Anglicanism in North America* (Detroit: Wayne State University Press, 1984). See also Carl Bridenbaugh, *Mitre and Sceptre: Transatlantic Faiths, Ideas, Personalities, and Politics, 1689–1775* (New York: Oxford University Press, 1962).

35. In 1773 Wentworth attempted to link the school with the Anglican church by having one of Wheelock's former students and a tutor at the college, Sylvanus Ripley, appointed as assistant and eventual successor to the rector of Anglican King's Chapel in Boston. Ripley considered the position but, knowing he would have to take orders in the Church of England, eventually decided against it. Wentworth, naturally, was disappointed with the decision. A friend of Ripley's wrote to Wheelock at the time: "The Governor it seems is not pleased to meet with a rebuff in his application for a Son of Dartmouth to become a Son of the Church. But he must have too much candor and Judgement to desire a man to strain his Conscience for the sake of swallowing a Gown. I wish he would send an Indian to Dartmouth and educate him with Episcopal money and then he might with a better face be sent home for orders." See Wheelock Papers,

303

773513, 774131, 774152, 774228.2, and Henry Caner to Wentworth, 25 Sept., 13 and 22 Nov., 6 Dec. 1773, and 14 Mar. 1774, Caner Letter Book, MSS. D.M. 388, University of Bristol Library.

304   36. Following an unsuccessful attempt to have the assembly make a grant to the college, Wentworth wrote to Wheelock: "Does it not prove the necessity of a college in a country where legislators will not grant an encouragement to Literature." See Wheelock Papers, 77129.1. Wheelock's appreciation of Wentworth and his endeavors for the college was made apparent in a letter he sent to fellow minister Soloman Williams. "The Governor," he wrote, "is a very Dear Man, and I think his Judgment is on the right side, and he appears unwearied in doing and endeavoring Good to this Cause." Ibid., 772209.1. See also ibid., 771555.1, 772558.1, 773612, 774672.1; NHPP, 7:260, 274, 314, 323; Chase, *Dartmouth College*, 2:648.

37. On John Wentworth's attendance at the first three commencements of the college, see Chase, *Dartmouth College*, 1:254–55, and Wheelock Papers, 771555.1, 772508.3. See also Chase, 1:253, 264–65, 291–93; Wheelock Papers, 773513; NHHS, *Collections*, 9:73.

38. *NHPP*, 7:232, 283–84.

39. Chase, *Dartmouth College*, 1:120; Daniell, "Eleazar Wheelock," 30.

40. Chase, *Dartmouth College*, 1:113, 121, 124–25, 132–33, 138–39, 141–42.

41. Ibid., 142–46.

42. Ibid., 147–53.

43. Wentworth to the earl of Hillsborough, 25 June 1768, Hammond Transcripts.

8. MAN IN THE MIDDLE

1. Wentworth to the earl of Shelburne, 17 June 1767, Transcripts of John Wentworth Letter Book no. 1, NHA, 2; Wentworth to Thomas Bell, 30 June 1767, ibid., 5–6; Wentworth to Major Robert Bayard, 19 Oct. 1767, ibid., 46–47.

2. *NHPP*, 7:8–9; Wentworth to Governor Bernard, 26 Aug., 10 Sept., 2 Oct. 1767, Letter Book no. 1, 33, 38–39, 43–45.

3. Wentworth to Peter Randolph, 10 July 1767, Letter Book no. 1, 10–11; Wentworth to Governor Bernard, 7 July 1767, ibid., 7; Wentworth to James Harbard, 10 July 1767, ibid., 12; Wentworth to Joshua Loring, 14 July 1767, ibid., 13–14; Wentworth to John Hill, 25 July 1767, ibid., 21–22; Wentworth to William Parker, 27 July 1767, ibid., 24; Wentworth to Jonathan Sewell, 19 Aug. 1767, ibid., 31–32; Wentworth to the Navy, Treasury, Admiralty, Board of Trade, and the earl of Shelburne, 3 Sept. 1767, ibid., 53–57. For additional evidence of Wentworth's energetic activities to enforce royal forest policy during the early months of his administration, see ibid., 7–39, passim.

Notes to Pages 136–41

4. Lawrence Henry Gipson, *The British Empire before the American Revolution*, vol. 10, *The Triumphant Empire: Thunder-Clouds Gather in the West, 1763–1766* (New York: Knopf, 1961), 378, 372, 374, 405, 391–92, 406. Grenville is quoted on p. 378, Walpole on p. 372, Hardwicke on p. 374, Sandwich on p. 405, and Camden on p. 406.

5. Wentworth to Alexander Yeats, 27 Oct., 4 Dec. 1767, Letter Book no. 1, 47, 53; Wentworth to Stephen Apthorp, 18 Aug. 1767, ibid., 28; Wentworth to Joshua Loring, 10 July 1767, ibid., 10.

6. Wentworth to the Board of Trade, 23 June 1767, Letter Book no. 1, 3–4; manuscript biography of Josiah Bartlett by his son, Levi Bartlett, Josiah Bartlett Papers, NHHS, 27–29. Thomas Westbrook Waldron in the years to come became one of Wentworth's close friends and confidants.

7. Wentworth to the Board of Trade, 30 Sept. 1767, Hammond Transcripts, NHHS; Wentworth to Stephen Apthorp, 18 Aug. 1767, Letter Book no. 1, 28. See also Wentworth to William Parker, 26 Aug. 1767, and to Richard Willis, 18 Aug. 1767, ibid., 32, 29.

8. Lawrence Henry Gipson, *The British Empire before the American Revolution*, vol. 11, *The Triumphant Empire: The Rumbling of the Coming Storm, 1766–1770* (New York: Knopf, 1965), 79–81, 99–104.

9. Ibid., 105–13. The preamble to the Townshend acts is quoted on p. 111n.

10. Townshend never knew the full extent of the opposition to his bill, for he died in September 1767 at the relatively young age of forty-two. Not universally admired, he was respected by most, including Edmund Burke, who said of him: "Perhaps there never arose in this country, nor in any country, a man of more pointed and finished wit; and (where his passions were not concerned) of a more refined, exquisite, and penetrating judgment." Ibid., 104, 116. Burke is quoted on p. 104.

11. Ibid., 139–43.

12. Wentworth to Peter Gilman, 25 Nov. 1767, Letter Book no. 1, 57–58.

13. Ibid.

14. Gipson, vol. 11, *Triumphant Empire: Rumbling*, 148–51, 166–69; H. Trevor Colbourn, *The Lamp of Experience* (Chapel Hill: University of North Carolina Press, 1965), 111–12.

15. Gipson, vol. 11, *Triumphant Empire: Rumbling*, 148–51, 166–69; NHPP, 7:152–53, 157, 165; *Journal of the House of Representatives . . . of Massachusetts Bay*, 25 May–30 June 1768 (Boston, 1768), Appendix 14. Hillsborough is quoted in Gipson, pp. 166–67.

16. Gipson, vol. 11, *Triumphant Empire: Rumbling*, 118–19, 181–82.

17. Ibid., 152–54; John R. Alden, *A History of the American Revolution* (New

York: Knopf, 1969), 98–100. For Harrison's firsthand account of the incident, see D. H. Watson, "Joseph Harrison and the Liberty Incident," *William and Mary Quarterly* 20 (October 1963): 585–95.

306   18. Wentworth to the earl of Shelburne, 25 Mar. 1768, Hammond Transcripts.

19. Wentworth to the marquis of Rockingham, 6 May 1768, Rockingham Correspondence, WWM, Sheffield Archives, R1–1047.

20. Wentworth to commissioners of the customs, 16 June 1768, PRO, CO5/945; commissioners of the customs to Wentworth, 18 June 1768, ibid.; resolution of the New Hampshire Assembly, General Court Records (Acts and Resolutions), NHA, n.d. For an excellent description of John Temple and his activities, see Charles W. Akers, "New Hampshire's 'Honorary' Lieutenant Governor: John Temple and the American Revolution," *Historical New Hampshire* 30 (Summer 1975): 79–99.

21. *Journal of the House of Representatives . . . of Massachusetts Bay*, 25 May–30 June 1768, Appendix 14; NHPP, 7:180, 186.

22. Wentworth to the earl of Hillsborough, 25 June 1768, PRO, CO5/935; *Journal of the House of Representatives . . . of Massachusetts Bay*, 25 May–30 June 1768, Appendix 14.

23. Wentworth to the earl of Hillsborough, 25 June 1768, PRO, CO5/935.

24. Clifford K. Shipton, *Sibley's Harvard Graduates* (Boston: Massachusetts Historical Society, 1968), 14:364. In 1766, while still in England, Wentworth expressed anxiety over his brother's health. See Wentworth to Hugh Hall Wentworth, 26 Aug. 1766, Miscellaneous Manuscripts, MHS. Not long after Thomas's death, Wentworth asked the Reverend Jeremy Belknap to take over the education of his seven-year-old nephew, Mark. See Wentworth to Jeremy Belknap, 1 Jan. 1770, Belknap Papers, MHS.

25. George B. Kirsch, "Jeremy Belknap and the Coming of the Revolution," *Historical New Hampshire* 29 (Fall 1974): 155; Portsmouth Town Records, vol. 2 (1695–1779), part 2, 226A, 226B, 227A, Historic Sites and Buildings of Portsmouth, WPA typescript, Portsmouth Public Library.

26. Wentworth to Anthony Belham, 9 Aug. 1768, Letter Book no. 1, 129–37.

27. Ibid.

28. *NHPP*, 7:186–90, 248–53.

29. Wentworth to the earl of Hillsborough, 1 Sept. 1768, PRO, CO5/930; Joseph Harrison to the marquis of Rockingham, 3 Nov. 1768, Rockingham Correspondence, WWM, R1–1111; Wentworth to the marquis of Rockingham, 13 Nov. 1768, ibid., R1–1118; NHG, 30 Sept. 1768. A portion of Wentworth's letter to Rockingham is printed in George T. Keppel, earl of Albemarle, *Memoirs*

of the Marquis of Rockingham and His Contemporaries (London: Richard Bently, 1852), 2:88–90.

30. Gipson, vol. II, *Triumphant Empire: Rumbling*, 164.

31. NHG, 14 Oct. 1768; Wentworth to the marquis of Rockingham, 13 Nov. 1768, Rockingham Correspondence, WWM, R1–1118; Wentworth to Paul Wentworth, 15 Nov. 1768, Letter Book no. 1, 152–53.   307

32. Wentworth to the marquis of Rockingham, 13 Nov. 1768, Rockingham Correspondence, WWM, R1–1118.

33. Wentworth to Paul Wentworth, 15 Nov. 1768, Letter Book no. 1, 152–53.

34. The earl of Hillsborough to Wentworth, 13 Aug. 1768, PRO, CO5/935.

35. Wentworth to the earl of Hillsborough, 7 Nov. 1768, Hammond Transcripts; NHPP, 7:248–49.

36. NHPP, 7:180; Charles H. Bell, *History of the Town of Exeter, New Hampshire* (Exeter, 1888), 82; NHG, 11 Mar. 1770. Parker and Livermore both received important judicial appointments from John Wentworth. Later, when Sheafe became active in the anti-British cause, he too was given an appointment by the governor. See Charles W. Brewster, *Rambles about Portsmouth* (1873; reprint, Somersworth: New Hampshire Publishing Co., 1971), 1:145; and Ransome B. True, "The New Hampshire Committee of Correspondence, 1773–1774" (Master's thesis, University of New Hampshire, 1969), 49–55, 62–68. Another reason for the assembly's seeming acquiescence in the suppression of the petition may reside in the fact that many House members were proprietors of land west of the Connecticut River, an area they hoped could be recovered from New York jurisdiction through the good offices of the governor. It was at that very time, late fall 1768, that New Hampshire's interest in the region was rekindled. See Jere R. Daniell, *Experiment in Republicanism: New Hampshire Politics and the American Revolution, 1741–1794* (Cambridge, Mass.: Harvard University Press, 1970), 71; John F. Looney, "The King's Representative: Benning Wentworth, Colonial Governor, 1741–1767" (Ph.D. diss., Lehigh University, 1961), 141; and NHPP, 10:215–17, and 18:587–88.

37. NHPP, 7:192.

38. "Portsmouth," Miscellaneous Town Papers, NHHS; NHG, 30 Sept. 1768; Jeremy Belknap, *The History of New Hampshire* (1831; reprint, New York: Johnson Reprint, 1970), 1:340; Daniell, *Experiment in Republicanism*, 54.

39. Wentworth to the marquis of Rockingham, 17 Nov. 1768, Rockingham Correspondence, WWM, R1–1120; Nathaniel Adams, *Annals of Portsmouth* (1825; reprint, Hampton, N.H.: Peter E. Randall, 1971), 224–25; Samuel Lane, *A Journal for the Years 1739–1803, by Samuel Lane of Stratham, New Hampshire*, ed. Charles

Lane Hanson (Concord: New Hampshire Historical Society, 1937), 79; Wentworth to Daniel Rindge, 30 Jan. 1769, Masonian Papers, N H A; New Hampshire Court Records, Case 4262, N H A; N H G, 6 Jan. 1769; *N H P P*, 7:206, 208; Wentworth to Clement March, 26 Dec. 1768, Letter Book no. 1, 171; Brewster, *Rambles about Portsmouth*, 1:290–92.

40. Daniell, *Experiment in Republicanism*, 40–41; the earl of Hillsborough to Wentworth, 15 Nov. 1768, P R O, C O 5/935; Wentworth to the earl of Hillsborough, 2 May 1769, Letter Book no. 1, 230–31. Wentworth's statement to Nathaniel Rogers that Trecothick refused to serve "unless with a Colleague" was likely an excuse for proposing Paul Wentworth as co-agent. See Wentworth to Nathaniel Rogers, 19 Dec. 1768, Letter Book no. 1, 169–71.

41. John Wentworth, *The Wentworth Genealogy* (Boston: Little, Brown, 1878), 3:8–13; *N E H G R* 38 (1884): 444–45.

42. Wentworth to Paul Wentworth, 13 Dec. 1768, Letter Book no. 1, 166–68; Wentworth to Nathaniel Rogers, 19 Dec. 1768, ibid., 169–71; Wentworth to the earl of Hillsborough, 2 May 1769, ibid., 230–31.

43. Wentworth to the earl of Hillsborough, 1 May 1769, and Hillsborough to Wentworth, 1 May 1769, P R O, C O 5/936; *N H P P*, 7:229–30, and 24:717–21; Wentworth to Paul Wentworth, 17 Sept. 1769, Letter Book no. 1, 274–75. When war finally came in America, Paul Wentworth became England's chief spy in France. He was known there as one of the "cleverest men in England." See Julian P. Boyd, "Silas Deane: Death by a Kindly Teacher of Treason," *William and Mary Quarterly* 16 (July 1959): 320n. On Paul Wentworth's connections in Europe and role as a spy, see Lewis Einstein, *Divided Loyalties: Americans in England During the War of Independence* (London: Cobden-Sanderson, 1933), 16–44. The name of the town of Trecothick was changed to Ellsworth, New Hampshire, early in the nineteenth century. See Elmer M. Hunt, *New Hampshire Town Names* (Peterborough: William L. Bauhan, 1970), 217–18.

44. Wentworth knew that reorganization of the ministry would not occur easily. In the spring of 1769 he remarked that John Fisher, then in England, "informs me that Adm[ini]s[tration] are very powerful & no appearances of any changes, and that it is probable Colony measures will not immediately be altered." See Wentworth to John Temple, 18 April 1769, Bowdoin-Temple Papers, M H S. See also Wentworth to Temple, 19 Mar. 1769, ibid. On the opposition role of the Rockingham party throughout the late 1760s and early 1770s and the ultimate failure of Rockingham to regain the government, see Peter D. G. Thomas, *The Townshend Duties Crisis: The Second Phase of the American Revolution, 1767–1773* (Oxford: Oxford University Press, Clarendon Press, 1987), passim.

9. A TIGHT ENGLISH REIN

1. Wentworth to the marquis of Rockingham, 16 Feb. 1769, Rockingham Correspondence, WWM, Sheffield Archives, R1–1159; Wentworth to Paul Wentworth, 17 Sept. 1769, Transcripts of John Wentworth Letter Book no. 1, NHA, 275.

309

2. Jeremy Belknap, *The History of New Hampshire* (1812; reprint, New York: Johnson Reprint, 1970), 2:11; NHPP, 7:222–26, 229; see also note 2, chapter eight. Wentworth later told Hillsborough that the assembly had agreed to leave open the question of payment for Rindge. There is no evidence for that or that the assembly reconsidered its negative vote. See Wentworth to the earl of Hillsborough, 3 July 1769, Letter Book no. 1, 251.

3. Wentworth to the earl of Hillsborough, 1 May 1769, PRO, CO5/930.

4. The best account of this case and of the events leading to it is chapter eleven, "Death Before Impressment," in Hiller B. Zobel, *The Boston Massacre* (New York: W. W. Norton, 1970), 113–31. I have relied heavily on Zobel's work. See also John Adams, *Legal Papers of John Adams*, ed. L. Kinvin Wroth and Hiller B. Zobel (Cambridge, Mass.: Harvard University Press, Belknap Press, 1965), 2:276–335. Evidence of those participating in the trial from New Hampshire is found in NHPP, 7:233, 236, 246; and MHS, *Proceedings* 44 (1910–1911): 438. Receipts for expenses incurred by Wentworth and George Jaffrey are found in Treasury Records, NHA.

5. MHS, *Proceedings*, 44:424.

6. The "Journal of the Times" is quoted in Oliver M. Dickerson, ed., *Boston under Military Rule, 1768–1769* (1936; reprint, Westport, Conn.: Greenwood, 1971), 104. See also Zobel, *Boston Massacre*, 109–11.

7. Quoted in Zobel, *Boston Massacre*, 122–23.

8. Dickerson, *Military Rule*, 110.

9. John Adams, *The Works of John Adams*, ed. Charles Francis Adams (Boston: Little, Brown, 1850), 2:226n. For Hutchinson's interpretation of the case, see Thomas Hutchinson, *The History of the Colony and Province of Massachusetts Bay*, ed. Lawrence Shaw Mayo (Cambridge, Mass.: Harvard University Press, 1936), 3:166–67.

10. Wentworth and Adams just two months earlier had had an opportunity to renew their friendship when Adams accepted an offer from the governor to prosecute a number of violations of the mast laws in the court of vice admiralty in Boston. Wentworth instructed his deputy to offer Adams "rather a generous fee, I'le reimburse." Adams responded, "I feel a great Inclination to be upon a footing with your Excellency and to be chatting about my self as I used twelve years ago." See Adams, *Legal Papers*, 2:259–64.

11. *Boston Gazette* and *Boston Evening Post*, 26 June 1769. See also *Boston Weekly News-Letter*, 29 June 1769; and Hutchinson, *History*, 3:174–75. For Wentworth's opinion of Bernard, see Wentworth to Paul Wentworth, 17 Sept. 1769, Letter Book no. 1, 275.

12. Wentworth to the earl of Hillsborough, 3 July 1769, PRO, CO5/930; Wentworth to Hillsborough, 22 Oct. 1770, PRO, CO5/227; Wentworth to John Henniker, 12 Jan. 1769, and to Messrs. Trecothick and Apthorp, 10 Apr. 1769, Letter Book no. 1, 178–79, 216–17.

13. Wentworth to Judge Auchmuty, 10 Apr. 1769, Letter Book no. 1, 215–16.

14. Wentworth to the earl of Hillsborough, 22 Oct. 1770, PRO, CO5/227.

15. Ibid.; Wentworth to Secretary of the Treasury John Robinson, 23 Mar. 1771, PRO, T1/484; Robert G. Albion, *Forests and Sea Power: The Timber Problem of the Royal Navy, 1652–1862* (Cambridge, Mass.: Harvard University Press, 1926), 248–50.

16. Wentworth to the earl of Hillsborough, 22 Oct. 1770, PRO, CO5/227; Wentworth to the marquis of Rockingham, 17 Sept. 1769, Rockingham Correspondence, WWM, R127–6. On the case involving the Kennebec proprietors, see Gordon E. Kershaw, "John Wentworth vs. Kennebec Proprietors: The Formation of Royal Mast Policy, 1769–1778," *The American Neptune* 33 (1973): 95–119. Wentworth seems to have set forth his plan for reserving forest lots in new townships on 13 January 1773, when he wrote to the lords of the admiralty and the treasury. See Letter Book no. 2, 41–47. This was not accomplished while he was governor, but he remained a proponent of the plan even after he had been forced by the outbreak of war to leave America. His fullest elaboration of it came in 1778 on consideration of a possible loyalist colony in Maine. See Wentworth to George Germain, 12 Oct. 1778, PRO, CO5/175.

17. Wentworth to the earl of Hillsborough, 1 May 1769, PRO, CO5/930.

18. The earl of Hillsborough to Wentworth, 15 July 1769, PRO, CO5/936.

19. Wentworth to the earl of Hillsborough, 17 Sept. 1769, PRO, CO5/936.

20. Wentworth to the marquis of Rockingham, 17 Sept. 1769, Rockingham Correspondence, WWM, R127–6.

21. Wentworth to Paul Wentworth, 17 Sept. 1769, Letter Book no. 1, 272–73.

22. Petition of Daniel Rindge to Governor Wentworth and the New Hampshire Council, 12 Oct. 1767, PRO, CO5/936. Throughout this period, illicit trade by New Englanders with the French in this region was a constant problem for England. See Lawrence Henry Gipson, *The Coming of the Revolution, 1763–1775* (New York: Harper and Row, 1954), 120–21. Rindge, nevertheless, insisted on his innocence.

23. Wentworth to the Honorable Hugh Palliser, Esq., 11 July 1767, Letter Book no. 1, 13; Wentworth to the earl of Shelburne, 5 Mar. 1768, PRO, CO5/936.

24. The earl of Hillsborough to Wentworth, 1 Mar. 1769, and pronouncement of the New Hampshire council on the admiralty case of Daniel Rindge, 15 Oct. 1767, PRO, CO5/936; the marquis of Rockingham to Wentworth, 19 May 1769, Wentworth Correspondence, WWM, Sheffield Archives.

25. Wentworth to the marquis of Rockingham, 17 Sept. 1769, Rockingham Correspondence, WWM, R127–6. See also Wentworth to Paul Wentworth, 13 Dec. 1768, Letter Book no. 1, 166–68; and Wentworth to Daniel Rindge, 30 Jan. 1769, Masonian Papers, NHA. Hillsborough made numerous enemies among the colonists. King George III at one point stated that he "did not know a man of less judgement." See Alan Valentine, *The British Establishment, 1760–1784: An Eighteenth-Century Biographical Dictionary* (Norman: University of Oklahoma Press, 1970), 1:453–54. Hillsborough angered many colonial officials by his strict interpretation of the currency laws, a fact Wentworth might have been able to glean some small satisfaction from had he been aware of it. See Peter D. G. Thomas, *The Townshend Duties Crisis: The Second Phase of the American Revolution, 1767–1773* (Oxford: Oxford University Press, Clarendon Press, 1987), 221.

26. Wentworth to Paul Wentworth, 17 Sept. 1769, Letter Book no. 1, 274–75.

27. Wentworth to the marquis of Rockingham, 17 Sept. 1769, Rockingham Correspondence, WWM, R127–6.

28. NHPP, 18:589–90.

29. Charles E. Clark, *The Eastern Frontier: The Settlement of Northern New England, 1610–1763* (New York: Knopf, 1970), 293–95.

30. Wentworth to Joseph Harrison, 24 Sept. 1769, Fulham Papers, Lambeth Palace Library, 6:106–7. Politics may have been the main reason behind Wentworth's interest in the Anglican church. At one time he told Daniel Rindge, "My heart knows no difference in Modes of Religion (save against those that are destructive of our civil rights and contrary to law)." See Wentworth to Rindge, 29 Nov. 1765, Masonian Papers.

31. D. H. Watson, "Barlow Trecothick and Other Associates of Lord Rockingham during the Stamp Act Crisis, 1765–1766" (Master's thesis, Sheffield University, 1958), 124; Wentworth to Joseph Harrison, 24 Sept. 1769, Fulham Papers, 6:106–7; Wentworth to the bishop of London, 28 April 1770, The Papers of Eleazar Wheelock, DCA, 770278.1; Belknap, *New Hampshire*, 1:324n; Moses Badger to the Society for the Propagation of the Gospel, 17 Dec. 1769, SPG Papers, NHHS, 99; Wentworth to SPG, 5 July 1773, 6 May 1774, ibid., 126–27, 139–41; Wardens of Queens Chapel, Portsmouth, N.H., to SPG, 2 July 1773, ibid., 124.

Ranna Cossit was very supportive of Wentworth's plan and agreed with the governor that the church would have a bolstering effect on government. See Cossit to SPG, 9 Mar 1773, Wheelock Papers, 773209, and 9 Oct. 1773, SPG Papers, 132.

312   32. Bernard Knollenberg, *Growth of the American Revolution, 1766–1775* (New York: Free Press, 1975), 221; the Reverend Arthur Browne to SPG, 15 Nov. 1770, SPG Papers, 109; NHHS, *Collections* 9 (1889): 55–57. Efforts to have Cosset made minister in Haverhill were not well received by some of the town's inhabitants. See resolution against John Hurd and Asa Porter, 28 Jan. 1775, Town Records, NHA.

33. Wentworth to Paul Wentworth, 27 Oct. 1769, Letter Book no. 1, 306. Wentworth was the highest ranking American official ever painted by Copley. The Boston artist produced portraits of a number of Portsmouth's elite, including Wentworth's sister, Anne. In 1765 he had painted Frances Wentworth Atkinson, Wentworth's future wife, and several years earlier, her first husband, Theodore Atkinson, Jr. In 1977, Copley's portrait of John Wentworth was donated to Dartmouth College by the family of a Wentworth descendant. On Copley and his paintings, see Jules David Prown, *John Singleton Copley*, 2 vols. (Cambridge, Mass.: Harvard University Press, 1966).

34. NHG, 3 Nov. 1769; NHPP, 7:247; Clifford K. Shipton, *Sibley's Harvard Graduates* (Boston: Massachusetts Historical Society, 1968), 14:131; Wentworth to the marquis of Rockingham, 2 Nov. 1770, Rockingham Correspondence, WWM, R1–1321.

35. Parochial Records of Queen's Chapel, Portsmouth, N.H., 1738–96, 116; Charles W. Brewster, *Rambles about Portsmouth* (1873; reprint, Somersworth: New Hampshire Publishing Co., 1971), 1:110–11.

36. Wentworth to the marquis of Rockingham, 2 Nov. 1770, Rockingham Correspondence, WWM, R1–1321; Parochial Records of Queen's Chapel, 81. Portsmouth lore, fabricated from few facts and much fiction over the nineteenth and twentieth centuries, has long titillated local residents with tales of Frances Wentworth's disreputable activities. Thomas H. Raddall found the lives of Frances and John Wentworth dramatic enough for a novel, *The Governor's Lady* (Garden City, N.Y.: Doubleday, 1960). In a chapter titled "Lady Frances, Sir John," Philip Young, in his *Revolutionary Ladies* (New York: Knopf, 1977), 87–141, has cast some healthy doubt on the myths surrounding the personal lives of John and Frances Wentworth.

37. Brewster, *Rambles*, 1:112–13; Wentworth to the marquis of Rockingham, 2 Nov. 1770, Rockingham Correspondence, WWM, R1–1321.

38. Wentworth to the earl of Hillsborough, 18 Feb. 1770, PRO, CO5/930; William G. Saltonstall, *Ports of Piscataqua* (1941; reprint, New York: Russell and

Russell, 1968), 87; NHPP, 7:232; Knollenberg, *Growth of the American Revolution*, 68–69.

10. PRESERVING A FRAGILE ORDER

1. For a detailed account of the immediate event, see Hiller B. Zobel, *The Boston Massacre* (New York: W. W. Norton, 1970), 180–205.

2. Arthur M. Schlesinger, *The Colonial Merchants and the American Revolution* (1918: reprint, New York: Atheneum, 1968), 194; NHG, 13 Apr. 1770; Portsmouth Town Records, vol. 2 (1695–1779): Part 2, 243A, 243B, 243C, 244A, Historic Sites and Buildings of Portsmouth, WPA Typescript, Portsmouth Public Library.

3. NHG, 13 Apr. 1770.

4. NHG, 11 May 1770; NHPP, 7:248–56.

5. Wentworth to the earl of Hillsborough, 12 Apr. 1770, PRO, CO5/937.

6. Ibid.; Zobel, *Boston Massacre*, 215.

7. Zobel, *Boston Massacre*, 215.

8. Nathaniel Adams, *Annals of Portsmouth* (1825; reprint, Hampton, N.H.: Peter E. Randall, 1971), 227; Lawrence Shaw Mayo, *John Langdon of New Hampshire* (1937; reprint, New York: Kennikat, 1970), 49; Lawrence Henry Gipson, *The Coming of the Revolution, 1763–1775* (New York: Harper and Row, 1954), 203–5; Bernard Knollenberg, *Growth of the American Revolution, 1766–1775* (New York: Free Press, 1975), 72–73.

9. Wentworth to the earl of Hillsborough, 28 Oct. and 20 Sept. 1770, PRO, CO5/930.

10. NHPP, 7:274, 276.

11. NHPP, 18:602, and 7:288, 294.

12. Wentworth to the earl of Hillsborough, 23 Sept. 1771, PRO, CO5/930; NHPP, 7:264–65, 268, 293–94. On the Holland map, see Julian W. Green, "A Map of New Hampshire—Spanning the Revolution," *Dartmouth College Library Bulletin* 16 (April 1976): 71–78. I am indebted to James L. Garvin for this reference.

13. Charles W. Akers, "New Hampshire's 'Honorary' Lieutenant Governor: John Temple and the American Revolution," *Historical New Hampshire* 30 (Summer 1975): 85–88; MHS, *Collections*, 6th ser., 9 (1897): 236–38. Wentworth also took this opportunity to send information with Temple for both the earl of Hillsborough and Edmund Burke. See Wentworth to Hillsborough, 4 Nov. 1770, PRO, CO5/930; and Wentworth to Burke, 18 Nov. 1770, Burke Papers, WWM, Sheffield Archives, 174.

14. NHG, 1 Mar. 1771.

15. Wentworth's account of this incident is found in his letter to the earl of Hillsborough, 15 Nov. 1771, PRO, CO5/930. See also NHPP, 18:606–7; Adams, *Annals*, 233; Mayo, *John Langdon*, 38–40.

16. Wentworth to the marquis of Rockingham, 2 Nov. 1770, Rockingham Correspondence, WWM, Sheffield Archives, R1–1321.

17. Wentworth to the marquis of Rockingham, 23 July 1771, Rockingham Correspondence, WWM, R1–1383.

18. Ibid.

19. The marquis of Rockingham to Wentworth, 9 Mar. 1771, Wentworth Correspondence, WWM, Sheffield Archives.

20. Matt B. Jones, *Vermont in the Making, 1750–1777* (Cambridge, Mass.: Harvard University Press, 1939), 77.

21. Ibid., 87. Optimism about the potential of the region between the Connecticut and Hudson rivers was borne out by the growth in population between 1763 and 1776 from approximately 120 families to 20,000 people. See Charles E. Clark, *The Eastern Frontier: The Settlement of Northern New England, 1610–1763* (New York: Knopf, 1970), 354.

22. Allen Soule and John W. Williams, eds., *State Papers of Vermont* (Montpelier, 1918–1969), 7:293, 341, 348–49; John F. Looney, "The King's Representative: Benning Wentworth, Colonial Governor, 1741–1767" (Ph.D. diss., Lehigh University, 1961), 141; Michael A. Bellesiles, *Revolutionary Outlaws: Ethan Allen and the Struggle for Independence on the Early American Frontier* (Charlottesville: University Press of Virginia, 1993), chapter 2. The John Wentworth listed as a proprietor is not the governor but his uncle. In 1769 Governor John Wentworth told a friend he "never held any lands on that side." See Wentworth to William Bayard, 23 Feb. 1769, Transcripts of John Wentworth Letter Book no. 1, NHA, 200. He did later, however, hold land west of the Connecticut River. See *Vermont State Papers*, 6:444. For an argument that New Hampshire did have a valid claim to land west of the Connecticut, see Allan R. Raymond, "Benning Wentworth's Claims in the New Hampshire–New York Border Controversy: A Case of Twenty-Twenty Hindsight?," *Vermont History* 43 (Winter 1975): 20–32.

23. Jones, *Vermont*, 97–101, 121–22; E. B. O'Callaghan, ed., *The Documentary History of the State of New York* (Albany: Charles Van Benthuysen, 1851), 4:577–78. For the best discussion of this entire dispute over the land west of New Hampshire, see Bellesiles, *Revolutionary Outlaws*.

24. Jones, *Vermont*, 125–26, 132–39; O'Callaghan, *Documentary History of New York*, 4:609–10.

25. NHPP, 10:215–17, and 18:587–88. At this very time, Theodore Atkinson wrote John Fisher that setting the boundary at the Connecticut River left New

Hampshire "too small to support the Charge of a Government & N. York as much too large to carry on affairs of Government with Comfort or Propriety." See Atkinson to Fisher, 13 Dec. 1768, Land Records (Vt.-N.H. Boundary), N H A.

26. Henry S. Wardner, *The Birthplace of Vermont: A History of Windsor* (New York: Charles Scribner's Sons, 1927), 131, 134.   315

27. Wardner, *Birthplace of Vermont*, 132; Wentworth to Nathaniel Rogers, 13 Jan. 1769, Letter Book no. 1, 190.

28. Wentworth to the earl of Hillsborough, 10 July 1769, P R O, C05/936; Wardner, *Birthplace of Vermont*, 137; Wentworth to Jared Ingersoll, 3 Feb. 1769, Letter Book no. 1, 190.

29. Wardner, *Birthplace of Vermont*, 133–36. The mastliner and Granger are quoted on pp. 133 and 136.

30. Wentworth to Jared Ingersoll, 3 Feb. 1769, Letter Book no. 1, 190; Wardner, *Birthplace of Vermont*, 106, 113–15.

31. Wentworth to William Bayard, 23 Feb. 1769, Letter Book no. 1, 199–200. Johnson is quoted in Jones, *Vermont*, 165.

32. Jones, *Vermont*, 171–74. As an example of the hardships suffered by New Hampshire grantees displaced by New York, see the petition of Andrew Powers to John Wentworth, 25 Mar. 1773, Executive Records (Petitions), N H A.

33. Wentworth to Jared Ingersoll, 10 Apr. 1769, Letter Book no. 1, 220–21; Wentworth to Judge Morris, 5 May 1769, ibid., 235; Wentworth to John Tabor Kempe, 24 June, 21 July 1769, ibid., 243, 257; Wentworth to the earl of Hillsborough, 10 July 1769, P R O, C05/936.

34. Jones, *Vermont*, 195; Wardner, *Birthplace of Vermont*, 108–9, 118–19. It might be questioned here whether Wentworth deliberately sought to trap the Deans in illegal cutting in order to use them in his efforts to regain jurisdiction for New Hampshire over the region disputed with New York. Dean later claimed that he only wanted to cut the timber so he could cultivate his land. According to his testimony, in spite of going himself to see Wentworth and repeated promises by the governor's deputies that they would survey his land, no one ever came. Was this an attempt by Wentworth to goad Dean into unlawful cutting and then catch him by surprise? On consideration of all the evidence, that conclusion appears unlikely. The failure of the deputies to show up on Dean's land was undoubtedly more the result of a rigorous schedule than of any preconceived scheme. Too, there is little doubt that Dean was in the lumber business. He and his sons had moved to Windsor with lumbering in mind, and they had made large contracts with dealers in Massachusetts. When Dean went to see Wentworth, it was to request an appointment as deputy surveyor, in which case he would be able to cut trees of any size with impunity. Further,

the story that he merely wanted to clear his land turned out to be a boldfaced lie when it was disclosed that most of the trees he had felled were on someone else's land. See Wardner, 107–18, 131–32, 135. The Deans were guilty, and every-
one involved in the case, whether they favored New Hampshire or New York, knew it. Given Wentworth's deep concern for enforcing the mast laws, there is no reason to question that he was at least as concerned with stopping the Deans' illegal cutting as with the broader implications of the case for the New Hampshire–New York land dispute.

35. See affadavits of Simon Stevens, Samuel Wells, and John Kelley in O'Callaghan, *Documentary History of New York*, 4:692, 698, 705. The petition circulated in the towns of Westminster and Rockingham is printed on pp. 672–75.

36. Wentworth to Paul Wentworth, 27 Feb. 1770, Letter Book no. 1, 324–25; Wentworth to the earl of Hillsborough, 18 Feb. 1770, PRO, CO5/930; Frederick Chase, *The History of Dartmouth College and the Town of Hanover*, ed. John K. Lord (Cambridge, Mass.: John Wilson Son, University Press, 1891), 1:141.

37. O'Callaghan, *Documentary History of New York*, 4:626–33; C. M. Hough, ed., *Reports of Cases in the Vice Admiralty of the Province of New York and in the Court of Admiralty of the State of New York, 1715–1788* (New Haven: Yale University Press, 1925), 227–33; Wentworth to the earl of Hillsborough, 22 Oct. 1770, PRO, CO5/227; Wardner, *Birthplace of Vermont*, 117–39. Wells and Grout were staunch supporters of New York and earlier had attempted to help the Deans escape from Wentworth's deputies. The governor developed a strong dislike for both men and for some time worked to have sanctions taken against them. Finding no sympathy among New York officials, he pursued that end in England. In his letter of 22 October 1770 to Hillsborough, Wentworth described Grout as a "petty fogging Lawyer . . . of deservedly infamous character" and, after explaining Wells's obstruction of his duties as surveyor general, noted that the judge's "character is by no means fair or honest in any other Province where he is known." In 1771 Wentworth wrote to John Robinson, secretary of the treasury, recommending that Wells be removed from the bench and that Grout be prohibited from practicing law. See Wentworth to John Robinson, 23 Mar. 1771, PRO, T1/484.

38. Wentworth to the earl of Hillsborough, 22 Oct. 1770, PRO, CO5/227; Wentworth to [William] Bayard, 6 Oct. 1769, Wentworth Papers, NHHS; O'Callaghan, *Documentary History of New York*, 4:621–26.

39. NYHS, *Collections* 10 (1877): 196–97, 213–14; O'Callaghan, *Documentary History of New York*, 4:623. For Wells's side of the story of his assistance to the Deans, see O'Callaghan, pp. 647–60.

40. Ira Allen, *The Natural and Political History of the State of Vermont* (London: J. W. Myers, 1798), 23–24; Charles A. Jellison, *Ethan Allen: Frontier*

Rebel (Syracuse: Syracuse University Press, 1969), 32–33; Jones, *Vermont*, 201–9; O'Callaghan, *Documentary History of New York*, 4:689. The most insightful account of Ethan Allen's importance in the transformation of the New Hampshire grants from a region contested by two colonies to an independent state can be found in Bellesiles, *Revolutionary Outlaws*.

41. Wardner, *Birthplace of Vermont*, 142–53; Jones, *Vermont*, 258–61, 284–91; Allen, *History of Vermont*, 24; O'Callaghan, *Documentary History of New York*, 4:689.

42. Wentworth to the earl of Hillsborough, 10 Oct. 1770, PRO, CO5/930; MHS, *Collections*, 6th ser., 9 (1897): 237–38.

43. Wentworth to Eleazar Wheelock, 29 Jan. 1771, Papers of Eleazar Wheelock, DCA, 771129.1. Governor Tryon of New York later accused Wentworth of deliberately making a false survey of the river in order to extend the jurisdiction of New Hampshire. Wentworth strongly denied the charge and said that if any error was made it was to the disadvantage of New Hampshire. See O'Callaghan, *Documentary History of New York*, 4:731–32; and NHPP, 10:217–20. For depositions attesting to deliberate fraud in the survey, see O'Callaghan, pp. 721–23.

44. O'Callaghan, *Documentary History of New York*, 4:663–68, 675–707; Eleazar Wheelock to Wentworth, 21 Jan. 1771, Wheelock Papers, 771121.1; earl of Hillsborough to Wentworth, 11 Dec. 1770, PRO, CO5/937; Hillsborough to Wentworth, 11 Feb. 1771, Hammond Transcripts, NHHS.

45. Report of the New Hampshire council, 16 Aug. 1771, and Wentworth to the earl of Hillsborough, 20 Aug. 1771, PRO, CO5/937.

46. Edwin A. Bayley, "An Address Commemorative of the Life and Public Services of Brig.-Gen. Jacob Bayley," *Proceedings of the Vermont Historical Society* (1918–1919): 61, 67; Chase, *Dartmouth College*, 1:435, 438–39.

47. Chase, *Dartmouth College*, 1:439–40. Bayley is quoted on p. 439. Wentworth's letter to Tryon is printed on pp. 441–42. It did not seem to matter to Bayley that in 1768, when he felt he had suffered a great loss from his land falling under New York jurisdiction and before Wentworth had given him any reason to believe it might revert to New Hampshire, Wentworth granted Bayley's petition for the town of Bath in New Hampshire just north of Haverhill. See NHPP, 11:165.

48. Chase, *Dartmouth College*, 1:440, 442. On Tryon's side of this controversy, see Paul David Nelson, *William Tryon and the Course of Empire: A Life in British Imperial Service* (Chapel Hill: University of North Carolina Press, 1990), 102–7.

49. O'Callaghan, *Documentary History of New York*, 4:712–17.

50. NHPP, 10:220; NYHS, *Collections* 2 (1869): 297; Wentworth to the earl of

Hillsborough, 8 May 1772, PRO, CO5/937; Wentworth to the earl of Dartmouth, 18 Dec. 1772, PRO, CO5/938; William L. Grant and James Munroe, eds., *Acts of the Privy Council, Colonial Series* (London: His Majesty's Stationery Office, 1912), 5:267–74. Wentworth's statements to Wheelock are quoted in Chase, *Dartmouth College*, 1:440–41.

51. Early in 1774 the New Hampshire assembly agreed to James Breakenridge's request that Paul Wentworth be appointed agent to petition the king for return of the land west of the Connecticut River to New Hampshire, but only on condition that Breakenridge pay for the effort himself. NHPP, 18:350–51.

52. In March 1772 Wentworth wrote again to Tryon seeking lands, this time for his wife's brother, young Benning Wentworth. See O'Callaghan, *Documentary History of New York*, 4:769. Benning's deceased father, the merchant Samuel Wentworth of Boston, had received a five-thousand-acre grant from his brother, Governor Benning Wentworth. John Wentworth now attempted to secure that land for Samuel's son. The request for five thousand acres was clearly illegal according to royal land granting instructions, which prohibited individuals from receiving more than five hundred acres. Wentworth did not worry about that, however, because the rule was generally ignored in America by all governors. Had it been enforced, few problems would have developed concerning speculative land holdings.

53. Wentworth to the earl of Hillsborough, 8 May 1772, PRO, CO5/937.

II. TROUBLE AT HOME

1. Wentworth to the marquis of Rockingham, 14 Feb. 1772 and 23 July 1771, Rockingham Correspondence, WWM, Sheffield Archives, R1–1395 and R1–1383. For Frances Wentworth's feelings about Wolfeboro, see her letter to Mrs. Woodbury Langdon printed in Lawrence Shaw Mayo, *John Wentworth, Governor of New Hampshire, 1767–1775* (Cambridge, Mass.: Harvard University Press, 1921), 92–94.

2. NHPP, 18:614; Board of Trade to Wentworth, 29 July 1772, PRO, CO5/943; Wentworth to the earl of Dartmouth, 28 Oct. 1772, PRO, CO5/938; Wentworth to the earl of Hillsborough, 9 May 1772, PRO, CO5/937.

3. Clifford K. Shipton, *Sibley's Harvard Graduates* (Boston: Massachusetts Historical Society, 1965), 13:261; Lawrence Shaw Mayo, "Peter Livius the Trouble-Maker," Colonial Society of Massachusetts, *Publications* 25 (1924): 126; Jere R. Daniell, *Experiment in Republicanism: New Hampshire Politics and the American Revolution, 1741–1794* (Cambridge, Mass.: Harvard University Press, 1970), 11–12, 67, 67n; NHHS, *Collections* 9 (1889): 308–9, 334, 358–63. As late as 1769 Livius was still trying to gain a foothold in the mast business. See Went-

worth to John Durand and Anthony Bacon, 17 July 1769, Transcripts of John Wentworth Letter Book no. 1, NHA, 262–64.

4. NHPP, 18:599–600, 616–17, 632–33; Peter Livius, *The Memorial of Peter Livius* (London, 1773), 8–13; NHHS, *Collections* 9 (1889): 324–25.

5. NHG, 2 Nov. 1770. Hurd is quoted in Daniell, *Experiment in Republicanism*, 68.

6. Wentworth to the marquis of Rockingham, 2 Nov. 1770 and 14 Feb. 1772, Rockingham Correspondence, WWM, R1–1321 and R1–1395. On Michael Wentworth, see D. H. Watson, "Barlow Trecothick and Other Associates of Lord Rockingham during the Stamp Act Crisis, 1765–1766" (Master's thesis, Sheffield University, 1958), 89–90; NEHGR 6 (1852): 213–14.

7. NHPP, 18:599, 624–30, 634; Livius, *Memorial*, 16.

8. In 1769 John Hurd was listed among the grantees of the town of Protectworth. See NHPP, 25:524–28. Seven months later, Hurd transferred twelve thousand acres in Protectworth to John Wentworth in exchange for one hundred pounds. See New Hampshire Province Deeds, 99:321–23, NHA. Wentworth later claimed that when he left New Hampshire in 1775 his land rights, beyond his large estate at Wolfeboro, totaled more than twenty-one thousand acres. See Gregory Palmer, *Biographical Sketches of Loyalists of the American Revolution* (Westport, Conn.: Meckler, 1984), 919.

9. See the New Hampshire town charters in NHPP, vols. 24 and 25.

10. NHHS, *Collections*, 9:325, 336–37, 341, 343–44, 350–51; NHPP, 7:274; Livius, *Memorial*, 26; Board of Trade to Wentworth, 29 July 1772, PRO, CO5/943.

11. NHPP, 18:623–25.

12. Wentworth to the earl of Dartmouth, 28 Oct. 1772, PRO, CO5/938; Wentworth to the marquis of Rockingham, 14 Dec. 1772, Rockingham Correspondence, WWM, R64–6.

13. Wentworth to the marquis of Rockingham, 14 Dec. 1772, Rockingham Correspondence, WWM, R64–6; NEHGR 33 (1879): 353; Wentworth to the earl of Dartmouth, 18 Dec. 1772 and 9 Jan. 1773, PRO, CO5/938; NHPP, 18:615–16, 630–38.

14. Wentworth to Eleazar Wheelock, 18 Dec. 1772, The Papers of Eleazar Wheelock, DCA, 772668; NHPP, 7:337, 343–44; NHHS, *Collections*, 9:327.

15. The various declarations and depositions on behalf of Wentworth referred to here are found in NHHS, *Collections*, 9:304–63; NHPP, 18:646–50; Rockingham Correspondence, WWM, R64–17, R64–18, R64–23, R64–24, R64–25; PRO, CO5/930, passim; MHS, *Collections*, 6th ser., 4 (1891): 42–43; Benjamin F. Parker, *History of Wolfeborough* (Wolfeborough, N.H.: by the town, 1901), 68.

16. NHHS, *Collections*, 9:329; Wentworth to the marquis of Rockingham,

14 Dec. 1772, Rockingham Correspondence, WWM, R64–6; NHPP, 18:637–38; Wentworth to the earl of Hillsborough, 12 Apr. 1770, and action of the king in council, 16 Nov. 1770, PRO, CO5/930.

320   17. *NHPP*, 18:645–46.

18. Thomas Macdonogh to the marquis of Rockingham, 8 Feb. 1773, and to the earl of Dartmouth, 28 Apr. 1773, Rockingham Correspondence, WWM, R64–7, R64–10, and also R64–5, R64–8, R64–9; John Wentworth's Bill of Costs at the Board of Trade, and Council Office, 1773, Executive Records, NHA; Livius, *Memorial*, 48–50; Wentworth to Eleazar Wheelock, 22 Apr. 1773, Wheelock Papers, 773272.

19. *NHPP*, 7:337–39.

20. Wentworth to Henry Bellew, 8 Apr. 1775, Letter Book no. 3, 83–84; *Public Advertiser*, 3 Aug. 1773; marquis of Rockingham to Wentworth, 30 July 1774, Rockingham Letters, Ramsden Records, Sheepscar Library, Leeds, 2B, no. 39.

21. Memorial to the king on behalf of Governor Wentworth, 12 June 1773, and John Pownall to Thomas Wentworth, Paul Wentworth, and Thomas Macdonogh, 24 June 1773, New Hampshire MSS, Courts, NYPL; William L. Grant and James Munroe, eds., *Acts of the Privy Council, Colonial Series* (London: His Majesty's Stationery Office, 1908–1912), 5:370–71; Thomas Macdonogh to the marquis of Rockingham, 6 July 1773, Rockingham Correspondence, WWM, R64–13; John Wentworth's Bill of Costs at the Board of Trade, and Council Office, 1773, Executive Records; *Dictionary of National Biography*, 11:802 and 18:360–61; George T. Keppel, Earl of Albemarle, *Memoirs of the Marquis of Rockingham and His Contemporaries* (London: Richard Bently, 1852), 2:106–10.

22. Rockingham Correspondence, WWM, R64–21; Ross J. S. Hoffman, *The Marquis: A Study of Lord Rockingham* (New York: Fordham University Press, 1973), 284–87. Rockingham is quoted on p. 285.

23. Grant and Munroe, *Acts of the Privy Council*, 5:370–71; *Public Advertiser*, 24 July 1773; Rockingham Correspondence, WWM, R64–22.

24. Edmund Burke, *The Correspondence of Edmund Burke*, ed. Thomas W. Copeland (Cambridge, England: Cambridge University Press, 1960), 2:469; the marquis of Rockingham to Wentworth, 30 July 1774, Rockingham Letters, Leeds, 2B, no. 39; Grant and Munroe, *Acts of the Privy Council*, 6:530–35; *Public Advertiser*, 2 Aug. 1773.

25. See especially *Public Advertiser*, 24, 28, 29 July, and 2, 3, 6 Aug. 1773.

26. Burke, *Correspondence*, 2:444; MHS, *Collections*, 6th ser., 4 (1891): 44–45; Wentworth to Eleazar Wheelock, 27 Sept., 7 Oct. 1773, Wheelock Papers, 773527, 773557; *NHPP*, 7:342.

27. Burke, *Correspondence*, 2:463–64; the marquis of Rockingham to the

duke of Portland, 29 Sept. 1773, Portland MSS, University of Nottingham Library.

28. NHPP, 7:340–42. Rockingham is quoted in Watson, "Barlow Treco-thick," 93.

29. The earl of Dartmouth to Wentworth, 28 Oct. 1773, PRO, C05/947; the earl of Dartmouth to Wentworth, 14 Jan. 1774, Wheelock Papers, 774114.1; Thomas Hutchinson, *The Diary and Letters of His Excellency Thomas Hutchinson, Esq.*, comp. Peter O. Hutchinson (Boston: Houghton Mifflin, 1884), 187; MHS, *Collections*, 6th ser., 4 (1891): 498–99; Grant and Munroe, *Acts of the Privy Council*, 5:464–71; Governor Wentworth's Subseqt. Bill in order to Recall Mr. Livius Appointment of Chief Justice of New Hampshire, 1774, Executive Records; NHG, 28 Jan. 1774.

30. NHG, 8 Oct. 1773; the marquis of Rockingham to Wentworth, 30 July 1774, Rockingham Letters, Leeds, 2B, no. 39. James Kirby Martin made a beginning at trying to understand the opposition to the dominance of the Wentworths in New Hampshire before the American Revolution. See "A Model for the Coming Revolution: The Birth and Death of the Wentworth Oligarchy in New Hampshire, 1741–1776," *Journal of Social History* 4 (Fall 1970): 41–60. The impression Martin creates, however, of an organized group of lesser officeholders impatiently looking for an opportunity to throw the Wentworths out and take over their offices is misleading. Martin writes, "Wentworth interrelationships stood out as the glaring factor convincing upwardly mobile outsiders that the government needed to be forced open"(p. 58). As shown, those relationships were a highly publicized issue in Livius's case against John Wentworth, yet none of the supposed opposition group took advantage of this opportunity to come out against the governor. Also, a third of the members of the group Martin lists as hoping to obtain the offices held by the Wentworth aristocracy (p. 56) wrote depositions in support of John Wentworth. So, too, did John Sullivan, the man Martin puts forward as archetypical of this class of "upwardly mobile" lesser officials. See NHHS, *Collections*, 9:304–63. On the other hand, the Langdon brothers, Woodbury and John, were not included in this group. There is need for a thorough study of the social and political groups in New Hampshire before the Revolution, especially the much discussed but still vaguely defined elite dominated by the Wentworth kinship network.

31. Wentworth was so sensitive to what was thought of him in England that even with a favorable verdict from the Privy Council, he was determined to return to the mother country to clear his name personally. See MHS, *Collections*, 6th ser., 4 (1891): 45–46.

32. Wentworth to the earl of Dartmouth, 9 Jan. 1773, PRO, C05/938.

33. MHS, *Collections* 4 (1891): 44–47; Shipton, *Sibley's Harvard Graduates*, 13:671.

34. Wentworth to Captain Hector McNeill, 10 Sept. 1773, Sir John Wentworth Misc. MSS, NYPL; *NHPP*, 7:336.

35. *NHPP*, 7:329–34; Henry Caner to Wentworth, 8 Nov. 1773, Caner Letter Book, MSS. D.M. 388, University of Bristol Library.

36. Bernard Knollenberg, *Growth of the American Revolution, 1766–1775* (New York: Free Press, 1975), 90–94.

37. Ibid., 95–96. The newspaper commentator is quoted on p.95.

38. Wentworth to the earl of Dartmouth, 17 Dec. 1773, PRO, CO5/938; *NHPP*, 7:333–34; Daniell, *Experiment in Republicanism*, 74–75; Arthur M. Schlesinger, *The Colonial Merchants and the American Revolution, 1763–1776* (1918; reprint, New York: Atheneum, 1968), 302.

39. Wentworth to the earl of Dartmouth, 17 Dec. 1773, PRO, CO5/938; Lawrence Shaw Mayo, *John Langdon of New Hampshire* (1937; reprint, New York: Kennikat, 1970), 45–46; Knollenberg, *Growth of the American Revolution*, 99–100. The most thorough account of the Boston Tea Party and the circumstances surrounding it is Benjamin Woods Labaree, *The Boston Tea Party* (New York: Oxford University Press, 1964).

12. REVOLUTION COMES TO NEW HAMPSHIRE

1. *NHPP*, 7:335.

2. Wentworth to the earl of Dartmouth, 1 Feb. 1774, Hammond Transcripts, NHHS.

3. *NHPP*, 7:350–58.

4. Jere R. Daniell, "Reason and Ridicule: Tea Act Resolutions in New Hampshire," *Historical New Hampshire* 20 (Winter 1965): 23; manuscript biography of Josiah Bartlett by his son, Levi Bartlett, Josiah Bartlett Papers, NHHS, 28.

5. Daniell, "Reason and Ridicule," 25; Henry Caner to Wentworth, 29 Feb., 14 Mar., 21 Apr. 1774, Caner Letter Book, MSS. D.M. 388, University of Bristol Library. The *New Hampshire Gazette* is quoted in Daniell, 27–28.

6. Wentworth to the earl of Dartmouth, 22 Apr. 1774, PRO, CO5/930; *NHPP*, 7:352; *NHG*, 18 Mar. 1774.

7. Jere R. Daniell, *Experiment in Republicanism: New Hampshire Politics and the American Revolution, 1741–1794* (Cambridge, Mass.: Harvard University Press, 1970), 78.

8. *NHG*, 25 Mar. 1774.

9. *NHPP*, 7:334–35, 359–60; Wentworth to the earl of Dartmouth, 28 Apr. 1774, PRO/938.

10. Wentworth to the earl of Dartmouth, 24 Apr. 1774, and Portsmouth's instructions to its representatives, 12 Apr. 1774, PRO, CO5/938.

11. Henry Caner to Wentworth, 21 Apr. 1774, Caner Letter Book. On Parker, Sherburne, and Cutts, see Ransom B. True, "The New Hampshire Committees of Correspondence, 1773–1774" (Master's thesis, University of New Hampshire, 1969), 38–55, 98–105. A debate in the *New Hampshire Gazette* made it clear that Langdon was a controversial figure. "An Independent Freeholder" urged that he not be elected. "Republicae Amicus" replied that such opposition came only from a "Junto of Wiseacres," which he identified with the New Hampshire council. *NHG*, 25 Mar., 1 Apr. 1774.

12. Wentworth to the earl of Dartmouth, 24 Apr. 1774, PRO, CO5/938.

13. Ibid.

14. Bernhard Knollenberg, *Growth of the American Revolution, 1766–1775* (New York: Free Press, 1975), 103–8.

15. *NHPP*, 7:362–69; Knollenberg, *Growth of the American Revolution*, 126; Sam Adams to the Portsmouth Committee of Correspondence, 12 May 1774, HLRO, 1775, no. 284; Wentworth to the earl of Dartmouth, 5 Aug. 1774, PRO, CO5/938. Wentworth told Dartmouth that to make up the difference needed for the supply, the assembly was willing "improvidently" to exhaust the remainder of the six thousand pounds granted the province by Parliament for its part in the last war. This decision was made in spite of the fact, Wentworth went on, that "the People are more able to pay their taxes for a reasonable supply then ever they were, and not unwilling."

16. *NHPP*, 7:369; the earl of Dartmouth to Wentworth, 6 Apr. 1774, PRO, CO5/947.

17. Knollenberg, *Growth of the American Revolution*, 126–28; *NHPP*, 7:369. The Virginia resolve is quoted in Knollenberg, 127.

18. Henry Caner to Wentworth, 16 June 1774, Caner Letter Book; *NHPP*, 7:406; Knollenberg, *Growth of the American Revolution*, 117–19.

19. Henry Caner to Wentworth, 16 June 1774, Caner Letter Book; Arthur M. Schlesinger, *The Colonial Merchants and the American Revolution* (1918; reprint, New York: Atheneum, 1968), 319, 325.

20. Samuel Cutts for the Portsmouth Committee of Correspondence, June 1774, PRO, CO5/938, and HLRO, 1775, no. 284; MHS, *Proceedings*, 2d ser., 2 (1885–1886): 481–86; Joseph B. Walker, "The New Hampshire Covenant of 1774," *The Granite Monthly* 35 (July 1903): 188–97. Concord is the only town other than

Portsmouth known to have signed the covenant. For some reason that I cannot explain, the copy of the covenant sent by Wentworth to England differs in wording and the date of implementation from the documents sent to Dover and Concord as published in the MHS, *Proceedings*, and Walker, "The New Hampshire Covenant."

21. The following incident concerning the importation of tea into New Hampshire in June 1774 is based largely on the following sources: Wentworth to the earl of Dartmouth, 4 July 1774, printed in Jeremy Belknap, *The History of New Hampshire* (1831; reprint, New York: Johnson Reprint, 1970), 2:314–18; Edward Parry to Wentworth, John Parker to Wentworth, and Wentworth to John Cochran, 29 June 1774, and John Cochran to Wentworth, 30 June 1774, HLRO, 1775, no. 284. See also NHPP, 7:408; NHG, 8 July 1774.

22. Wentworth did not indicate whether the councillor mentioned was Daniel or Jonathan Warner. See Wentworth to the earl of Dartmouth, 4 July 1774, in Belknap, *New Hampshire*, 2:317.

23. This incident in New Hampshire, in fact, was not overlooked by the radicals in Massachusetts. See NHG, 29 July 1774.

24. Knollenberg, *Growth of the American Revolution*, 128; Order of the New Hampshire Committee of Correspondence, 25 June 1774, Personal Records, John Pickering, NHA.

25. Wentworth to the earl of Dartmouth, 6 July 1774, in Belknap, *New Hampshire*, 2:318–19; NHPP, 7:400.

26. Wentworth to the earl of Dartmouth, 13 July 1774, in Belknap, *New Hampshire*, 2:319; NHPP, 7:407–8.

27. Wentworth to the earl of Dartmouth, 13 July 1774, in Belknap, *New Hampshire*, 2:319; Wentworth to William Williams, 22 July 1774, quoted in Clifford K. Shipton, *Sibley's Harvard Graduates* (Boston: Massachusetts Historical Society, 1965), 13:664.

28. The marquis of Rockingham to Wentworth, July 1774, Rockingham Letters, Ramsden Records, Sheepscar Library, Leeds, 2B, no. 40.

29. Shipton, *Sibley's Harvard Graduates*, 13:664, 655.

30. The earl of Dartmouth to Wentworth, 6 July, 3 Aug. 1774, PRO, CO5/938; the earl of Dartmouth to Wentworth, 8 Sept. 1774, PRO, CO5/947; David McClure to Eleazar Wheelock, 24 Aug. 1774, The Papers of Eleazar Wheelock, DCA, 774474; Wentworth to the earl of Dartmouth with enclosures, 29 Aug. 1774, HLRO, 1775, no. 284. Wentworth's letter is printed alone in Belknap, *New Hampshire*, 2:320–22.

31. The following account of the tea incident is derived from these sources: Wentworth to the earl of Dartmouth, 13 Sept. 1774, HLRO, 1775, no. 284;

Edward Parry to Wentworth, 8 Sept. 1774, ibid.; Minutes of the Council, 9 Sept. 1774, ibid.; *NHPP*, 7:415–16; Wentworth to Corbyn Morris, 16 Nov. 1774, Transcripts of John Wentworth Letter Book no. 3, NHA, 15.

32. Knollenberg, *Growth of the American Revolution*, 138–62. For the Suffolk 325 resolves, see p. 249.

33. *NHPP*, 7:417; *NHG*, 18 Nov. 1774.

34. MHS, *Collections*, 4th ser., 4 (1858): 74–77; Wentworth to Thomas W. Waldron, 25 Oct. 1774, ibid., 6th ser., 4 (1891): 58; Lawrence Shaw Mayo, *John Langdon of New Hampshire* (1937; reprint, New York: Kennikat, 1970), 59–60; Wentworth to the earl of Dartmouth, 15 Nov. 1774, in Belknap, *New Hampshire*, 2:325.

35. Henry Caner to Wentworth, [4?] Oct. 1774, Caner Letter Book; Wentworth to Thomas W. Waldron, 25 Oct. 1774, MHS, *Collections*, 6th ser., 4 (1891): 56–57.

13. FALL FROM AN "HONORABLE PRECIPICE"

1. *NHG*, 28 Oct., 11 Nov. 1774; Wentworth to the marquis of Rockingham, 9 Nov. 1774, *NEHGR* 23 (1869): 275; Wentworth to the earl of Dartmouth, 15 Nov. 1774, in Jeremy Belknap, *The History of New Hampshire* (1831; reprint, New York: Johnson Reprint, 1970), 2:326; Wentworth to Thomas W. Waldron, 25 Oct. 1774, MHS, *Collections*, 6th ser., 4 (1891): 56–57; Wentworth to Henry Rust, 15 Nov. 1774, Transcripts of John Wentworth Letter Book no. 3, NHA, 14.

2. Wentworth to Thomas W. Waldron, 26 Nov., 25 Oct. 1774, MHS, *Collections*, 6th ser., 4 (1891): 66, 57; Wentworth to the marquis of Rockingham, 9 Nov. 1774, *NEHGR* 23 (1869): 275; Wentworth to the earl of Dartmouth, 15 Nov. 1774, in Belknap, *New Hampshire*, 2:326–27. Wentworth's young friend from Concord, Benjamin Thompson, whom he had awarded a major's commission in the militia, was the governor's point man in returning British deserters. Thompson visited Gage early in November but shortly after was arrested and imprisoned in the town of Woburn, Massachusetts, as an enemy of the colonies. See Wentworth to General Gage, 2 Nov. 1774, Letter Book no. 3, 1; and *NHPP*, 7:419. Thompson gained his release, and when the British army finally evacuated Boston, he went to England. A scientist and inventor of repute, he was one of the most successful of all the loyalists. During the Revolutionary War he served as undersecretary of state to George Germain, was appointed a lieutenant colonel in the King's Dragoons, and in 1784 was knighted. Moving to Munich, where he remained for eleven years serving in various positions of Bavarian service including minister of war, he gained the title *Count von Rumford*. In 1799 Went-

worth's old friend John Adams, then president of the fledgling United States of America, asked Thompson to direct the new military academy at West Point, but he declined. See *Dictionary of National Biography*, 19:685–88; NHHS, *Proceedings* 5 (1917): 312–17. There are numerous biographies of Benjamin Thompson, Count Rumford.

326

3. Wentworth to the marquis of Rockingham, 9 Nov. 1774, NEHGR 23 (1869): 275; Eleazar Wheelock to Wentworth, 6 Nov. 1774, in Frederick Chase, *The History of Dartmouth College and the Town of Hanover*, ed. John K. Lord (Cambridge, Mass.: John Wilson Son, University Press, 1891), 1:324–25. Ironically, Woodbury Langdon, always a trimmer, was at this time also procuring blankets for the British army. See Lawrence Shaw Mayo, *John Langdon of New Hampshire* (1937; reprint, New York: Kennikat, 1970), 61. See also Wentworth to Thomas W. Waldron, 26 Nov. 1774, MHS, *Collections*, 6th ser., 4 (1891): 66–67.

4. Wentworth to Captain [Lieutenant] Mowat, 7 Nov. 1774, Letter Book no. 3, 3; Wentworth to Corbyn Morris, 16 Nov. 1774, ibid., 15; Wentworth to the earl of Dartmouth, 15 Nov. 1774, in Belknap, *New Hampshire*, 2:327; Edward D. Boylston, *Historical Sketches of the Hillsborough County Congresses* (Amherst, N.Y.: Farmer's Cabinet Press, 1884), 8; NHG, 18 Nov. 1774; Proceedings of Durham town meeting and order of provincial committee of correspondence, HLRO, 1775, no. 284.

5. Wentworth to the marquis of Rockingham, 9 Nov. 1774, NEHGR 23 (1869): 275; Wentworth to Eleazar Wheelock, 18 Nov. 1774, in Chase, *Dartmouth College*, 1:325; Wentworth to Jeremy Belknap, 18 Nov. 1774, MHS, *Collections*, 6th ser., 4 (1891): 65.

6. Wentworth to Jeremy Belknap, 18 Nov. 1774, MHS, *Collections*, 6th ser., 4 (1891): 65; Wentworth to Thomas W. Waldron, 26 Nov. 1774, ibid., 67.

7. Lawrence Henry Gipson, *The British Empire before the American Revolution*, vol. 12, *The Triumphant Empire: Britain Sails into the Storm, 1770–1776* (New York: Knopf, 1965), 248–50.

8. Gipson, vol. 12, *Triumphant Empire: Britain Sails*, 259–60, 342; Wentworth to Thomas W. Waldron, 26 Nov. 1774, MHS, *Collections*, 6th ser., 4 (1891): 68. Dartmouth is quoted in Gipson, p. 250.

9. Wentworth to Thomas W. Waldron, 26 Nov. 1774, MHS, *Collections*, 6th ser., 4 (1891): 67.

10. Gipson, vol. 12, *Triumphant Empire: Britain Sails*, 270–71, 172; Wentworth to Thomas W. Waldron, 9 Dec. 1774, MHS, *Collections*, 6th ser., 4 (1891): 69; Bernhard Knollenberg, *Growth of the American Revolution, 1766–1775* (New York: Free Press, 1975), 169, 421–22 n.5.

11. Paul Wilderson, "The Raids on Fort William and Mary: Some New Evidence," *Historical New Hampshire* 30 (Fall 1975): 186–87; and "John Wentworth's Narrative of the Raids on Fort William and Mary," ibid., 32 (Winter 1977): 230. The Boston committee sent a similar message to Salem, Massachusetts, at the same time, complete with assurances that the British soldiers that had embarked on Sunday were headed for that port or Marblehead. See Timothy Pickeren, Jr., to John Langdon, 12 Dec. 1774, John Langdon Letter Book, NYPL, 33–35. On the raids on Fort William and Mary, see also Charles L. Parsons, "The Capture of Fort William and Mary, December 14 and 15, 1774," NHHS, *Proceedings* 4 (1906): 18–47; Elwin L. Page, "The King's Powder, 1774," *New England Quarterly* 18 (March 1945): 83–92; and the first three articles in *Historical New Hampshire* 29 (Winter 1974). Parsons's valuable article was reprinted in booklet form by the New Hampshire American Revolution Bicentennial Commission (1974). 327

12. Wilderson, "The Raids on Fort William and Mary," 187–88, and "John Wentworth's Narrative," 230.

13. Wilderson, "The Raids on Fort William and Mary," 188–90.

14. Wilderson, "The Raids on Fort William and Mary," 191–92, and "John Wentworth's Narrative," 231–32.

15. Wentworth to General Gage, 14 Dec. 1774, in Belknap, *New Hampshire*, 2:328–30; John Cochran to Wentworth, 14 Dec. 1774, ibid., 330–31; NHPP, 7:421; Wilderson, "John Wentworth's Narrative," 232.

16. Wilderson, "John Wentworth's Narrative," 232–33. Wentworth was not completely forthcoming when he denied that any ships were headed for the Piscataqua to secure the armaments at Fort William and Mary. On 9 December, he had written to Thomas Waldron: "I am in expectation of a man-of-war in this port next Sunday." See MHS, *Collections*, 6th ser., 4 (1891): 69. General Gage, nevertheless, continued to disavow any intent to confiscate provincial arms. Writing to Wentworth on 19 December he decried the "Falsehood of the Reports about seizing either Arms or Ammunition in the Provincial Forts." See PRO, CO5/930.

17. Wilderson, "John Wentworth's Narrative," 233–34, and "The Raids on Fort William and Mary," 192–94.

18. Wilderson, "John Wentworth's Narrative," 234; Wentworth to the earl of Dartmouth, 20 Dec. 1774, PRO, CO5/939. A portion of Wentworth's letter to Dartmouth is printed in *NEHGR* 23 (1869): 276–77. Indicative of the angry disposition of the crowd in Portsmouth on 16 December was the treatment of William Pottle of Stratham. Denounced as a "Tory" for his alleged opposition to aid for Boston and to the tea boycott, Pottle was pulled from his horse,

roughed up by the mob, and chased out of town. See Charles W. Brewster, *Rambles about Portsmouth* (1873; reprint, Somersworth: New Hampshire Publishing Co., 1971), 1:198–99.

19. Wentworth to Thomas W. Waldron, 30 Dec. 1774, MHS, *Collections*, 6th ser., 4 (1891): 70; Wentworth to the earl of Dartmouth, 20 Dec. 1774, PRO, CO5/939; Josiah Bartlett to militia officers of Sandown, 15 Dec. 1774, Josiah Bartlett Papers, NHHS; Wilderson, "John Wentworth's Narrative," 231–32; NHPP, 7:423. Two students of the raids on Fort William and Mary have come to the "inescapable conclusion" that a large number of the men involved were from the "upper-middle and upper classes." See Theodore Crackell and Martin Andresen, "Fort William and Mary: A Case Study in Crowd Behavior," *Historical New Hampshire* 29 (Winter 1974): 220. Wentworth placed much of the blame on Sullivan and Folsom, the delegates to the Continental Congress, who he concluded took "a more active part in the violences . . . with a view to Secure and promote a popular interest in this convention." See Wentworth to the earl of Dartmouth, 28 Dec. 1774, PRO, CO5/939. See also Wentworth to Dartmouth, 20 Dec. 1774, and Wentworth to General Gage, 29 Dec. 1774, ibid. Names of the participants in the raids can be found in Crackel and Andresen, "Fort William and Mary," and Wilderson, "The Raids on Fort William and Mary."

20. Belknap, *New Hampshire*, 1:353–54; Wentworth to the earl of Dartmouth, 20 Dec. 1774, PRO, CO5/939; Wilderson, "John Wentworth's Narrative," 234–35; Wentworth to George Irving, 5 Jan. 1775, NEHGR 23 (1869): 277.

21. Wilderson, "John Wentworth's Narrative," 234–35; Wentworth to General Gage, 29 Dec. 1774, and Admiral Graves to Wentworth, 2 Jan. 1775, PRO, CO5/939; Wentworth to Admiral Graves, 30 Dec. 1774, and Admiral Graves to the Admiralty, 8 Jan. 1775, HLRO, 1775, no. 296. When Lieutenant Mowat did attempt to bring the *Canceaux* closer to town at Wentworth's request, the ship ran aground at low tide and suffered damage to her keel. She was extricated a day later, but only after an unusually high tide and jettisoning her iron ballast. See Admiral Graves to Philip Stephen, 15 Jan. 1775, in William Bell Clark, ed., *Naval Documents of the American Revolution* (Washington, D.C.: Government Printing Office, 1964), 1:62–63.

22. Wentworth to Thomas W. Waldron, 30 Dec. 1774, MHS, *Collections*, 6th ser., 4 (1891): 71.

23. Ibid., 70.

24. Ibid., 71; Wentworth to General Gage, 29 Dec. 1774, PRO, CO5/939.

25. Wentworth to the earl of Dartmouth, 14 Jan. 1775, and Wentworth to General Gage, 21 Jan. 1775, PRO, CO5/939; Kenneth Scott, "Tory Associators of Portsmouth," *William and Mary Quarterly* 17 (1960): 507–15; Wentworth to

General Gage, 20 Jan. 1775, Letter Book no. 3, 50. Scott provides a detailed list of the associators, their occupations, and their relationship to the governor.

26. *NHPP*, 7:442–44.

27. Wentworth to Thomas W. Waldron, 27 Jan. 1775, MHS, *Collections*, 6th ser., 4 (1891): 73; John Wentworth's Proclamation, 22 Feb. 1775, PRO, CO5/939; General Gage to Wentworth, 24 Jan. 1775, ibid.; Wentworth to the earl of Dartmouth, 10 Mar. 1775, ibid.; *NHPP*, 7:370–71. It is questionable whether the members elected from Orford and Lyme were supportive of the governor. When objections were raised against them in the assembly, they did not force the issue but instead declined to take their seats. See Richard F. Upton, *Revolutionary New Hampshire* (1936; reprint, New York: Octagon, 1971), 25. Some forty-five unrepresented towns were larger than those three Grafton County communities. See Jere R. Daniell, *Experiment in Republicanism: New Hampshire Politics and the American Revolution, 1741–1794* (Cambridge, Mass.: Harvard University Press, 1970), 87n.

28. *NHPP*, 7:445; Ezra S. Stearns, *History of Plymouth, New Hampshire* (Cambridge, Mass.: University Press, 1906), 1:69; Wentworth to General Gage, 16 Dec. 1774, in Belknap, *New Hampshire*, 2:331. On Fenton see also Hugh Edward Egerton, ed., *The Royal Commission on the Losses and Services of American Loyalists, 1783 to 1785* (1915; reprint, New York: Arno, 1969), 194–96.

29. Wentworth to the earl of Dartmouth, 10 Mar. 1775, PRO, CO5/939; Wentworth's Proclamation, 22 Feb. 1775, ibid.; General Gage to Wentworth, 23 Feb. 1775, ibid.; *NHG*, 10 Feb. 1775. See also Gage to Wentworth, 28 Jan., 6 Feb. 1775, PRO, CO5/939, and Wentworth to Gage, 3 and 23 Feb. 1775, ibid., for a discussion of the possibility of sending troops to New Hampshire.

30. Wentworth to Thomas W. Waldron, 20 Jan. 1775, MHS, *Collections*, 6th ser., 4 (1891): 72; Wentworth to Waldron, 8 Feb. 1775, ibid., 80; Elizabeth Wentworth to Mrs. Nathaniel Ray Thomas, 2 Feb. 1775, in John Wentworth, *The Wentworth Genealogy* (Boston: Little, Brown, 1878), 1:317n. On Hall Jackson, see J. Worth Estes, *Hall Jackson and the Purple Foxglove: Medical Practice and Research in Revolutionary America, 1760–1820* (Hanover, N.H.: University Press of New England, 1979), and Clifford K. Shipton, *Sibley's Harvard Graduates* (Boston: Massachusetts Historical Society, 1968), 14:177–81.

31. Wentworth to Thomas W. Waldron, 27 Jan. 1775, MHS, *Collections*, 6th ser., 4 (1891): 73–74; Wentworth to Waldron, 8 Feb. 1775, ibid., 81. If Wentworth still loved the people of New Hampshire, a letter to him in mid-March from "The Spectator" indicated that respect for him had been given up only reluctantly. Heaping high praise on the governor, Spectator then listed his alleged offenses of recent months and wondered why it was necessary for the executive to "echo

the voice of a despotick Minister." Touching on the futility and tragedy of the situation that had produced this unnatural estrangement, Spectator lamented, "I . . . pity the person appointed to preside, and the unhappy people who are called to obey." The Spectator to Governor Wentworth, Peter Force, comp., *American Archives*, 4th ser. (Washington, D.C.: M. St. Clair Clarke and Peter Force, 1839), 2:159–60.

32. Gipson, vol. 12, *Triumphant Empire: Britain Sails*, 301–6; the marchioness of Rockingham to Edmund Burke, 29 Mar. 1775, *The Correspondence of Edmund Burke*, ed. Thomas W. Copeland (Cambridge, England: Cambridge University Press, 1961), 3:146. Distrusting her own political knowledge, Lady Rockingham decided to delete this passage from her letter to Frances Wentworth. The quotation from Burke is found in Gipson, p. 303.

33. Nathaniel Adams, *Annals of Portsmouth* (1825; reprint, Hampton, N.H.: Peter E. Randall, 1971), 251; NHPP, 7:453–54; John Hurd to Joshua Brackett, 6 May 1775, MHS, *Proceedings*, 1st ser., 5 (1860–1862): 2–3; Wentworth to the earl of Dartmouth, 26 Apr. 1775, PRO, CO5/939. Wheelock is quoted in Chase, *Dartmouth College*, 1:326.

34. NHPP, 7:372–75, 9:714–15.

35. Wentworth to the earl of Dartmouth, 17 May 1775, PRO, CO5/939.

36. Wentworth to the earl of Dartmouth, 17 May 1775, PRO, CO5/939; Deposition of Dr. Josiah Pomeroy, 16 May 1775, ibid.; George Meserve and Robert Trail to Commissioners of Customs, Boston, 18 May 1775, PRO, TI/513.

37. Wentworth to the earl of Dartmouth, 17 May 1775, PRO, CO5/939; NHPP, 7:473, 481, 485, 487.

38. Arthur M. Schlesinger, *The Colonial Merchants and the American Revolution* (1918; reprint, New York: Atheneum, 1968), 556; NHPP, 7:480.

39. *Letters and Papers of Major-General John Sullivan*, ed. Otis G. Hammond (Concord: New Hampshire Historical Society, 1930), 1:61–62 (vol. 13, NHHS, *Collections*); NHPP, 7:509–10; Resolves of the Committee of Safety of Henniker, 12 June 1775, Town Records, NHA. Shortly after Lexington and Concord, Oliver Parker of Stoddard was accused of being unfriendly to the colonial cause for, among other things, stating "his opinion the govenor had a good right to Cuddle on both sides of the Question—for this reason if he should stick to the province (meaning New Hampshire) the king would Take his Commission from him—and thereby he would Lose his Bread—and further if he should openly stick to the king the people would Quarril him away and so he would again lose his Bread." Deposition of John Robb, 10 Mar. 1777, General Court Records (Minutes), NHA.

40. Wentworth to the earl of Dartmouth, 3 June 1775, PRO, CO5/939; NHPP,

7:375–77, 18:663–74; Captain Barkley to Admiral Graves, 30 May 1775, in Clark, *Naval Documents*, 1:567–68. An attempt had been made in England to exclude from the Restraining Act shipments of needed food, but it was voted down by a margin of nearly four to one. See Gipson, vol. 12, *Triumphant Empire: Britain*   331
Sails, 294–300.

41. Wentworth to the earl of Dartmouth, 3 June 1775, PRO, CO5/939; NHPP, 7:376–77; David McClure to Eleazar Wheelock, 15 Aug. 1775, The Papers of Eleazar Wheelock, DCA, 775465.1.

42. Wentworth to the earl of Dartmouth, 3 June 1775, PRO, CO5/939; Captain Barkley to Admiral Graves, 5 June 1775, in Clark, *Naval Documents*, 1:612–13.

43. NHPP, 7:377–81.

44. Gipson, vol. 12, *Triumphant Empire: Britain Sails*, 296–97; NHPP, 7:380. Hartley is quoted in Gipson, p. 296.

45. Jere R. Daniell, "Lady Wentworth's Last Days in New Hampshire," *Historical New Hampshire* 23 (Spring 1968): 21–22; Wentworth to the earl of Dartmouth, 14 June 1775, PRO, CO5/939; NHPP, 7:381; Upton, *Revolutionary New Hampshire*, 25–26. Fenton had spent the previous three weeks aboard the *Scarborough* for protection but had felt confident enough to go into town on the thirteenth to attend the assembly. See Captain Barkley to Admiral Graves, 16 June 1775, in Clark, *Naval Documents*, 1:689.

46. Daniell, "Lady Wentworth's Last Days," 22; Wentworth to the earl of Dartmouth, 14 June 1775, PRO, CO5/939; Captain Barkley to Admiral Graves, 16 June 1775, in Clark, *Naval Documents*, 1:689; Brewster, *Rambles about Portsmouth*, 1:98.

47. Admiral Graves to Wentworth, 23 June 1775, PRO, CO5/939; Captain Barkley to Wentworth, 27 June 1775, ibid.; Wentworth to Admiral Graves, 29 June 1775, ibid.; NEHGR 23 (1869): 278; NHPP, 7:381–82.

48. Wentworth to Timothy Ruggles, 3 July 1775, Letter Book no. 3, 122–23; Wentworth to the earl of Dartmouth, 20 July 1775, PRO, CO5/939; George Jaffrey to Wentworth, 4 July 1775, ibid.; Isaac Rindge to Wentworth, 11 July 1775, ibid.; Joseph Peirce to Wentworth, 15 July 1775, ibid.; William Parker to Wentworth, 15 July 1775, ibid.; Deposition of Samuel Hale, Jr., 11 July 1775, ibid.; NHPP, 18:665–71; Theodore Atkinson to the provincial congress, 4 July 1775, Wentworth Papers, NHHS (letter not forwarded).

49. NHPP, 7:383–86; Wentworth to the earl of Dartmouth, 17 July 1775, PRO, CO5/939.

50. Wentworth to the earl of Dartmouth, 17 July 1775, PRO, CO5/939; Wentworth to Captain Barkley, 17 July 1775, Letter Book no. 3, 125–26; Wentworth to Tristram Dalton, 31 July 1775, ibid., 128–29; Wentworth to Newcastle Select-

men, 17 Aug. 1775, Wentworth Papers, Newcastle Town Archives; NEHGR 23 (1869): 278; NHPP, 7:381; David McClure to Eleazar Wheelock, 15 Aug. 1775, Wheelock Papers, 775465.1.

51. Wentworth to the earl of Dartmouth, 8 and 18 Aug. 1775, PRO, CO5/939.

52. Wentworth to the earl of Dartmouth, 18 Aug. 1775, PRO, CO5/939; Portsmouth Town Meeting, 10 Aug. 1775, ibid.

53. Wentworth to the earl of Dartmouth, 18 Aug. 1775, PRO, CO5/939; Meeting of New Hampshire council, 11 Aug. 1775, ibid.; Newcastle Selectmen to Wentworth, 13 Aug. 1775, Wentworth Papers, Newcastle Town Archives; NHPP, 7:389.

54. Wentworth to the earl of Dartmouth, 18 Aug. 1775, PRO, CO5/939; David McClure to Eleazar Wheelock, 15 Aug. 1775, Wheelock Papers, 775465.1.

55. Wentworth to Newcastle Selectmen and Newcastle Selectmen to Wentworth, 17 Aug. 1775, Wentworth Papers, Newcastle Town Archives; Wentworth to the earl of Dartmouth, 29 Aug. 1775, PRO, CO5/939; NHPP, 7:390; Remarks on board the *Scarborough*, 24 Aug. 1775, in Clark, *Naval Documents*, 1:1219.

56. Wentworth to the earl of Dartmouth, 29 Aug., 29 Sept. 1775, PRO, CO5/939; Wentworth to Theodore Atkinson, 21 Sept. 1775, Wentworth Papers, NHHS; NHPP, 7:393–94.

EPILOGUE

1. Wentworth to the marquis of Rockingham, 4 Dec. 1775, Rockingham Correspondence, WWM, Sheffield Archives, R1–1634.

2. Wilbur H. Seibert, "Loyalist Troops of New England," *New England Quarterly* 4 (January 1931): 134–36; Edward C. Boulter, "The Loyalists of New Hampshire" (Master's thesis, University of New Hampshire, 1949), 98–100. A pay record for these troops can be found in the Public Record Office, AO1/325, no. 1288.

3. Mary Beth Norton, *The British Americans: The Loyalist Exiles in England, 1774–1789* (Boston: Little, Brown, 1972), 187; NHPP, 8:810.

4. Brian C. Cuthbertson, *The Loyalist Governor: Biography of Sir John Wentworth* (Halifax: Patheric Press, 1983), 27; Wentworth to Daniel Rindge, 29 Sept. 1783, Masonian Papers, NHA.

5. Robert G. Albion, *Forests and Sea Power: The Timber Problem of the Royal Navy, 1652–1862* (Cambridge, Mass.: Harvard University Press, 1926), 350–52; Earl Fitzwilliam Papers, WWM, F128–86; Rockingham Correspondence, WWM, R157–1, R157–3, R157–4, R157–5, R157–6, R157–9, R157–10, R157–12, R157–13, R157–18.

6. Neil MacKinnon has dealt thoroughly with this loyalist immigration in *This Unfriendly Soil: The Loyalist Experience in Nova Scotia, 1783–1791* (Kingston and Montreal: McGill-Queens University Press, 1986).

7. Cuthbertson, *The Loyalist Governor*, 48–50.

8. Ibid., 78–84.

9. Ibid., 108–11. The quotation is from p. 108.

10. J. Holland Rose, A. P. Newton, E. A. Benians, eds., *The Cambridge History of the British Empire*, vol. 6, *Canada and Newfoundland* (Cambridge, England: Cambridge University Press, 1930), 213–14.

11. Cuthbertson, *The Loyalist Governor*, 59, 139.

12. Ibid., 137–39.

13. Ibid., 139–40. The most thorough work on Wentworth's years in Canada is Cuthbertson, *The Loyalist Governor*. See also Clifford K. Shipton, *Sibley's Harvard Graduates* (Boston: Massachusetts Historical Society, 1965), 13:671–81; Sir Adams Archibald, "The Life of Sir John Wentworth: Governor of Nova Scotia, 1792–1808," Nova Scotia Historical Society, *Collections*, 20 (1921): 43–109; Lawrence Shaw Mayo, *John Wentworth: Governor of New Hampshire, 1767–1775* (Cambridge, Mass.: Harvard University Press, 1921), 162–95; Margaret Ells, "Governor Wentworth's Patronage," in *Historical Essays on the Atlantic Provinces*, ed. G. A. Rawlyk (Toronto: McClelland and Stewart, 1967), 61–81.

14. Earl Fitzwilliam Papers, WWM, F128–94, F128–95, F128–98, F128–99, F128–102, F128–103, F128–104, F128–105, F128–106.

15. Wentworth to Jeremy Belknap, 15 May 1791, MHS, *Collections*, 6th ser., 4 (1891): 497–500; Wentworth to John Peirce, 25 May 1791, Peirce-Rindge Papers, NHA.

16. Wentworth to Jeremy Belknap, 15 May 1791, MHS, *Collections*, 6th ser., 4 (1891): 499. See also Wentworth to John Peirce, 9 Mar. 1786, 17 May 1786, 21 Jan. 1788, 25 May 1791, Peirce-Rindge Papers; Frances Wentworth to John Peirce, 8 Aug. 1786, and John Peirce to Frances Wentworth, [15?] Oct. 1786, ibid.; Wentworth to President Wheelock, 24 Dec. 1783, The Papers of Eleazar Wheelock, DCA, 783674.1.

333

BIBLIOGRAPHY

MANUSCRIPTS

"American Loyalists." Transcript of the Manuscript Books and Papers of the Commission of Enquiry into the Losses and Services of the American Loyalists. New York Public Library. New York.

Bartlett, Josiah, Papers. New Hampshire Historical Society. Concord.

Belknap, Jeremy, Papers. Massachusetts Historical Society. Boston.

Bowdoin-Temple Papers. Massachusetts Historical Society. Boston.

Boyd, George, Letter Book, 1773–1775. New Hampshire Historical Society. Concord.

Burke Papers. Wentworth-Woodhouse Muniments. Sheffield Archives. Sheffield City Libraries. Sheffield, England.

Caner Letter Book. MSS. D.M. 388. University of Bristol Library. Bristol, England.

Executive Records. New Hampshire Archives. Concord.

Fitzwilliam, Earl, Papers. Wentworth-Woodhouse Muniments. Sheffield Archives. Sheffield City Libraries, Sheffield, England.

Fulham Papers. Lambeth Palace Library. London.

General Court Records: Minutes. New Hampshire Archives. Concord.

Hammond Transcripts. Transcripts from the Public Record Office. New Hampshire Historical Society. Concord.

Harvard University Archives. Cambridge.

House of Lords Record Office. No. 284, 296. London.

Land Records. New Hampshire Archives. Concord.

Langdon, John, Letter Book. New York Public Library. New York.

Masonian Papers. New Hampshire Archives. Concord.

Miscellaneous Manuscripts. Massachusetts Historical Society. Boston.

Miscellaneous Town Papers. New Hampshire Historical Society. Concord.

Moffatt, Whipple, and Mason Papers. New Hampshire Historical Society. Concord.

New Hampshire Court Records. New Hampshire Archives. Concord.

New Hampshire Manuscripts. New York Public Library. New York.

New Hampshire Town Records. New Hampshire State Library. Concord. Microfilms of transcripts from town records.

Parochial Records of Queen's Chapel, Portsmouth, N.H., 1738–1796. St. John's Church. Portsmouth.

Peirce Papers. Portsmouth Athenaeum. Portsmouth, N.H.

336   Peirce-Rindge Papers. New Hampshire Archives. Concord.

Personal Papers. New Hampshire Archives. Concord.

Portland Manuscripts. University of Nottingham Library. Nottingham, England.

Portsmouth Town Records. "Historic Sites and Buildings of Portsmouth." WPA typescript. Portsmouth Public Library. Portsmouth, N.H.

Public Record Office. Colonial Office 5/ 175, 227, 928, 930, 934, 935, 936, 937, 938, 939, 942, 943, 947; Treasury 1/ 484, 493, 513; Audit Office 1/ 325. London.

Rockingham Correspondence. Wentworth-Woodhouse Muniments. Sheffield Archives. Sheffield City Libraries. Sheffield, England.

Rockingham Letters. Ramsden Records. Sheepscar Library. Leeds, England.

Society for the Propagation of the Gospel Papers. Transcripts from manuscripts in the Library of Congress; Lambeth Palace Library, London; and St. John's Church, Portsmouth, N.H. New Hampshire Historical Society. Concord.

Town Records. New Hampshire Archives. Concord.

Treasury Records. New Hampshire Archives. Concord.

Wentworth Correspondence. Wentworth-Woodhouse Muniments. Sheffield Archives. Sheffield City Libraries. Sheffield, England.

Wentworth, John, Letter Book, 1767–1778. Transcript of first three volumes of nine volumes in Nova Scotia Public Records, Halifax. New Hampshire Archives. Concord.

Wentworth Papers. Newcastle Town Archives. Newcastle, N.H.

Wentworth Papers. New Hampshire Historical Society. Concord.

Wentworth, Sir John, Miscellaneous Manuscripts. New York Public Library. New York.

Wentworth-Woodhouse Muniments. Sheffield Central Library. Sheffield, England.

Wheelock, Eleazar, Papers. Dartmouth College Archives. Hanover, N.H.

PRINTED PRIMARY SOURCES

Adams, John. *The Diary and Autobiography of John Adams.* Edited by Lyman H. Butterfield. 4 vols. Cambridge, Mass.: Harvard University Press, 1961.

———. *The Earliest Diary of John Adams.* Edited by Lyman H. Butterfield. Cambridge, Mass.: Harvard University Press, 1966.

———. *Legal Papers of John Adams.* Edited by L. Kinvin Wroth and Hiller B.

Zobel. 3 vols. Cambridge, Mass.: Harvard University Press, Belknap Press, 1965.

———. *The Works of John Adams.* Edited by Charles Francis Adams. 10 vols. Boston: Little, Brown, 1850–1856.

Allen, Ira. *The Natural and Political History of the State of Vermont.* London: J. W. Myers, 1798.

Batchellor, A. S., and Henry H. Metcalf, eds. *The Laws of New Hampshire, 1689– 1835.* 10 vols. Manchester, Concord, and Bristol, N.H., 1904–1922.

Belknap, Jeremy. *The History of New Hampshire.* 3 vols. Dover, N.H., 1812, 1831. Reprint (3 vols. in 2). New York: Johnson Reprint, 1970.

Boswell, James. *Boswell's London Journal, 1762–1763.* Edited by Frederick A. Pottle. New York: McGraw-Hill, 1950.

Bouton, Nathaniel, et al., eds. *Documents and Records Relating to New Hampshire, 1623–1800 (New Hampshire Provincial and State Papers).* 40 vols. Concord and Manchester: by the state, 1867–1941.

Burke, Edmund. *The Correspondence of Edmund Burke.* Edited by Thomas W. Copeland. 9 vols. Cambridge, England: Cambridge University Press, 1958– 1970.

Clark, William Bell, ed. *Naval Documents of the American Revolution.* Vol. 1, *American Theater: Dec. 1, 1774–Sept. 2, 1775; European Theater: Dec. 6, 1774– Aug. 9, 1775.* Washington, D.C.: Government Printing Office, 1964.

Daniell, Jere R. "Lady Wentworth's Last Days in New Hampshire." *Historical New Hampshire* 23 (1968): 14–25.

Dickerson, O. M., ed. *Boston under Military Rule, 1768–1769.* Boston: Chapman and Grimes, 1936. Reprint. Westport, Conn.: Greenwood Press, 1971.

Dwight, Timothy. *Travels in New England and New York.* Edited by Barbara M. Solomon. 4 vols. Cambridge, Mass.: Harvard University Press, 1969.

Egerton, Hugh Edward, ed. *The Royal Commission on the Losses and Services of American Loyalists, 1783 to 1785.* Oxford, 1915. Reprint. New York: Arno Press, 1969.

Force, Peter, comp. *American Archives.* 9 vols. Washington, D.C.: M. St. Clair Clarke and Peter Force, 1837–1853.

Franklin, Benjamin. *The Papers of Benjamin Franklin.* Edited by Leonard W. Labaree, et al., 14 vols. New Haven: Yale University Press, 1959–1970.

Giffen, Jane C., ed. "The Estate of Madam Elizabeth Wentworth of Portsmouth." *Historical New Hampshire* 23 (Spring 1968): 31–49.

Grant, William L., and James Munroe, eds. *Acts of the Privy Council, Colonial Series.* 6 vols. London: His Majesty's Stationery Office, 1908–1912.

Hammond, Otis G., ed. *Letters and Papers of Major-General John Sullivan.* 3 vols.

Concord: New Hampshire Historical Society, 1930–1939. Same as *Collections*, vols. 13–15, New Hampshire Historical Society.

Hough, C. M., ed. *Reports of Cases in the Vice Admiralty of the Province of New York and in the Court of Admiralty of the State of New York, 1715–1788*. New Haven, 1925.

Hutchinson, Thomas. *The Diary and Letters of His Excellency Thomas Hutchinson, Esq*. Compiled by Peter O. Hutchinson. Boston: Houghton Mifflin, 1884.

———. *The History of the Colony and Province of Massachusetts Bay*. Edited by Lawrence Shaw Mayo. 3 vols. Cambridge: Harvard University Press, 1936.

Journals of the House of Commons. Vol. 30. London, 1803 (microprint).

Lane, Samuel. *A Journal for the Years 1739–1803 by Samuel Lane of Stratham, New Hampshire*. Edited by Charles Lane Hanson. Concord: New Hampshire Historical Society, 1937.

Livius, Peter. *The Memorial of Peter Livius*. London, 1773.

Massachusetts Historical Society. *Collections* 4th ser., vol. 4 (1858); 6th ser., vols. 4 (1891), 9 (1897).

Massachusetts Historical Society. *Proceedings* 1st ser., vol. 5 (1860–1862); 2d ser., vol. 2 (1885–1886); 3d ser., vol. 44 (1910–1911).

McClure, David. *Diary of David McClure*. Edited by Franklin B. Dexter. New York: Knickerbocker Press, 1899.

New England Historical and Genealogical Register. Vols. 4 (1850), 5 (1851), 6 (1852), 18 (1864), 23 (1869), 28 (1874), 33 (1879), 38 (1884).

New Hampshire Historical Society. *Collections*. Vols. 3 (1832) and 9 (1839).

New Hampshire Historical Society. *Proceedings*. Vol. 5 (1917).

New-York Historical Society. *Collections*. Vols. 2 (1869) and 10 (1877).

O'Callaghan, E. B. *The Documentary History of the State of New York*. 4 vols. Albany: Charles Van Benthuysen, 1851.

Saunders, William L., ed. *The Colonial Records of North Carolina*. 10 vols. Raleigh, 1886–1890.

Soule, Allen, and John A. Williams, eds. *State Papers of Vermont*. 17 vols. Montpelier: 1918–1969.

Warren, Mercy Otis. *History of the Rise, Progress and Termination of the American Revolution*. 3 vols. Boston, 1805. Reprint. New York: AMS Press, 1970.

Watson, Derek H. "John Wentworth's Description of the American Colonies in 1765." *Historical New Hampshire* 27 (Fall 1972): 141–66.

Wilderson, Paul. "John Wentworth's Narrative of the Raids on Fort William and Mary." *Historical New Hampshire* 32 (Winter 1977): 228–36.

———. "The Raids on Fort William and Mary: Some New Evidence." *Historical New Hampshire* 30 (Fall 1975): 178–202.

NEWSPAPERS

Boston Evening Post.
Boston Gazette.
Boston Weekly News-Letter.
Massachusetts Gazette and Boston News-Letter.
New Hampshire Gazette.
Public Advertiser (London).

SECONDARY SOURCES

Abbot, Wilbur C. Conflicts with Oblivion. New Haven: Yale University Press, 1924.

Abbot, W. W. The Royal Governors of Georgia, 1754–1775. Chapel Hill: University of North Carolina Press, 1959.

Adams, Nathaniel. Annals of Portsmouth. 1825. Reprint. Hampton, N.H.: Peter E. Randall, 1971.

Akers, Charles W. "New Hampshire's 'Honorary' Lieutenant Governor: John Temple and the American Revolution." Historical New Hampshire 30 (Summer 1975): 79–99.

Albion, Robert G. Forests and Sea Power: Timber Problems of the Royal Navy, 1652–1862. Cambridge, Mass.: Harvard University Press, 1926.

Alden, John R. A History of the American Revolution. New York: Knopf, 1969.

Alumni Oxonienses: The Members of the University of Oxford, 1715–1886. Later ser. Vol. 4. Oxford: James Parker, 1891.

Archibald, Sir Adams. "Life of Sir John Wentworth: Governor of Nova Scotia, 1792–1808." Nova Scotia Historical Society, Collections 20 (1921): 43–109.

Axtell, James. "Dr. Wheelock's Little Red School." In The European and the Indian: Essays in the Ethnohistory of Colonial North America, 87–109. New York: Oxford University Press, 1981.

Bailyn, Bernard. The Ordeal of Thomas Hutchinson. Cambridge, Mass.: Harvard University Press, 1974.

———. The Origins of American Politics. New York: Knopf, 1968.

Battis, Emery. Saints and Sectaries: Anne Hutchinson and the Antinomian Controversy in the Massachusetts Bay Colony. Chapel Hill: University of North Carolina Press, 1962.

Bayley, Edwin A. "An Address Commemorative of the Life and Public Services of Brig.-Gen. Jacob Bayley." Proceedings of the Vermont Historical Society (1918–1919): 57–92.

Bell, Charles H. History of the Town of Exeter, New Hampshire. Exeter: by the town, 1888.

Bellesiles, Michael A. *Revolutionary Outlaws: Ethan Allen and the Struggle for Independence on the Early American Frontier.* Charlottesville: University Press of Virginia, 1993.

340   Binney, Marcus. "Wentworth Woodhouse Revisited—I," and "Wentworth Woodhouse Revisited—II." *Country Life* (17 and 24 March 1983): 624–27, 708–11.

Botsford, J. B. *English Society in the Eighteenth Century.* 1924. Reprint. New York: Octagon Books, 1965.

Boulter, Edward C. "The Loyalists of New Hampshire." Master's thesis, University of New Hampshire, 1949.

Bowen, Catherine Drinker. *John Adams and the American Revolution.* Boston: Little, Brown, 1950. Reprint. New York: Grossett and Dunlap, 1973.

Boyd, Julian P. "Silas Deane: Death by a Kindly Teacher of Treason? Part II." *William and Mary Quarterly,* 3d ser., 16 (July 1959): 319–42.

Boylston, Edward D. *Historical Sketch of the Hillsborough County Congresses.* Amherst, N.H.: Farmer's Cabinet Press, 1884.

Brewster, Charles W. *Rambles about Portsmouth.* 2d ser., 1859 (rev. 1873), 1869. Reprint. Somerworth, N.H.: New Hampshire Publishing Co., 1971, 1972.

Bridenbaugh, Carl. *Cities in the Wilderness: The First Century of Urban Life in America, 1625–1742.* 1938. Reprint. Oxford: Oxford University Press, 1971.

———. *Mitre and Sceptre: Transatlantic Faiths, Ideas, Personalities, and Politics, 1689–1775.* New York: Oxford University Press, 1962.

———. *Peter Harrison: First American Architect.* Chapel Hill: University of North Carolina Press, 1949.

The Bulletin of the Metropolitan Museum of Art in New York 33 (1938): 21–23.

Bullion, John L. *A Great and Necessary Measure: George Grenville and the Genesis of the Stamp Act, 1763–1765.* Columbia: University of Missouri Press, 1982.

Butts, R. Freeman, and Lawrence A. Cremin. *A History of Education in American Culture.* New York: Holt, Rinehart, and Winston, 1953.

Calhoon, Robert McCluer. *The Loyalists in Revolutionary America, 1760–1781.* New York: Holt, Rinehart, and Winston, 1973.

The Cambridge History of the British Empire. Edited by J. Holland Rose, A. P. Newton, and E. A. Benians. Vol. 6, *Canada and Newfoundland.* Cambridge, England: Cambridge University Press, 1930.

Cashin, Edward J. "Sowing the Wind: Governor James Wright and the Georgia Backcountry on the Eve of the Revolution." In *Forty Years of Diversity: Essays on Colonial Georgia,* edited by Harvey H. Jackson and Phinzey Spalding, 233–50. Athens, Georgia: The University of Georgia Press, 1984.

Chase, Frederick. *The History of Dartmouth College and the Town of Hanover.*

Edited by John K. Lord. Vol. 1. Cambridge, Mass.: John Wilson Son, University Press, 1891.

Clark, Charles E. *The Eastern Frontier: The Settlement of Northern New England, 1610–1763.* New York: Knopf, 1970.

Clark, Charles E., and Charles W. Eastman, Jr., eds. *The Portsmouth Project.* Somersworth: New Hampshire Publishing Co., 1974.

Colbourn, H. Trevor. *The Lamp of Experience: Whig History and the Intellectual Origins of the American Revolution.* Chapel Hill: University of North Carolina Press, 1965.

Crackell, Theodore, and Martin Andresen. "Fort William and Mary: A Case Study in Crowd Behavior." *Historical New Hampshire* 29 (Winter 1974): 203–26.

Cremin, Lawrence A. *American Education: The Colonial Experience, 1607–1783.* New York: Harper and Row, 1970.

Cuthbertson, Brian C. *The Loyalist Governor: Biography of Sir John Wentworth.* Halifax: Patheric Press, 1983.

Cutter, William R. *A History of the Cutter Family of New England.* Boston, 1871.

Daniell, Jere R. *Colonial New Hampshire.* Millwood, N.Y.: KTO, 1981.

———. "Eleazar Wheelock and the Dartmouth College Charter." *Historical New Hampshire* 24 (Winter 1969): 3–31.

———. *Experiment in Republicanism: New Hampshire Politics and the American Revolution, 1741–1794.* Cambridge, Mass.: Harvard University Press, 1970.

———. "Politics in New Hampshire under Governor Benning Wentworth, 1741–1767." *William and Mary Quarterly,* 3d ser., 20 (January 1966): 76–105.

———. "Reason and Ridicule: Tea Act Resolutions in New Hampshire." *Historical New Hampshire* 20 (Winter 1965): 23–28.

Dickerson, O. M. "Use Made of the Revenue from the Tax on Tea." *New England Quarterly* 31 (June 1958): 232–43.

DiRenzo, Gordon J., ed. *Personality and Politics.* Garden City, N.Y.: Anchor Press/Doubleday, 1974.

Dunbar, Louise. "The Royal Governors in the Middle and Southern Colonies on the Eve of the Revolution: A Study in Imperial Personnel." In *The Era of the American Revolution,* edited by Richard B. Morris, 214–68. New York: Columbia University Press, 1939.

Einstein, Lewis. *Divided Loyalties: Americans in England during the War of Independence.* London: Cobden-Sanderson, 1933.

Ells, Margaret. "Governor Wentworth's Patronage." In *Historical Essays on the Atlantic Provinces,* edited by G. A. Rawlyk, 61–81. Toronto: McClelland and Stewart, 1967.

Estes, J. Worth. *Hall Jackson and the Purple Foxglove: Medical Practice and Research in Revolutionary America, 1760–1820.* Hanover, N.H.: University Press of New England, 1979.

342 Fliegelman, Jay. *Prodigals and Pilgrims: The American Revolution against Patriarchal Authority, 1750–1800.* Cambridge, England: Cambridge University Press, 1982.

Foss, Gerald D. *Three Centuries of Freemasonry in New Hampshire.* Somersworth: New Hampshire Publishing Co., 1972.

Fry, William H. *New Hampshire as a Royal Province.* New York: Columbia University Press, 1908. Reprint. New York: AMS Press, 1970.

Garvin, James L. "Portsmouth and the Piscataqua: Social History and Material Culture." *Historical New Hampshire* 26 (Summer 1971): 3–48.

Giffen, Jane C., and Harriet S. Lacy. "The Governor Wentworth House in Portsmouth." *Historical New Hampshire* 23 (Spring 1968): 50–54.

Gipson, Lawrence Henry. *American Loyalist: Jared Ingersoll.* 1920. Reprint. New Haven: Yale University Press, 1971.

———. *The British Empire before the American Revolution.* 15 vols. Caldwell, Idaho: Caxton Printers; and New York: Knopf, 1936–1970.

———. *The Coming of the Revolution, 1763–1775.* New York: Harper and Row, 1954.

Goldthwaite, James W. "The Governor's Road from Rochester to Wolfeboro." *New Hampshire Highways* (May 1931): 2–5.

Green, Julian W. "A Map of New Hampshire—Spanning the Revolution." *Dartmouth College Library Bulletin* 16 (April 1976): 71–78.

Greene, Evarts B. *The Provincial Governor in the English Colonies of North America.* Harvard Historical Studies, vol. 7. New York, 1898.

Guttridge, George H. *The Early Career of Lord Rockingham, 1730–1765.* University of California, *Publications in History*, vol. 44. Berkeley: University of California Press, 1952.

———. *English Whiggism and the American Revolution.* 1942. Reprint. Berkeley: University of California Press, 1966.

Hall, David D., ed. *The Antinomian Controversy, 1636–1638: A Documentary History.* Middletown, Conn.: Wesleyan University Press, 1968.

Hammond, Otis G. "The Mason Title and its Relations to New Hampshire and Massachusetts." *Proceedings of the American Antiquarian Society* 26 (April–October 1916): 245–63.

Hoffman, Ross J. S. *The Marquis: A Study of Lord Rockingham.* New York: Fordham University Press, 1973.

Hofstadter, Richard. *America at 1750: A Social Portrait.* New York: Knopf, 1971.

Howells, John M. *The Architectural Heritage of the Piscataqua.* 1937. Reprint. New York: Architectural Book Publishing Co., 1965.

Hunt, Elmer M. *New Hampshire Town Names.* Peterborough, N.H.: William L. Bauhan, 1970.

Jellison, Charles A. *Ethan Allen: Frontier Rebel.* Syracuse: Syracuse University Press, 1969.

Jervey, Theodore. "Barlow Trecothick." *South Carolina Historical and Genealogical Magazine* 32 (July 1931): 157–69.

Jones, Matt B. *Vermont in the Making, 1750–1777.* Cambridge, Mass.: Harvard University Press, 1939.

Kammen, Michael G. *A Rope of Sand: The Colonial Agents, British Politics and the American Revolution.* Ithaca, N.Y.: Cornell University Press, 1968.

Keppel, George T., Earl of Albemarle. *Memoirs of the Marquis of Rockingham and His Contemporaries.* 2 vols. London: Richard Bently, 1852.

Kershaw, Gordon E. "John Wentworth vs. the Kennebec Proprietors: The Formation of Royal Mast Policy, 1769–1778." *The American Neptune* 33 (April 1973): 95–119.

Kirsch, George B. "Jeremy Belknap and the Coming of the Revolution." *Historical New Hampshire* 29 (Fall 1974): 151–72.

Knollenberg, Bernhard. *Growth of the American Revolution, 1766–1775.* New York: The Free Press, 1975.

———. *Origin of the American Revolution, 1759–1766.* New York: The Free Press, 1960.

Labaree, Benjamin Woods. *The Boston Tea Party.* New York: Oxford University Press, 1964.

Labaree, Leonard W. *Royal Government in America.* New Haven: Yale University Press, 1930. Reprint. New York: Frederick Ungar, 1958.

Langford, Paul. *The First Rockingham Administration, 1765–1766.* Oxford: Oxford University Press, 1973.

Lillywhite, Bryant. *London Coffee Houses: A Reference Book of the Coffee Houses of the Seventeenth, Eighteenth, and Nineteenth Centuries.* London: George Allen and Unwin, 1963.

Looney, John F. "The King's Representative: Benning Wentworth, Colonial Governor, 1741–1767." Ph.D. diss., Lehigh University, 1961.

MacKinnon, Neil. *This Unfriendly Soil: The Loyalist Experience in Nova Scotia, 1783–1791.* Kingston and Montreal: McGill-Queens University Press, 1986.

Malone, Joseph J. *Pine Trees and Politics: The Naval Stores and Forest Policy in Colonial New England, 1691–1775.* Seattle: University of Washington Press, 1964.

Marshall, Dorothy. *Eighteenth-Century England.* London: Longman, 1962.

343

Martin, James Kirby. "A Model for the Coming Revolution: The Birth and Death of the Wentworth Oligarchy in New Hampshire." *Journal of Social History* 4 (Fall 1970): 41–60.

Mayo, Lawrence Shaw. *John Langdon of New Hampshire*. 1937. Reprint. Port Washington, N.Y.: Kennikat Press, 1970.

——. *John Wentworth: Governor of New Hampshire, 1767–1775*. Cambridge, Mass.: Harvard University Press, 1921.

——. "Peter Livius the Trouble-Maker." Colonial Society of Massachusetts, *Publications* 25 (1924): 125–29.

Meader, Robert F. *The Saga of a Palace: The Story of Wentworth House at Wolfeboro, New Hampshire*. Wolfeboro: Wolfeboro Historical Society, 1962.

Middlekauf, Robert. *Ancients and Axioms: Secondary Education in Eighteenth-Century New England*. New Haven: Yale University Press, 1963.

Morgan, Edmund S., and Helen M. Morgan. *The Stamp Act Crisis: Prologue to Revolution*. Chapel Hill: University of North Carolina Press, 1953. Reprint. New York: Collier, 1963.

Morison, Samuel Eliot. *Three Centuries of Harvard, 1636–1936*. Cambridge, Mass.: Harvard University Press, 1936.

Morrison, Hugh. *Early American Architecture: From the First Colonial Settlements to the National Period*. New York: Oxford University Press, 1952.

Nelson, Paul David. *William Tryon and the Course of Empire: A Life in British Imperial Service*. Chapel Hill: University of North Carolina Press, 1990.

Norton, Mary Beth. *The British-Americans: The Loyalist Exiles in England, 1774–1789*. Boston: Little, Brown, 1972.

Oedel, Howard T. "Portsmouth, New Hampshire: The Role of the Provincial Capital in the Development of the Colony (1700–1775)." Ph.D. diss., Boston University, 1960.

Olson, Alison Gilbert. *Anglo-American Politics, 1660–1775: The Relationship between Parties in England and Colonial America*. New York: Oxford University Press, 1973.

——. "The London Mercantile Lobby and the Coming of the American Revolution." *The Journal of American History* 69 (June 1982): 21–41.

Page, Elwin L. *Judicial Beginnings in New Hampshire, 1640–1700*. Concord: New Hampshire Historical Society, 1959.

——. "The King's Powder, 1774." *New England Quarterly* 18 (March 1945): 83–92.

Palmer, Gregory. *Biographical Sketches of Loyalists of the American Revolution*. Westport, Conn.: Meckler, 1984.

Bibliography

Parker, Benjamin F. *History of Wolfeborough*. Wolfeborough, N.H.: by the town, 1901.

Parsons, Charles L. "The Capture of Fort William and Mary, December 14 and 15, 1774." New Hampshire Historical Society, *Proceedings* 4 (1906): 18–47.

Prown, Jules David. *John Singleton Copley*. 2 vols. Cambridge, Mass.: Harvard University Press, 1966.

Quilici, Ronald H. "A Voyage to Antigua: A Social and Economic Study of the Maritime Activities of Colonial Portsmouth, New Hampshire." Master's thesis, University of New Hampshire, 1973.

Raddall, Thomas H. *The Governor's Lady*. Garden City, N.Y.: Doubleday, 1960.

Raymond, Allen R. "Benning Wentworth's Claims in the New Hampshire–New York Border Controversy: A Case of Twenty-Twenty Hindsight?" *Vermont History* 43 (Winter 1975): 20–32.

Richardson, A. E. *Georgian England*. 1931. Reprint. Freeport, N.Y.: Books for Libraries Press, 1967.

Sabine, Lorenzo. *Biographical Sketches of Loyalists of the American Revolution*. 2 vols. Boston: Little, Brown, 1864.

Sachse, William L. *The Colonial American in Britain*. Madison: University of Wisconsin Press, 1956.

Saltonstall, William G. *Ports of Piscataqua*. Cambridge, Mass.: Harvard University Press, 1941. Reprint. New York: Russell and Russell, 1968.

Sanborn, Frank B. *New Hampshire: An Epitome of Popular Government*. Boston: Houghton Mifflin, 1904.

Schlesinger, Arthur M. *The Colonial Merchants and the American Revolution, 1763–1776*. 1918. Reprint. New York: Atheneum, 1968.

Scott, Kenneth. "Tory Associators of Portsmouth." *William and Mary Quarterly*, 3d ser., 17 (October 1960): 507–15.

Shipton, Clifford K. *Biographical Sketches of Those Who Attended Harvard College (Sibley's Harvard Graduates)*. 17 vols. Boston: Massachusetts Historical Society, 1873–1975.

———. *New England Life in the Eighteenth Century: Representative Biographies from Sibley's Harvard Graduates*. Cambridge, Mass.: Harvard University Press, 1963.

Siebert, Wilbur H. "Loyalist Troops of New England." *New England Quarterly* 4 (January 1931): 108–47.

Skemp, Sheila L. *William Franklin: Son of a Patriot, Servant of a King*. New York: Oxford University Press, 1990.

Smith, Page. *John Adams*. 2 vols. Garden City, N.Y.: Doubleday, 1962.

345

Sosin, Jack M. *Agents and Merchants: British Colonial Policy and the Origins of the American Revolution, 1763–1775*. Lincoln: University of Nebraska Press, 1965.

Starbuck, David R., ed. *America's First Summer Resort: John Wentworth's Eighteenth Century Plantation in Wolfeboro, New Hampshire*. Vol. 30 of *The New Hampshire Archeologist*, no. 1. New Hampshire Archeological Society, 1989.

Stearns, Ezra S. *History of Plymouth, New Hampshire*. Vol. 1. Cambridge, Mass.: University Press, 1906.

Strawbery Banke: Official Guidebook. Portsmouth, N.H.: Strawbery Banke, 1982.

Suffern, Winslow. *From Graces to Gargoyles: A Social Essay on the Theater in Portsmouth, New Hampshire, 1762–1850*. Portsmouth, N.H.: Seacoast Arts Council, 1972.

Summerson, John N. *Architecture in Britain, 1530–1830*. 1953. Reprint. Harmondsworth, Middlesex: Penguin Books, 1970.

Szasz, Margaret Connell. *Indian Education in the American Colonies, 1607–1783*. Albuquerque: University of New Mexico Press, 1988.

Thomas, P. D. G. *British Politics and the Stamp Act Crisis: The First Phase of the American Revolution, 1763–1767*. Oxford: Oxford University Press, Clarendon Press, 1975.

Thomas, Peter D. G. *The Townshend Duties Crisis: The Second Phase of the American Revolution, 1767–1773*. Oxford: Oxford University Press, Clarendon Press, 1987.

True, Ransom B. "The New Hampshire Committees of Correspondence, 1773–1774." Master's thesis, University of New Hampshire, 1969.

Turberville, A. S., ed. *Johnson's England: An Account of the Life and Manners of His Age*. 2 vols. 1933. Reprint. Oxford: Oxford University Press, Clarendon Press, 1952.

Tyler, John W. *Smugglers and Patriots: Boston Merchants and the Advent of the American Revolution*. Boston: Northeastern University Press, 1986.

Upton, Richard Francis. *Revolutionary New Hampshire*. 1936. Reprint. New York: Octagon, 1971.

Valentine, Alan. *The British Establishment, 1760–1784: An Eighteenth-Century Biographical Dictionary*. 2 vols. Norman: University of Oklahoma Press, 1970.

Walker, Joseph B. "The New Hampshire Covenant of 1774." *The Granite Monthly* 35 (October 1903): 188–97.

———. *New Hampshire's Five Provincial Congresses, July 21, 1774–January 5, 1776*. Concord, N.H.: Rumford Printing Co., 1905.

Wardner, Henry S. *The Birthplace of Vermont: A History of Windsor*. New York: Charles Scribner's Sons, 1927.

Waterhouse, Ellis. *Painting in Britain, 1530 to 1790.* Baltimore: Penguin Books, 1953.

Watson, D. H. "Barlow Trecothick." *Bulletin of the British Association for American Studies,* n.s. 1 (September 1960): 36–49, and (March 1961): 29–39.

——— . "Barlow Trecothick and Other Associates of Lord Rockingham during the Stamp Act Crisis, 1765–1766." Master's thesis, Sheffield University, 1958.

——— . "Joseph Harrison and the Liberty Incident." *William and Mary Quarterly,* 3d ser., 20 (October 1963): 585–95.

Watson, J. Steven. *The Reign of George III, 1760–1815.* Oxford: Oxford University Press, Clarendon Press, 1960.

Wentworth, John. *The Wentworth Genealogy.* 3 vols. Boston: Little, Brown, 1878.

Woolverton, John Frederick. *Colonial Anglicanism in North America.* Detroit: Wayne State University Press, 1984.

Young, Philip. *Revolutionary Ladies.* New York: Knopf, 1977.

Zobel, Hiller B. *The Boston Massacre.* New York: W. W. Norton, 1970.

INDEX

Adams, John: background compared to Wentworth's, 14, 15; correspondence with Wentworth, 37–38, 42; defense counsel in Boston admiralty case, 157–59; at Harvard, 29, 32, 33, 35; and Harvard M.A., 38; in opposite political camp from Wentworth, 159; in Paris, 13, 14; as prominent attorney in Massachusetts, 159; Wentworth renews friendship with, 156, 159

Adams, Samuel, 157, 226

admiralty case in Boston, 156–59

admiralty court: and Daniel Rindge case, 167–68; and Dean case, 190–91. *See also* vice-admiralty court

agricultural expansion in N.H., 107–108, 109–10, 133; for export, 110, 114

Albany, N.Y.: site of ejectment suits, 194

Allen, Ethan, 194, 195, 199

Allen, Ira, 194

Androscoggin River, 163

Anglican Church, 170–71. *See also* Anglicanism; Church of England

Anglicanism: and Benning Wentworth, 169; spread of in N.H., 131; Wentworth as proponent of, 131; Wentworth's plan to advance, 169–71; Wentworth relates

to politics in N.H., 170. *See also* Anglican Church; Church of England; Society for the Propagation of the Gospel (SPG)

Apthorp, Stephen, 137–38

assembly. *See* House of Representatives, N.H.

Atkinson, Frances Wentworth, 173. *See also* Wentworth, Frances

Atkinson, Theodore, Jr.: as college roommate of Wentworth, 34; death of, 171–73; marriage to Frances Deering Wentworth, 45; and N.H. petition against Townshend acts, 144

Atkinson, Theodore, Sr.: attempt to transfer office to son, 47; defends Wentworth against Livius, 204; letters of introduction for Wentworth from, 49, 52; and marriage of Wentworth, 173; as member of anti-Massachusetts faction, 17; and N.H. petition against Townshend acts, 144; as proprietor west of Connecticut River, 187; ridiculed by John Langdon, 246; sends Wentworth's defense to Barlow Trecothick, 207; and Stamp Act, 70; trade with John Thomlinson, 24; Wentworth sends note to, 265

Auchmuty, Robert, 156

University Press of New England
publishes books under its own imprint and is
the publisher for Brandeis University Press,
Brown University Press, University of Connecticut,
Dartmouth College, Middlebury College Press,
University of New Hampshire, University of Rhode
Island, Tufts University, University of Vermont,
and Wesleyan University Press.

Library of Congress
Cataloging-in-Publication Data
Wilderson, Paul W.
Governor John Wentworth and the Ameri-
can Revolution
The English connection / by Paul W. Wilderson.
p. cm.
Includes bibliographical references and index.
ISBN 0-87451-656-0
1. Wentworth, John, 1737-1820. 2. Governors –
New Hampshire – Biography.
3. New Hampshire – Politics and government –
To 1775. 4. Great Britain –
Colonies – America – History. I. Title.
F37.W46W55 1993
974.1'03'092 – dc20 [B] 93-19717